AN ANTHROPOLOGY OF ANTHROPOI

by ROB BOROFSKY

ENDORSEMENTS BY

35 PROMINENT ANTHROPOLOGISTS FROM

AUSTRALIA, CANADA, FRANCE, NORWAY, UNITED KINGDOM, and UNITED STATES

Anthropology as a discipline should have far greater impact on the world today, both in its elucidation of the nature of humanity, and its application to specific human needs. To this end, Borofsky provides a trenchant critique of current ideology and practice in anthropology. In calling for increased attention to Public Anthropology, he explains why anthropologists have not fulfilled their promise in improving the human understanding and the human condition. This book is both an incisive critique of anthropology and a call for action. It should be widely read and taken to heart.

**WILLIAM O. BEEMAN,** Co-President of the Association for the Anthropology of Policy; Professor of Anthropology, University of Minnesota

. . .

Borofsky's call for a public anthropology with real human, political and intellectual stakes is inspiring. His rich documentation of the history of anthropology and his critique of the propensity for elite academics to pursue irrelevant trendy theory that advances careers instead of useful, knowledge helpful to the people anthropologists study is right on point. Please read this book and engage with the world on behalf of social justice.

**PHILIPPE BOURGOIS,** Director of the Center for Social Medicine and Humanities, UCLA; Author of *In Search of Respect: Selling Crack in El Barrio* and *Righteous Dopefiend*

. . .

This book is a timely call to action for all of us who want to see anthropology become a discipline that engages the public and does good in the world. Please read it; please teach it to your students!

**NINA BROWN,** Professor of Anthropology, Community College of Baltimore County-Essex; Editor, Anthropology of Work Review; Co-Editor, *Perspectives: An Open Invitation to Cultural Anthropology*

. . .

*An Anthropology of Anthropology* is a work of clarity and impressive scholarship. It makes a powerful case for anthropologists to contribute, and to look for validation, beyond their narrow professional world. In fact, Borofsky's argument for a public anthropology which aims not just to do no harm, but positively to benefit others, could be read with profit by any social scientist, and especially by those who now feel themselves trammeled by the inward turn toward theory which presently dominates so much of social science. I very much hope the book reaches a wide audience.

**MICHAEL CARRITHERS,** Fellow of the British Academy; Professor of Anthropology, Durham University

. . .

Never has the time been as ripe for anthropologists, both as scholars and citizens, to turn their unique human, humane insight toward urgent public issues in our world. Seldom has the case for such a turn been as boldly or persuasively made as in this book.

**JEAN COMAROFF,** Alfred North Whitehead Professor of African and African American Studies and of Anthropology, Harvard University

. . .

Robert Borofsky's book is an invitation to dialogue on some of the most vexing issues on the place of anthropology as disciplinary knowledge and as practice in the first half of the twenty-first century. Passionate in its advocacy for making anthropology open to other disciplines, it should inspire a debate that goes beyond narrow preoccupations of the increasing tendency to accommodate to an accounting culture and its application of neoliberal models to the production of knowledge.

**VEENA DAS,** Krieger-Eisenhower Professor of Anthropology, Johns Hopkins University

. . .

It is hard to take the 'publish or perish' model of academic anthropology seriously these days when the actual lives of many of the people that we work with around the globe are at stake. Borofsky provides us with a timely and much needed road map for how anthropology can best move forward in an era when our insights into the shared human condition are not simply intellectual food for thought, but crucial to the survival of our species and our planet.

**JASON DE LEÓN,** Arthur F. Thurnau Professor, University of Michigan

. . .

Borofsky asks us to address vitally important issues—regarding disciplinary relevance, accountability and accessibility—at a critical time. An intrepid scholar, he is not content simply to call for a publicly engaged anthropology; he provides ways forward to accomplish it. One of the book's most valuable contributions is its refusal to get drawn into an easy opposition between academic and engaged work. Instead the book, in drawing both together, seeks an ever-critical, publicly engaged relevance that reinvigorates the discipline. We should embrace *An Anthropology of Anthropology's* call for change.

**SIMONE DENNIS,** Head of School, Archaeology and Anthropology, The Australian National University

. . .

Rob Borofsky's clarion call for a more engaged public anthropology asks some of the necessary hard questions: What are anthropology's evidentiary standards and characteristic inferential leaps? How do academic publishing and the new emphasis on metrics bolster individual careers while sidelining the broader community? Why do universities and foundations so often stifle scholars' desires to speak to audiences beyond academia? Readers of this insightful book will encounter an erudite, critical voice that questions many of the discipline's fundamental practices. An Anthropology of Anthropology is a book well worth reading.

**MARC EDELMAN,** Professor of Anthropology, Hunter College and CUNY Graduate Center; President, American Ethnological Society

. . .

Public anthropology's long-serving ambassador weighs in on issues that have shaped the discipline's place in the world. Using American anthropology as a case study, the book merits careful consideration by anyone interested in how cultural anthropology might transform itself.

**HARRI ENGLUND,** Professor of Social Anthropology, University of Cambridge

. . .

This book is a rare treasure. Mild-mannered and provocative, learned and playful, well documented and well written, acutely timely yet timeless, Borofsky showcases the magic of anthropological knowledge and the need for anthropology to be engaged and public, yet he also argues that contemporary anthropology suffers from cocooning and internal fragmentation. Through a wealth of stories, cases and analytical perspectives, Borofsky shows why everybody deserves to have a little bit of anthropology in their lives.

**THOMAS HYLLAND ERIKSEN,** Professor of Social Anthropology, University of Oslo

. . .

For the past century, anthropology has established itself within and through universities. But what, fundamentally, is anthropology's purpose beyond the classroom? In an important rethinking of a field he loves, Borofsky has thrown down the gauntlet, arguing that a field devoted to the understanding of cultures and the diverse ways people behave must be held to a higher standard. The challenge of fashioning an anthropology accountable to a broader public isn't new, as readers of the discipline's major figures, from Boas to Mead, know. But Borofsky shakes up the debate in new and engaging ways. As you will see, the book offers much food for thought. I truly enjoyed this book. I hope it finds a wide readership.

**PAUL FARMER**, MD, PhD, Kolokotrones University Professor, Harvard University

. . .

Champion of public anthropology, Rob Borofsky delivers in this book his long-awaited program for a renewal of the discipline. Starting with a critical state of the art, he then defends and illustrates an alternative paradigm, which would involve a radical transformation of the way in which the academia considers its responsibility toward society. Rich in numerous case studies, this book will undoubtedly give rise to valuable discussions among anthropologists.

**DIDIER FASSIN**, Professor of Social Science at the Institute for Advanced Study

. . .

A spirited challenge to anthropology's public image and efficacy, one that should stir up vigorous controversy and renewed public engagement.

**MICHAEL M.J. FISCHER**, Andrew W. Mellon Professor in the Humanities, Professor of Anthropology and Science and Technology Studies, MIT

. . .

This is a very important critique of the decline of anthropological thinking into the shrinking corridor of careerism in which quantity has replaced quality, in which creativity and pathbreaking ideas have become a relic of the past. Borofsky makes a strong plea for redirecting anthropology into the world beyond the academy that is our object of study in order to produce knowledge that has a real impact on others and is not simply focused on our own social status and career steps.

**JONATHAN FRIEDMAN**, Distinguished Professor of Anthropology, U.C. San Diego, Directeur D'études, *École des Hautes Études en Sciences Sociales*, Paris

. . .

Anthropology is turning in on itself and this is deeply problematic. The field has become overly specialized and narrow at a time when it needs to convey its insights to those beyond the discipline. It needs to ask big questions that matter to others. Rob Borofsky asks why cultural anthropology falls short of this potential. In his search to answer this question, he challenges the university-based contexts that shape the field—what he terms the fields "self-affirming myths" and its limited sense of objectivity. Building on case studies, he explores an alternative paradigm that could bring cultural anthropology closer to fulfilling its potential. Borofsky has proposed a very valuable way forward and we thank him for it.

**MAURICE GODELIER,** Professeur d'Anthropologie and Directeur, *École des Hautes Études* en Sciences Sociales, Paris

. . .

There is a general consensus that anthropology is in trouble. It is a discipline sitting on top of a vast compendium of accumulated knowledge about human social and cultural achievement and possibility, increasingly uncertain as what, precisely, was supposed to be the point of compiling it. In this admirable volume, Robert Borofsky suggests one possible way out: one that anthropologists would do well to take very seriously.

Anthropologists have now spent a generation reflecting on power dynamics "in the field"—that is, where there are unlikely to be any real-world consequences because we are the ones with all the power - but written almost nothing about conditions of work, patronage, funding, institutional hierarchy in the academy—that is, the power relations under which anthropological writing is actually produced. Robert Borofsky is one of the few who's had the requisite courage to do so.

**DAVID GRAEBER,** Professor of Anthropology, London School of Economics

. . .

*An Anthropology of Anthropology* raises important, provocative questions about the future of anthropology and contributes to a much-needed conversation about the discipline's relevance to critical social and political issues of our time. It offers much food for thought.

**SETH HOLMES,** Martin Sisters Endowed Chair; Co-Director, Berkeley Center for Social Medicine; Associate Professor of Medical Anthropology and Public Health, U.C. Berkeley

. . .

With a brisk look at anthropology's past, a sharp critique of its present, and a clear recipe for its immediate future, Borofsky catches a sea change in the discipline's perception of itself. The book will surely be much used in the classroom, and its arguments much debated.

**MICHAEL LAMBEK,** Canada Research Chair, University of Toronto Scarborough

. . .

*An Anthropology of Anthropology* is a thoughtful, provocative book. When you finish it, I expect you will be much more strongly inclined to agree on the paramount need for the field to work at building an explicit consensus about what an anthropology degree signals to the world and also agree that the standards of accountability we set for ourselves go well beyond bibliometrics to include the ways in which our work contributes to a more just and sustainable global community.

**EDWARD LIEBOW,** Executive Director at American Anthropological Association

. . .

Rob Borofsky's timely book calls for a paradigm shift in cultural anthropology, one in which emphasis is given to a "public anthropology" designed expressly to benefit the lives of others. Findings shown to be clearly beneficial to research subjects are stressed and, further, a critique is made of a tendency among anthropologists towards self-aggrandizement at the expense of covering the entirety of relevant fields in a just manner. This book will make a major contribution to cultural anthropology.

**MARGARET LOCK,** Marjorie Bronfman Professor Emerita, McGill University; Fellow of the Royal Society of Canada

. . .

Many observers think that anthropology is in a state of crisis. Robert Borofsky suggests a way forward—ditching scholarship as usual, increasing scientific collaboration and comparison, and evaluating scholars on the value of their real-world impact. This is a thoughtful, provocative, challenging intervention into a conversation we must have.

**TANYA MARIE LUHRMANN,** Howard H. and Jessie T. Watkins University Professor of Anthropology, Stanford University

. . .

I am inspired by the faith Rob Borofsky places in what anthropologists can do in bringing professional and activist roles together—what I termed in the 1990s 'circumstantial activism'—for the benefit of both publics and anthropology. There is a fearless, yet well informed, judgment here about the value of the paths that various anthropological traditions of scholarship have taken. There is a call for explicit acts of public service built into anthropological research drawn from an informed reading of its history.

Many anthropologists are self-identified activists. But all works of anthropological scholarship have publics within them who are inadequately addressed or recognized. What if these works were articulated as both scholarly and public at the same time? This is the fearless and difficult challenge—in a hopeful voice—that Borofsky has been proposing to anthropology for some time.

Far from being a 'turn' as many advocated trends are termed , this is a call to make an explicit part of the discipline's research as currently performed something that has lain embedded in the ethos of being an anthropologist all along. As anthropology seeks a way forward in difficult times, this is an important book to read.

**GEORGE E. MARCUS,** Founding Editor, Cultural Anthropology; Chancellor's Professor, UC Irvine

. . .

In *An Anthropology of Anthropology*, Borofsky challenges us to apply anthropological theories and methods to our discipline. Full of new interpretations of old anthropological chestnuts, the book is immediately a compendium of public anthropology stories, and examples of our best and worst practices. It is perfect for teaching and for reflecting on the state of our profession, both inside and outside of the classroom. More broadly, this book is call for a more effective public anthropology. Indeed, Borofsky stresses, as anthropologists, we must work better to address and solve the world's problems.

**TAD McILWRAITH,** Associate Professor, Guelph University; Co-Editor, *Perspectives: An Open Invitation to Cultural Anthropology*

. . .

In this thoughtful book Borofsky challenges the field of cultural anthropology to finally be true to its core values by boldly moving past the "do no harm" seemingly neutral stance of the academy, to a more proactive "do good!" model of anthropology with no apologies. He challenges us to reclaim our own unique research tools such as ethnography and participant observation, increasingly used by other fields without attribution. Using theoretical concepts such as Kuhn's notion of paradigm and Gramsci's notion of hegemonic type structures, the book charts a roadmap for us as anthropologists to pursue, "the road not taken" as he calls it, to implement an authentic public anthropology. Please consider its message!

**YOLONDA MOSES,** Professor of Anthropology and Associate Vice Chancellor, U.C. Riverside; Past President of the American Anthropological Association, the American Association for Higher Education, and the City University of New York

. . .

Borofsky argues that anthropology needs more engagement with the world outside academia. The public needs to hear from us directly—a more public anthropology. A must read!

**LAURA NADER,** Professor of Anthropology, U.C. Berkeley

. . .

Borofsky offers a richly narrated guide to anthropology that succeeds equally as an introduction to the discipline for students and as a guide to its reform for those who practice it. His account of the place of public anthropology in the face of unprecedented challenges to public discourse and the integrity of scholarship is informative, timely, and inspiring.

**RONALD NIEZEN,** Katharine A. Pearson Chair in Civil Society and Public Policy, McGill University

. . .

This book offers tough love for anthropology. Borofsky shows us how the structures of academic "success" harness anthropologists to the production of our own irrelevance. He challenges us to do more to realize cultural anthropology's untapped public potential. It is a, timely, important contribution.

**ANDREW ORTA,** Acting Director, Center for Latin American and Caribbean Studies; Professor of Anthropology, University of Illinois

. . .

An impassioned critique of insular social science from one of public anthropology's staunchest allies. Borofsky's book provides both a lucid diagnosis of the field's professional dynamics and crucial ways to nurture more socially engaged and responsive scholarship.

**ANAND PANDIAN,** Associate Professor and Director of Undergraduate Studies, Johns Hopkins University

. . .

The message of this provocative, suggestive book is "go public or perish." Anthropologists are called to deploy their scholarship to impact the world. There is much food for thought as well as action in *An Anthropology of Anthropology*. Well worth reading!

**JAMES PEACOCK,** Kenan Professor of Anthropology, emeritus, University of North Carolina at Chapel Hill; Past President of the American Anthropological Association

. . .

A unique and inspiring book of research, vision, and heart. *An Anthropology of Anthropology* lays bare how the political economy of promotion in the academy equates quantity and quality and distracts anthropology from applying its truths to helping a world that needs us. Borofsky urges anthropologists to move beyond the enslaving metrics of the academy towards projects grappling with changing the world. Required reading for any anthropologist struggling with not only understanding the world, but with how to change it.

**DAVID PRICE,** Professor of Anthropology and Sociology, Saint Martin's University; Author of *Cold War Anthropology: The CIA, the Pentagon,* and *The Growth of Dual Use Anthropology and Weaponizing Anthropology: Social Science in Service of the National Security State*

. . .

Borofsky's book is brimming with ideas for redefining anthropology. He shows close up through case studies how the institutional structures of the academy have controlled and restricted anthropology as an intellectual discipline. He asks tough questions about individual accountability, ethics, and self-interests. Has anthropology made real intellectual breakthroughs in recent decades? He confronts anthropologists asking them to reassess and to renew our social contract with the public good so that our ethnographic engagements can enrich the broader society as well as anthropology. For many years Rob Borofsky has been a necessary critic to the profession that he so clearly loves. Once again, he is pushing the envelope toward a more critically interpretive, ethical, and public anthropology for the people—the people they study and for the people who dedicate themselves to the 'difficult science' of ethnography.

I recommend this incisive and valuable book to anyone who cares about the future of our field. Once you read it, you will see why.

**NANCY SCHEPER-HUGHES;** Chancellor's Professor of Medical Anthropology Emerita, U.C. Berkeley

. . .

Robert Borofsky makes a powerful case for a more outwardly focused and publicly relevant anthropology showing how it can contribute to the major public policy issues of our times. This book offers a refreshing reminder of what makes cultural anthropology distinctive among the human sciences, the richness of anthropology's methodologies, and how these can be harnessed to improve people's lives. This book should be read by all those who care about the future of anthropology, the academy and the uses of publicly-funded research.

**CRIS SHORE,** Department of Anthropology, Goldsmiths University of London

. . .

"Reach out to others or become irrelevant!" is Rob Borofsky's take home message for American cultural anthropologists. He believes the discipline has shot itself in the foot: producing abstruse publications on topics of little value to the broader world, read only by an insular anthropological audience, and written primarily for the sake of narrow professional advancement. His manifesto is grounded in the conviction that knowledge in the social sciences is best advanced through research that aims to help others. While it remains to be seen whether a morally or politically motivated "mend the world" action anthropology will save our discipline from itself, what is not in doubt (even for a skeptic such as myself) is that *An Anthropology of Anthropology* is a welcome contribution to the crisis literature in cultural anthropology. It is well worth reading and debating.

**RICHARD A. SHWEDER,** Harold Higgins Swift Distinguished Service Professor, Comparative Human Development, University of Chicago

. . .

Borofsky gives us a sharp-sighted analysis of anthropology's by turns admirable and troubled history and a way forward based in a new commitment to principles of public engagement and social justice. His book is a valuable, important contribution to the great unfinished project of rethinking our field and its place in the world.

**ORIN STARN,** Professor of Cultural Anthropology and History, Duke University

# AN ANTHROPOLOGY
# OF ANTHROPOLOGY

**PUBLIC ANTHROPOLOGY: An Open Access Series**

The series embraces the hope that anthropology has value to those beyond the discipline, beyond the university. It is one thing to write a thoughtful book. It is another to do so in a manner that attracts the attention and collaboration needed to help address a problem. The focus is on publications that matter to other people—by the power of their ideas and by how, with the help of others, they transform peoples' lives for the better.

SERIES EDITOR: ROBERT BOROFSKY
(CENTER FOR A PUBLIC ANTHROPOLOGY)

*An Anthropology of Anthropology: Is It Time to Shift Paradigms?* by Robert Borofsky

# AN ANTHROPOLOGY OF ANTHROPOLOGY

## Is It Time to Shift Paradigms?

**ROBERT BOROFSKY**

To Nancy,
for Florida

The only people who see the whole picture are the ones who step outside the frame.

SIR SALMAN RUSHDIE, British-Indian novelist and essayist

When you go to Haiti, when you go to Africa . . . they do not ask you how much do you feel for my people, how much have you studied . . . my people, they say have you brought anything?

With all this privilege, with this fantastic education we have gotten, what is the nature of our responsibility to the rest of the world?

What makes a great leader? It is not just charisma; it is not just the people who can produce interesting banter. It's people who will take responsibility for a situation and move it to a place where it is better than it was before. That is something for every single person to aspire to.

JIM YONG KIM, cofounder of Partners in Health and former president of the World Bank

# CONTENTS

Preface  /  xi

Acknowledgments  /  xiii

1  Exploring Cultural Anthropology's
Academic Contexts  /  1

2  Who Are the Main Beneficiaries of Cultural
Anthropology's Many Publications?  /  41

3  Shifting the Paradigm Toward Public
Anthropology  /  123

4  Making Your Voice Count  /  173

5  Two Roads Diverged . . .  /  195

References  /  231

Index  /  331

About the Author  /  347

# PREFACE

**AS THE TITLE SUGGESTS**, this book uses anthropological methods and insights to study the practice of anthropology as an academic discipline. It considers the contexts that shape the discipline, especially its beliefs, its publications, and the degree to which what it produces is of value to others. *An Anthropology of Anthropology* explores alternative ways to assess the intellectual productivity of faculty besides measuring how many publications they produce in what period of time. It focuses on outcomes—what results from anthropological publications and projects.

Given anthropology's precarious position—being small in size with limited funding but, at the same time, possessing great potential—this book calls for a paradigm shift, away from the publication treadmill, toward a more profile-raising paradigm that focuses on addressing a broad array of social concerns in meaningful ways. The book seeks to shift cultural anthropology's paradigm from one focusing on "do no harm" to one emphasizing a "public anthropology" focused on benefitting others. Drawing on an anthropological dictum relating to exogamy—to marry out or die out—the book suggests anthropology needs to engage more effectively with the broader world. The alternative is to turn in on itself, diminishing its public importance and funding.

Rather than considering the discipline as a whole, the book narrows its focus to American cultural anthropology as a case study—so it can dig deeply into the field's dynamics. It explores trends within the field over several decades and, in discussing them, includes over a thousand references. Since in the United States cultural anthropologists constitute roughly two-thirds of the discipline, the focus on cultural anthropology seems reasonable. Still, cultural and social anthropologists in other countries as well as archaeologists, physical anthropologists, and linguists may find certain themes relevant—especially the book's focus on moving beyond judging faculty by the number of publications produced to assessing whether their work actually advances knowledge and/or helps others. Stylistically, it is awkward to repeatedly refer to "cultural anthropology" when one might use "anthropology." ("An anthropology of anthropology" sounds more appealing than "a cultural anthropology of cultural anthropology.") When I refer to "anthropology" in the text, I mostly mean "cultural anthropology" especially as practiced in the United States.

In brief, *An Anthropology of Anthropology* provides readers with much food for thought regarding the present state of cultural anthropology and its future possibilities. Being an open-access book is simply an added bonus.

# ACKNOWLEDGMENTS

THERE ARE MANY PEOPLE whom I wish to thank for helping to shape this book. I appreciate the thoughtful comments offered by Amelia Borofsky, Philippe Bourgois, Nancy Scheper-Hughes, Paul Farmer, Marshall Sahlins, Didier Fassin, George Marcus, Nina Brown, Tad McIlwraith, Antonio De Lauri, Ellen Moodie, Todd Sanders, Michael Fischer, and Russell Bernard. They have proved most helpful.

In producing this book, I would like to thank Dave Peattie of BookMatters for his careful, thoughtful efforts to bring it to fruition and Nicole Hayward for her delightful design work. At the Center for a Public Anthropology, I appreciate the support of Stan Bowers and Joe Esser. I have worked for so long with David Maliachi and Matt Sproat, of Adaptium, that many of the Center's projects are now theirs as much as mine. David has opened up new worlds to explore through the internet.

I also wish to acknowledge various individuals who through their friendship and insightful conversations have shaped much of my intellectual work. This book would not have taken the shape it has without their help: Bruce Albert, Fredrik Barth, Philippe Bourgois, Nina Brown, Greg Dening, Paul Farmer, Maurice Godelier, Marvin Harris, Alex Hinton, Alan Howard, Claude Lévi-Strauss, Robert Levy, Richard Lieban, Carolyn Nordstrom, Douglas Oliver, George Marcus, Tad McIlwraith, Laura Nader, Roy Rappaport, Boyce Rensberger, Marshall Sahlins, Nancy Scheper-Hughes, Stanley Tambiah, and Valery Tishkov.

In Hawaii, I am indebted for the enduring support of my immediate family— Amelia, Robyn, Sam, Caleb, Tad, Yinale, Reva, and especially Nancy, my wife for more than forty-five years. This book is dedicated to her. At Hawaii Pacific, I wish to thank David Lanoue, Mathew Liao-Troth, John Fleckles, and Bill Potter. More broadly, I appreciate the support provided by Mark Hannington, Taro Takahashi, Calvert Hung, Josh Schuette, and Amanda Iames. Thank you!

Finally, I want to express my appreciation to Victor Englebert for allowing me to use photographs from his outstanding ethnographic collection. For more information on Victor Englebert and his books, please refer to https://www.ama zon.com/Victor-Englebert/e/B001HP9ZZS?ref=dbs_p_pbk_r00_abau_000000

For a selection of his photographs and a way to contact him, please see https:// www.asmp.org/portfolio/victor-englebert/ .

The **Chapter 1 photo** is from Bali, Indonesia. An older man is herding his ducks along the edge of a rice paddy. The **Chapter 2 photo** is from Chombote, Peru. At dawn, fishermen unload the catch from their fishing boats onto the rowboats that then take the fish to the beach.

The **Chapter 3 photo** is from Cuenca, Ecuador. The three women are waiting outside a church for the bus on market day. The **Chapter 4 photo** is from the Amazon rain forest, Roraima, Brazil, portrait of a young Yanomami man. The **Chapter 5 photo** is from the Niger Republic, Sahara Desert. A young Tuareg woman is pulling a baby camel away from its mother after nursing so the woman's relatives can milk the mother camel.

# 1

# EXPLORING CULTURAL ANTHROPOLOGY'S ACADEMIC CONTEXTS

**CULTURAL ANTHROPOLOGY**, the focus of this book, has tremendous potential. With its in-depth research techniques and broad comparative insights, it can make a difference—a real difference—in the lives of many people around the world. At its best, cultural anthropology represents an antidote to hate, provincialism, and despair. In stressing the fluid nature of group identities through time and space, it helps soften ethnic violence. In valuing cultural diversity for how it enriches our world, cultural anthropology fosters tolerance of difference. In emphasizing how context shapes behavior, it encourages people to reshape the contexts needed to reshape their lives—medically, economically, socially— so as to find new meaning, opportunity, and hope. But unfortunately, cultural anthropology frequently falls short of this potential. A key question this book deals with is *why*. What are the structural impediments that, despite the best intentions, limit the field's development—fragmenting its intellectual focus and limiting its public support and significance? Understanding how these structural impediments operate and how they might be lessened, perhaps even overcome to some degree, is the second concern of this book. It seeks to offer a path forward for revitalizing the field.

The book's two concerns are relevant to those who wish to escape prominent constraining structures in the field today—especially the metrics that assess faculty productivity and shape their intellectual lives. Ignoring, or even dismissing, these structures may feel good, but it will not make them disappear. These assessment standards are now being significantly shaped by forces beyond the academy. They impact our research, careers, and, more broadly, the field's dynamics. Given the stresses they engender, *An Anthropology of Anthropology* offers hope in a time of uncertainty and doubt.

Chapter 1 sets the stage for the following chapters. It uses anthropology's tools to understand the university-based contexts that shape cultural anthropology— its definition, its self-affirming myths, and its sense of objectivity. In addition, the chapter sets out the book's broader framework—discussing two prominent paradigms and why the first, given that it is embedded in key academic-based structures, dominates cultural anthropology to the field's current detriment.

Chapter 2 focuses on a set of case studies. Because it challenges a widely held affirmation—that the field is continually building cumulative knowledge and refining key concepts—I add supporting data indicating this criticism also holds for other disciplines. The chapter discusses five intellectual trends as a way of assessing what the field has, and has not, accomplished in recent years. It suggests the limited results relate to how key structures, tied to the dominant paradigm, shape the field and impede its intellectual development.

Chapter 3 explores an alternative paradigm for the field that could bring cultural anthropology closer to fulfilling its potential. Case studies highlight the points made. This alternative paradigm, the book suggests, holds promise for enlarging the field's public significance and, at the same time, making it more coherent.

Chapter 4 builds on the previous chapter. Through a number of case studies, it discusses how cultural anthropologists can make their voices count, increase their public impact, and expand their public support.

Chapter 5 starts with the recent increase in metric assessments of faculty productivity—in terms of publications, funding, and citations—and the distortions fostered by them. Despite their negative impact and faculty frustrations with these assessments, overturning them has proved problematic. The chapter explores why and asks if instead of directly confronting the political and financial supporters of metric assessments, it might be wiser to draw these supporters to a new paradigm, one that measures faculty productivity less in terms of publications and more in terms of what impact they, and the field, have on the larger society. Finally, drawing on Robert Frost's "The Road Not Taken," the chapter suggests the professional and personal value in embracing this alternative paradigm.

## Cultural Anthropology's Ethnographic Tools

*This section discusses cultural anthropology's three central methodological tools: participant-observation, contextual understanding, and comparison. Through participant-observation, anthropologists come to understand the people they work with, not as strangers but as colleagues. Placing behaviors within their contexts offers a better understanding of why people behave the way they do. Comparisons, especially controlled comparisons, allow anthropologists to step back from a range of details to see the underlying dynamics at work.*

At first glance, reviewing the field's ethnographic tools may seem unnecessary. They tend to be well known. But there is a reason. I want to stress there is much value in using anthropological tools to study anthropology. They illuminate underlying structural dynamics that shape the practice of cultural anthropology today. The Bronislaw Malinowski quote below regarding participant-observation is well known. What many may not realize is the degree to which participant-observation has become a key tool in a host of other disciplines, allowing authors in these disciplines to produce perceptive analyses that gain wide, public recognition and facilitate change.

The second tool, understanding cultural context, is again well known within the field. The examples here suggest how Pukapukans acquire and validate knowledge overlaps with the ways anthropologists do (as readers will see in Chapter 2). They both have some of the same strengths and limitations. The third tool, comparative analysis, especially controlled comparison, for decades has been in decline. Older readers may recall the examples presented. Younger readers might wonder why the approach, with such insights, has gone out of style.

What we need to keep in mind, as we move through various chapters in this book, is the power of the field's ethnographic tools to help us see cultural anthropology in a new light. Why have other disciplines often made better use of these tools—in facilitating effective public discourse, providing important social insights—than cultural anthropology?

## PARTICIPANT-OBSERVATION

Malinowski, a prominent early twentieth-century anthropologist, famously stated his goal in anthropology was "to grasp the native's point of view ... to realize *his* vision of *his* world."[1] To do this, Malinowski lived as a participant as well as an observer for roughly two years—between 1915 and 1918—among the Trobriand Islanders of Papua New Guinea in the South Pacific. He wrote:

> There is all the difference between a sporadic plunging into the company of na-
> tives, and being really in contact with them. ... Soon after I had established myself
> in [the village of] Omarakana (Trobriand Islands), I began to take part, in a way, in
> the village life, to look forward to the important or festive events, to take personal
> interest in the gossip and the developments of the small village occurrences; to
> wake up every morning to a day, presenting itself to me more or less as it does to
> the native. ...
>
> It must be remembered that as the natives saw me constantly every day ...
> [they] ceased to be interested or alarmed, or made self-conscious by my presence
> and I ceased to be a disturbing element in the tribal life ... altering it by my very
> approach, as always happens with a new-comer to every [such] ... community.
> In fact, as they knew that I would thrust my nose into everything, even where a
> well-mannered native would not dream of intruding, they finished by regarding
> me as part and parcel of their life, a necessary evil or nuisance, mitigated by dona-
> tions of tobacco. ... Whatever happened was within easy reach, and there was no
> possibility of its escaping my notice. ... Really important quarrels and rifts within
> the community, cases of illness, attempted cures and deaths, magical rites ... all
> these I had not to pursue, fearful of missing them, but they took place under my
> very eyes, at my own doorstep, so to speak.[2]

## UNDERSTANDING CULTURAL CONTEXT

In cultural anthropology, understanding is often achieved by placing various beliefs and behaviors within their cultural contexts. What may seem strange and exotic to those unfamiliar with a group's practices often makes sense when placed within indigenous contexts of meaning. That is why anthropologists spend considerable space in their ethnographies discussing indigenous terms and conveying the subtleties and complexities of indigenous perceptions. It clar-

---

1    Malinowski (1922[1961]:25).
2    Malinowski (1922[1961]:7–8).

ifies, to quote Clifford Geertz, a sense of "what goes on in such places . . . what manner of [people] are these?"[3]

Two examples from my fieldwork illustrate contextual analyses. I spent forty-one months (almost three-and-a-half years) conducting research on a small Polynesian atoll in the northern Cook Islands called Pukapuka. To explain how Pukapukans acquire and validate knowledge of the past, I described what life was like on the atoll when I lived there. The first example discusses the playful status rivalry regarding the display of knowledge that takes place on the atoll. The second example considers how Pukapukans, while feeling free to assert their opinions, also tend to defer to those they deem as "experts":

[Example 1]
As Molingi was trying to make a particular [traditional] string figure (waiwai), Nimeti, her husband, jokingly criticized her efforts. When she failed to do it right the first time and had to try over again, he turned to me and stated she did not know how to make such things. Here was the proof; she could not do a string figure. Molingi appeared to ignore his comments. She seemed absorbed in trying to work out where she had gone wrong in making the figure. Again Nimeti criticized her efforts. Finally Molingi turned to him and stated that he was getting senile. (Both of them [were] in their seventies.) Didn't Nimeti recognize, she rhetorically asked, that she was an expert on traditional matters?

As a result of Molingi's comment, Nimeti picked up a string and started making a figure himself. Molingi scoffed at his efforts. My daughter, Amelia, came by and asked Nimeti what he was doing. He proudly showed her his figure. Molingi criticized Nimeti's string figure as something any child could do. Finally Molingi finished her figure and showed it to me. She pointedly noted that Nimeti did not know how to make one like hers. Nimeti laughed at the implied challenge and began to work on a different string figure. Here was another one, he commented, that Molingi did not know.[4]

[Example 2]
One day, after gathering some poles in Loto's public reserve to build the roof of my cook house, I stopped at a pule guardhouse to rest and talk with two of the guards. They were both women, one in her late thirties and the other in her late twenties. One thing led to another and we started discussing whether it was the legendary

3    Geertz (1973:16).
4    Borofsky (1987:78).

figure Waletiale or Malangaatiale who possessed an enlarged penis. Both of them asserted that it was Malangaatiale. They admitted uncertainty as to exactly who Waletiale was, but basically felt that he was another character entirely. I, on the other hand, asserted that Waletiale possessed the enlarged penis and that the legend of Malangaatiale concerned a man struck by lightning.

We discussed our differences of opinion for a while without coming to any agreement. Then the younger of the two women asked me how I knew my version of the two legends was correct. I replied that this was what several old people, especially Petelo and Molingi, had told me.

As I listened to them, they again discussed the whole issue between themselves. What I had said did not really seem right to them. But they admitted that they themselves were not that sure of either legend. Finally, they decided that I might indeed be right. Unlike them, I had discussed the issue with Petelo and Molingi, both recognized experts on Pukapukan legends.[5]

Observing how a group of people interact in a number of situations, such as these, anthropologists are able to make sense—and convey that sense to others—of how people in a group go about their daily lives in ways that are different from but understandable by us.[6]

## CONTROLLED COMPARISONS

The third anthropological tool, comparison, compares behaviors and beliefs in one group of people with related data from another group (or groups). By bringing more than one case to bear on a problem, anthropologists perceive suggestive possibilities for explaining how cultural trait A influences B or how trait C causes D. In "controlled comparisons," anthropologists explore a select number of related contexts involving a limited number of differences and/or similarities to better understand key cultural dynamics across the groups studied. Here are three examples.

The first involves British anthropologist S. F. Nadel's study of witchcraft among four African societies.[7] (Because of length considerations, I limit my summary to the two West African societies he discusses.) The Nupe and Gwari, Nadel

---

5    Borofsky (1987:111).

6    In relation to contextual analysis, Alfred Kroeber writes that Franz Boas insisted "that phenomena can properly be dealt with only in their adhering context" (Kroeber [1943:6]).

7    Nadel (1952).

notes, share a number of cultural similarities regarding social, economic, and political organization. But they differ on a significant point. Among the Nupe only women are witches, but among the Gwari both men and women are. Why the difference? Nadel points out that Nupe women are traders, and this trading often provides them with economic power and wealth. Moreover, it allows Nupe women the freedom to become involved in a number of extramarital liaisons. Gwari women lack this power and freedom. They are unable to challenge the cultural norm of male dominance existing in both cultures. Nadel suggests that the gap between the ideal power of men and the real power of women focused witchcraft accusations on female traders among the Nupe. Social stresses among the Gwari are more diffuse and as a result so are the witchcraft accusations.

In the second example, Eric Wolf uses historical material to compare responses to colonization in Mesoamerica and Central Java. He suggests that a type of peasant village—called "closed corporate communities"—arose in both locales due to similar pressures during the colonial era. Closed corporate communities, as defined by Wolf, were communities with communal jurisdiction over land, restricted membership, redistributive mechanisms for surplus, and barriers against outside goods and ideas. Part of the reason they developed, he suggests, was because of administrative efforts to restrict the power of colonial settlers. "By granting relative autonomy to the native communities," Wolf writes, "the home government could at one and the same time ensure the maintenance of cultural barriers against colonist encroachment, while avoiding the huge cost of direct administration."[8] Wolf highlights another formative factor: an economic split in the organization of colonial society, involving a dominating entrepreneurial sector and a dominated peasant sector. Indigenous peasants were relegated "to the status of part-time laborers, providing for their own subsistence on scarce land, together with the imposition of charges levied and enforced by . . . local authorities."[9] In brief, using comparison, Wolf perceived important dynamics shaping peasant communities during the colonial era in diverse parts of the world.

The third example emphasizes that comparison (or a comparative consciousness) can be used as a tool of control. Laura Nader discusses how Western women perceive themselves as freer than Muslim women while Muslim women

8    E. Wolf (1957:10).
9    E. Wolf (1957:12).

hold the reverse perspective. "Female subordination is increasingly rationalized in terms of the other," she writes. "Downtrodden Arab females make Muslim culture in general seem less human, and by comparison the treatment of Western women seem more human, and more enlightened. The reverse is also true; images of the West are of a barbaric and immoral people. The result of using comparison as control I argue is *perpetuation of female subordination in both East and West*."[10] As Nader explains:

> The West plays an important part in the Islamic construction of Islamic womanhood and as I show is key to holding Western women in place. Paradigms are legitimated by their very contrast with the West, especially a barbaric, materialistic West. . . . American women are sex objects and cite the multi-billion dollar pornography industry as evidence. Women in the West are said to be under daily threat of rape, while they are not in Cairo. U.S. incest and family violence rates are cited, and always we are reminded that the portrayal of women in American magazines is disrespectful.
>
> The Western media reciprocate, and their images show that the East plays an important part in the construction of Western womanhood. Images of the Muslim woman show her as pitiable and downtrodden. Usually these media images focus on selected areas of comparison (contrast). Muslim women wear the veil, a symbol of subordination for the Western observer. Islamic society fixates on the cult of virginity, and female children are abused by various techniques such as *Jabr* or forced marriage, or by clitoridectomy. Also polygamy and easy divorce subjugate women psychologically and materially.[11]

## Highlighting Cultural Anthropologists Who Have Made Valuable Contributions to the Broader Society

*This section discusses three prominent scholar-activists in anthropology— Franz Boas, Margaret Mead, and Paul Farmer—who have made significant contributions to the wider society. Boas emphasized that behavior is more culturally, than racially, determined. Mead described how cultural dynamics often play a critical role in shaping behavior. Farmer developed a healthcare system that emphasizes local participation as much as national and international resources.*

---

10    Nader (1994:92, emphasis in the original).
11    Nader (1994:91–92).

Anthropology is a historically unique project. No intellectual effort in recorded history has involved as many scholars striving to understand people living in different locales on their own terms. In discussing the practice of anthropology, it is important to emphasize that several anthropologists have effectively spoken out publicly regarding key issues of our time. They illustrate cultural anthropology's potential in making a real difference in other people's lives.

There are a number of individuals one might cite: Nancy Scheper-Hughes disclosing the international buying and selling of kidneys; Carolyn Nordstrom illuminating the illegal networks that perpetuate Third World armed conflicts; Philippe Bourgois providing insight into the dynamics of drug dealing and the survival strategies of homeless drug addicts; Alex Hinton explaining the killing fields of Cambodia; or Harri Englund describing why many human rights NGOs (nongovernmental organizations) are ineffective in Third World settings.[12]

Boas opposed racist theories of development. As Nazism strengthened its hold on Germany, he appeared on the cover of *Time* magazine in May 1936. *Time* called Boas's *The Mind of Primitive Man* (originally published in 1911) "the Magna Carta of self-respect" for non-Western peoples.[13] Based on years of study, Boas emphasized that "physiological, mental and social functions are highly variable, being dependent upon external conditions so that an intimate relation between race and culture does not seem plausible."[14] A well-known somatological study of European immigrants Boas conducted for the United States Immigration Commission (published in 1912) confirmed this point. He spoke out on this issue in letters and articles to the *New York Times*, the *Nation*, and *Dial*.[15] He wrote an open letter to Germany's President Hindenburg denouncing Nazism. He was the catalyst behind a 1938 "Scientists' Manifesto" opposing any connection between race and intelligence that was signed by 1,284 scientists from 167 universities.[16]

Margaret Mead was a cultural icon. In her time she was the most widely known and respected anthropologist in the world. At her death in 1978, there

---

12    Bourgois (2000, 2002); Bourgois and Schonberg (2009); Scheper-Hughes (2000, 2003); Lawless (n.d.); Nordstrom (2004, 2007); Hinton (2004); Englund (2006).

13    Baker (2004:42).

14    Boas (1938:145).

15    Boas (1945).

16    Baker (2004:43). Boas was involved with the NAACP and wrote the lead article for its journal's second issue (Lewis [2001b]:455). He publicly challenged Columbia University's president and trustees when they sought to fire a faculty member for opposing American entry into World War I (Lewis [2001b]:457).

were tributes not only from the president of the United States but the secretary-general of the United Nations.[17] In 1979 she was posthumously awarded the United States's highest civilian honor, the Presidential Medal of Freedom.[18] The American Museum of Natural History (where Mead worked from 1926 until her death) described her this way: "[She] brought the serious work of anthropology into the public consciousness. . . . A deeply committed activist, Mead often testified on social issues before the United States Congress and other government agencies."[19] She brought an understanding of culture—especially how it shaped human differences—to an international audience eager, in the aftermath of World War II, to address the ills of the world in less violent terms. Her intellectual output was staggering. She wrote forty-four books and more than a thousand articles. She was a monthly columnist for the popular *Redbook* magazine from 1961 until 1978. She reputedly gave as many as 110 public lectures a year.[20] She was a leader in the feminist movement. Mead's 1928 book, *Coming of Age in Samoa*, is one of the best-selling books by an American anthropologist.

Paul Farmer is well known and widely respected in Western medical circles.[21] Through his work as a medical doctor/anthropologist and in Partners in Health (a nonprofit organization he helped found), Farmer has played a central role in improving the health care of millions. The *New York Times* reports: "If any one person can be given credit for transforming the medical establishment's thinking about health care for the destitute, it is Paul Farmer." Working through Partners in Health, Farmer and others have been able to lower the price of drugs for the sick in Third World countries as well as change the World Health Organization's guidelines for treating the poor. The *New York Times* continues: "Dr. Farmer and his Partners in Health have shown that a small group of committed individuals . . . can change the world."[22] According to the Partners in Health website, "We build on the strengths and the communities by working within public health systems and serving where there are gaps . . . we invest directly in the communities we serve by training and employing a cadre of local community health workers to accompany our patients and their families through

17    Whitman (1978).
18    Ciano (2001).
19    Mead (n.d.).
20    WIC, Margaret Mead (n.d.).
21    Sixty Minutes (2008).
22    P. Cohen (2003).

their care."[23] This radically different—but very anthropological—perspective has transformed health care in several Third World settings.[24]

## Why Do More Anthropologists Not Follow in the Footsteps of Boas, Mead, and Farmer?

*The problem, at least in part, centers around how objectivity is defined within the academy. Objectivity arises when people independently confirm a research project's results. In contrasting objectivity with advocacy, many universities have sought to limit faculty activism. But objectivity does not preclude activism and activism does not preclude objectivity.*

Anthropologists such as Boas, Mead, and Farmer have always remained a minority within cultural anthropology. The problem is that the context within which anthropology generally operates today (i.e., universities) often undermines political engagement and addressing important social concerns in effective ways. In the mid- to late-nineteenth century, as disciplines took shape, social scientists often lacked an aura of public credibility. They were deemed to be amateurs—unprofessional in orientation and training—who might peddle this or that view but who lacked the proper credentials to get others to take them seriously. In joining universities, they raised their status and their salaries.

But becoming a credible professional in a university meant establishing a disinterested, "objective" attitude toward the subject studied. The politics involved in this can be seen in Mary Furner's study of early social scientists, *Advocacy and Objectivity: A Crisis in the Professionalization of American Social Science, 1865–1905.* This book won the Frederick Jackson Turner Award from the Organization of American Historians. I present four quotations from Furner's book so that she herself can explain what transpired:

(1) Establishing scientific authority [in the 1870s and 1880s] was . . . difficult for . . . [amateur social scientists] because many of them were publicly connected with controversial political positions. No matter how hard pre-academic social scientists tried to change their image . . . anyone who resented their findings . . .

23   Dahl (2008).
24   Readers interested in exploring this topic further might refer to Arnst (2006); Boas (1912); Economist (2003); Farmer (2004, 2010, 2013, 2015); Hyatt (1990); Kidder (2004); Lewis (2001a, 2001b); Lowie (1944); David Mills (2008); Time (2005); Williams (1991).

could easily cast doubt on their objectivity by hurling the reliable epithet, "reformer."[25]

(2) By the end of the 1890s professional status and security competed with ideological . . . considerations as values [for social scientists]. . . . Direct appeal to the public . . . was retained as a theoretical right but . . . [social scientists in universities] were expected to channel most of their reform efforts through government agencies or private organizations where scholars could serve inconspicuously as technical experts, after the political decisions had been made, rather than as reformers with a new vision of society.[26]

(3) Objectivity . . . [became] part of . . . [an] emerging professional identity, but . . . [university] leaders defined it in a special way. It restricted open public advocacy of the sort that allied . . . [social scientists] with reforms that threatened the status quo.[27]

(4) The tension between advocacy and objectivity which characterized the professionalization process altered the mission of social science. Only rarely [as the twentieth century proceeded] did professional social scientists do what no one else was better qualified to do: bring expert skill and knowledge to bear on cosmic questions pertaining to the society as a whole. Instead, studies and findings tended to be internal, recommendations hedged with qualifiers, analyses couched in jargon that was unintelligible to the average citizen. A fundamental conservatism developed in the academic social science professionals. . . . The academic professionals, having retreated to the security of technical expertise, left to journalists and politicians the original mission—the comprehensive assessment of industrial society—that had fostered the professionalization of social sciences [in the first place].[28]

In brief, to gain academic security and respectability, academics were drawn to behave in "professionally objective" ways. They were seduced away from social activism by the comforts and financial stability of university positions.

One can follow this process by examining the late-nineteenth-century case of Richard T. Ely, a prominent tenured economist at the University of Wisconsin.[29] Ely, as Furner remarks, "was more active than anyone else [in economics]

25    Furner (1975:3–4).
26    Furner (1975:259).
27    Furner (1975:290–291).
28    Furner (1975:324).
29    Furner (1975:147–158).

in taking his findings directly to the people and advocating specific reforms."[30] When one of the University of Wisconsin's regents charged Ely with unprofessional behavior (including being an anarchist) in 1894, the university's Board of Regents held a trial to decide whether to dismiss him. Ely's most vigorous support came from nonacademic economists rather than academic economists who were afraid his case might undermine their status as reputable, objective scholars. Ely was cleared of the specific charges laid against him. But after the trial he became more conservative in his views and turned toward writing scholarly publications rather than engaging in reformist activities.

"Objectivity" came to mean avoiding politically charged topics that might seriously threaten the "powers that be" in universities. But objectivity doesn't lie in avoiding certain topics, in appearing respectable. The issue isn't whether one does (or doesn't) have a political agenda. To some degree, everyone has biases of one sort or another. Being a "disinterested" professional doesn't mean being uninterested in the world outside one's laboratory. It means putting the larger society's interests ahead of one's own interests or the interests of those one works for. Objectivity derives from the open, public analysis of differing accounts—not from what we assert or suspect to be true. We know an account is more objective, more credible, more scientific, after other researchers—whatever their personal biases—independently confirm the claims being made.

Take the controversy surrounding breast implants. Legal suits worth millions of dollars have been brought against breast implant manufacturers based on the claim that breast implants harm a woman's health. Marcia Angell, former editor of the *New England Journal of Medicine*, writes: "The idea that breast augmentation caused connective tissue disease has a superficial plausibility."[31] However, she continues: "None of the epidemiological studies has been able to demonstrate a clear link between breast implants and connective tissue disease or suggestive symptoms."[32] The FDA concurs: "Based on the totality of the evidence, the FDA believes that silicone gel-filled breast implants have a reasonable assurance of safety and effectiveness when used as labeled."[33] If the studies contradicted one another in various ways, we might search for an explanation in the biases of this or that researcher. But all the major research studies, espe-

30  Furner (1975:147).
31  Angell (1996:104).
32  Angell (1996:27); see, e.g., Gabriel et al. (1994).
33  FDA (2011:31).

cially the retrospective ones that looked at thousands of cases, came to the same basic conclusion. Despite what readers might personally wish to believe, there is no objective support for an association between breast implants and connective tissue disease.

In some complex cases, retesting claims may not be possible because the data are difficult to replicate. In such cases the solution is to have conversations among those of divergent perspectives regarding what caused their results to diverge in unexpected ways. We see this in the Redfield-Lewis controversy. Two anthropologists, Robert Redfield and Oscar Lewis, wrote ethnographies of a Mexican village, Tepoztlán. However, their accounts differed in significant ways.[34] Most anthropologists would agree that the process of sorting through their differences led to a more objective account of Tepoztlán's dynamics. It didn't matter that Lewis was of a more liberal persuasion than Redfield. What mattered was that various anthropologists, poring over the same material, found a way to make sense of the differences. Lewis, it turned out, focused more on actual behavior; Redfield, on ideal norms.

Objectivity, in brief, derives from the independent retesting of claims and/ or the negotiated conversations arising out of this process. Advocacy has little, if anything, to do with objectivity. The opposition isn't between objectivity and advocacy. The opposition is between claiming objectivity and substantiating it. It is rubbish to assert that if one thinks objectively, that if one acts in a seemingly "disinterested" manner, if one avoids any hint of social advocacy, then one is objective. We might note the example of Linus Pauling. Pauling was a prominent scientist who won a Nobel Prize for his contributions to chemistry. But he was also a political activist who won the Nobel Peace Prize for his opposition to aboveground nuclear testing. No one has challenged the value of Pauling's contributions to chemistry because he campaigned against the dangers of nuclear fallout.

Or take Noam Chomsky, one of the most prominent linguists of the twentieth century. He is widely viewed as having revolutionized the study of language. He is also a political activist of considerable renown. He is a leading critic of American foreign policy as well as of American media, viewing the media as often a propaganda machine for supporting the power elite. Yet his political activism hasn't cast doubt on his intellectual work. In a 2005 poll by *Prospect/Foreign Pol-*

34    O. Lewis (1951, 1960); Redfield (1930, 1956).

*icy*, Chomsky was voted the leading public intellectual alive.[35] He has received honorary degrees from over thirty universities worldwide and won a number of prestigious prizes. He is also a member of both the American Academy of Arts and Sciences and the National Academy of Sciences.[36]

## Additional Ways Academic Contexts Shape the Practice of Cultural Anthropology

*The academic departmental structure plays a key role in determining who is and isn't perceived as an anthropologist as well as what is and isn't perceived as anthropology. Despite various efforts to foster interdisciplinary studies, they have not replaced discipline-based departments because departments usually control the tenure and promotion process. The specializations and subspecializations now common in cultural anthropology likely grew out of the need for anthropologists to differentiate themselves within a department. As departments grew in size, so did the specializations.*

The university-based departmental structure shapes the discipline's definition and self-image in definite ways. In the social sciences, topics of study frequently cut across various disciplines. You would be hard pressed to find a topic anthropologists study that some other discipline doesn't also study in some form. Power? Anthropologists study that; but so do political scientists. Economic exchanges? Both anthropologists and economists study them. Clyde Kluckhohn, a noted post–World War II anthropologist, suggested that a degree in anthropology provided an "intellectual poaching license" to explore areas of interest in other disciplines.[37] Clifford Geertz observed: "People who watch

35    D. Campbell (2005).

36    Wikipedia, s.v. "Noam Chomsky." Readers interested in exploring this topic further might refer to Anonymous (1919); Bannister (1976); T. Bender (1993); Bousquet (2002); Brock (1994); F. Brown (1954); Calhoun (1976); Content (1976); Critser (2003); Dykstra (1976); Economist (2008d, 2008l); Floridi (2001); Furner (1999); Gerber (1991); Grafton (1997, 2007); Haskell (1977, 1998); Jordanova (2000); M. R. Kaplan (1974); Katz (2002); Kuklick (1976); M. Marshall (1989); McFeely (2001); McMurty (2001); Mills (2008); Noble (1978); Oleson and Voss (1979); D. Ross (1976, 1978, 1991); Scull (1990); Silva and Slaughter (1984); Silver (1979); Simpson (1999); M. Smith (1994); Veblen (1918); Veysey (1975); Watkins (1976); Westbrook (1992, 1994); Williams and Ceci (2007).

37    "Clyde Kluckhohn once said about anthropology—that it's an intellectual poaching license" (Geertz 1983:21).

baboons copulate, people who rewrite myths in algebraic formulas, people who dig up Pleistocene skeletons, people who work out decimal point correlations between toilet-training practices and theories of disease, people who decode Maya hieroglyphics, and people who classify kinship systems into typologies in which our own comes out as 'Eskimo,' all call themselves anthropologists."[38]

How does one decide who is an anthropologist? If an individual wants a position as an anthropologist—in an academic or a nonacademic context—that individual generally needs a graduate degree in anthropology at the master's or doctoral level. To practice anthropology, in other words, one generally needs to be credentialed by an anthropology department. Once credentialed, the individual can legitimately study a wide range of subjects and still claim to be an anthropologist. An individual may assert that she or he is an anthropologist. But to be seen by others—and, critically, to obtain employment as an anthropologist—the key is having a graduate degree in the discipline at either the master's or doctoral level. It is like the old baseball saying that a pitch isn't a strike until the umpire calls it a strike. An individual isn't considered a professional anthropologist—no matter what she or he does—until some anthropology department grants that individual a graduate degree. Anthropology departments, then, are central to anthropology's efforts to reproduce itself. Quoting the sociologist Andrew Abbott:

> Non-disciplinary intellectuals have difficulty reproducing themselves because the American open market for public intellectuals is incapable of supporting more than a tiny handful of nonacademic writers and has no organized means of re-production and exchange beyond some tenuous referral networks. Academia is, to all intents and purposes, the only practical recourse for American intellectuals. And being an academic means willy-nilly being a member of a discipline. There have indeed been great interdisciplinary geniuses, even within academia; Gregory Bateson is an obvious example. But they have no obvious mode of reproduction. They simply arise, revolutionize two or three disciplines, and leave magical memories behind.[39]

---

38    Geertz (1985:623). Wolf once wrote: "The result of anthropology's eclecticism is that the field continues to astound by its diverse and colorful activity" (E. Wolf [1980:20]).

39    Abbott (2001:130).

Perceiving anthropology in this way helps make sense of applied anthropology's straddling of the academic/nonacademic divide. As the journal *Applied Anthropology* (later renamed *Human Organization*) indicated in its opening editorial in 1941: "*Applied Anthropology* is designed . . . for those concerned with putting plans into operations . . . and all those who as part of their responsibility have to take action in problems of human relations."[40] Despite a determined effort to reach beyond the academy, a sizable number of applied anthropologists remain university based. Why? Because the field can only reproduce itself if a sizable number of applied anthropologists remain within the academy and train new generations of applied anthropologists.

Given anthropologists go off in all sorts of different intellectual directions, study all sorts of interesting topics, how should we define anthropology? Anthropology departments demarcate which topics are and are not perceived as proper anthropology. Let me explain. If you look at the course offerings of different anthropology departments at different universities, you will notice that many courses have similar titles. Most departments, for example, teach introductory anthropology as well as courses in economic anthropology, religion, and anthropological theory. But if you examine the reading lists and the topics covered by courses with the same title, you will find tremendous diversity in respect to the books assigned, locales studied, and issues addressed. As long as teachers stay within certain departmentally defined parameters—have a recognized title for the course or make passing reference to material that might be perceived as anthropological—they are pretty much free to frame their courses as they wish and still call them anthropology.

This brings me to a definition of anthropology. If a particular topic is taught as part of an anthropology course by an anthropologist within an anthropology department, it is generally perceived as anthropology. Phrasing this another way, if some anthropologist in some anthropology department somewhere teaches a particular subject, who is to say that what the teacher is teaching, or what the students are learning, isn't anthropology? Most people—inside and outside anthropology, inside and outside the university—would concur. Such a definition doesn't have the liberating sense of saying anthropologists do almost anything. But it cuts through the complications of deciding which topics "belong" to the discipline.

40   Applied Anthropology (1941:2).

I offer two personal examples. I once taught an anthropology course at Hawaii Pacific University called "Is Global Citizenship Possible?" with the former dean of the College of Natural Sciences. It covered a wide range of topics and involved readings from diverse disciplines. But no one ever questioned whether the course was "really" anthropology, at least to my face. I also taught a course called "Managing Our Mortality" with a registered nurse. It was a cross-listed course in both nursing and anthropology. Most nurses I talked to wanted to make sure there was a nursing component to the course. But the nurses never questioned whether the course was anthropological. They assumed that if it was labeled as an anthropology course and was taught by a professional anthropologist, it must be anthropology.

Various anthropologists define themselves and their discipline in broad, encompassing ways that enhance their intellectual freedom. But that doesn't mean that others—especially outside the discipline—accept their definitions. The assertions of this or that individual aren't what makes others accept particular definitions. What brings public consensus is when the definitions are embedded in publicly accepted social structures. The departmental structure has the authority to define who is (and is not) an anthropologist as well as what is (and is not) anthropology. Basically, anthropology is what anthropology departments say it is.

Much money and energy has been put into developing university-based interdisciplinary studies. Today, centers—such as Centers of Latin American Studies—draw various disciplines together to address common problems. Some suggest this interdisciplinary movement will eventually dominate university life. Disciplinary-based departments, such as anthropology, will die out. They should not count on it. The interdisciplinary movement has been part of academic life for decades. But, even at its high point, in the years following World War II, it never came to dominate academic life. Interdisciplinary centers may coexist with departments but, because of their limited control over tenure and promotion, they are not able to challenge the dominance of disciplinary-based departments within universities.

Readers may not be aware that some of the major specializations within cultural anthropology—medical anthropology, political anthropology, and economic anthropology, for example—are relatively recent. The expansion of specializations within cultural anthropology occurred during the 1960s. As university enrollments increased, anthropology departments expanded, and they hired more faculty. Faculty members in the same department tended to carve out distinct areas of expertise. To advance their careers, new faculty often preferred publishing on topics different from their colleagues, thus avoiding intellectual conflicts that might disrupt their careers. Whatever intellectual justifications one might offer for the division of cultural anthropology into specializations and subspecializations, departmental demographic pressures—an increase in the number of faculty within departments—helped drive the process forward.[41]

## How the Departmental Structure Shapes the Discipline's Self-Image

*This section discusses two myths anthropologists affirm about their past to reinforce departmental solidarity. These myths function as charters for affirming the present departmental organization while allowing modern anthropologists to pursue their personal interests. These myths also highlight that anthropologists, rather than confronting disciplinary problems head on, sometimes lean toward myth-making to address them.*

While many anthropologists might disagree—because it goes against the scholarly traditions they grew up with as graduate students—an outsider might well perceive certain mythic elements in the discipline's depiction of its past. Take, for example, the assertion that Franz Boas is the father of American anthropology. One sees reference to Boas as the "father of American anthropology" in textbooks, in various disciplinary journals, book advertisements, even in Wikipedia.[42] However, it is not true.

Housing anthropology in university departments is today portrayed as an important step forward in the discipline's progress as a profession. The image frequently conveyed is that, prior to the establishment of university anthropology departments, anthropology was full of unprofessional amateurs. For anthropology departments to retain control over the training (and reproducing) of anthropologists, they need to create barriers against amateurs training themselves. After all, if people can become anthropologists by reading books and

41    Readers interested in further exploring this topic might refer to: Barnett (1940); Boettke (2002); Bulmer (2001); Chaney (1993); Collins (2002); Gulbenkian Commission (1996); Eriksen (1992); Glenn (2002, 2008a); Lamont (2009); Mann (1993); David Mills (2008); Petrie (2007); Pieters and Baumgartner (2002); Rensburger (1996); Sica (2001); D. Smith (1993); Taylor (1993); Wallerstein (2001); and Wikipedia, s.v. "anthropology."

42    E.g, see Cole (1995); Holloway (1997); Hyatt (1990); Paredes (2006); D. Schneider (n.d.); Williams (1991); and Wikipedia, s.v. "Franz Boas."

doing fieldwork on their own, why go through the effort of getting an expensive departmental degree? Anthropology departments emphasize that they provide the training that turns amateurs into professionals. A Boas obituary makes this point: he "found anthropology a collection of wild guesses and a happy hunting ground for the romantic lover of primitive things; he left it a discipline in which theories could be tested and in which he had delimited possibilities from impossibilities."[43]

In actual fact, there were a number of prominent anthropologists before Boas who exerted important influences on the discipline's development. Boas deserves to be recognized for establishing the first anthropology department (at Columbia University in New York City). But that doesn't mean he deserves to be called "the father of American anthropology." The nineteenth century had a number of prominent anthropologists that were not trained in university settings; they were mostly self-taught. These included important theorists such as Lewis Henry Morgan and significant ethnographers such as James Mooney, Frank Hamilton Cushing, and Henry Rowe Schoolcraft. William Fenton writes of Lewis Henry Morgan, a lawyer turned anthropologist, "to say that Morgan was the most important social scientist in nineteenth century America is an understatement."[44] Morgan's *League of the Iroquois* was a precedent-setting ethnography, as was Mooney's *The Ghost-Dance Religion and the Sioux Outbreak of 1890*. John Wesley Powell helped establish the premier anthropological research unit of the nineteenth century in the United States, the Bureau of American Ethnology (housed in the Smithsonian Institution).[45] While neither Morgan nor Powell worked in academic settings and they embraced a form of evolution that was anathema to Boas, they certainly were not unprofessional "amateurs." In many ways they were the true founding fathers of the discipline in the United States.

The positioning of Boas as the "father of anthropology" was facilitated, in part, by Boas producing the first generation of academically based anthropologists. His students came to control the American Anthropological Association (AAA) as well as many of the academic departments in the country. They rewrote the discipline's history in their own image. We can see the Boasian

43    Lowie (1947:311) suggests Boas would have disagreed with this statement. Boas appreciated earlier contributors to the discipline.

44    Fenton (1962:viii). Readers might note that Ewers (1960:703) perceives Morgan as the "father of American Anthropology" in a review of Morgan's *Indian Journals*.

45    Interested readers might refer to Worster (2001).

academic branding of the field through a small, rarely noticed detail. Once the Boasians gained control of the AAA, its officers were no longer identified in the association's publications by their hometowns but rather by their institutional affiliations.

As a way of introducing the second mythic assertion, I note that various textbooks conceive of the discipline's subfields in different ways. Alfred Kroeber, the foremost anthropologist of the post–World War II period, divided anthropology into race, language, culture, psychology, and prehistory. Ralph Linton, another prominent anthropologist during the same period, wrote, "the two great divisions of anthropology . . . are known as physical anthropology and cultural anthropology." Cultural anthropology he divided into archaeology, ethnology, and linguistics. (After noting that linguistics was "the most isolated and self-contained" of anthropology's "subsciences," he dropped further discussion of it.) Carol and Melvin Ember and Peter Peregrine today divide anthropology into biological anthropology and cultural anthropology. Cultural anthropology they further divide into archaeology, linguistics, and ethnology. Cutting across these four fields, they add a fifth field: applied anthropology.[46]

These different ways for organizing the subfields point to a contradiction within the discipline. Anthropology is committed to intellectual progress and change. Yet it is centered in a bureaucratic structure—academic departments—that doesn't readily facilitate change. When anthropology departments were created, they drew together scholars from an array of backgrounds to facilitate the examination of a set of intellectual concerns centered on the "cultural roots" of non-Western groups without recorded history. That is the reason researchers from cultural anthropology, archaeology, physical anthropology, and linguistics were included in anthropology departments. The difficulty anthropology faces today—especially in cultural anthropology, which constitutes two-thirds of the discipline—is that many anthropologists have gone on to other questions, other concerns. As a result, they are now less interested in the problems that interest their departmental colleagues in other subfields.

During the eighteenth and nineteenth centuries, Europe went through a major transformation. Unified nation-states were created out of fragmented, local-based communities. "The inhabitants of Wales, of Scotland and of England," writes the historian Linda Colley, "were separated from each other . . . [by] different folklores, different sports, different costumes, different building

---

46    Kroeber (1948); Linton (1945:5,7); Ember, Ember, and Peregrine (2007:3).

styles, different agricultural practices, different weights and measures, and different cuisines."[47] To smooth the transition to unified nation-states—to make a cohesive emotional, cultural, and intellectual union out of such differences— scholars searched for cultural "roots" that validated the new nation-states. When anthropologists studied non-Western groups during the early twentieth century, they tended to carry the European search for cultural traditions over to the people they studied. You needed biological, linguistic, archaeological, and cultural clues to infer a group's origins and migrations. As one anthropologist phrased it, a primary task of American anthropology was to determine questions of origins. How did they do this? "By the study of the physical types of the people, their archaeological remains, their languages, and their customs— the four fields of anthropology."[48] What does an anthropology department do when a large percentage of its members move off in new intellectual directions that separate them from others in the department? Do anthropologists reorganize themselves into separate, smaller, departments? As George Stocking observes: "Any movement in ethnology [or sociocultural anthropology] away from historical reconstruction could not help but have implications for the unity of anthropology."[49] Bureaucratically, anthropology departments are set up to defend anthropology—its funding, its faculty positions, its status in wider settings—against competitors. They aren't set up to continually change with changing trends, especially when one subfield moves off in a different intellectual direction.

How do anthropologists deal with this bureaucratic problem? Some ignore it, but many embrace a myth of disciplinary integration in times past. Anthropologist Eric Wolf expressed this myth in an often-cited introduction to the field: "In contrast to the anthropological traditions of other countries, anthropology in the United States always prided itself upon its role as the unified and unifying study of several subdisciplines. In combining the pursuits of human biology, linguistics, prehistory, and ethnology, American anthropology put a premium on intellectual synthesis, upon the tracing out of connections where others saw only divergence."[50] However, if we examine the 3,252 articles published from 1899 to 1998 in the *American Anthropologist*, the discipline's flagship journal,

47    Colley (1992:13–14).
48    Bourguignon (1996:7).
49    Stocking (1976:24).
50    E. Wolf (1974:x).

perhaps only 308 substantially draw on more than one anthropological subfield in the analysis of their data.[51] That is to say, over a hundred-year period, perhaps only 9.5 percent of the articles published in the *American Anthropologist* bring the discipline's subfields together in any significant way. Most of the articles focus on narrow subjects and use the perspectives and tools of only one subfield. These articles are narrowly framed and narrowly presented, with relatively little synthesis across subfields.

Up until the 1970s, the total number of collaborative subfield articles decade by decade in the *American Anthropologist* was lower than 9.5 percent. Only eight times in the past one hundred years has the number of collaborative articles— across subfields—reached at least 20 percent of the total articles published in the journal—in 1974, 1975, 1979, 1980, 1981, 1984, 1986, and 1989. True, early anthropologists often published articles in more than one subfield. But the critical point is that they rarely brought the subfields together in the same article, using different subfield perspectives to develop a broader synthesis. In the *American Anthropologist* from 1899 to 1998, collaboration across the subfields was a distinctly minority affair.

The lack of subfield integration in times past is readily apparent when you read through old issues of the *American Anthropologist*. So why would anthropologists affirm something about the past—that the subfields previously collaborated in significant ways—that is clearly at variance with established fact? The myth of an earlier "golden age" of disciplinary integration constitutes a "social charter" for today's departmental structure: It holds up an ideal. Disciplinary integration is imposed on the past—an "invention of tradition," to quote Eric Hobsbawm and Terence Ranger.[52] But it also does more. It implicitly represents a call for more disciplinary integration to resolve the current problem of departmental fragmentation. The myth allows anthropologists to address a problem of social structure—intellectual fragmentation within a department—without the pain of anyone actually having to change. It allows them to pretend that they all once worked together as a team.[53]

---

51    Borofsky (2002).
52    Hobsbawm and Ranger (1983).
53    Readers interested in exploring this topic further might refer to Economist (2005c); Leerssen (2007); Powell (1888); Rogge (1976).

# The Book's Broader Framework:
# Kuhn, Gramsci, and Hegemonic-Like Structures

*Thomas Kuhn's concept of paradigm and Antonio Gramsci's concept of hegemon (or hegemony) frame points made throughout this book. A new paradigm arises when it proves better at addressing critical problems left unsolved by the existing paradigm. Hegemonic-like structures within the academy shape the academy's production of knowledge as well as the behavior of those who produce it.*

The approach taken up to this point might be termed an "anthropology of anthropology." It uses anthropological methods and concepts to analyze the discipline's ideology. We see how certain structures shape the discipline's view of itself—what is and is not viewed as anthropology as well as who is and is not viewed as an anthropologist. Drawing on work by Malinowski and Lévi-Strauss, this approach perceives certain myths affirmed by anthropologists as reinforcing the discipline's ambiguous departmental structure. The approach taken is no different than the approach many anthropologists apply in analyzing other social groups.

Turning now to the book's broader framework, I begin with the book's theoretical underpinning—specifically Kuhn's concept of paradigm and Gramsci's concept of hegemony. Kuhn states that paradigms focus on solving particular problems. He observes, in a postscript to his 1970 work, that a sympathetic reader "concluded the term [paradigm] is used [in his book] in at least twenty-two different ways." I focus on paradigms as "constellation of beliefs, values, techniques, and so on shared [to a large degree] by members of a given community." Kuhn perceives paradigms as providing "models from which spring coherent traditions of scientific research." He notes paradigms are often "sufficiently open-ended to leave all sorts of problems for . . . [a] group of practitioners to resolve."[54]

It is important to note, for points made later in the book, that Kuhn asserts "paradigms gain their status because they are more successful than their competitors in solving a few problems that the group of practitioners has recognized as acute." Furthermore, he writes: "Probably the single most prevalent claim advanced by the proponents of a new paradigm is that they can solve the problems that have led the old one to a crisis." In respect to such crises, Kuhn asserts that "paradigm-testing occurs only after persistent failure to solve a noteworthy

54   Kuhn (1970:181, 175, 10, 10).

puzzle has given rise to a crisis. And even then, it occurs only after the sense of crisis has evoked an alternative candidate paradigm."[55]

As I elaborate later, most universities assess a faculty member's intellectual competence by the publications produced. Focusing on publications resolves an important problem for universities: how to convey accountability to outside supporters while reinforcing their own agenda and perspectives. Following Mary Furner, we might perceive the piles of publications—with their technical language—as conveying a sense of academic excellence without overly threatening financial and political supporters of their universities. (Most academic publications go unread by the public at large.) Quoting Furner, after the move into universities, social science "studies tended to be internal, recommendations hedged with qualifiers, analyses couched in jargon that was unintelligible to the average citizen."[56]

Gramsci's open-ended sense of hegemony, especially as espoused in his *Prison Notebooks*, involves two key elements useful for making sense of why so many academics accept accountability in terms of publications. Hegemony can be seen as "the 'spontaneous' consent given by the great masses of the population to the general direction imposed on social life by the dominant fundamental group"—with the dominant group, in this case, being key university administrators. When this "spontaneous" consent fails, Gramsci continues, there is "the apparatus of state [in this case, administrators'] coercive power which 'legally' enforces discipline on those groups who do not 'consent' either actively or passively."[57] We see this coercive power in tenure, promotion, and hiring procedures—usually initiated by departments but supervised by administrators above the departmental level. Departments do not hire, promote, or grant tenure on their own. These decisions are almost always reviewed by administrators at a higher level.

I refer to these structural constraints within academia as *hegemonic-like* because, while they provide broad constraints on behavior, they lack the general sense of hegemon as the term is commonly used—relating to the political, economic, and intellectual dominance of one country over another or one social group over another within a society. Here, the focus is narrower. It is on the academy, especially in the United States, and how certain academic structures shape the production of knowledge within cultural anthropology. Publications

---

55    Kuhn (1970:23, 153, 145).
56    Furner (1975:147).
57    Gramsci (1971:12).

are a key measure of intellectual competence within the academy. The open-ended creative element that is embodied in both Kuhn's concept of paradigm and Gramsci's concept of hegemony can be seen in the following example from the *Economist*:

> One thing that determines how quickly a researcher climbs the academic ladder is his publication record. . . . A long list of papers attached to a job application tends to impress appointment committees, and the resulting pressure to churn out a steady stream of articles in peer-reviewed journals often leads to the splitting of results from a single study into several "minimum publishable units," to the unnecessary duplication of studies and to the favouring of work that is scientifically trivial but easy to publish.
>
> There is another way to pad publication lists: coauthoring. Say you write one paper a year. If you team up with a colleague doing similar work and write two half-papers instead, both parties end up with their names on twice as many papers, but with no increase in workload. [*The Economist* found for thirty-four million publications examined between 1996 and 2015,] the average number of authors per paper grew from 3.2 to 4.4. At the same time, the number of papers divided by the number of authors who published in a given year (essentially, the average author's overall paper-writing contribution) fell from 0.64 to 0.51. The boom in coauthorship more than compensated for the drop in individual productivity, so that the average researcher notched up a slightly higher number of papers for his curriculum vitae: 2.3 a year compared to 2.1 two decades earlier.
>
> One particular trend behind these numbers is the rise of "guest authorship," in which a luminary, such as the director of a research centre, is tagged on as an author simply as a nod to his position or in the hope that this signals a study of high quality. That can lead to some researchers becoming improbably prolific. For example, between 2013 and 2015 the 100 most published authors in physics and astronomy from American research centres had an average of 311 papers each to their names. The corresponding figure for medicine, though lower, was still 180. . . .
>
> Another trend is that the meaning of authorship in massive science projects is getting fuzzier. Particle physics and genomics, both of which often involve huge transnational teams, are particularly guilty here. A paper on the Higgs boson published in 2015 in *Physical Review Letters* holds the record, with 5,154 coauthors . . . a genomics paper on Drosophila, a much-studied fruitfly, also published in 2015, has 1,014 authors, most of them students who helped with various coding tasks. Such studies are paragons of scientific collaboration and the exact opposite of

creating minimum publishable units. But they list as authors people who have contributed only marginally to the success of the project—roles that, in the past, were simply acknowledged in a thanks-to-all sentence but are now the bricks from which careers may be built.[58]

This example illustrates the innovative lengths academics may go to in order to lengthen their publication records and advance their careers. Digging a bit deeper, we might also perceive a darker side in this push to publish. Benefits to the larger society sometimes seem to be set aside.

## Two Paradigms

*Two paradigms are key to understanding cultural anthropology, and more broadly, the social sciences today. The dominant paradigm today—labeled "do no harm"—is defined by those within universities to not only enhance their power and significance but also to soften dynamics that might disrupt the university's normal functioning and those who support it. Recently, the paradigm has been reframed to stress quantitative measurements in assessing faculty productivity. The "public anthropology" paradigm focuses on serving the broader public that tends to fund key university resources and research.*

Two distinct paradigms are present in cultural anthropology today. The first paradigm—"do no harm"—takes its name from a common medical saying ("first do no harm" enunciated by Sydenham in the seventeenth century) as well as various phrasings of the American Anthropological Association's codes of ethics in 1998, 2009, and 2012. While its focus appears to be on protecting research participants, as practiced today in academia this paradigm often involves maintaining the general status quo. It includes both a university's financial and political backers and, to a certain degree, its administrators and faculty. Nontenured faculty especially should avoid seriously disrupting the social arrangements that facilitate their university's functioning. We saw that in the case of the economist Richard Ely discussed earlier by Furner. We see the pattern again in Yale University's refusal to extend David Graeber's contract (discussed in Chapter 5).

It is important to note that, until recently, the standards of intellectual and professional accountability were mostly defined by universities in ways that enhanced these universities' missions. Chapter 3 suggests, at least in cultural

58    Economist (2016b).

anthropology, there is a self-serving element to embracing the "do no harm" ethic in fieldwork. The "do no harm" paradigm centers on two principles. The first stresses the importance of keeping up appearances that depict academia, and especially one's university, in a positive light. Universities often portray themselves as centers of meritocracy. Competency trumps status. That may be how academia likes to portray itself, but it is not necessarily how academia operates. The inequalities of a self-serving elite patronage system are frequently disguised behind a rhetoric of equality. Take faculty hiring as an example. In principle, any PhD can apply for a position at any school and expect to be taken seriously. But in actual fact, hiring is often based on a patronage system dominated by elite schools. As Chad Wellmon and Andrew Piper report:

> Several recent studies have shown a high degree of concentration of academic hires from a small number of PhD-granting institutions. One recent study of placement data on nearly 19,000 tenure or tenure-track faculty in history, business, and computer science departments found that faculty hiring "follows a common and steeply hierarchical structure," reflecting "profound social inequality." Only 25 percent of institutions produced 71 to 86 percent of all tenure-track faculty. And the top ten institutions produced 1.6 to 3.0 times more faculty than the second ten. Another study of political science programs in the United States found that the top five programs placed 20 percent of all academics at research institutions; a different study found that graduates of eight universities were hired for half of all tenure-track jobs. These studies have demonstrated the role of institutional prestige and the dominance of a very few institutions in academic faculty hiring.[59]

The same holds true in respect to publishing. The standard image, once again, is that quality trumps prestige. In publishing, a faculty member's innovative insights should count, not the status of the school at which the faculty member is employed. Yet as Wellmon and Piper observe, faculty at high-status universities have significantly more papers accepted for publication in prominent journals than faculty at less prestigious universities. For Wellmon and Piper, what should be an open, objective evaluation of a proposed publication's worth tends to be dominated by status concerns. They write:

> Historically, university reformers from the eighteenth to the twenty-first century have touted publication as a corrective to concentrations of power and patronage

---

59    Wellmon and Piper (2017) includes three references that relate to quotes and assertions made. Readers are encouraged to refer to these for further detail.

networks. An increased emphasis on more purportedly transparent or objective measures provided by publication have long been cast as an antidote to cronyism and connections. . . . However, current data suggest that publication patterns largely reproduce significant power imbalances within the system of academic publishing. Systems of academic patronage as well as those of cultural and social capital seem not only to have survived but flourished in the modern bureaucratic university, even if in different form. When, as our data show, Harvard University and Yale University exercise such a disproportionate influence on . . . publishing patterns, academic publishing seems less a democratic marketplace of ideas and more a tightly controlled network of patronage and cultural capital.[60]

In addition, despite the appearance of embracing foreign as well as domestic authors, a national bias often exists. Tobias Opthof, Ruben Coronel, and Michiel Janse state, in respect to their study of 3,444 manuscripts, that "manuscripts receive significantly higher priority ratings when reviewers and authors originate from the same country."[61] To quote Pierre Bourdieu: judgments of quality and value are "contaminated . . . by knowledge of the position [an individual] occupies in the instituted hierarchies."[62]

Most universities portray themselves as centers of intellectual endeavor to advance knowledge and through such efforts to advance the interests of the larger society that funds much university-based research. I challenge this image in Chapter 2. Based on a set of case studies over several decades, the chapter suggests many faculty, despite appearances to the contrary, tend to be more focused on advancing their careers than on refining anthropological perspectives or building cumulative knowledge. Quoting Deborah Rhode: "Faculty have incentives to churn out tomes that will advance their careers regardless of whether they will also advance knowledge."[63] (We saw this point made in a slightly different way in the *Economist* quote above relating to how academics seek to enlarge their publications.)

The second principle frames academic accountability primarily in terms of publications: how many are produced in what types of journals over what period of time. Universities might consider other standards for judging intellectual competence, such as the quality of the publications produced or what

60    Wellmon and Piper (2017).
61    Opthof, Coronel, and Janse (2002:345).
62    Cited in Wellmon and Piper (2017); see also Bourdieu (1975:20; 1988).
63    Rhode (2006:11).

impact they have had on the world beyond the academy. But intellectual competence mostly tends to be assessed in terms of publications, especially with certain journals and presses. Universities have a long history of using publications not only to assess faculty but also to enhance their status within the broader society. Wellmon and Piper observe: "Publications are discrete objects that can be compared. They have become the academy's ultimate markers of value."[64] Or as Ivan Oransky, head of Retraction Watch (discussed in Chapter 2), puts it: "Everything in science is based on publishing a peer-reviewed paper in a high-ranking journal. Absolutely everything. . . . You want to get a grant, you want to get promoted, you want to get tenure. That's how you do it. That's the currency of the realm."[65]

Describing the roots of the modern university, William Clark writes: "After 1740 Prussia mandated publication [to gain a faculty position]. The regulation of 1749 set a minimum of two disputation-dissertations [or publications] to be a lecturer."[66] Wellmon and Piper, in discussing early universities such as Göttingen (founded in 1734), note that "printed publications were one of the university's key commercial goods . . . professors . . . should be 'focused more than ever on writing and the development of individual works of excellence so that the University remains fresh in the minds of the public and they can see that talented and hard-working men are employed there.'"[67] In other words, from early on faculty publications constituted a way for enhancing university prestige.

Until recently, the standards for assessing publications—in terms of their quality, their intellectual competence—tended to be a vague mixture of quality and quantity. Quality tended to involve who published a faculty member's books or articles, what senior colleagues thought of these publications, and how well the books were reviewed in various journals as well as by selected outside reviewers. Quantity tended to focus on the number of publications produced. The number of colleagues citing a faculty member's work counted as well. It was interpreted as a sign of intellectual respect.

This vague, somewhat informal system is changing, however. As I discuss in Chapter 5, metric assessments of faculty productivity now dominate. In cultural anthropology these assessments are causing considerable concern and stress among faculty, who perceive their intellectual competence being judged

64    Wellmon and Piper (2017).
65    Oransky in Achenbach (2015).
66    W. Clark (2006:259).
67    Wellmon and Piper (2017).

primarily by the number of publications produced, not by these publications' quality. Deborah Rhode cites a Carnegie Foundation report that indicates more than a third of university faculty believed their publications are mostly assessed in terms of quantity rather than quality. (At schools with doctoral programs, the figure is over 50 percent.) [68] This puts faculty in an awkward position. They are trying to produce quality work that is published in quality journals and/or by quality presses. But rather than being assessed on the quality of their ideas, the quality of their insights, they are being judged on the number of publications produced. Many cultural anthropologists are deeply upset by this turn to quantification in assessing intellectual competence.

The second paradigm focuses less on quantitative measures, less on maintaining the status quo and more on how the publications benefit others beyond the academy. Chapter 3 deals extensively with this "public anthropology" paradigm. Briefly, the chapter highlights four strategies for resisting (and, if possible, overturning) the dominant "do no harm" paradigm.

- *Benefitting others.* Moving beyond a "do no harm" ethos to striving to benefit others, especially the broader society that supports anthropological research.
- *Fostering alternative forms of faculty accountability.* Moving beyond judging faculty primarily by the number of academic publications produced to also emphasizing the social impact of their work.
- *Transparency.* Not only uncovering the underlying patronage systems that dominate hiring and publishing but also allowing others to investigate how the work's conclusions were reached—thereby offering a means to assess that work's value and validity (a point stressed in Chapter 2).
- *Collaborating with others.* Moving beyond primarily working alone to working with others beyond the academy to facilitate significant change.

## The Academy's Hegemonic-Like Structures

*Key hegemonic-like structures shape the academy's operation. Funding agencies, while appearing to channel funding to projects that serve the broader society, are less than careful to check that the projects actually do. Universities, while appearing to advance "the common good," often assess faculty productivity in ways that, while serving their own ends, leave faculty*

68    Rhode (2006:46).

*frustrated in respect to arbitrary definitions of quality. Despite their lofty mission statements, many academic publishers judge an author's intellectual potential on the ability to produce book sales. The combination of ennobling ideals and limited follow-through not only reinforces the "do no harm" paradigm but limits the faculty's ability to disrupt existing power structures.*

It is important to understand that paradigms discussed here do not float above social structures and social institutions. They are embedded in them.[69] Key to understanding the dominance of the "do no harm" paradigm within the academy is understanding how it fits with funding agencies, universities, and academic publishers. The three, while distinct from one another, are also entwined in a mutually reinforcing triadic infrastructure. They collectively focus on high-sounding aspirations about benefitting the broader society while displaying limited accountability for implementing these aspirations, leading often to a focus on their own aggrandizement. Below surface appearances, the hegemonic-like structures discussed here often seem to benefit themselves as much as those beyond the academy.

## FUNDING AGENCIES

A number of government and private groups provide substantial support for university-based research. Using data from the National Science Foundation (NSF), in 2012 they collectively provided over fifty billion dollars (universities provided another thirteen billion).[70] Few believe these groups' funding is provided carte blanche. There is an implicit sense of accountability. The funding is expected to lead, in one way or another over time, to results that have positive benefits for the larger society—not just positive benefits for the individuals receiving the money.

At times, the accountability may be quite explicit. The America Competes Act of 2007, Section 7010, specifies that "all final project reports and citations of published research documents resulting from research funded, in whole or in part, by the Foundation [i.e., the NSF], are made available to the public in a timely manner."[71] Fitting with this law, the NSF requires proposals and final reports to specify the "broader impacts" of their research defined as encom-

---

69    Kuhn dealt with what he termed "scientific communities" and with their intellectual contexts and problems. He did not directly deal with the broader social and historical factors shaping these communities and the problems they were addressing; see, e.g., Kuhn (1970:10, 164, 168).

70    See NSF (2015).

71    See Public Law (2007).

passing "the potential to benefit society and contribute to the achievement of specific, desired, societal outcomes."[72] The National Institutes of Health (NIH) "looks for grant proposals of high scientific caliber that are relevant to public health needs" and support its mission, which seeks "to expand the knowledge base in medical and associated sciences in order to enhance the Nation's economic well-being and ensure a continued high return on the public investment in research."[73]

It is important to note that the details of this accountability are often imprecisely defined. There can be serendipitous events in which something is unexpectedly discovered—such as with Fleming's accidental discovery of penicillin. Cultural anthropologists have gone into the field expecting to study one topic and then found it advantageous to focus on another. Defining accountability too narrowly limits the possibility of unexpected discoveries—hence the open-ended nature of the phrase "broader impacts." It is clear that a number of funding agencies place greater emphasis on funding research than on assessing what their funding has accomplished. The NSF requires all grantees to submit a Project Outcomes Report upon completion of their research. Yet, as discussed in Chapter 4, a substantial number of grantees do not.[74]

Despite this positive rhetoric of funding agencies seeking to produce benefits for the broader society, one has to wonder to what degree these agencies are actually focused on ensuring this occurs. One might perceive a parallel to what happens with governmental and private funding to development agencies. Quoting David Keen: "Because aid is politically accountable to Western electorates—which consume only the images and reports of its impact and not the real things—there are few incentives to make it work better."[75] To stay in business, aid agencies often have an investment in aid seeming to address important problems without ever really solving them.

I do not want to overstate the case. NIH is concerned about the limited replicability of studies—how some studies suggest startling results that then get

72    See NSF (2013).

73    NIH (2017). Paralleling these perspectives, the United Kingdom's Research Councils (n.d.) stresses a commitment "to supporting and rewarding researchers to engage with the public."

74    For the publicly available figures, see the Project Outcome Reports for each of the years listed plus the reporting regulations for Project Outcome Reports listed under the National Science Foundation's Proposal and Award Policies and Procedures Guide for the respective year, "Research Spending & Results," https://www.research.gov/research-portal/appmanager/base/desktop?_nfpb =true&_eventName=viewQuickSearchFormEvent_so_rsr (accessed August 9, 2018).

75    Keen (1999:28).

further funding but never pan out. Francis Collins, NIH's director, states: "We can't afford to waste resources and produce non-reproducible conclusions."[76] The *Chronicle of Higher Education* reports: "The NIH's response is wide-ranging. Its institutes are revising how they review grants, requiring far more data on experimental design, including validation of past findings that studies purport to build upon. . . . It is pressing journals to raise their review standards. . . . And it is experimenting with different ways of financing research."[77] Fitting with this trend, the journal *Science* reports: "The U.S. National Institutes of Health (NIH) has imposed unusual new requirements on researchers based at Duke University in Durham, North Carolina, who receive federal funds. . . . NIH now requires Duke researchers to obtain prior approval for any modifications to new and existing grants. And any Duke researcher submitting a so-called 'modular application' for a grant worth less than $250,000 per year must include 'detailed budgets' justifying the costs."[78]

Still, the basic pattern remains. Fitting with the "do no harm" paradigm, there is a focus on appearances over objective, substantiated facts. Accountability is often defined in vague terms. The appearance of knowledge is what mostly counts. Having enough transparency so others can confirm important results is not necessarily emphasized. (Chapter 2 elaborates on this point in respect to cultural anthropology.)

## UNIVERSITIES

As NSF's "Institutional Rankings" indicate, the billions of dollars for research are channeled through universities and university-affiliated institutions.[79] Universities generally possess their own standards for accountability. Especially in the social sciences, they tend to measure benefits less in terms of broad national agenda than in terms of standards that highlight the university's intellectual excellence. In judging excellence, universities lean toward certain metrics—such as the number and quality of academic publications their faculty produce. Quality is generally assumed if an article is published in a high-status journal or a book is published by a high-status academic press as well as being cited by aca-

76    Collins as quoted in Voosen (2015:A12).

77    Voosen (2015:A12).

78    McCook (2018a). Also note McCook (2018b) in respect to Ohio State, although intriguingly Ohio State did not stop the work of Dr. Carlo Croce, perhaps because of his status and substantial funding (see Glanz and Armendariz [2017]).

79    NSF (2015).

demic colleagues.[80] Chapter 2 makes clear that these are imperfect measures at best, certainly the citation count. What makes publications particularly salient for administrators is that ready metrics exist to measure them. Trying to judge "broader impacts"—such benefitting others—is less easy to quantify.

Research transparency—the details behind the collection of data for a publication—are generally limited. This not only holds for anthropology. It occurs in a number of fields, including the life sciences. The *Economist* recently reported, based on a study by Ben Goldacre and Anna Powell-Smith, that "half of clinical trials do not have their results published. . . . Proportionally, the worst culprits are government and academia."[81] This leaves readers to puzzle over not only how to interpret the data the authors publish but also what to infer about the data they do not. How objective can a study be if readers are left unclear as to what it confirms when we only see its positive results, not the negative ones? Without transparency, measures of accountability often break down. As the *New York Times* reports:

> The past several years have been bruising ones for the credibility of the social sciences. A star social psychologist was caught fabricating data, leading to more than 50 retracted papers. A top journal published a study supporting the existence of ESP that was widely criticized. The journal *Science* [one of the world's leading journals] pulled a political science paper on the effect of gay canvassers on voters' behavior because of concerns about faked data. Now, a painstaking years long effort to reproduce 100 studies published in three leading psychology journals has found that more than half of the findings did not hold up when retested.[82]

For some, limited transparency serves a positive end. It fosters creative publications. Researchers are able to publish what they wish without having to provide detailed confirming data. This can be a significant plus professionally because innovative approaches may well draw in new funding. Innovative publications are often well cited by others.

Chapter 2 demonstrates it is not always clear the degree to which faculty publications actually advance knowledge (versus simply claiming to). *The Lancet*, one of the world's leading medical journals, reports that perhaps two hundred billion dollars—which constitutes about 85 percent of all global research spending—is likely wasted on poorly designed and reported research studies. Paul Glasziou

---

80    See, e.g., Voosen (2015:12).
81    Economist (2016a).
82    Carey (2015a).

states that "a research publication can both communicate and miscommunicate. Unless research is adequately reported, the time and resources invested in the conduct of research is wasted. . . . Adequate reports of research should clearly describe which questions were addressed and why, what was done, what was shown, and what the findings mean. However, substantial failures occur in each of these elements."[83] This holds for other fields as well as articles by Paul Romer on macroeconomics, and a book by Lee Smolin on string theory in physics suggest this holds in other fields as well.[84]

Measuring accountability in terms of publications produced—independent of their transparency, quality, objectivity, and benefits—cannot be laughed off. Given one's publications are the basis for promotion and tenure (as well as being hired) at most universities, it embodies a strong coercive element. Academics need to take these standards seriously, very seriously. It forms the basis for how they are judged professionally. Once again, we see the concern with appearances. There is less focus on finding ways to qualitatively assess publications. Intellectual competence is often judged by how many publications a faculty member produces. Transparency—which would allow for some form of confirmation— is downplayed. Behind the appearances, behind the limited accountability, Furner's point holds: universities tend to support those who support them, not only financially and politically but also in enhancing their status. The social scientists they employ should be cautious about destabilizing or upsetting the structures that support their supporters.

## ACADEMIC PUBLISHING

Academic publishers are often caught in a balancing act. The University of California Press portrays itself as "one of the most forward-thinking scholarly publishers, committed to influencing public discourse and challenging the status quo."[85] Harvard University Press asserts that it is "driven by the belief that books from academic publishers are more essential than ever before for understanding critical issues facing the world today."[86] And the University of Chicago Press perceives its mission as publishing "serious works that promote education, foster

---

83    Macleod et al. (2014:101). See also Chalmers and Glaziou (2009:88); Belluz (2015).

84    Romer (2016); Smolin (2007); see also Economist (2018b).

85    "About UC Press," https://www.ucpress.edu/about (accessed August 6, 2018).

86    "About Harvard University Press," http://www.hup.harvard.edu/about/ (accessed August 6, 2018).

public understanding, and enrich cultural life."[87] But in truth, most of the books these presses publish are aimed at being used in academic courses. Most of their authors are not only academics but academics who are seeking promotions, tenure, and/or increased status vis-à-vis colleagues. These authors frequently write in an academic style so as to convey intellectual competence to their peers. Some of the books these presses produce sell well beyond the academy. But most academic presses make their profit from selling academic books to students taking academic courses.

Let me take a specific example. In my early years as editor of the California Series in Public Anthropology, I sought out books that would do exactly what the University of California Press states above. The series' statement of purpose reads: "The California Series in Public Anthropology emphasizes the anthropologist's role as an engaged intellectual. It continues anthropology's commitment to being an ethnographic witness, to describing in human terms how life is lived beyond the borders of many readers' experiences. But it also adds a commitment through ethnography to reframing the terms of public debate—transforming received, accepted understandings of social issues with new insights, new framings."[88] Two presidents (Mikhail Gorbachev and Bill Clinton) as well as three Nobel laureates (Amartya Sen, Jody Williams, and Gorbachev) contributed to the series either through books or forewords. Some of the leading figures in anthropology—Paul Farmer, Philippe Bourgois, Arthur Kleinman, Seth Holmes, Carolyn Nordstrom, Didier Fassin, Aihwa Ong, and Margaret Lock—have written for the series. In an effort to draw in more publicly accessible books, before they are framed as academic works for academics, the series has held an annual international competition asking for proposals so the press could help guide authors to reach a wider audience. The competition has been successful in drawing a large number of proposals from five different continents. It has inspired a host of students and faculty to address broader problems.

But despite this well-intentioned effort, the series is still mainly an academic series for academics. The junior authors, who might be most open to the series' attempts to reach a wider readership, also desired promotions and tenure. Writing for a large public audience often is a "bridge too far" for them given this

---

87    "About the Press," http://www.press.uchicago.edu/press/about.html (accessed August 6, 2018).

88    Lock (2001: front matter).

agenda. They need to impress the academic colleagues more than offer understandable insights to the broader public.

In respect to academic writing, Victoria Clayton observes in *The Atlantic*: "A disconnect between researchers and their audiences fuels the problem . . . academics, in general, don't think about the public; they don't think about the average person, and they don't even think about their students when they write. . . . Their intended audience is always their peers. That's who they have to impress to get tenure." She continues: "It's easy to be complex, it's harder to be simple. . . . It would make academics better researchers and better writers, though, if they had to translate their thinking into plain language . . . it would probably also mean more people . . . would read their work."[89] So for academic presses the focus is also often on appearances. There is inspirational talk of high purpose, trying to reach out to the public in important ways that matter. But many of the books and articles produced embody an academic style of presentation that cuts them off from the broader public. The focus tends to be narrow, specialized topics. Because transparency is limited, readers are drawn to trusting an author—even when they do not understand the data supporting her or his conclusions.

Most academic presses emphasize the use of blind peer reviews in which a prospective author is subject to two outside reviews (who remain anonymous to the author) followed, at least in the case of the University of California Press, by a faculty board member's review. In principle, this process provides a professional assessment of a professional work. Most academic publishers take pride in upholding this standard. But it is unclear if the review process is all that it claims to be.[90] Paul Basken observes that "researchers show a growing resistance to serving as reviewers or devoting adequate time to the task. One result: The notion of what it means to have a highly respected 'peer reviewed' work . . . has become diminished, if not lost entirely." He continues: "At the same time, many journals and universities cling to the idea that a final published article that passes some measure of 'peer review' remains a defining measure of academic accomplishment—even in the face of growing evidence that the standards of those reviews are slipping." Basken notes: "There appears to be little coordinated effort to determine what, exactly, 'peer review' should look like in the future.

89   Clayton (2015). In relation to Clayton's statements, Hawkins (2018) presents an interesting piece.

90   Howsam (2009) offers a historical perspective on publishing standards.

Even among journals that make a good-faith effort at peer review, there's no common understanding of whether the process should mean a single reader giving a quick scan for obvious errors, a team of highly qualified reviewers offering multiple rounds of feedback to the author, or something in between."[91]

The *Economist* writes that "'peer review' is supposed to spot mistakes and thus keep the whole process honest. The peers in question, though, are necessarily few in number, are busy with their own work, are expected to act unpaid—and are often the rivals of those whose work they are scrutinising."[92] But that may not be the worst of it. The *Economist* recently reported: "A rising number of journals that claim to review submissions . . . do not bother to do so. Not coincidentally, this seems to be leading some academics to inflate their publication lists with papers that might not pass such scrutiny." The article continues: "According to Brian Nosek, head of the Centre for Open Science . . . many institutions that hire and promote researchers seem unconcerned about where those researchers have been publishing—a problem made worse by recent requirements by the American and Canadian governments that taxpayer-funded research must be published in open-access journals." When asked what might be done about the problem, Dr. Pyne, an economist at Thompson Rivers University in Canada, suggested that "too many academic administrators have no research experience, and so either cannot tell good publications from bad, or do not care."[93]

For many academic publishers, a book's quality is often judged by its sales and, to a lesser degree, the publicity the book generates for the author and the press. If book sales number over ten thousand, it is perceived as a good book—a solid investment of the press's time and money. If book sales reach over fifty thousand, it is perceived as impressive, financially and intellectually.

### Where Do We Go from Here?

Using cultural anthropology's ethnographic tools, this chapter analyzed the field of cultural anthropology. It also discussed the intellectual framework that shapes the book. Chapter 2 addresses the "do no harm" paradigm's claim to advancing knowledge through a host of publications. The chapter shows that in cultural anthropology the paradigm does not necessarily work as appearances suggest.

91   Basken (2018:16–18, 19).

92   Economist (2014b:72).

93   Economist (2018c:67–68); https://vancouversun.com/news/local-news/investigation-launched -into-possible-breach-of-b-c-profs-academic-freedom.

Instead of advancing knowledge, it has significant dysfunctional elements that produce unsubstantiated assertions of uncertain, ambiguous value. What the push to publish does do, quite well, is advance the careers of anthropologists. It is the broader public, that funds anthropological research, that tends to lose out.

Chapters 3 and 4 embrace an alternative paradigm, one focused on public anthropology. Chapter 3 elaborates on four principles of this paradigm—benefitting others, alternative forms of accountability, transparency, and collaboration—illustrating each principle with a host of anthropological examples. In seeking to add strength to this alternative paradigm, Chapter 4 uses case studies to suggest ways to make one's voice count in addressing social problems beyond the academy.

Chapter 5 is the key chapter around which earlier chapters revolve. It starts by discussing the administrative embracing of metric standards for assessing faculty productivity. It considers how this change came about and the frustrations many faculty feel with it. The chapter asks: Have faculty frustrations with metric standards generated enough of a crisis (following Kuhn) to move cultural anthropologists to explore an alternative paradigm, a paradigm in which they will be less vulnerable to the caprices of quantitative assessments? The chapter offers points to ponder in this regard.

In essence, this book uses anthropological techniques to analyze anthropology's current predicament in which the "do no harm" paradigm, especially in its present form involving metric assessments, has become an albatross around the necks of many faculty. In its place, the book calls for a public anthropology paradigm that reframes faculty accountability in ways that draw support from those beyond the academy that fund faculty research and lessens the arbitrariness of how administrators judge their intellectual competence. Change takes time. Many often resist it. Still, as readers will see, it is unlikely that faculty can go back to a time when they had more control over how they were assessed. Shifting paradigms, I suggest, can be more than a time of despair. It can also be a time of hope.

# 2

## WHO ARE THE MAIN BENEFICIARIES OF CULTURAL ANTHROPOLOGY'S MANY PUBLICATIONS?

**THIS CHAPTER ASKS** whether the plethora of publications produced in cultural anthropology live up to the "do no harm" paradigm's claim of advancing knowledge in ways that benefit the broader community. The chapter suggests, for the decades studied, this has not always been the case. We see the paradigm's basic pattern—claiming to hold high ideals while, in fact, embodying self-serving concerns that mostly advance individual careers and existing power structures. Because this chapter challenges certain accepted assumptions, it offers considerable documentation so readers can, if they wish, review the supporting data and draw their own conclusions.

Before turning to this issue, however, let me briefly note the considerable publications produced each year—both in general and specifically within cultural anthropology. Given the difficulties in collecting comprehensive data, it is not entirely clear how many publications are produced annually. Still, there are estimates. Gabriel Zaid suggests, based on the UNESCO *Statistical Yearbook*, that perhaps one million books were published throughout the world in 2000, or one every thirty seconds.[1] The *New York Times* reports that 175,000 books were published in the United States in 2003, or roughly twenty per hour.[2] Drawing on data from the International Association of Scientific, Technical, and Medical Publishers, the *Economist* in 2005 reported that the sixteen thousand journals tracked by the association annually produce 1.2 million articles.[3] In 2017 the journal *Science* reported that "the world's academic libraries pay some €7.6 billion in subscription fees for access to between 1.5 million and 2 million new papers annually" that are not open-access.[4]

Where does cultural anthropology fit into this picture? To get a rough idea, I counted the number of articles in the twenty journals published in 2016 by the American Anthropological Association that seem to fit within the field. The number of clearly defined articles (excluding pieces that might be viewed as commentaries) approached five hundred. It is not unreasonable to assume that the overall number of articles published by cultural anthropologists is at least twice that number—given the other relevant journals, both in the United States and abroad, in which cultural anthropologists publish. For 2016 there were roughly 250 book reviews in the *American Anthropologist*. Since the *American Anthropologist* only reviews some books (intriguingly it never reviewed Clifford Geertz's *The Interpretation of Cultures* nor Eric Wolf's *Europe and the People Without History*), we might speculate, doubling that figure, that the number of books published relating to cultural anthropology in 2016 was between four hundred and five hundred.[5] Both these numbers are likely conservative estimates. Taken as a whole, these data suggest that a considerable number of articles and books are published each year in cultural anthropology.

Succinctly stated, I highlight four points in this chapter:

- How the focus of funding agencies on producing social benefits becomes transformed into advancing the interests of individual faculty in their pursuit of status.
- Cultural anthropologists have raised all sorts of interesting possibilities in their publications. But few have been systematically substantiated. We

---

1  Zaid (2003).
2  L. Miller (2004).
3  Economist (2005e).
4  Vogel and Kupferschmidt (2017).
5  Geertz (1973); Wolf (1982).

remain uncertain as to which assertions we can collectively trust—which possess a reasonable degree of validity and which do not.

- The constant criticizing of established formulations and the seeking of new, innovative formulations in a pursuit of status is feasible because of the way accountability and credibility are assessed in cultural anthropology. Accountability is mostly framed in terms of producing publications. Tearing down old frameworks and erecting new ones provides plenty of publishing opportunities. In respect to credibility, anthropological data tend to be accepted on trust. (Anthropologists rarely restudy the same topic in the same locale.) This means that an author's perspective is primarily "authenticated" by her or his own assertions. The process encourages a creative, entrepreneurial freedom while downplaying a systematic building and/or refining of knowledge that supports someone else's perspective.

- The way this system plays out benefits those within the academic community—foremost, individual anthropologists but, secondarily, their departments and universities. It is far more questionable to what degree the publications produced benefit the larger society that, more than likely, funded the research on which the publications are based.

## Questioning the Intellectual Advances Generated by the Many Publications Produced Each Year

*Cultural anthropology's intellectual progress in the past sixty-plus years may seem self-evident. And yet it remains open to question. This section discusses prominent anthropologists who raise questions about the field's systematic progress. Many publications do not produce more knowledge. Rather, they often produce unsubstantiated assertions of uncertain, ambiguous value.*

Most cultural anthropologists embrace a tale of progress, emphasizing the significant intellectual advances the field has made since the 1950s. The hegemonic-like framework of progress that pervades the larger society shapes this discussion. But it is far from clear that the degree of progress espoused in the discipline's histories has actually occurred. Emphasizing intellectual progress is not a new academic goal. Noted British historian Peter Burke in *A Social History of Knowledge* dates this academic ideal of progress back to the seventeenth and eighteenth centuries, highlighting Francis Bacon's 1605 *The Advancement of Learning* as a prominent example. Burke writes that today "intellectual innovation, rather than the transmission of tradition, is considered one of the major functions of institutions of higher education, so that candidates for higher degrees are normally expected to have made a 'contribution to knowledge,' and there is pressure on academics . . . to colonize new intellectual territories rather than to continue to cultivate old ones."[6]

Fitting with this hegemonic-like perspective, funding agencies assess grant applications by whether they advance human understanding. As noted earlier, the National Science Foundation (NSF) considers how important a proposed activity is by whether it helps advance knowledge.[7] The Social Sciences and Humanities Research Council of Canada asks what is the "expected contribution to the advancement of knowledge."[8] The Wenner-Gren Foundation asks: "How does your research build on existing scholarship in anthropology and closely related disciplines?"[9] We do not know what various cultural anthropologists secretly affirm in their hearts. But it is clear that most publicly frame their requests for funding in ways that fit with the expectations of major funding agencies.

Intellectual histories of the field affirm this progressive development. "The intellectual adventure of cultural anthropology," one noted historian of the discipline states, "has exhibited a continuous . . . advance in perspective."[10] Two others assert that while "we do not consider the history of anthropology to be a linear tale of progress . . . we believe that there has been a steady, cumulative growth in knowledge and understanding within the subject."[11] More broadly, James Rule writes in *Theory and Progress in Social Science*:

> Pretensions of progress are pervasive in the images we project of our work. Conferences are convened, and volumes of studies commissioned, purporting to extend the "frontiers" of knowledge in one or another domain. Yearbooks are published documenting "advances" in the discipline. Journal submissions, books, and doctoral dissertations are assessed in terms of whether they constitute "contributions" to existing knowledge. Such language obviously presumes movement in the direction of fuller, more comprehensive, more *advanced* understanding. The notion of a "contribution" implies not just the sheer addition of another book, ar-

---

6   Burke (2000:114).
7   NSF (2013); see also NSF (2004).
8   Social Sciences and Humanities Research Council of Canada (2009).
9   Wenner-Gren Foundation (n.d.).
10   Voget (1975:795).
11   Eriksen and Nielsen (2001:viii).

ticle, or research report to an ever-lengthening bibliography, but a meaningful step forward in a direction shared by all. And claims to participate in such advances, I hold, are central to the justifications most of us would put forward for our work.[12]

The host of citations in books and articles published by cultural anthropologists suggest they are using other scholars' publications as reference points and building on them. Otherwise, why would cultural anthropologists cite so many publications in their publications?

And yet, within cultural anthropology, some prominent scholars have doubts. I am certainly not the first to question whether cultural anthropology, with its piles of publications, is significantly advancing knowledge. Eric Wolf asserts: "In anthropology, we are continuously slaying paradigms [or trends], only to see them return to life, as if discovered for the first time. As each successive approach carries the axe to its predecessors, anthropology comes to resemble a project of intellectual deforestation."[13] The noted Berkeley anthropologist Elizabeth Colson writes:

Rapid population growth and geographical dispersal [within cultural anthropology] have been associated with the emergence of a multitude of intellectual schools, each of which stresses both its own uniqueness and superiority and the need for the whole of the social/cultural community to accept its leadership. This never happens, and even the most successful formula rarely predominates for more than a decade: At the moment when it appears to triumph, it becomes redefined as an outmoded orthodoxy by younger anthropologists who are attempting to stamp their own mark upon the profession. This has the therapeutic effect of outmoding most of the existing literature, by now too vast to be absorbed by any newcomer, while at the same time old ideas continue to be advanced under new rubrics.[14]

The Canadian anthropologist Philip Carl Salzman observes:

A well-known and occasionally discussed problem is the fact that the vast multitude of anthropological conferences, congresses, articles, monographs, and collections, while adding up to mountains of paper . . . do not seem to add up to a substantial, integrated, coherent body of knowledge that could provide a base for the further advancement of the discipline. L. A. Fallers used to comment that we

---

12    Rule (1997:25).

13    E. Wolf (1990:588). Kroeber phrases it more gently. He states that sciences such as anthropology "are subject to waves of fashion" (1948:391).

14    Colson (1992:51).

seem to be constantly tooling up with new ideas and new concepts and never seem to get around to applying and assessing them in a substantive and systematic fashion. John Davis, over two decades ago in *The Peoples of the Mediterranean*, seemed on the verge of tears of frustration during his attempts to find any comparable information in the available ethnographic reports that might be used to put individual cases into perspective and be compiled into a broader picture. Nor is there confidence in the individual ethnographic reports available: We cannot credit the accounts of I. Schapera, because he was a functionalist, or that of S. F. Nadel because he was an agent of colonialism, or J. Pitt-Rivers because he collected all his data from the upper-class señoritos . . . or M. Harris because he is a crude materialist, etc. etc. So we end up without any substantive body of knowledge to build on, forcing us to be constantly trying to make anthropology anew.[15]

In assessing the discipline's theoretical development, Stanley Barrett states: "We keep discovering old truths, and long-abandoned orientations pop up again, often under new labels. By the conventional criteria used to measure theoretical progress—simplicity, elegance, accuracy, scope, and fruitfulness—the discipline appears to have stood still: or, more aptly, to have rocked back and forth without gaining ground."[16] Boyce Rensberger, the former science editor of the *Washington Post* and former director of the Knight Science Journalism Fellowships at MIT, offers an outsider's view:

> One of the questions frequently put to me by anthropologists is why the press doesn't capitalize more on anthropological insights and expertise about various stories in the news. In my experience, anthropology is still so riven with rival "schools of thought" that it is almost always possible to find a well-credentialed anthropologist to dispute anything said by any other well-credentialed anthropologist. This gives the impression that anthropology hasn't got its act together or isn't a mature science. Consequently, science writers tend to think that readers (and viewers) will not be well-served simply by putting up contrary points of view that explain nothing.
>
> There is controversy on the frontiers of the "hard" sciences but not on a steadily growing body of accepted textbook knowledge—hard facts. In physics no one doubts that $F=ma$. In chemistry, redox reactions always happen the same way, and nobody claims they don't. In biology, RNA always transcribes DNA the same way.

---

15    Salzman in Borofsky (1994:34).
16    Barrett (1984:76).

It doesn't seem that anthropology can point to a large body of knowledge that explains a lot about humans and is solidly accepted by all anthropologists.

I offer this commentary from a point of view of great sympathy with anthropology.[17]

## BROADENING THE CRITIQUE

Turning to the life and natural sciences, we also see considerable questioning of intellectual progress. John Ioannidis is a prominent figure in this movement. One might suspect that a scientist, at the University of Ioannina in Greece, might not draw much positive attention, especially in North America, for a short 2005 article published in *PLoS Medicine* titled "Why Most Published Research Findings Are False."[18] How did leading scholars react to his provocatively titled work? It turns out, that article is the journal's most downloaded technical paper. Wikipedia reports that "Ioannidis is one of the most-cited scientists across the scientific literature, especially in the fields of clinical medicine and social sciences, according to Thomson Reuters' Highly Cited Researchers 2015." Ioannidis is now a professor at Stanford University and codirector of the Meta-Research Innovation Center at Stanford (METRICS). His 2005 article directly relates to cultural anthropology. He writes: "A research finding is less likely to be true when the studies conducted in a field are smaller; when effect sizes are smaller; . . . where there is greater flexibility in designs, definitions, outcomes, and analytical modes; when there is greater financial and other interest and prejudice; and when more teams are involved in a scientific field in chase of statistical significance. Simulations show that for most study designs and settings, it is more likely for a research claim to be false than true."[19]

Quoting from a 2013 *Economist* article titled "Trouble in the Lab":

A few years ago scientists at Amgen, an American drug company, tried to replicate 53 studies that they considered landmarks in the basic science of cancer, often cooperating closely with the original researchers to ensure that their experimental technique matched the one used first time round. According to a piece they wrote last year [2012] in *Nature*, a leading scientific journal, they were able to reproduce the original results in just six. . . . Fraud is very likely second to incompetence in generating erroneous results. . . . Dr. Fanelli has looked at 21 different surveys of

17    Rensburger (1996).
18    Wikipedia, s.v. "John Ioannidis."
19    Ioannidis (2005b).

academics. . . . Only 2% of respondents admitted falsifying or fabricating data, but 28% of respondents claimed to know of colleagues who engaged in questionable research practices.[20]

In Chapter 1, I touched on a publication in the journal *Lancet*. I elaborate on that article in Chapter 3, but here I highlight a brief statement: "In 2009, Chalmers and Glasziou identified some key sources of avoidable waste in biomedical research. They estimated that the cumulative effect was that about 85% of research investment—equating to $200 billion of the investment in 2010—is wasted."[21] In physics, Lee Smolin, in *The Trouble with Physics*, argues "that fundamental physics—the search for the laws of nature—is losing its way. Ambitious ideas about extra dimensions, exotic particle, multiple universes, and string have captured the public's imagination—and the imagination of experts. But these ideas have not been tested experimentally, and some, like string theory, seem to offer no possibility of being tested. Yet these speculations dominate the field, attracting the best talent and much of the funding . . . the situation threatens to impede the very progress of science."[22]

Similar questions are raised in the social sciences. In Chapter 1, I quoted the *New York Times* regarding the degree to which prominent studies in psychology cannot be reconfirmed. The Center for Open Science's study "Estimating the Reproducibility of Psychological Science" in *Science* reports that of one hundred experimental and correlational studies published in three psychological journals, "Ninety-seven percent of original studies had significant results (p < .05). Thirty-six percent of replications had significant results."[23] In 2018, the *Washington Post* reported on:

> a research project [that] attempted to replicate 21 social science experiments published between 2010 and 2015 in the prestigious journals *Science* and *Nature*. Only 13 replication attempts succeeded. The other eight were duds, with no observed effects consistent with the original findings . . . the authors also noted that even in the replications that succeeded, the observed effect was on average only about 75 percent as large as the first time around. . . . This latest project provides a reminder that the publication of a finding in a peer-reviewed journal does not make it true. . . . The advocates for greater reproducibility believe that publication pres-

20   Economist (2013a).
21   Macleod et al. (2014:101). See also Chalmers and Glasziou (2009:88); Belluz (2015).
22   Smolin (2007:back cover of book).
23   Open Science Collaboration (2015:943).

sures create an environment ripe for false positives. Scientists need to publish, and journal editors are eager to publish novel, interesting findings.[24]

Finally, the sociologist Andrew Abbott (referred to in Chapter 1) suggests that the social sciences "pretend to perpetual progress while actually going nowhere at all, remaining safely encamped within a familiar world of fundamental concepts." Abbott writes: "The young build their careers on forgetting and rediscovery, while the middle-aged are doomed to see the common sense of their graduate school years refurbished and republished as brilliant new insights."[25] Clearly, some prominent scholars have spoken out about the limited progress being made in the natural, medical, and social sciences. The following analysis of cultural anthropology fits this trend.[26]

## The Standards to Measure Intellectual Advances in Cultural Anthropology

*Cultural anthropology has two coexisting and, at times, overlapping traditions. One focuses on interpretation and understanding; the other on the scientific accumulation of knowledge. The first standard considers to what degree a set of publications refines a particular trend's approach by addressing key conceptual problems within it. The second standard involves establishing objective accounts through one anthropologist systematically building on the work of another.*

The degree to which one perceives significant intellectual advances in the piles of publications produced by cultural anthropologists depends on how one measures these advances. The term "progress" is held by some anthropologists to imply a positivist perspective—a perspective that, even though most anthropologists are committed to advancing knowledge, they reject because it connotes an overly scientific orientation. As Roy Rappaport observes, there are two basic traditions in anthropology. One is "influenced by philosophy, linguistics, and the

---

24    Achenbach (2018). For the actual study, see Camerer et al. (2018). Intriguingly, Achenbach adds: "The researchers asked more than 200 peers to predict which studies would replicate and to what extent the effect sizes would be duplicated. The prediction market got it remarkably right. The study's authors suggest that scientific journals could tap into the 'wisdom of crowds' when deciding how to treat submitted papers with novel results."

25    Abbott (2001:147–148).

26    Readers interested in exploring this topic further might refer to P. Campbell (1999); Colson (1989); Kuper (2007); Ortner (1984); Rensburger (1996); Voget (1973); and E. Wolf (1969).

humanities, and open to more subjectively derived knowledge, attempts interpretation and seeks to elucidate meanings." The other is "objective in its aspirations and inspired by the biological sciences, seeks explanation and is concerned to discover causes, or even, in the view of the ambitious, laws."[27] Adam Kuper frames the difference between them as follows: "The first [is] . . . concerned with description and interpretation rather than with explanation, and with the particular rather than with the general. . . . The second . . . seeks general principles and models itself on the natural sciences rather than on the humanities."[28]

Each tradition has its own view of what it means to advance knowledge. In the first tradition, often termed "interpretivist," understanding an action "requires reference to its larger context . . . the aim is not to uncover universals or laws but rather to explicate context." "Interpretive explanation," Clifford Geertz asserts, "trains its attention on what institutions . . . mean to those whose institutions . . . they are."[29] "It is not against a body of uninterpreted data, radically thinned [or superficial] descriptions, that we must measure the cogency of our explications," he states, "but against the power of the scientific imagination to bring us into touch with the lives of strangers."[30] Geertz is not anti-science. "I do not believe that anthropology is not or cannot be a science," he writes, " . . . that the value of anthropological works inheres solely in their persuasiveness."[31] But he is against what he views as method-obsessed quantification and rigid law-seeking.

The second tradition, in its positivist, empirically oriented form, can be viewed as a set of working principles for building cumulative knowledge. It emphasizes that (a) theory formation should be based on inductions from observation; (b) in case of theoretical disputes, they should be resolved by empirical tests; and (c) since theoretical disputes are resolvable, scientific knowledge can be cumulative and progressive over time. The positivist perspective is expressed by Marvin Harris. Scientific knowledge, Harris states, "is obtained by public, replicable operations." And "the aim of scientific research is to formulate explanatory theories which are . . . testable (or falsifiable) . . . [and] cumulative within a coherent and expanding corpus of theories."[32]

27    Rappaport (1994:154).
28    Kuper (1994:113).
29    Geertz (1983:22).
30    Geertz (1973:16).
31    Geertz in Carrithers (1990:274).
32    M. Harris (1994:64).

In assessing the trends discussed below, I ask: To what degree does a particular trend represent a significant advance in knowledge? This is a question funders raise about projects that apply for funding? They, like many others, ask: What are anthropologists producing of value through their various publications?

Some readers might perceive the first standard below as leaning toward the interpretivist tradition; the second toward the positivist. A closer examination, however, suggests they do not fit easily into an either/or dichotomy. I believe most anthropologists would in principle embrace at least one of these standards. Many might embrace both. They affirm anthropology's value. They emphasize anthropological publications are not simply works of fiction but involve valuable research. The first standard for assessing intellectual advances considers to what degree a set of publications relating to a trend refines that trend's perspective. Take, for example, the transmission of Franz Boas's skepticism regarding historical speculation used in wide-ranging comparisons. Boas castigated the conjectural analyses of early evolutionists. In "The Limitations of the Comparative Method of Anthropology," he critiqued the abandon with which certain scholars compared different cultures across time and space. Boas was concerned with understanding specific patterns in specific cultures before offering broad generalizations about the dynamics at work across a panoply of cultures. He wrote: "When we have cleared up the history of a single culture and understand the effects of environment and the psychological conditions that are reflected in it, . . . we can then investigate in how far the same causes . . . [are] at work in the development of other cultures."[33]

Having spent years examining Native American societies during the early part of his career, Boas's first student at Columbia, Alfred Kroeber, in *Configurations of Culture Growth,* explored whether there were common patterns of development in Old World civilizations. Rather than postulating possible configurations, Kroeber immersed himself in the historical specifics of ancient Egypt, Mesopotamia, Greece, and Rome, detail after detail to build his analysis. Julian Steward, Kroeber's first student at the University of California–Berkeley, exhibited the same Boasian caution toward comparative conjectures. Steward's book, *Theory of Culture Change,* had as its subtitle *The Methodology of Multilinear Evolution* to make clear that he was not proposing a grand theory of change but a method for studying detailed cases of change. One of Steward's students

33   Boas (1896[1940]:279).

at Columbia, Eric Wolf, continued the Boasian tradition of rejecting conjectural histories. In *Europe and the People Without History*, Wolf showed specific ways that Western economies shaped the development of non-Western groups. He focused on detailed historical records to make his case. We see in the procession of anthropologists—Boas teaching Kroeber teaching Steward teaching Wolf—a concern with actual histories over conjectural ones. But each refined Boas's perspective in a particular way to address a set of problems that interested him.

The second standard for assessing intellectual progress considers whether a set of publications builds a cumulative body of knowledge in respect to a specific group or topic. A good example of this second standard is Annette Weiner's research among the Trobrianders of Papua New Guinea. By the time of her fieldwork in the early 1970s, the Trobrianders had become well known, thanks to the writings of Bronislaw Malinowski. His *Argonauts of the Western Pacific* (1922), *The Sexual Life of Savages in North-Western Melanesia* (1929), and *Coral Gardens and Their Magic* (1935) are seen as classics in the field. But that didn't mean Weiner could not add to them. She writes: "Although Malinowski and I were in the Trobriands at vastly different historical moments and there also are many areas in which our analyses differ, a large part of what we learned in the field was similar. From the vantage point that time gives me, I can illustrate how our differences, even those that are major, came to be." She states: "My most significant . . . departure from [Malinowski] . . . was the attention I gave to women's productive work." Weiner continues: "My taking seriously the importance of women's wealth not only brought women . . . clearly into the ethnographic picture [which was not the case in Malinowski's accounts] but also forced me to revise many of Malinowski's assumptions about Trobriand men."[34] In short, building on Malinowski's classic writings, Weiner extended and refined the analysis of Trobriand society.

Marshall Sahlins's *Social Stratification in Polynesia* constitutes another example. Building on accounts of individual Polynesian atolls, Sahlins perceived a generalized pattern of social organization. The atolls have, he writes, "a number of interlocking social groups, each dedicated to the exploitation of a particular resource or resource area."[35] Sahlins suggested that the pattern of interlocking ties between descent and residential groups on these atolls constituted an adaptation to high-population densities with limited food surpluses and periodic

---

34   Weiner (1988:5); see also Weiner (1976).
35   Sahlins (1958:245).

conditions of scarcity. Building on the work of earlier scholars studying separate atolls, Sahlins suggested a general process—adaptation—that lay behind the shared social structures of several Polynesian atolls. Leonard Mason subsequently took Sahlins's insight regarding Polynesian atolls and applied it to Micronesian atolls. He found that Micronesian atolls responded in a related way to many of the same pressures.[36]

I presume that one or both of these two standards seem reasonable to most readers. They should. The two standards fit with what the broader public presumes anthropology does: advance knowledge. Some anthropologists might wander from these standards. They might view their ethnographies as a form of poetic license, where they can write what they want how they want. But most anthropologists cannot openly move far from these standards and still expect to receive funding for their research and/or academic promotions.

## Assessing Whether Researchers Are Living Up to These Standards

*Cultural anthropology rarely has the smoking gun—the convincing evidence of unethical and/or fraudulent behavior—that convinces editors to retract an article. Because few anthropologists restudy a group studied by another anthropologist, anthropologists tend to produce unverified assertions of uncertain, ambiguous value. When we have more than one account of a group—whether the accounts agree or disagree—we gain a better sense of the group being studied and the scholars studying it.*

The standard way researchers determine the degree to which a new study advances knowledge is to assess its validity. For some this involves other researchers replicating the study. This approach does not address the complex factors often involved in anthropological fieldwork. But starting with this as a point of reference, we can explore why certain published studies are deemed invalid or fallacious and, as a result, retracted from publication. Recently, there has been an increase in journal retractions within the medical, natural, and social sciences. Benedict Carey, in reporting on the website Retraction Watch, notes the site "has charted a 20 to 25 percent increase in retractions across 10,000 medical and science journals in the past five years: 500 to 600 a year today from 400 in 2010." Carey reports that "the pressure to publish attention-grabbing findings is

36   Mason (1959).

stronger than ever. . . . Retraction Watch's records suggest that about a third of retractions are because of errors, like tainted samples or mistakes in statistics, and about two-thirds are because of misconduct or suspicions of misconduct."[37]

John Ioannidis noted in *JAMA* that in three leading medical journals, "6% of the top-cited clinical research articles on postulated effective medical interventions that have been published within the last 15 years have been contradicted by subsequent clinical studies and another 16% have been found to have initially stronger effects than subsequent research" confirmed.[38] An article in the *Economist* reports, based on a meta-analysis conducted by Daniele Fanelli: "About 10% confessed to questionable practices, such as 'dropping data points based on a gut feeling' or 'failing to present data that contradict one's previous research.'" In respect to those who had seen colleagues "running experiments with deficient methods, failing to report deficiencies or misrepresenting data, the straight average suggested that 46% of researchers had seen others get up to such shenanigans. In only half of the cases, though, had the respondent to a survey tried to do anything about the misconduct he said he had witnessed."[39]

A prominent example of retracted research involves Victor Ninov, a world-renowned expert on atomic particles working at the respected Lawrence Berkeley National Lab. He played a prominent role in the seeming discovery of a new atomic element, Number 118. The discovery was announced in *Physical Review Letters*, the foremost journal in its field, with fourteen coauthors. The discovery received worldwide attention. For an element to be allocated a name (rather than just a number) the same result needs to be produced by a different laboratory. Both GSI in Germany and the Riken Institute in Japan tried to do this but failed. As the *New York Times* reported, "these negative results were not necessarily fatal. Events like these are exceedingly rare, and it was possible that Dr. Ninov and his colleagues had just been luckier than the others." It was further complicated by the fact that Ninov used a sophisticated software program, Goosy, to process the results, that few besides Ninov knew how to use effectively. It took four review committees assessing the research before things could be sorted.

"What turned out to be the smoking gun," the *New York Times* reported, "was a computer 'log file'—a diary automatically generated by Goosy of everything that had occurred during the handling of the data. . . . According to this history, an analysis performed around noon on May 7 indeed showed what appeared

37  Carey (2015a).
38  Ioannidis (2005a).
39  Economist (2009a).

to be an element 118 decay chain. But when the very same data was analyzed again, a few hours later, the chain was not there. A closer look showed that it was the earlier record that had been altered; page lengths were inconsistent, and the timing of some of the events was off."[40] On this basis, the discovery of the atomic element 118 was denied. *Physical Review Letters* retracted the publication announcing the discovery. A researcher quoted in the *New York Times* piece commented that it was fortunate that Glenn T. Seaborg—a world-famous scientist at the Berkeley lab who holds the Guinness world record for discovering the most elements—"died before this, because he would have been one of the co-authors" too.[41]

It was not the inability to reproduce the results of a world famous physicist that led to the detection of fraud. Rather, it was the discovery of contextual factors associated with the discovery—changes in the computer code. If Ninov had not sought to make such a prominent discovery—had not sought to win a heated competition with other labs trying to discover new elements and, because of the discovery's importance, needed repeated review committees to ascertain the results—his fraud might never have been discovered.

Let's examine the case of *The Lancet* retracting an article affirming a relationship between autism and vaccines. From the *New York Times*:

> The retraction by *The Lancet* is part of a reassessment that has lasted for years of the scientific methods and financial conflicts of Dr. Andrew Wakefield, who contended that his research showed that the combined measles, mumps and rubella vaccine may be unsafe. . . . Despite a wealth of scientific studies that have failed to find any link between vaccines and autism, [some] parents [still] fervently believe that their children's mental problems resulted from vaccinations. . . .
> A British medical panel concluded . . . that Dr. Wakefield had been dishonest, violated basic research ethics rules and showed a "callous disregard" for the suffering of children involved in his research. Dr. Richard Horton, editor in chief of *The Lancet*, said that until that decision, he had no proof that Dr. Wakefield's 1998 paper was deceptive. . . . An investigation by a British journalist found financial and scientific conflicts that Dr. Wakefield did not reveal in his paper. For instance, part of the costs of Dr. Wakefield's research were paid by lawyers for parents seeking to sue vaccine makers for damages. Dr. Wakefield was also found to have patented in

40   Johnson (2002).
41   Johnson (2002).

1997 a measles vaccine that would succeed if the combined vaccine was withdrawn or discredited.[42]

Again, we see that contextual factors were important in forcing the article's retraction, not simply the fact that it went against a large amount of highly credible research. See the accompanying footnote here for a list of additional retractions.[43]

In the social sciences, another retraction stands out: *Science*'s retraction of Michael LaCour's asserting that gay canvassers can influence voters' attitudes on gay marriage. Since LaCour erased his raw data—preventing any confirmation of his results—the breadth of his falsifications is unclear. (He had been asked by his coauthor to store his raw data in an academic databank but deleted them instead.) An investigation into other aspects of the research, Carey reports in the *New York Times*, uncovered that "three funding sources that Mr. LaCour listed as providing support for his published paper denied . . . that they had done so" and "the survey company he told the Los Angeles LGBT Center he was working with did not have any knowledge of his project."[44] Once again, it was not the data themselves that led to the retraction but contextual factors surrounding the research.

A final example involves the work of Brian Wansink, the former head of Cornell University's prestigious Food and Brand Lab. Wansink became famous for his various food studies, drawing attention from *Oprah Magazine*, the *Today Show*, and the *New York Times*. His well-publicized work attracted millions in grants, numerous awards, and a distinguished chair at Cornell. His basic theme, according to Stephanie Lee of *BuzzFeed*, was that "weight loss is possible for anyone willing to make a few small changes to their environment, without need for strict diets or intense exercise." But rather than testing the hypothesis seriously, Wansink would keep "messaging" various experimental data until he found something exciting to report. Lee reports:

> Interviews with a former lab member and a trove of previously undisclosed emails
> show that, year after year, Wansink and his collaborators at the Cornell Food and
> Brand Lab have turned shoddy data into headline-friendly eating lessons that
> they could feed to the masses. In [email] correspondence between 2008 and 2016,
> the renowned Cornell scientist and his team discussed and even joked about ex-

42    Harris (2010).
43    Roston (2015).
44    Carey (2015b).

haustively mining datasets for impressive-looking results. They strategized how to publish subpar studies, sometimes targeting journals with low standards. And they often framed their findings in the hopes of stirring up media coverage to, as Wansink once put it, "go virally big time."[45]

What brought this email correspondence to light, and led to several publications being retracted, were record requests from the University of New Mexico, which employs one of Wansink's longtime collaborators. Wansink's email exchanges became public. Brian Nosek, of the Center for Open Science, observed: "It is difficult to read these emails and avoid a conclusion of research misconduct . . . this is not science, it is storytelling."[46]

## CULTURAL ANTHROPOLOGY

Turning to cultural anthropology, let me highlight three points. First, while cultural anthropology embodies alternative approaches to those used in the physical and life sciences, ferreting out fallacious claims frequently depends on contextual factors. Few researchers make their raw data openly available and few have others restudy their field sites, especially from a different perspective. Some researchers may feel under pressure to come up with exciting, new results to enhance their careers. But there is no reason to presume they are being dishonest. Most anthropologists believe other anthropologists, when reporting on their research, are honest; their accounts are reliable.

Because an anthropological journal's reviewers rarely have visited the field site of work being reviewed, they are often drawn, as in the above examples, into relying on contextual factors to assess the work. Cultural anthropologists often assess credibility by whether the author is familiar with certain references. Presumably, that is the reason why authors refer to a number of prominent figures in their publications. It makes them appear knowledgeable. An author's research data should also fit within expected norms. It should seem "reasonable" to other anthropologists familiar with the ethnographic region. The author should also convey a familiarity with the indigenous language to emphasize the author understood the group she or he worked with.

45    S. Lee (2018); see also Bartlett (2017).

46    S. Lee (2018). Readers interested in related examples might read Stapel (2014), which is the author's account of how, while fabricating more than fifty studies in social psychology, he became famous—until the fabrications were uncovered. More unsettling are Madrick (2014) and Harvey and Liu (2014) in economics. See also https://thewire.in/science/replication-crisis-science.

The most prominent case of "seeming fraud" in cultural anthropology involves Carlos Castaneda's *The Teachings of Don Juan*. In 1968, Castaneda, with a PhD in anthropology from UCLA, wrote *The Teachings of Don Juan*. The book has sold over twenty-five million copies. Many anthropologists today suspect the book and its sequels are works of fiction. Wikipedia provides a good overview of problems involved in assessing Castaneda's work:

> At first, and with the backing of academic qualifications and the UCLA anthropological department, Castaneda's work was critically acclaimed. Notable anthropologists like Edward Spicer (1969) and Edmund Leach (1969) praised Castaneda, alongside more alternative and young anthropologists. Castaneda's books and the man himself became a cultural phenomenon. . . . Despite [their] widespread popularity . . . some critics questioned the validity of Castaneda's books. . . . In a series of articles, R. Gordon Wasson, who had . . . originally praised Castaneda's work, questioned the accuracies of Castaneda's botanical claims.
>
> The authenticity of Don Juan was accepted for six years, until Richard de Mille and Daniel Noel both published their critiques of the Don Juan books in 1976. Later anthropologists specializing in Yaqui Indian culture (William Curry Holden, Jane Holden Kelley and Edward H. Spicer), who originally supported Castaneda's account as true, questioned the accuracy of Castaneda's work. . . . Criticisms of Castaneda's work include[d] the total lack of Yaqui vocabulary or terms for any of his experiences, and his refusal to defend himself against the accusation that he received his PhD from UCLA through deception. . . . Dr. Clement Meighan, one of Castaneda's professors at UCLA, and an acknowledged expert on Indian culture in the U.S., Mexico, and other areas in North America, up to his death, never doubted that Castaneda's work was based upon authentic contact with and observations of Indians. . . .

A March 5, 1973, *Time* article by Sandra Burton, looking at both sides of the controversy, stated:

> [The credibility of Castaneda's work] hinges on the credibility of Don Juan as a being and Carlos Castaneda as a witness. Yet there is no corroboration beyond Castaneda's writings that Don Juan did what he is said to have done, and very little that he exists at all. A strong case can be made that the Don Juan books are of a different order of truthfulness. . . . Where, for example, was the motive for an elaborate scholarly put-on? *The Teachings* were submitted to a university press [the University of California Press], an unlikely prospect for best-sellerdom. Besides,

getting an anthropology degree from UCLA is not so difficult that a candidate would employ so vast a confabulation just to avoid research. A little fudging perhaps, but not a whole system in the manner of *The Teachings*, written by an unknown student with, at the outset, no hope of commercial success.[47]

While the credibility of Castaneda's work has been called into question, we only have contextual factors to assess the validity of his work. We know enough to be suspicious. But we do not know enough to claim outright fraud.[48]

The second point is that because anthropologists tend to work in different field sites, they are often caught in what might be termed a "comparative fallacy." In seeking to enlarge the relevance of their research, anthropologists frequently relate their work to the work of prominent researchers on the same topic—often emphasizing how their work challenges these figures' conclusions. The implication, speaking in general terms, is that since both field sites deal with human beings and humans share certain traits, the new research can act as a test of a prominent figure's work. The difficulty with this assumption is that it flies in the face of accepted anthropological knowledge that people in different cultural groups often act differently. They may not. But this cannot be assumed. It must be proven. To use one group to verify data in another group—not directly connected to it in time, space, or context—makes little sense. To draw an effective comparison, we need detailed knowledge of how the two groups overlap—in what ways, to what degree—to understand, as we did with Nadel, Nader, and Wolf (in Chapter 1), the value of the comparison being drawn.

Cultural anthropologists frequently claim to "build" on or refine earlier work while altering two variables—both the location and the topic. If an anthropologist went back to the same field site as another anthropologist, or in moving to a different site addressed the same topic in the same exact way, we might gain a reasonable idea of how one study relates to the other. But anthropologists often don't do this. They tend to select a new locale and a related, but somewhat differently framed, research problem. As a result, we are often unsure how one study relates to another—a point Salzman noted above.

The third point, building on this, when a restudy of a group presents a different perspective from the original study, it is sometimes perceived as a controversy

---

47    Wikipedia, s.v. "Carlos Castaneda."

48    One might compare this controversy with that surrounding *On the Run: Fugitive Life in an American City* by Alice Goffman. I personally take a positive view of her work and recommend Lewis-Kraus's (2016) thoughtful overview of the issues involved.

(or even perhaps a "scandal"). I would avoid such rhetoric. It seems reasonable that given the prominence of intracultural diversity, and the point Rensberger made earlier (regarding the diverse stances anthropologists take on a topic), that there would be divergent accounts. It is an act of hubris to assert a single anthropologist can completely and accurately report on the cultural behaviors and beliefs of a group of people numbering from perhaps two hundred to two thousand after a year or two of research. In an early period, cultural anthropologists wrote general ethnographies of a group; today their ethnographies often focus on narrower topics. Either way, the picture they present of a group is, more than likely, incomplete. There is no reason to assume two anthropologists researching the same group will come to the same conclusions. Human groups involve complex interactions through time. Though not always emphasized, they also possess considerable internal variability.

## THREE EXAMPLES

Rather than viewing discrepant accounts between anthropologists of a group as a negative, the discrepancies should be viewed as a positive. They enlarge our understanding of the group, the anthropologists who studied it, and, more broadly, cultural anthropology. I offer three examples. The Redfield-Lewis controversy, noted in Chapter 1, involved the rural Mexican village of Tepoztlán.[49] Robert Redfield, a noted anthropologist at the University of Chicago, studied Tepoztlán in 1926–1927. He wrote an ethnographic description of the village that focused on normative rules. Redfield portrayed neighbors as living in relative harmony. In 1943 another anthropologist, Oscar Lewis (affiliated with the Inter-American Indian Institute and a different political perspective), conducted research in the village. Focusing on observed behavior rather than ideal norms, Lewis painted a picture of conflict and factionalism.

As Redfield emphasized, the differing accounts led to a better understanding of the village: "The principle conclusion that I draw from this experience is that we are all better off with two descriptions of Tepoztlán than we would be with only one of them. More understanding results from the contrast and complementarity that the two together provide. In the cases of most primitive and exotic communities we have a one-eyed view. We can now look at Tepoztlán with somewhat stereoscopic vision."[50] Having two accounts—even if they

---

49    Redfield (1930, 1956); O. Lewis (1951, 1960); also note Butterworth (1972).
50    Redfield (1956:136).

disagree—is better than having one account because they provide a richer, fuller, more textured account of a group. As far as I know, no one has ever accused Redfield or Lewis of fraud because their accounts differ.

As an aside, I note that while many anthropologists (especially those trained before 1990) know of the controversy, it is rarely highlighted in introductory textbooks or disciplinary histories today. I examined twenty-six introductory texts. None of them refer to the controversy.[51] I also examined thirteen disciplinary histories.[52] Two, written by European anthropologists, refer to the controversy.[53] None written by American anthropologists do, despite the fact that Redfield and Lewis were both prominent American anthropologists. Perhaps many anthropologists feel uneasy with discussing a case in which two prominent anthropologists described the same field site in two different ways. It challenges the credibility of the disciplinary paradigm that one anthropologist is sufficient for describing a whole cultural group.

The second example draws on my own fieldwork. It discusses the residence patterns on the atoll of Pukapuka—comparing the field notes of Pam and Earnest Beaglehole with my own. According to the Beagleholes—who worked on the island for seven-and-a-half months in 1934–1935—informants reported Pukapukan postmarital residence as patrilocal. Census data collected from fifty-four households mostly in Ngake and Yato villages, they state, confirmed this assertion. In respect to kin affiliation (the reason a person affiliated with one household rather than another at the time of their census), the Beagleholes indicate 82.5 percent (of the 348 people examined) lived patrilocally. The atoll's patrilocal emphasis fits nicely with the anthropological emphasis on Polynesian patrilineality common in the 1930s.

My research suggested a somewhat different pattern, however. Patrilineality is less dominant on the atoll than the Beagleholes conveyed. First, a problem exists in fitting the somewhat fluid, ambiguous data from both our research into

51   See Bates (2003); Bohannan (1992); Ember and Ember (2002, 2007); Ember, Ember, and Peregrine (2007); Ferraro (2004); M. Harris (1993); Harris and Johnson (2007); Haviland (1996); Heider (2007); Hicks and Gwynne (1994); F. Keesing (1958); R. Keesing (1981); Kottak (1997, 2005); Lassiter (2002); B. Miller (2005); Nanda and Warms (2004); Omohundro (2008); Peoples and Bailey (2009); R. Robbins (2001, 2009); Rosman and Rubel (1998); Schultz and Lavenda (2001); Scupin (2008); and Spradely and McCurdy (1975).

52   Barnard (2000); Carneiro (2003); Darnell (2001); Erickson and Murphy (1998); Eriksen and Nielsen (2001); M. Harris (1968); Hatch (1973); Langness (1987); Layton (1997); Leaf (1979); McGee and Warms (2000); J. Moore (2004); and Patternson (2001).

53   Eriksen and Nielsen (2001); Barnard (2000).

neat ethnographic categories. The anthropological image implied in postmarital residence patterns—of stable groupings in which the only significant residence change occurs at marriage—oversimplifies a rather complex situation in Pukapuka. When I did my research for forty-two months from 1977–1981, individual Pukapukans resided in a variety of locations, even in a variety of villages, prior to marriage. Once married, moreover, the couple might not stay put in a single location. They might make two or three subsequent moves. The terms "patrilocal" and "matrilocal" obscure residence options that have rather different implications with respect to group formation. Moving into one's husband's father's household (viri-patrilocality) implies a different form of kin affiliation than moving into one's husband's mother's household (viri-matrilocality).

Given these ambiguities, the Beagleholes made two choices that, while facilitating the presentation of their data in statistical form, raise doubts, I suggest, regarding their conclusions. First, they generally used a person's place of birth as his premarital residence. Second, when both spouses were born in the same village—which meant postmarital residence could not be determined from their census data—they listed the couple's residence as patrilocal. When I reclassified their census data to allow this latter category to stand simply as unclear (rather than subsuming it under patrilocality), postmarital residence was 49 percent patrilocal (i.e., virilocal), 17 percent matrilocal (i.e., uxorilocal), and 33 percent unclear.

The atoll's overwhelming patrilocality, in other words, appears less definite when, based on my own research, I reanalyzed their data. The pattern of residence seems more ambiguous, more fluid, than the uniform, structured account the Beagleholes presented. It does not mean that they were ultimately wrong. But it does mean that in analyzing their data for publication, for presentation to an audience of Western scholars, they tended to fit their data into somewhat arbitrary, inaccurate categories that overstated the degree to which Pukapukan households were patrilocal. As with Tepoztlán, having two divergent accounts clearly allows us to gain a better sense of a group's social dynamics and how anthropologists present them.

The final example is more complicated. It involves what has been termed the Sahlins-Obeyesekere controversy.[54] The controversy centers on Captain James Cook's arrival and subsequent murder at Kealakekua Bay (on the "big island" of Hawaii) in 1778–1779. Marshall Sahlins, one of the discipline's leading anthro-

---

54  For additional information on this controversy, refer to Borofsky (1997).

pologists, uses Cook's seeming apotheosis as *Lono* to illuminate broad themes of cultural process in which efforts to reproduce the social order often lead to changes in it. Or as Sahlins writes in *Historical Metaphors and Mythical Realities*: "The great challenge to an historical anthropology is not merely to know how events are ordered by culture, but how, in that process, the culture is reordered?"[55] Hawaiian efforts to cope with the anomalies of Cook's visit—by incorporating him into their cultural order—led, over time, to transformations in that order.

Two sets of concerns have been raised regarding Sahlins's analysis of Cook's visit, especially by Gananath Obeyesekere, another prominent anthropologist. The first questions the tightness of Hawaiian cultural structures. The plethora of sources cited by Sahlins (in confirmation of his thesis), Obeyesekere suggests, could be interpreted in a number of ways. "The very possibility of a plausible alternative interpretation," he writes, "is at the very least a demonstration of the folly of attempting any rigid interpretation of symbolic form."[56] The second concern challenges Sahlins's interpretation of the historical data, especially that Cook was seen as a manifestation of the *akua Lono*. Obeyesekere asserted that Cook's apotheosis was based on European, not Hawaiian, myth-making: "To put it bluntly, I doubt that the natives created their European god; the Europeans created him for them. This 'European god' is a myth of conquest, imperialism, and civilization."[57]

The overall tone in the more than twenty-nine reviews of Obeyesekere's critique of Sahlins—in *The Apotheosis of Captain Cook*—support Obeyesekere's position.[58] Being unfamiliar with specific aspects of Hawaiian historical ethnography, many Pacific specialists tended to evaluate the controversy in broad terms. There are two elements of Obeyesekere's analysis that resonated with these reviewers. The first emphasizes the problematic nature of the historical material—a prominent postmodern concern. "One must probe into the hidden agendas underlying the writing of [historical] . . . texts," Obeyesekere notes. For Obeyesekere, historical accounts "have to be *deconstructed* before they can be effectively *reconstructed* as reasonable history." Second, Obeyesekere suggests that various agents of Western expansion—explorers, traders, and missionaries—misperceived Hawaiians' understandings of Cook. He

---

55   Sahlins (1981:8).
56   Obeyesekere (1992:82).
57   Obeyesekere (1992:3).
58   For a list of them, see Borofsky (1997).

asserted the apotheosis of Cook "was created in the European imagination of the eighteenth century . . . based on antecedent 'myth models' pertaining to the redoubtable explorer cum civilizer who is a god to the 'natives.'"[59] The notion that European explorers would see themselves as gods to Pacific Islanders made sense to these reviewers given the prominence of postcolonial critiques in the discipline at the time.[60]

One of the intriguing aspects of the controversy is that the differences between Obeyesekere and Sahlins—on certain issues—are not necessarily that great. It is a small step, for example, from saying Cook was perceived as a chief named Lono (Obeyesekere's position) to saying Cook was perceived as a manifestation of the *akua Lono* (Sahlins's position) if one accepts some chiefs were perceived as possessing divine qualities. Obeyesekere acknowledges this in passing: "It is possible that Hawaiians had some notion of divinity inherent in chiefs of high descent."[61] It is likely many of the *kamaʻaina*, people of the land or commoners, were puzzled as to what nature of being Cook was. But the documentary material makes clear the priests of Lono at Kealakekua Bay (e.g., Kanekoa, Kuakahela, Kaʻōʻō, Keliʻikea, and Omeah)—because they were the priests of Lono—had the authority to emphasize Cook's *akua* status at this time. They were, as Sahlins notes, Lono's "legitimate prophets."[62] (Though *akua* is often translated into English as "god," it should be stressed that Hawaiian and English conceptions of divinity differ.) For the *kamaʻaina*, to publicly challenge Cook's association with Lono would be to directly challenge the priests at the height of their power during the Makahiki, a religious holiday dedicated to Lono. Few would risk it.

Whether Obeyesekere's or Sahlins's analysis fits better with current anthropological trends is not the central issue. What we need focus on is which analysis accords better with Hawaiian and British understandings of 1778–1779 as they have come down to us through time.[63] It should be noted that serious problems exist with Obeyesekere's argument. Geertz's statement that Obeyesekere's argument follows the "beat-the-snake-with-whatever-stick-is-handy" strategy catches the sense of Obeyesekere's presentation.[64] Obeyesekere's subarguments do not necessarily hold together. Important discrepancies and contradictions

59    Obeyesekere (1992:66, 144, 3).

60    Obeyesekere (1992:123).

61    Obeyesekere (1992:198), cf. Obeyesekere (1992:91) and Sahlins (1995:128).

62    Sahlins (1985:122).

63    Cf. Sahlins (1995:127, 151–152).

64    Geertz (1995a:4).

exist. His central premise that a European myth depicted Europeans as gods to savage people faces a basic contradiction. Both Sahlins and Obeyesekere agree that nowhere else in Polynesia did the British describe Cook as being taken for a god.[65] This is so, even where indigenous populations might well have held such an opinion.[66] If Cook's apotheosis was a European myth (rather than a Hawaiian assertion), should it not have also been noted elsewhere as well? The myth also runs counter to a sense among many in England during this period—particularly among those of "middling" rank—that it was improper to place oneself at the level of a god. What is intriguing is that documentation for this point—a frequently cited passage by Cowper, a popular poet—is right in Obeyesekere.[67] One need not really reach beyond Obeyesekere's own volume, in other words, to counter his thesis.

Though these contradictions and gaps in argumentation are fairly evident, few of the twenty-nine reviews of Obeyesekere's book refer to them. The dearth of critical comment on Obeyesekere's arguments, I suspect, stems from two factors. First, Obeyesekere's style and perspective fit with existing intellectual trends in the discipline. That fact lulled many reviewers into accepting Obeyesekere's views because they fit with their own perspectives. Second, many were focused on pursing their personal research. They did not have the time to fully check the sources cited by Sahlins and Obeyesekere. While they were interested in asserting their competence in reviewing the controversy, for these reviewers the large number of citations to unpublished and/or unfamiliar historical material likely proved intimidating.

What I find particularly interesting about the controversy is that despite the wealth of British and Hawaiian data supporting Sahlins's position, various anthropologists persist in affirming Obeyesekere is correct (and Sahlins wrong). When I ask them why they side with Obeyesekere, they emphasize a "gut feeling" or make reference to their own fieldwork from another part of the Pacific. They seem unwilling to believe the journals from Cook's third voyage as well as the relevant Hawaiian data that challenge Obeyesekere's position. They fall prey to the above-noted *comparative fallacy*. Even without empirical support, they connect their own research experiences with those of the Hawaiians in 1778–1779.

65   Obeyesekere (1992:87); Sahlins (1995:178).

66   See, e.g., Salmond (1993:51).

67   Regarding Cowper, see, e.g., Beaglehole (1964:289); Obeyesekere (1992:126); cf. Sahlins (1995:200).

The groups of people anthropologists study are complex. Having more than one perspective of a group allows us to better appreciate cultural subtleties—both of the people themselves and the people describing them. Fitting with this point, I would not totally dismiss Obeyesekere's work. I believe Obeyesekere was correct in asserting that the British were engaged in their own myth-making. Cook, though of "middling background," was a highly respected figure in British society in the late 1700s—a proud example of British upward mobility. But with the French Revolution and its aftermath, there was a renewed focus on social stability in British society. Cook's status declined. In sharp contrast to Lord Nelson, my research suggests, prominent public statues were not erected to Captain Cook with civic funds until early into the twentieth century in the United Kingdom.

## Five Dominating Trends in Cultural Anthropology

Turning from these general statements, regarding the degree to which cultural anthropology is advancing knowledge, we now examine five trends that dominated the field from the 1930s through the 1990s. The first trend—Culture and Personality—was popular from the 1930s into the early 1960s. It explored the relationships between culture on the one hand and personality on the other. The second trend—Cultural Ecology—was prominent from the 1960s into the 1970s. It focused on environmental and evolutionary explanations for cultural phenomena. The third trend—Interpreting Myths, Symbols, and Rituals—was prominent from the late 1960s into the 1970s. It explored how myths, symbols, and rituals provided insights into the dynamics of both specific cultural groups and, more generally, the workings of human society. The fourth trend—a turn toward historical analysis, which I term a (Re)Turn to History because it renewed an earlier anthropological concern with history—was prominent from the 1970s into the 1990s. The fifth trend—Postmodernism—was prominent from the late 1980s through the 1990s. It emphasized the role the knower (the anthropologist) played in the construction of the known (the description of a cultural group).

These trends represent a special time in cultural anthropology. By the 1930s the discipline had coalesced professionally and was embedded in university departments. It was striving to demonstrate its value to others within and beyond the university. For the decades discussed here, many cultural anthropologists shared a set of common concerns and addressed a set of common problems. As a result, we can gain a reasonable sense of the degree to which there was intellectual advancement within the field. Today, cultural anthropology seems fragmented into subcohorts and sub-subcohorts going off in diverse directions. With less binding different cohorts together, it is less certain clear standards now exist for assessing the field's advances.

## ASSESSING CULTURE AND PERSONALITY

*Three leading figures of the Culture and Personality trend were Margaret Mead, Cora Du Bois, and Anthony Wallace. Mead demonstrated that the gender stereotypes we associate with men and women in America don't hold for all societies. Du Bois showed that particular types of child-rearing practices could lead to certain types of adult personalities and beliefs. And Wallace indicated that people within the same small cultural group do not necessarily share the same personality traits. There was not a one-to-one relationship between culture and personality. In a vague sort of way, we can perceive a progressive refining of their frames of analysis through time. But anthropologists involved with this trend did not systematically refine the analytical framework used by their predecessors, nor did they return to previously studied groups to develop a more substantive body of ethnographic knowledge on them.*

One might describe the trend of Culture and Personality as an effort by American anthropologists from the 1930s into the early 1960s to explore relationships between personality and culture. It offered a number of suggestive answers as to how culture shaped personality and how personality in turn shaped culture. Margaret Mead's *Sex and Temperament in Three Primitive Societies* explores the ways cultures patterned male and female behavior. As Mead recollected in her autobiography, *Blackberry Winter*, she went to the East Sepik region of Papua New Guinea "to study the different ways in which cultures patterned the expected behavior of males and females."[68] She reasoned that "if those temperamental attitudes which we have traditionally regarded as feminine—such as passivity, responsiveness, and a willingness to cherish children—can so easily be set up as the masculine pattern in one tribe, and in another be outlawed for the majority of the women . . . we no longer have any basis for regarding such aspects of behavior as sex linked." In the East Sepik, Mead "found three tribes all conveniently within a hundred mile area. In one [the Arapesh], both men and women act as we expect women to act—in a mild parental responsive way; in the second [the Mundugumor], both act as we expect men to act—in a fierce

---

68   Mead (1972:196).

initiating fashion; and in the third [the Tchambuli], the men act according to our stereotype for women—or, as she phrased it, "catty, wear curls, and go shopping, while the women are energetic, managerial, unadorned partners."[69] These data led Mead to conclude that overall "male and female personality are socially produced."[70] But while emphasizing the importance of cultural conditioning, Mead does not elaborate on how specific cultural mechanisms shape particular personality traits.

Cora Du Bois, in *The People of Alor*, addresses the problem of specifying the cultural mechanisms shaping personality—the problem Mead left unaddressed. On the Indonesian Island where Du Bois conducted her research, she describes how specific cultural institutions shaped personality traits and how these personality traits in turn shape other cultural institutions. Working with 180 inhabitants in a village cluster called Atimelang, roughly fifty miles from the coast on Alor, Du Bois collected considerable ethnographic material: observations of child-rearing practices, life histories of eight adults, and important psychological test data (involving thirty-seven Rorschachs, fifty-five Porteus mazes, thirty-six word association protocols, and fifty-five children's drawings). Du Bois frames her analysis in terms of the Freudian psychiatrist Abram Kardiner's assertion that certain primary institutions, such as economic organization, shape child-rearing practices resulting in certain adult personality traits, which in turn shape certain secondary institutions, such as religion and myth.[71]

Du Bois discovered that a mother's economic responsibilities—taking care of the family's horticulture gardens—meant she spent relatively little time with an infant child during the day. That child was mostly the responsibility of an older sibling who, more often than not, was inconsistent in disciplining the child. Instead of offering love and affection, the older child often emphasized ridicule and teasing. This sort of child rearing, Du Bois suggests, resulted in an emotionally shallow adult with limited self-confidence who distrusted deep relationships. The psychological test data were not analyzed by Du Bois but by another researcher to avoid biasing the results. Still, they confirm her impressions of Atimelanger personality, thereby strengthening her assessment. Emil Oberholzer, the psychiatrist who analyzed the Rorschachs, describes the Atimelangers as "suspicious and distrustful . . . not only toward everything that is unknown and new . . . but also among themselves. Not one will trust another." Fitting with

69    Mead (1935[1950]:190, 6).
70    Mead (1935[1950]:210).
71    Du Bois (1944[1961]:xxi–xxii).

this pattern (and perpetuating it), Atimelang men were involved in a precarious status-wealth system based on chicanery and deceit. In accord with Kardiner's perspective, the Atimelangers frequently framed relations with supernatural beings in terms of manipulation and exploitation.[72]

As Du Bois herself came to recognize, her impressive results were tarnished by sampling problems. Focusing on eight adult autobiographies or even thirty-seven Rorschachs in a group of 180 villagers (within a larger cluster of six hundred people) meant that it was difficult to assess the modal, or average, Atimelang personality. Complicating her research further was the fact that most of the culturally successful individuals—those in the thick of the village's business and dynamics—were too busy to be interviewed.[73]

Anthony Wallace addresses Du Bois's sampling problem in a study of the Tuscarora Indians in upstate New York. Focusing on a Tuscarora reservation of roughly six hundred people near Niagara Falls—a group perceived as being culturally homogeneous—Wallace found significant variation in personality traits (as judged by Rorschach protocols). Only 37 percent of the seventy interviewed possessed what might be termed a modal, or average, personality—their collective responses (in terms of twenty-one identifiable Rorschach categories) fell within a modal range. Another 23 percent fell within the modal range for some Rorschach categories but not others. Wallace refers to these as "submodal." And a final 40 percent fell completely outside the model range. These he called "deviant."

The results (published in *The Modal Personality of the Tuscarora Indians* in 1952) led Wallace to make a critical distinction in a later book, *Culture and Personality* (in 1961). He differentiates between two models for conceptualizing the "relation between cultural systems and personality systems." The first he terms "the replication of uniformity" in which "the society may be regarded as

---

72    Du Bois (1944[1961]:549, 596).

73    When one looked closer at the various interpretations of the interpreters, they did not all agree. Where Kardiner found much neurotic anxiety, Oberholzer found little. Du Bois, reflecting on her study "two decades later" wrote: "It seems highly probable that the range of trait distributions with any moderately complex society is greater than multimodal differences between societies" (Du Bois 1944[1961]:xx)—that there may be as much diversity within as between groups. And there remained the question of whether certain cultural institutions did indeed engender certain personalities. In her review of *The People of Alor*, Powdermaker doubted whether the absence of the mother in infancy, common among Melanesian horticultural groups, would necessarily foster being perceived as a frustrating object by the child (Powdermaker 1945:160). Barnouw added that during the dry season, with less horticultural work, the mother likely spent considerably more time with her infant (Barnouw 1963:116).

culturally homogeneous and the individuals will be expected to share a uniform nuclear character . . . [what researchers needed to study were the] . . . mechanisms of socialization by which each generation becomes, culturally and characterologically, a replica of its predecessors." In "the organization of diversity," or second model, a group's psychological diversity is stressed and researchers need to examine "how . . . various individuals organize themselves culturally" given such diverse personalities. This second model, Wallace indicates, emphasizes "when the process of socialization is examined . . . it becomes apparent that . . . it is not a perfectly reliable mechanism for [cultural] replication."[74]

Wallace, in other words, reframed how anthropologists might perceive the relationship between culture and personality, offering two models of socialization instead of one and highlighting the presence of psychological diversity within a seemingly culturally homogeneous group. It is a powerful perspective, and Wallace gained considerable respect for enunciating it. But few anthropologists built on Wallace's work. One of the key figures in the field, George Spindler, in reviewing Culture and Personality, suggests that Wallace had unnecessarily dichotomized the issue.[75]

Should we view these culture and personality studies as collectively embodying intellectual progress—either in terms of refining certain perspectives or in terms of building cumulative knowledge? It is possible to perceive—in a vague sort of way—a progressive refining of the frames of analysis in the Culture and Personality trend. Mead sets out a cultural position regarding the development of personality. She demonstrated that given the variations in gender temperaments, culture must logically play a key role in shaping gender-oriented behavior. But she does not describe specific mechanisms by which this occurred. Du Bois shows that certain Freudian-based assumptions about child rearing explain developmental processes shaping adult Atimelanger personalities. Her analysis is strengthened by the fact that a psychiatrist, relying solely on her test data, comes to the same general conclusion as she did. Her study failed, however, to deal with intracultural variation. Wallace makes intracultural variation the focus of his study. He uses the results of his Tuscarora research to conceptualize a new way for looking at the relationship between culture and personality.

74    Wallace (1961:27–28).
75    Spindler (1955a:1321–1322).

But I would be cautious about perceiving substantive intellectual progress by the terms defined in this chapter. It would be fairer to suggest that, in an effort to conduct innovative research, there was a vague refining of earlier perspectives but in different locales. They didn't directly address earlier research in its own terms except to criticize it. If Du Bois and Wallace had gone back to New Guinea where Mead did her work, and redone her study, then in a very real sense one could view their collective studies as cumulative.[76] When Du Bois and Wallace cite earlier research, it is generally in a critical way that places their own work at center stage. Wallace's *Culture and Personality* refers to Du Bois's work, but only to emphasize that the autobiographies she collected showed diverse personality types. To view their collective works as progress—as defined here—is to fall victim to the comparative fallacy.

When we discuss other trends, I offer more systematic data on how various colleagues did or did not build on the work of a trend's key figures. But since the Culture and Personality trend started before the Social Sciences Citations Index (now ISI's Web of Science)—the source used in this study—was fully functional, I can only offer an impression. "The Six Cultures Project" published by John and Beatrice Whiting in the early 1960s is perhaps the most comprehensive culture and personality research project ever undertaken.[77] Rather than returning to any of the above studied sites, the six researchers chose new locations for their research. It is interesting to note that the key books describing the project's theoretical and ethnographic underpinnings do not seriously engage with any of the above authors' writings, even though Du Bois worked in the same department (at Harvard) as the Whitings. The Whitings conclude from their work that "the question of the correspondence of . . . variables within and across cultures remains unanswered."[78] In other words, the "Six Cultures Project" leaves unanswered the very question Mead and Du Bois left unanswered in their research.

---

76    Roughly fifty years later, Gewertz and Errington (1987), based on their fieldwork among the Chambri (Mead's Tchambuli), did a reanalysis of Mead's data on the group. They emphasized an alternative perspective from Mead. They examined a question related to the one Mead asked—regarding how "the personalities of the two sexes are socially produced" (Mead 1935[1950]:209). But they did not take the same comparative approach of focusing on three neighboring groups as Mead did, nor did they focus as much on child rearing in their analysis.

77    See Whiting (1963); Whiting et al. (1966).

78    Whiting, Whiting, and Longabaugh (1975:135). Reflecting on the Six Culture's data, Minturn and Lambert (1964:293) write, in considering questions needing to be addressed in the future, "our message to anthropologists . . . [is] not to ignore the precise measurement of individuals

Wallace formulated an answer, but few (including the Whitings) seemed interested in following up on his perspective.[79]

## ASSESSING CULTURAL ECOLOGY

*Four of the leading figures of the Cultural Ecology trend were Elman Service, Marshall Sahlins, Roy Rappaport, and Marvin Harris. Service and Sahlins played a key role in initiating the trend by seeking to reinvigorate the evolutionary approach in anthropology. Service elaborated on this approach by setting out evolutionary stages of human social organization as well as their characteristics. Rappaport emphasized that ritual often possesses important ecological functions. Harris reframed the discipline's history in evolutionary terms.*

*As with the previous trend, we might perceive in a vague sort of way a degree of intellectual refinement and development. But I question whether the trend's central works embody significant intellectual advances through time, at least by the assessment standards of this chapter. First, the key figures deal with different ethnographic areas in their research. Second, with two exceptions, these figures do not seriously engage with each other's work. Third, the trend's key figures never seriously come to terms with the trend's key problem—assuming adaptive value without supporting diachronic data. They instead focused on unsubstantiated conjectures.*

The trend of Cultural Ecology was prominent from the 1960s into the 1970s. Though the field has been called by different names—cultural evolution, neo-evolution, and cultural materialism—its adherents tended to share certain perspectives. Anthropologists associated with this trend often (a) perceived themselves as building on the works of Leslie White and/or Julian Steward and (b) focused on environmental adaptation as an explanation for certain cultural institutions.

Marshall Sahlins and Elman Service's *Evolution and Culture* helped initiate the trend.[80] Their purpose, as they state in that book's introduction, "is not to describe the actual evolution of culture, but rather to argue in favor of several

---

that specifies variation of behavior among people who share a common culture"—the problem Wallace and Du Bois emphasized.

79   Readers interested in exploring this topic further might refer to Milton Singer (1961); Barnouw (1963); Le Vine (1963, 1997); Rossi (1976b); Spiro (1968); Wallace (1962); Kiefer (1977); Pelto (1967); and Spindler ed. (1978).

80   Sahlins and Service (1960).

general principles that we believe are fundamental to the theory of cultural evolution." Chapters in *Evolution and Culture* discuss "the principle of stabilization," "the law of cultural dominance," and "the law of evolutionary potential." The most-cited chapter involves Sahlins's effort to bring White's and Steward's differing approaches into a common framework. Sahlins sees White's work as involving general evolution and Steward's as concerning specific evolution. Quoting Sahlins: "General cultural evolution . . . [involves the] passage from less to greater energy transformation. . . . Specific evolution is the . . . ramifying, historic passage of culture along its many lines, the adaptive modification of particular cultures." Where specific evolution might be perceived as adaptation moving from more homogeneous structures toward more heterogeneous ones, general evolution involves a progressive movement toward "all-around adaptability." Drawing on an idea from Steward, Sahlins suggests a proposition that is later elaborated on by Service: Different societies have different levels of social integration.[81]

In *Primitive Social Organization: An Evolutionary Perspective*, Service describes three stages of cultural evolution—bands, tribes, and chiefdoms.[82] He suggests that each stage has its own distinct form of social integration. He writes that hunters and gatherers form cohesive bands as a result of "familistic bonds of kinship and marriage which by their nature can integrate only the relatively small and simple societies that we call bands." Tribal social solidity is based on "pan-tribal solidarities which can integrate several bandlike societies" into one unit. Chiefdoms, by contrast, involve "specialization, redistribution, and the related centralization of authority." Service contrasts chiefdoms with states that have "a bureaucracy employing legal force."[83]

What did their colleagues make of these ideas? The *American Anthropologist* reviews of *Evolution and Culture* and *Primitive Social Organization* focused on a continuing problem with the trend. The review of *Evolution and Culture* claimed that "the authors haven't seriously investigated any of [the] principles [discussed], nor do they give any sign of an intention to do so, nor do they express any diffidence about the usefulness of their untested concepts or the validity of their untested hypotheses."[84] The review of *Primitive Social Organization*

---

81    Sahlins in Sahlins and Service (1960:38, 16, 37, 21–22).

82    Service (1962). One might note Service helped establish the popularity of these perceived stages through his 1958 textbook (Service 1958) and Service (1962); cf. Ortner (1984:132).

83    Service (1962:181).

84    Naroll (1961:390).

states: "Chapters 3, 4, and 5 dealing with bands, tribes, and chiefdoms . . . [are mostly] devoted to defining the criteria of the specific levels [of integration]. This leaves little [room for] . . . more than a listing of . . . examples with discussion devoted primarily to problem cases. The reader, in effect, is left to accept the type societies on authority."[85] Of the five trends discussed in this chapter, Cultural Ecology is the one most tied to archaeological research and the one most cited by archaeologists. Yet the archaeological record—which, through its concern with temporal transformations, could provide empirical substantiation to Sahlins's and Service's claims—is rarely cited by them. The adaptive significance of particular cultural forms tends to be mostly postulated, not demonstrated.

Roy Rappaport's *Pigs for the Ancestors* approached cultural adaptation differently, emphasizing the regulatory role of ritual in maintaining a community's ecological viability.[86] He perceives the two hundred Tsembaga he studied in highland New Guinea as more than simply a cultural collectivity. Rappaport views them as a biotic community that seeks to stay in balance with its environment. Addressing the flaw in the two works just cited, he focuses on the specific ethnographic "processes by which systems maintain their structure." He summarizes his thesis as follows: "The regulatory function of ritual among the Tsembaga . . . helps to maintain an undegraded environment, limits fighting to frequencies that do not endanger the existence of the regional population, adjusts man-land ratios, facilitates trade, distributes local surpluses of pig . . . and assures people of high-quality protein when they most need it."[87]

Clarifying these remarks, in a subsequent commentary written sixteen years later, Rappaport adds: "The aim of the book was not to account for either the presence or the origin of the ritual cycle, and it was not asserted that the regulatory functions ascribed to the cycle could not be fulfilled by other mechanisms. The ritual cycle was taken as a given and the aim of the book was simply to elucidate its place in the operation of a particular system during a particular period in its history." He emphasizes he is more concerned with "the processes by which

---

85   Lane (1964:152). Readers might note that Service did warn readers: "This book is rife with speculation and conjecture," he wrote in the first chapter. And in concluding the book, Service (1962:10, 184) added: "What seem to be needed are more evolutionary studies designed to reveal those things that actually *are* related, for only in the course of evolutionary change are such functional connections fully revealed."

86   Rappaport (1968[1984]:224, 374, 38ff.).

87   Rappaport (1968[1984]:224).

systems maintain their structure" rather than with adaptive "change in response to environmental pressures."[88]

Criticisms of *Pigs for the Ancestors* center on the degree to which Rappaport moves beyond simply suggesting that certain rituals have ecological functions to confirming they actually do. Today the book remains a descriptive tour de force. But critics feel that Rappaport never proves the postulated cause-and-effect relationships between ritual and environment. They perceive the relationship as mostly conjectural. Rappaport himself came to realize that the explanatory power of his ecological formulation is, as he phrased it, "exaggerated."[89]

Marvin Harris, in *The Rise of Anthropological Theory*, writes a history of the discipline emphasizing ecological/evolutionary theory (which he termed "cultural materialism").[90] Harris writes: "The reader. . . [is] forewarned that, while this book is a history of anthropological theories, it is intended to prove a point" relating to cultural materialism. "The essence of cultural materialism is that it directs attention to the interaction between behavior and environment [and emphasizes] . . . that group structure and ideology are responsive to . . . material conditions." Harris continues: "The vindication of the strategy of cultural materialism . . . lies in the capacity of the approach to generate major explanatory hypotheses which can be subjected to the tests of ethnographic and archaeological research."[91] Harris published his book in 1968, a critical period in anthropology. With the discipline expanding in the late 1960s, a new recounting of its past was needed to convey a new sense of respectability. Harris's account filled this need in a way that thrilled supporters of the evolutionary approach.

But Harris never really put his explanatory principles to a test. He wrote best-selling books (such as *Cows, Pigs, Wars, and Witches* and *Cannibals and Kings*) that offered suggestive, provocative explanations for a host of cultural

---

88    Rappaport (1984[1968]:354, 241, cf. 414).

89    Rappaport accepted Friedman's criticism that "while it is valid to *describe* . . . the ritual as operating to keep the pig population below a certain level, it is incorrect to claim that it is a *homeostat* [or regulator] . . . when no relation has been shown to exist between the limit and the triggering of the cycle." He continued: "I showed no intrinsic relation between women's labor [which was asserted to be a key element in precipitating the *kaiko* ritual] and carrying capacity [the reputed triggering mechanism for the ritual to rebalance human-pig populations], and there may not be any" (Rappaport 1968[1984]:334, 406); see Friedman (1974); A. Strathern (1985); and Watson (1969).

90    One need only read Lowie's *The History of Ethnological Theory* (1937) to see how it had been marginalized by the Boasians in their tellings and retellings of the discipline's history.

91    M. Harris (1968: 659, 687; see also 4–5, and 520).

phenomena.[92] But though he espoused a concern for examining changes through time (especially in *Cannibals and Kings*), the brief anecdotal explanations he offers for this cultural behavior or that pattern do not meet this standard. One intriguing suggestion is piled on top of another, but they are not systematically tested in the ethnographic and archaeological record.

Do these studies in Cultural Ecology embody significant intellectual advances, either in terms of refining certain perspectives or in terms of building cumulative knowledge? In a vague sort of way, we might perceive a certain degree of intellectual refinement. All these books refer back to the work of Leslie White and/or Julian Steward. Sahlins offers a thoughtful way to conceptualize White's and Steward's differences. In *Primitive Social Organization*, Service presents a set of cultural stages that, in drawing on Sahlins's development of Steward's work, helps to order a diverse set of social units into the relatively ordered categories of bands, tribes, and chiefdoms. Rappaport builds on Steward's ideas while moving toward what some have called a "new ecology," focusing on biotic communities and the role that rituals (not just technoecological/economic structures) play in maintaining a group's ecological/cultural viability. Harris innovatively describes the discipline's history in evolutionary/ecological terms that draw on Steward's framework and research.

But I question the degree to which their collective work represents significant intellectual progress through time. It would be closer to the mark to suggest that, rather than cumulative progress, White's and Steward's writings offer different authors different possibilities that they then mine, in their own interesting ways. Service builds on the work of Sahlins and Service in developing the levels of integration concept; but one would be hard pressed to demonstrate that Service, Rappaport, and Harris built on each other's work. They all seemed to go off in different directions. The three authors deal with different ethnographic locales. If Rappaport had worked among one of the tribal groups discussed by Service, or if Harris, following on Rappaport's heels, had offered a detailed cultural materialistic reinterpretation of Rappaport's work among the Tsembaga that brought new data to light, then we could perceive some sense of intellectual progress. But that is not what occurred. Rappaport worked in a totally different locale from White, Steward, Sahlins, Service, and Harris. Harris, in *Cows, Pigs, Wars, and Witches*, addresses Rappaport's analysis. But he doesn't really present new data. Rather, he seeks to turn Rappaport's analysis on its head by making ecological

92  M. Harris (1974, 1977).

concerns—particularly population pressure and land-carrying capacity—the reasons for certain rituals, even though, as Harris admits, the ritual occurs well *before* "the onset of actual nutritional deficiencies or the actual beginning of irreversible damage to the environment."[93] Harris is simply offering an alternative speculation to that offered by Rappaport. He isn't building on Rappaport's work in a cumulative way.

Aside from Harris's reinterpretation of Rappaport's analysis and Service building on Sahlins's suggestion, these authors don't seriously engage with each other's work. Rappaport briefly cites Sahlins and Service in a critical footnote and adds a citation to Harris in the revised 1984 edition of *Pigs for the Ancestors*.[94] But he ignores Harris's explanation in *Cows, Pigs, Wars, and Witches* and doesn't even list the book in his 1984 bibliography. Harris briefly discusses Sahlins's analysis in *Evolution and Culture* of general and specific evolution, but he is critical of the analysis, asserting that a different approach would be better.[95] The authors all grapple with the same problem: assuming adaptive value without offering supporting diachronic data. Unfortunately, they all fall back on unsubstantiated conjectures. We are left with much to ponder but little proven. New possibilities keep piling up, but the underlying criticisms of the trend don't seem to be seriously addressed.

Another way to examine whether these authors' works collectively constitute a significant intellectual advance by the chapter's standards is to consider to what degree these figures' colleagues seriously engage with these figures' key works. To make the task manageable, I limited myself to five journals: the *American Anthropologist*, *American Ethnologist*, *Current Anthropology*, *Man*, and (because these authors are frequently cited in archaeology) *American Antiquity*. I collected citations from five, ten, and fifteen years out from these publications. My examination of the citations to these figures suggests that other anthropologists rarely build on Service's, Rappaport's, or Harris's work. Rather, they cite these figures mainly in passing, as a way of showing they are familiar with these

---

93　M. Harris (1974:66). "There is not great mystery," he asserts, regarding how this *kaiko* became part of Tsembaga life: "As in the case of other adaptive evolutionary novelties, groups that invented or adopted growth cutoff institutions survived more consistently than those that blundered forth across the limit of carrying capacity" (M. Harris 1974:66). Extensive diachronic data—that showed how the *kaiko* ritual varied with ecological conditions through time—would buttress Harris's suggestion. But he offers none.

94　Rappaport (1968[1984]:xi, 350).

95　M. Harris (1968:651–653).

figures' work. (The dates in parentheses represent the years the books are published or republished.)

If we look at to what degree (of the total articles in which these figures were cited) the authors of these articles make a sustained attempt to develop the work of one of the figures—specified as involving at least *three* sentences of discussion—we get the following percentages:

| SERVICE (1962/71) | RAPPAPORT (1968/84) | HARRIS (1968) |
|:---:|:---:|:---:|
| 4% | 5% | 0% |

The specific citations for Service (1962/71), Rappaport (1968/84), and Harris (1968) are listed in the footnote.[96]

---

96   SERVICE (1962/71): (a) Number of citations examined in five leading journals five, ten, and fifteen years following dates of publication: 24. (b) A sustained attempt to DEVELOP one of the three authors' work in a specific way (through reinterpreting, building on, or criticizing their respective work). Involves at least *three* sentences of discussion of the specified author's work [4 percent]: Snow (1969). (c) A sustained attempt to DISCUSS one of the three authors' work—in a review of the literature—before presenting the anthropologist's own perspective. Involves at least *three* sentences of discussion of the specified author's work [8 percent]: Gibbon (1972), Hines (1977). (d) Relevant author's work CITED ONLY IN PASSING as a way of demonstrating the anthropologist's own competence and credibility—by indicating her or his familiarity with the relevant literature. Often embedded in a list of citations, but may be referred to separately in one or, on a rare occasion, two sentences in passing as the anthropologist is developing a certain point [88 percent]: Bettinger (1977), Chilungu (1976), Y. Cohen (1969), Earle and Preucel (1987), Gilman (1981), Hage (1977), Haviland (1977), Janes (1977), Kirch and Green (1987), Knauft (1987), Lancaster (1976), Martin (1969), Mosko (1987), O'Brien (1987), Peebles and Kus (1977), Price (1977), P. Rice (1981), Sidrys (1976), Steponaitis (1981), J. Thomas (1987), and Whalen (1981)

RAPPAPORT (1968/84): (a) Number of citations examined in five leading journals five, ten, and fifteen years following dates of publication: 21. (b) A sustained attempt to DEVELOP one of the three authors' work in a specific way (through reinterpreting, building on, or criticizing their respective work). Involves at least *three* sentences of discussion of the specified author's work [5 percent]: Hallpike (1973). (c) A sustained attempt to DISCUSS one of the three authors' work—in a review of the literature—before presenting the anthropologist's own perspective. Involves at least *three* sentences of discussion of the specified author's work [5 percent]: Kim (1994). (d) Relevant author's work CITED ONLY IN PASSING as a way of demonstrating the anthropologist's own competence and credibility—by indicating her or his familiarity with the relevant literature. Often embedded in a list of citations, but may be referred to separately in one or, on a rare occasion, two sentences in passing as the anthropologist is developing a certain point [90 percent]: Abruzzi (1982), Boeck (1994), Boehm (1978), Brosius (1999a), Diener and Robkin (1978), Ellen (1978), Feil (1978), Hawkes (1977), Ingold (1983b), Irons (1977), C. Jenkins (1983), H. Leach (1999), Lightfoot and Feinman (1982), LiPuma (1983), O'Hanlon (1992), Price (1982), Read and LeBlanc (1978), Sorenson (1972), Steadman and Merbs (1982).

In other words, most of the citations to these figures' key works were of the "bump and go" variety, to use an American football metaphor. Authors mostly refer to them to convey they are aware of the relevant literature related to the topic they are writing about. But few seek to systematically engage with the ideas in these figures' key works for more than two sentences. Volume 101 of the *American Anthropologist* (dated 1999) published several articles honoring Rappaport. Examining these articles offers an opportunity for exploring to what degree anthropologists build on a prominent figure's work when honoring him. In terms of the authors who dealt with Rappaport's classic *Pigs for the Ancestors*, 50 percent of them sought to develop his ideas, 33 percent discussed them in a review of the literature, and 17 percent cited his key work only in passing as these authors were developing their own ideas.[97]

One might interpret the special issue of the *American Anthropologist* as reinforcing a sense of intellectual progress. That, I think, is the dominant trend of

---

HARRIS (1968): (a) Number of citations examined in five leading journals five, ten, and fifteen years following dates of publication: 16. (b) A sustained attempt to DEVELOP one of the three authors' work in a specific way (through reinterpreting, building on, or criticizing their respective work). Involves at least *three* sentences of discussion of the specified author's work [0 percent]. (c) A sustained attempt to DISCUSS one of the three authors' work—in a review of the literature—before presenting the anthropologist's own perspective. Involves at least *three* sentences of discussion of the specified author's work [0 percent]. (d) Relevant author's work CITED ONLY IN PASSING as a way of demonstrating the anthropologist's own competence and credibility—by indicating her or his familiarity with the relevant literature. Often embedded in a list of citations, but may be referred to separately in one or, on a rare occasion, two sentences in passing as the anthropologist is developing a certain point [100 percent]: Begler (1978), Chaney (1978b), Diener and Robkin (1978), Dunnell (1978), Epstein (1973), Freed and Freed (1983), Hoffman (1973), Hsu (1973), Ingold (1983a), Jarvie (1983), Mundkur (1978), Nash and Wintrob (1972), Ruyle (1973), Stahl (1993), Thornton (1983), and Wobst (1978).

97    *RAPPAPORT FESTSCHRIFT*: (a) A sustained attempt to DEVELOP one of the three authors' work in a specific way (through reinterpreting, building on, or criticizing their respective work). Involves at least *three* sentences of discussion of the specified author's work: Gezon (1999); Kottak (1999); E. Wolf (1999). (b) A sustained attempt to DISCUSS one of the three authors' work—in a review of the literature—before presenting the anthropologist's own perspective. Involves at least *three* sentences of discussion of the specified author's work: Biersack (1999a); Ernst (1999). (c) Relevant author's work CITED ONLY IN PASSING as a way of demonstrating the anthropologist's own competence and credibility—by indicating her or his familiarity with the relevant literature: Biersack (1999b). (d) I left out from the categorization percentages Watanabe and Smuts (1999) because while I viewed it as belonging with the "sustained attempt to DEVELOP" category, it did not focus on *Pigs for the Ancestor*. I also left out Brosius (1999b) in fairness because it was dealing, again, with a different focus than *Pigs for the Ancestor*. It seemed reasonable not to obscure the categorization percentages by casually including articles that did not precisely fit the categorization criteria.

the articles. However, works dedicated to honoring a specific figure (they are termed Festschrifts) are rarely published today. Even in the case discussed here, only 50 percent of the authors embraced Rappaport's major work in developing their own. Not one of the anthropologists honoring Rappaport went back to his Tsembaga field site and sought to confirm or rebut his analysis.[98]

## ASSESSING INTERPRETATIONS OF MYTHS, SYMBOLISM, AND RITUAL

*This third trend was prominent from the late 1960s into the 1970s. Claude Lévi-Strauss, Victor Turner, and Clifford Geertz were its dominant figures. Lévi-Strauss suggests that myths often express underlying social contradictions in groups. These myths do not resolve such contradictions, but highlighting them, they help people to deal with them more effectively. Turner examines the structured rituals of the social order as well as "anti-structural rituals" that emphasize alternative forms of human relations, community, and bonding. Geertz explores how symbols reflect and reinforce certain cultural preoccupations within a group.*

*While these three figures suggest interesting possibilities, one might again hesitate to view their collective efforts as representing intellectual progress as specified in this chapter. First, despite the fact that Lévi-Strauss, Turner, and Geertz discuss a wide range of ethnographic materials, there is little overlap in their analyses. Second, while these authors take note of each other's writings, they seem mostly focused, in their discussions, on affirming their own positions. And third, the incisive insights proffered by these writers don't resolve the trend's underlying problem: How to evaluate one interpretative analysis against another; how to assess their validity?*

The third trend—focused on myths, symbols, and rituals—was prominent in cultural anthropology from the 1960s into the 1970s. While Claude Lévi-Strauss, Victor Turner, and Clifford Geertz take different approaches, they share a con-

---

98    Readers interested in exploring this topic further might refer to Bennet (1998); Burger (1974); Carneiro (1968, 1979); Clifton (1976); Darnell (1977); Durham (1990, 1992); Earle (1987); Haddon (1934); M. Harris et al. (1968); H. R. Hays (1964); Heider (1972); R. Keesing (1974); Kemper and Phinney (1977); Lange (1965); Mead and Bunzel (1960); Murphy (1967, 1979); Orlove (1980); Rappaport (1999); Rossi (1976a); Sahlins (1964); Salome (1976); Sanderson (1977, 1997); Service (1968); Spindler and Spindler (1959); Sponsel (1977); Steward (1968); Voget (1963); Westen (1984); L. White (1959, 1968); and Zubrow (1972).

cern for demonstrating how the analysis of symbols, myths, and rituals provides important insights into the dynamics of specific cultural groups and, more broadly, the workings of human society. Lévi-Strauss was a widely recognized French scholar. No other anthropologist—*ever*—has represented his government abroad as a cultural attaché, been the subject of a Susan Sontag essay and a Robert Lowell poem, or been cited in an Agatha Christie mystery. Lévi-Strauss's hundredth birthday was a national occasion for celebration, with the president of France making a personal home visit.[99] In inventing structuralism, Lévi-Strauss created "the only genuinely original social science paradigm . . . in the twentieth century," one prominent American anthropologist suggested.[100]

The corpus of Lévi-Strauss's work is wide-ranging, subtle, and complex. In respect to myths, the topic dealt with here, he argues that "the true constituent units of a myth are not isolated relations but bundles of . . . relations . . . [that] produce a meaning."[101] Lévi-Strauss views myth in terms of a musical composition in which, as in music, different variants of the myth represent variations on an underlying theme—frequently addressing a particular social contradiction. He suggests that myths do not usually resolve the contradiction. Rather, the myth and its variants tend to soften a contradiction's polarizing tensions in a way that allows people to better cope with them.[102]

In the "Overture" to his 1969 work *The Raw and the Cooked*, Lévi-Strauss addresses a question frequently raised by his critics: Whose understanding of a myth is being represented in his analyses—his own or that of the people he is studying? He offers an intriguing answer: "If the final aim of anthropology is to contribute to a better knowledge of objectified [human] thought . . . it is in the last resort immaterial whether in this book the thought processes of the South American Indians take shape through the medium of my thought, or whether mine take place through the medium of theirs. What matters is that the human mind, regardless of the identity of those who happen to be giving it expression, should display an increasingly intelligible structure as a result of the doubly reflexive forward movement of two thought processes acting one upon the other."[103]

99   While Lévi-Strauss was of course gracious on this occasion, I note that he personally did not particularly enjoy celebrating his birthday.

100   Ortner (1984:135).

101   Lévi-Strauss (1963:211).

102   Lévi-Strauss (1969:26, 10); Lévi-Strauss (1967:27–28).

103   Lévi-Strauss (1969:13).

In his 1969 book *The Ritual Process*, Turner focuses on rituals as a way of understanding broader social dynamics. He suggests that the structured, hierarchical order of everyday life is counterbalanced by a more communally oriented sharing (or anti-structure) that temporarily unites people without the differentiations or hierarchy of the normal social order. In the early 1900s the Belgian anthropologist Arnold Van Gennep postulated three stages to rituals of passage (or *rites de passage*). These are separation (i.e., exclusion from the society), margin (i.e., liminality), and aggregation (i.e., reintegration into the society). Turner builds on Van Gennep's work focusing on the middle or liminal state, which he feels embodies an anti-structural quality—a way of relating distinct from the demarcations and separations of normal social structures. "The liminal group," Turner writes, "is a community . . . of comrades and not a structure of hierarchically arrayed positions. This comradeship transcends distinctions of rank, age, [and] kinship position."[104]

Turner perceives "two alternative 'models' for human interrelatedness, juxtaposed to one another. The first involves society as a structured, differentiated, and often hierarchical system of politico-legal-economic positions. . . . The second, which emerges recognizably in the liminal period, is of society as an unstructured or rudimentarily structured and relatively undifferentiated *communitas*, community, or even communion of equal individuals." He suggests that for both religious and secular groups, "a fairly regular connection is maintained between liminality, structural inferiority, lowermost status, and structural outsiderhood . . . [involving] . . . such universal human values as peace and harmony . . . fertility, health of mind and body, universal justice . . . and brotherhood."[105]

In concluding *The Ritual Process*, Turner suggests that society "seems to be a . . . dialectical process with successive phases of structure and communitas. There would seem to be—if one can use such a controversial term—a human 'need' to participate in both modalities." It is a powerful vision that gave new impetus to the study of rituals especially when Turner extended his approach, as he did in later work, to include historical events in Western societies. (He analyzes Saint Francis of Assisi, Thomas Becket, and the Hell's Angels.)[106] But Turner falls prey to the same criticisms as Lévi-Strauss does regarding why we

---

104   Turner (1967:100). In a quirk of history, Turner first discovered Van Gennep's work in the Hastings (England) Public Library while waiting for an American visa to take up a position at Cornell (Deflem 1991:7).

105   Turner (1969:96, 134).

106   Turner (1969:203); Turner (1974).

should trust his interpretations. Turner cannot demonstrate that his analyses are anything more than symbolic guessing.

Believing that humans are caught up in webs of meaning that they themselves shape (as well as are shaped by), Geertz seeks to interpret the webs of meaning that bind people together in groups. Geertz, who conducted fieldwork in sites ranging from Bali to Morocco, has been described as "one of the foremost figures in the reconfiguration of the boundary between the social sciences and the humanities in the second half of the twentieth century."[107] I focus on his most famous volume, *The Interpretation of Cultures*, specifically on its two most famous chapters, "Thick Description" and "Deep Play" (which covers Balinese cock fighting). "When scholars from the humanities . . . cite an anthropologist," one anthropologist notes, "it is more often than not Geertz . . . and usually it is Geertz on thick description or Geertz on the cockfight."[108] (Intriguingly, it appears the *American Anthropologist* never reviewed Geertz's *The Interpretation of Cultures*.)

Believing "that man is an animal suspended in webs of significance he himself has spun," Geertz writes in a famous passage, "I take culture to be those webs and the analysis of it to be . . . not an experimental science in search of law but an interpretive one in search of meaning." In discussing "thick" description, Geertz continues, "it is not against a body of uninterpreted data, radically thinned descriptions, that we must measure the cogency of our explications, but against the power of the scientific imagination to bring us into touch with the lives of strangers."[109] Geertz interprets the Balinese cockfight as a dramatization of status concerns and fears enacted on a public stage. He writes: "Attending cockfights and participating in them is, for the Balinese, a kind of sentimental education. What he [a Balinese] learns there is what his culture's ethos and his [private] sensibility . . . look like when spelled out externally in a collective text." Building on this point, Geertz writes, "the culture of a people is an ensemble of texts . . . which the anthropologist strains to read over the shoulders of those to whom they properly belong."[110]

He suggests that "cultural analysis is (or should be) guessing at meanings."[111] But there remains the question of how we should judge Geertz's guesses. In

107  Ortner, ed. (1999:1); see also Lindholm (1997:214).
108  Spencer (1996:538).
109  Geertz (1973:5, 16).
110  Geertz (1973:449, 452).
111  Geertz (1973:20).

respect to his Balinese material, other anthropologists have challenged Geertz's interpretation on a number of points. One writes: "When Geertz discusses the aims and nature of interpretive theory, he seems more interested in possibility than in tangibility."[112] Readers are left—as with Lévi-Strauss and Turner—wondering why one particular interpretation is more valid than another. Should we view these myth, symbolism, and ritual studies as embodying significant intellectual progress—either in terms of refining certain perspectives or in terms of building cumulative knowledge?

We can, speaking positively, perceive in some vague general sense progress in the work of the cited figures. Turner gives analytical grounding to Lévi-Strauss's abstract analyses of myth, describing symbolism in action. Geertz broadens the symbolic discourse, viewing the everyday worlds anthropologists encounter, in all their diversity, as ripe for interpretive analysis as texts—a framework that appeals to academics in the humanities. However, despite the fact that Lévi-Strauss, Turner, and Geertz discuss a wide range of ethnographic materials— from the Amazon to Bali to California's Hell's Angels—there is little overlap in their analyses. It would be one thing if all three worked in one locale with one set of rituals or myths. Then we could see up close how their approaches overlap. Working with these data, readers could weigh one interpretation against another.

Moreover, while these three authors take note of each other's writings (more so than the cultural ecologists did), they do not overtly build on one another's work. In discussing each other's work, they mostly seem bent on affirming their own perspectives. In a critique of Lévi-Strauss, Geertz writes: "That Lévi-Strauss should have been able to transmute the romantic passion of *Tristes Tropiques* into the hypermodern intellectualism of *La Pensée Sauvage* is surely a startling achievement. But there remain questions one cannot help but ask. Is this transmutation science or alchemy?"[113] Geertz remarks that Turner "can expose some of the profoundest features of social process, but at the expense of making vividly disparate matters look drably homogeneous."[114] Lévi-Strauss criticizes Turner, noting that "ritual is not a reaction to life; it is a reaction to what thought has made of life. It is not a direct response to the world . . . it is a response to the way

---

112    Shankman (1984:264); see also Ortner, ed. (1999:1); Shankman (1984:265).
113    Geertz (1973:359).
114    Geertz (1983:28).

man thinks of the world."[115] From the literature I have examined, Lévi-Strauss appears not to have engaged with Geertz.

Turner is the most positive of the three. He affirms his agreement with Geertz on certain points and acknowledges Lévi-Strauss's criticism of his work. But nowhere in the citations and comments I have examined is there a direct exchange, at the ethnographic level, regarding how one author's writings relate to another's or how one author's work might build on another's.[116]

And finally, the incisive insights offered by these writers do not resolve the trend's underlying problem: How do readers evaluate one interpretative analysis against another? When we set aside the intellectual glitter each presents, it remains uncertain to what degree we find ethnographic validation that extends beyond an author's own assertions. If the three had collectively examined the same myth, ritual, or symbol, we might be able to effectively address that problem. If we apply the strategy used with the cultural ecologists—seeing how other anthropologists refer to these figures' work—we come to a roughly similar conclusion. I examined citations five, ten, and fifteen years out from Lévi-Strauss's, Turner's, and Geertz's key works in some of the discipline's leading journals: the *American Anthropologist, American Ethnologist, Current Anthropology,* and *Man.* Rather than refer to an archaeologically based journal, it seemed appropriate, given the trend's orientation, to use one focused on psychological anthropology. Hence, the fifth journal examined was *Ethos,* the journal of the Society for Psychological Anthropology.

My survey of citations suggests that other anthropologists tend not to directly build on Lévi-Strauss's, Turner's, and Geertz's work. Rather, these anthropologists cite them mainly in passing—as a way of showing they are familiar with their work. The notable exception is Lévi-Strauss. Perhaps having offered one of the most original perspectives in cultural anthropology—certainly for the trends discussed here—he has stirred up more discussion and debate among his colleagues. If we look at to what degree (of the total articles in which the trend's three leading figures are cited) the authors of the articles make a sustained attempt to develop one of the figure's ideas—involving at least *three* sentences of discussion of the specified author's work—we get the following percentages:

| LÉVI-STRAUSS (1969) | TURNER (1969) | GEERTZ (1973) |
|:---:|:---:|:---:|
| 18% | 6% | 5% |

---

115 Lévi-Strauss (1981:681).
116 Turner (1975:147–148).

The specific citations for Lévi-Strauss,[117] Turner,[118] and Geertz[119] are listed in the footnotes.

117   LÉVI-STRAUSS (1969): (a) Number of citations examined in five leading journals five, ten, and fifteen years following dates of publication: 17. (b) A sustained attempt to DEVELOP one of the three authors' work in a specific way (through reinterpreting, building on, or criticizing their respective work). Involves at least *three* sentences of discussion of the specified author's work [18 percent]: Gould (1978); Hage (1979); Spiro (1979). (c) A sustained attempt to DISCUSS one of the three authors' work—in a review of the literature—before presenting the anthropologist's own perspective. Involves at least *three* sentences of discussion of the specified author's work [13 percent]: Guindi and Read (1979); Utley (1974). (d) Relevant author's work CITED ONLY IN PASSING as a way of demonstrating the anthropologist's own competence and credibility—by indicating her or his familiarity with the relevant literature. Often embedded in a list of citations but may be referred to separately in one or, on a rare occasion, two sentences in passing as the anthropologist is developing a certain point [69]: R. Bolton (1984); M. Brown (1984); Carroll (1978, 1979); Fernandez (1974); Hartzler (1974); J. Hill (1984); Hooper (1983); D. Kaplan (1974); Luhrman (1984); Peacock (1984); and Wierzbicka (1984).

118   TURNER (1969): (a) Number of citations examined in five leading journals five, ten, and fifteen years following dates of publication: 18. (b) A sustained attempt to DEVELOP one of the three authors' work in a specific way (through reinterpreting, building on, or criticizing their respective work). Involves at least *three* sentences of discussion of the specified author's work [6 percent]: Holloman (1974). (c) A sustained attempt to DISCUSS one of the three authors' work—in a review of the literature—before presenting the anthropologist's own perspective. Involves at least *three* sentences of discussion of the specified author's work [6 percent]: Hazan (1984). (d) Relevant author's work CITED ONLY IN PASSING as a way of demonstrating the anthropologist's own competence and credibility—by indicating her or his familiarity with the relevant literature. Often embedded in a list of citations but may be referred to separately in one or, on a rare occasion, two sentences in passing as the anthropologist is developing a certain point [89 percent]: Aguilar (1984); Bledsoe (1984); Da Matta (1979); Firestone (1978); Fluehr-Lobban (1979); Guyer (1984); Hanna (1979); Karp (1974); Knauft (1979); Kolenda (1984); Lebra (1978); Marcus (1978); Peacock (1984); Stirrat (1984); Wengle (1984); and Westen (1984).

119   GEERTZ (1973): (a) Number of citations examined in five leading journals five, ten, and fifteen years following dates of publication: 38. (b) A sustained attempt to DEVELOP one of the three authors' work in a specific way (through reinterpreting, building on, or criticizing their respective work). Involves at least *three* sentences of discussion of the specified author's work [5 percent]: Asad (1983); W. Keller (1983). (c) A sustained attempt to DISCUSS one of the three authors' work—in a review of the literature—before presenting the anthropologist's own perspective. Involves at least *three* sentences of discussion of the specified author's work [5 percent]: Chaney (1978b); Kennedy (1978). (d) Relevant author's work CITED ONLY IN PASSING as a way of demonstrating the anthropologist's own competence and credibility—by indicating her or his familiarity with the relevant literature. Often embedded in a list of citations but may be referred to separately in one or, on a rare occasion, two sentences in passing as the anthropologist is developing a certain point [89]: Abeles (1988); Adams (1978); Atkinson (1983); Boddy (1988); Boehm (1978); Chaney (1978a); Drummond (1977); Evens (1983); Galaty (1983); Godelier (1978); Hefner (1983a, 1983b); Hendricks (1988); Hollan (1988); Knapp (1988); Lambek (1988); Low (1988); W. Mitchell (1988); Myers (1988); S. Parker (1988); Potter (1988); Rice (1983); Ridington (1988); Rodin, Michaelson, and Britan (1978);

In other words, except in the case of Lévi-Strauss, the authors citing the above figures in the sample do so mostly in passing, usually in a list with other citations. Within the sample examined, there is limited substantive intellectual engagement with these figures' ideas as they discuss them in their books.[120]

## ASSESSING THE (RE)TURN TO HISTORY

*The (Re)Turn to History trend, popular from the late 1970s into the 1990s, built on the historical work of earlier anthropologists. Key figures were the French philosopher/historian Michel Foucault and two Americans, Eric Wolf and Marshall Sahlins. Foucault explores how a "political economy of the body"—that is, how the body is regulated (such as in prisons)—relates to the political economy of French society during the rise of capitalism. Wolf shows how many of the societies perceived as uninvolved in Western systems of exchange after 1492 were, in fact, intimately connected to them and in many cases transformed by them. Sahlins demonstrates, using the example of the 1779 murder of Captain Cook in Hawaii, how one might understand the history of contact—especially what the "other (or non-Western) side" thought during contact—through an understanding of the rituals and behaviors involved in their interactions.*

*Reviewing these three writers and their work, it is easy to be impressed. But, once again, their collective efforts mostly represent limited intellectual progress—by the terms specified earlier in this chapter. First, despite the fact that Foucault, Wolf, and Sahlins discuss a wide range of historical material, there is little overlap in their analyses. Second, while they take note of each other's writings, they seem to mostly focus on affirming their own positions. And third, while the data the authors refer to are often massive, others perceive their efforts as a little "quick of foot"—skimming over important details that might disrupt the neat perspectives enunciated. We are left with an uncertainty as to whether we should trust their analyses. Where does truth leave off and imagination begin in their writings? There is, however, a surprise—an exception*

Rosaldo (1983); Sangren (1988); Schieffelin (1983); Schwartzman (1977); B. Shore (1983); Milton Singer (1977); Tennekoon (1988); Thayer (1983); Whiteley (1987); and Wierzbicka (1988).

120   Readers interested in exploring this topic further might refer to Alexander (1991); Anonymous (n.d.); Biersack (1989); Boyer (1996); Crapanzano (1995); Crick (1982); Foster (1985); Geertz (1968); Josselin de Jong (1996); R. Keesing (1974, 1985, 1987); E. Leach (1965, 1970, 1989); Maranda (1979); Oliver (1959); Peacock (1968); Pouillon (1996); Robinson (1983); Scheper-Hughes (1995); Shweder (1985, 1988); Turner (1968); and Yalman (1964).

*to the pattern. In the controversy between Sahlins and Obeyesekere, there is a clear refining of how one might examine the history and politics of "first contact" in Hawaii and a clear building up of cumulative knowledge.*

The (Re)Turn to History trend was popular in cultural anthropology from the 1970s into the 1990s. The French philosopher/historian Michel Foucault is well cited in the United States for his historical analyses. Among American anthropologists, Eric Wolf and Marshall Sahlins are the trend's most prominent proponents. Before discussing them, however, it is important to recognize that this trend's turn toward history is far from new. A concern for the temporal dimension in anthropology is almost as old as the discipline itself. Few readers will recognize all the individuals or studies referred to here. But just seeing the names and dates should convey that the historical analyses of this trend are following in the footsteps of earlier works—works, I note, these later authors rarely cite.

Among the early works are Clark Wissler's *The American Indian* (1917), Alfred Kroeber's *Cultural and Natural Areas of North America* (1939), and Kroeber and Harold Driver's *Quantitative Expression of Cultural Relationships* (1932) as well as the Kulturkreis analyses of Fritz Graebner's *Methode der Ethnologie* (1911). There were also important acculturation studies such as James Mooney's *The Ghost-Dance Religion and the Sioux Outbreak of 1890* (1896), Ralph Linton's *Acculturation in Seven American Indian Tribes* (1940), and Godfrey Wilson and Monica Wilson's *The Analysis of Social Change, Based on Observations in Central Africa* (1945). We should also acknowledge the work of ethnohistorians, such as William Fenton on the Iroquois and Jan Vansina on Central Africa.[121] We might also highlight two works that few cite today. But in their time, they impressed the field: Wissler's 1914 article "The Influence of the Horse in the Development of Plains Culture" and Richardson and Kroeber's 1940 book *Three Centuries of Women's Dress Fashions*. As far back as 1908, Bernheim emphasized a theme that Wolf makes famous in his 1983 book (discussed below). Bernheim asserts: "There are no peoples without history."[122]

Turning first to Foucault, he uses history to discover how submerged structures of power shape important Western (especially French) institutions—from the treatment of the insane to the development of the medical profession to patterns of imprisonment. While Foucault isn't technically an anthropologist,

---

121    Fenton (1941, 1957, 1987, 1998); Vansina (1961, 1966, 1968).
122    Bernheim is in W. Thomas, ed. (1956:169), quoted by Koppers.

he has an air "of the anthropologist about him," as a reviewer noted in the *New York Times*.[123] His 1977 book *Discipline and Punish* is the most cited by anthropologists. It concerns a transformation in the way criminals were punished in France. "At the beginning of the nineteenth century," Foucault writes, "the great spectacle of physical punishment disappeared." Torture stopped. It was replaced "by a punishment that acts in the depth on the heart, the thoughts, the will, the inclinations"—the "soul rather than the body." Foucault is referring to the individual learning to control his own behavior in prison rather than having it controlled by physical punishment.[124] He frames what he perceived as changes in the "political economy of the body"—how the body is controlled and regulated by others—in terms of changes in the political economy of society. "Is it surprising," he asks in respect to the rise of capitalist orientations in industry, "that prisons resemble factories, schools, barracks, [and] hospitals" in respect to the rise of new disciplined regimes such as organizing behavior according to regimented time schedules?[125]

Reviewers repeatedly highlight two problems regarding *Discipline and Punish*. First, Foucault tends to work by analogy, showing how similar processes operate in different areas of French society rather than demonstrating historical or causal connections between the two. One reviewer notes: "He constructs his argument not by mapping precise lines of influence from one institution to another but by defining broad similarities of approach."[126] Second, Foucault asserts, "where there is power there is resistance." While readers can find suggestions of resistance—in public disruptions of royal hangings, for example—the resistance he describes tends to be at a vague, abstract level. We don't see real people taking real actions. A reviewer observed: "Foucault's is a history without significant actors, a history filled with disembodied . . . forces."[127]

In Eric Wolf's 1982 book *Europe and the People Without History*, Wolf demonstrates that non-Western groups do not lack history in our sense of the term. In

123  Rothman (1978:1).

124  Foucault (1979:14, 16).

125  Foucault (1979:77, 87, 228); see also Foucault (1979:138, 22, 265, 304, 224).

126  Rothman (1978:26); see also Goldstein (1979:117).

127  Goldstein (1979:117); see also Shelley (1979). Perhaps it is for this reason that his English translation (but not the original French version) ends with the assertion: his book "serve[s] as a historical background to . . . studies of . . . power . . . and the formation of knowledge in modern society" (Foucault 1979:308).

fact, for the past five hundred years their history has been part of our history—they have been entwined with Western systems of trade and exchange.[128] Take, for example, the early American fur trade. Wolf writes: "Wherever it went, the fur trade brought with it contagious illness and increased warfare. Many native groups were destroyed, and disappeared entirely; others were decimated, broken up, or driven from their original habitats. Remnant populations sought refuge with allies or grouped together with other populations, often under new names and ethnic identities." In respect to the African slave trade, Wolf observes: "The Tallensi [a group described in two famous ethnographies by Fortes] . . . were formed from a fusion of original inhabitants of the country with immigrants headed by slave-taking chiefs." His point is that the groups anthropologists study are frequently the "outcome of a unitary historical [economic] process" or, phrased another way, "the global processes set in motion by European expansion constitute *their* history" as well as *our* history. We have shaped their history and vice versa.[129]

Beyond doubt, *Europe and the People Without History* is a powerful work, with its reconceptualization of West-Rest relations combined with a broad range of ethnographic examples.[130] (Though viewed as a critically important book

---

128   As Worsley noted in his review of *Europe and the People Without History*: "After . . . [Wolf's] book, anthropology will never be quite the same" (Worsley 1984:170). Asad provides a fair summary of Wolf's project: "to demonstrate that societies typically studied by anthropologists have been continuously changed over the past five centuries by global political-economic forces . . . two explicit assumptions are made . . . first, that no society is completely self-contained or unchanging, and, second, that a proper understanding of societal linkages and transformations must start from an analysis of the material processes in which all social groups are involved—the production, circulation, and consumption of wealth" (Asad 1987:594; cf. E. Wolf 1982:390).

129   E. Wolf (1982:230, 230, 385), emphasis in the original.

130   In contrast to such world systems theorists as Andre Gunder Frank (1970, 1998) and Immanuel Wallerstein (1974, 1980, 1989), Wolf is interested not only in how forms of production in the European periphery effected the development of European capitalism at the European center but in the variable reactions that took shape across the breadth of the periphery from center-periphery interactions: how, in his words, "a general dynamic, capitalism . . . gave rise to a variability of its own" (E. Wolf 1982:266). To give his wide-ranging chronological and ethnographic analysis intellectual coherence, Wolf focuses on the interactions, through time, of three "modes of production" that allow him to "deal with the spread of the capitalistic mode and its impact on world areas where social labor was allocated differently" (E. Wolf 1982:76). The capitalist mode, he perceives, controls the "means of production, buys labor power, and puts it to work continuously expanding surpluses by intensifying productivity through an ever-rising curve of technological inputs" (E. Wolf 1982:78). The tributary mode entails a primary producer, such as a cultivator or herdsmen, who "is allowed access to the means of production, while tribute is exacted from him by political or military means"

within the discipline, like Geertz's *Interpretation of Cultures*, it also appears to have never been reviewed by the *American Anthropologist*.)

The book's problem is that, in a manner not dissimilar to Foucault, Wolf tends to discuss the abstract dynamics of capitalism rather than how real people in specific locations had their lives shaped and reshaped by capitalistic forces. A reviewer of *Europe and the People Without History* phrases it this way: "The work . . . ends with the movement of commodities and with the movement of people as just another commodity. There is little about the self-movements of people."[131] Like Foucault, Wolf has bowled readers over with the power of his vision. Many stand in awe of what he has produced. Still, it is one thing to suggest that Tallensi are a cultural construction of the slave trade. It is another to substantiate this assertion.[132]

Through two key books—*Historical Metaphors and Mythical Realities* (1981) and *Islands of History* (1985)—Marshall Sahlins demonstrates how bringing cultural structures together with historical events allows us to better understand these events, especially in terms of indigenous responses to Western contact. Sahlins focuses on Captain James Cook's 1778–1779 visit to Hawaii. As previously noted, in the interactions of Europeans with Hawaiians, Sahlins suggests "a possible theory of history?" He writes: "The great challenge of a historical anthropology is not merely to know how events are ordered by culture, but how, in that process the culture is reordered. How does the reproduction of a structure become its transformation?"[133]

But there is a problem, a problem that exists with most records of contact: How can we know "the other's" understandings beyond the historical records of Europeans or those written by indigenous descendants years later? Sahlins's solution is to focus on Hawaiian myths and rituals, as they were recorded by later Hawaiians and Europeans, in an attempt to grasp the cultural understandings of Hawaiians during Cook's 1778–1779 visit. Cook was drawn into the Makahiki, a Hawaiian ritual celebrating the New Year, during his visit to Kealakekua Bay. He is perceived, according to both British and Hawaiian accounts, as a manifestation of the Hawaiian *atua* Lono. Sahlins suggests that Cook's murder, at Kealakekua Bay on February 14, 1779, "was not premeditated . . . but neither was

---

(E. Wolf 1982:80). And a kinship mode involves "shareholders in social labor . . . through marriage and filiation" or, claims to resources through a "kinship license" (E. Wolf 1982:92, 91).

131   Worsley (1984:173); see also Asad (1987:607).

132   See E. Wolf (1982:230 vs. 412–413).

133   Sahlins (1985:138, 1981:7–8).

it an accident, structurally speaking. It was the Makahiki in a historical form" in which Lono was praised with offerings and then symbolically dismissed (or killed) to return again the following year.[134]

As with Foucault and Wolf, there is an element of intimidation in the historical references Sahlins brings to bear on his analysis. The number of references he cites, especially as they focus on a limited set of events few anthropologists know about, are impressive. Still, a number of anthropologists are skeptical about Sahlins's interpretation of whatever data he presents. The order he portrays seems too neat, too structurally "snug." This became clear when, as noted earlier, Obeyesekere challenged Sahlins's interpretation and few came to Sahlins's defense.[135]

Should we view these (Re)turn to History studies as embodying significant intellectual progress—either in terms of refining certain perspectives or in terms of building cumulative knowledge? Reviewing these three writers and their work, it is easy to be impressed: Drawing inspiration from a range of sources, they raise important questions. And, equally important, they suggest thoughtful answers. Once again, however, I am skeptical as to the degree we can perceive significant intellectual progress in their collective efforts. There is little direct engagement

---

134 Sahlins (1981:24).

135 Reading reviews of Sahlins's *Historical Metaphors and Mythical Realities* by Marcus (1982) and of Sahlins's *Islands of History* by Friedman (1988) and Toren (1988), I am puzzled at times by their critiques. Throughout his writings, Sahlins asserts the importance of historical contingencies: He emphasizes, for example, Hawaiians were entwined with performative structures—structures that "tend to assimilate themselves to contingent circumstances . . . [and] are . . . open to negotiation." He asserts: "The cultural order reproduces itself" in Hawaii "in and as change" (Sahlins 1985:xii). Yet these reviews criticize his overly static and structural portrayals of Hawaiian ritual. They perceive, at the ethnographic level, little of the fluid, agency-led sense of ritual he affirms in the abstract. The resolution of the problem returns us to Sahlins's need to grasp Hawaiian understandings through the formalistic accounts of later writers. Hawaiians' agency to shape and reshape their rituals—on which both Sahlins and his critics concur—tends to get lost in the shuffle. One is trying to infer process while giving due credence to fairly static depictions of the contact era. Still, if one looks carefully, it remains possible to see agency. One of the unanimously agreed-upon facts—if I dare use this phrase—surrounding the events at Kealakekua Bay is that the priests of Lono (specifically Kanekoa, Kuakahela , Kaöö, Keli'ikea, and Omeah) supported the British well after Cook's murder. In doing so, they were challenging—as an expression of their own agency—the very ritual cycle that gave them power. They were continuing their alliance with Cook—that is to say, after he was ritually out of season, out of sequence. The Makahiki might have been over, but the priests of Lono continued to demonstrate respect for Cook up to and well after his death. We see people resisting the accepted ritual sequence and thereby undermining the cultural basis for their own ritual power. (It eventually cost them—see Sahlins 1995:256.)

among them. Nor do they really engage with earlier anthropologists' writing on the same topic. Wolf wrote that an "older anthropology had little to say . . . about the major forces driving the interaction of cultures since 1493."[136] A host of earlier works directly address this issue, in fact. (Wolf preferred to not refer to them.) Sahlins's perspective on Cook, without the sophisticated theory or the abundance of details, was outlined by Gavan Daws in 1968. Still such silencing doesn't detract from the power of these authors' ideas. But it does highlight an important point. These authors' ideas are less innovative than some imply.

Repeating the pattern, the three authors tend to talk past one another. It is reasonable not to expect Foucault to take note of Wolf's and Sahlins's work, given that Foucault wrote his book before the others. But Wolf doesn't cite Foucault, even though they both address the "discipline" instilled by capitalism into Western institutions during the eighteenth and nineteenth centuries. Sahlins, in *Islands of History* (which came out three years after Wolf's book), offers a brief one-sentence nod to Wolf's perspective. Sahlins is concerned with Cook's role as "Adam Smith's global agent"—as a spreader of capitalism—but he never seriously takes up Wolf's analysis of capitalism.[137] And while concerned with how Cook used "tolerance for the pursuit of domination," Sahlins never refers to Foucault (though other writings demonstrate that he is clearly familiar with his work).

One might hope that there would be some ethnographic overlap to let readers compare—and thereby assess—one perspective vis-à-vis another. But only once or twice do the authors' data overlap ethnographically. Wolf makes reference to Hawaiian political transformations brought on by the acquisition of European weaponry in a single paragraph. It is a tangential reference made only in passing. Sahlins ignores it. Wolf refers in passing to French political consolidation as well as industrialization. But he focuses his analysis on industrialization and the rise of capitalism in England and the United States.

To determine to what degree other scholars citing Foucault, Wolf, and Sahlins directly engage with their work, I examined citations five, ten, and fifteen years after the publication dates for the books referred to here in the discipline's leading journals: the *American Anthropologist*, *American Ethnologist*, *Current Anthropology*, and *Man*. For the fifth journal, I chose one of the trend's popular forums, *Comparative Studies in Society and History*. If we look at to what

---

136    One might note Mooney (1896[1965]); Barber (1941); and Hill (1944) on the ghost dance religion, or, more broadly, Service (1955) and E. Wolf (1957) himself on how Europeans shaped postconquest social organization in the Americas.

137    Sahlins (1985:131).

degree (of the total articles in which these figures are cited) the authors of these articles make a sustained attempt to develop some portion of the figure's key work—involving at least *three* sentences of discussion of the specified author's work—we get the following percentages:

FOUCAULT (1977/79)      WOLF (1982)      SAHLINS (1981/85)
0%                      0%                2%

The specific citations for Foucault,[138] Wolf,[139] and Sahlins[140] are listed in the footnotes.

138   FOUCAULT: (a) Number of citations examined in five leading journals five, ten, and fifteen years following dates of publication: 18. (b) A sustained attempt to DEVELOP one of the three authors' work in a specific way (through reinterpreting, building on, or criticizing their respective work). Involves at least *three* sentences of discussion of the specified author's work [0 percent]. (c) A sustained attempt to DISCUSS one of the three authors' work—in a review of the literature—before presenting the anthropologist's own perspective. Involves at least *three* sentences of discussion of the specified author's work [0 percent]. (d) Relevant author's work CITED ONLY IN PASSING as a way of demonstrating the anthropologist's own competence and credibility—by indicating her or his familiarity with the relevant literature. Often embedded in a list of citations but may be referred to separately in one or, on a rare occasion, two sentences in passing as the anthropologist is developing a certain point [100 percent]: Bentley (1984, 1987); Bercovitch (1994); Desjarlais (1994); Donham (1994); Edwards (1989); Farnell (1994); Harkin (1994); Jacquemet (1992); Knauft (1987); Kurtz and Nunley (1993); Mitchell (1989); Ortner (1984); Peteet (1994); Rushforth (1994); Scheper-Hughes (1987); D. Scott (1992); and Yang (1989).

139   WOLF: (a) Number of citations examined in five leading journals five, ten, and fifteen years following dates of publication: 37. (b) A sustained attempt to DEVELOP one of the three authors' work in a specific way (through reinterpreting, building on, or criticizing their respective work). Involves at least *three* sentences of discussion of the specified author's work [0 percent]. (c) A sustained attempt to DISCUSS one of the three authors' work—in a review of the literature—before presenting the anthropologist's own perspective. Involves at least *three* sentences of discussion of the specified author's work [5 percent]: Cowlishaw (1987); Kelly (1992). (d) Relevant author's work CITED ONLY IN PASSING as a way of demonstrating the anthropologist's own competence and credibility—by indicating her or his familiarity with the relevant literature. Often embedded in a list of citations but may be referred to separately in one or, on a rare occasion, two sentences in passing as the anthropologist is developing a certain point [95 percent]: Ammerman (1987); Asad et al. (1997); B. Bender (1992); Bentley (1987); Brumfiel (1992); Burton (1992); Carrier (1992); Christian (1987); Colby (1987); Comaroff and Comaroff (1987); Conklin (1997); Durrenberger and Palsson (1987); Durrenberger and Tannenbaum (1992); Earle and Preucel (1987); Edens (1992); Ernest (1997); Friedman (1992); Gold and Gujar (1997); Griffith (1987); Griffith, Pizzini, and Johnson (1992); Headland (1997); Kurtz (1987); R. Lee (1992); Medick (1987); Messick (1987); Nader (1997); Nettle (1997); Rodman (1987); Roseman (1996); Rutz (1987); Shott (1992); P. Smith (1987); Swidler (1992); Trautmann (1992); and R. White (1992).

140   SAHLINS: (a) Number of citations examined in five leading journals five, ten, and fifteen years following dates of publication: 47. (b) A sustained attempt to DEVELOP one of the three

In other words, the authors citing these figures in the sample do so mostly in passing, usually in a list with other citations. There is little substantive engagement—of more than two sentences—in the sample examined. Still, the unfolding of history is not always a neatly ordered affair. In the (Re)turn to History trend, there is an exception to the pattern. A Princeton-based Sri Lankan anthropologist, Gananath Obeyesekere, challenges Sahlins's interpretation of Cook's "apotheosis" as the *atua* Lono. Obeyesekere views Sahlins as presenting a Western rather than a Third World perspective.

Instead of being dependent on Sahlins's field notes, scholars were able to study the documentation in the British Public Records Office and the libraries of Hawaii. Scholars could make their own independent assessments of what the material did and did not affirm in respect to each author's assertions. Rather than the tendency toward limited intellectual engagement, the Sahlins-Obeyesekere controversy has led to real intellectual progress that even the most skeptical of readers can acknowledge. The difference is that both sides could examine the same material. People could engage with one another using the same ethnographic data.[141]

--------

authors' work in a specific way (through reinterpreting, building on, or criticizing their respective work). Involves at least *three* sentences of discussion of the specified author's work [2 percent]: Ohnuki-Tierney (1995). (c) A sustained attempt to DISCUSS one of the three authors' work—in a review of the literature—before presenting the anthropologist's own perspective. Involves at least *three* sentences of discussion of the specified author's work [6 percent]: Martha Kaplan (1990); Lampland (1991); Rumsey (2000). (d) Relevant author's work CITED ONLY IN PASSING as a way of demonstrating the anthropologist's own competence and credibility—by indicating her or his familiarity with the relevant literature. Often embedded in a list of citations but may be referred to separately in one or, on a rare occasion, two sentences in passing as the anthropologist is developing a certain point [91 percent]: Astuti (1995); Barber (1996); Basso (1989); Bauer (1996); Besteman (1996); De Munck (1996); Desjarlais (1996); Dixon (1991); Finney (1991); Gillespie (2000); Gulbrandsen (1995); Habe, Harary, and Milicic (1996); Hantman (1990); Hastrup and Elsass (1990); Heald (1991); Keane (1991); Kipp (1995); Kuper (1986); Lominitz-Adler (1991); Maddox (1995); Mageo (1996); Malarney (1996); Masco (1995); Daniel Miller (1991); Mosko (1991, 1995); Munn (1990); Orlove (1986); Ortner (1995); Pauketat and Emerson (1991); Piot (1995); Redman (1991); Robben (1989); Roberts (1985); Sanjek (1991); Saris (1996); Saunders (1995); Sivaramakrishnan (1995); Sutton (1990); N. Thomas (1996); Trigger (1991); Whitehead (1995); and E. Wolf (1990).

141    Readers interested in exploring this topic further might refer to Bergendorff, Hasager, and Henriques (1988); Bernstein (1995); C. Brown (1976); Burke, ed. (1992); Carmack (1972); Clemons (1978); Edgerton (1995); Fagan (1995); Faubion (1993); Geertz (1978, 1982, 1995a, 1995b); Gledhill (1999); Hacking (1995); Hanson (1982); Hooper (1996); A. Howard (1982); K. Howe (1995); Jackson (1978); Kelly (1990); Krech (1991); Laughlin (1975); Levy (1992); Lingua Franca (1995); Lomnitz (1996); Marcus (1995); W. Marshall (1999); Nash (1981); Newbury (1982); Ortner (1985); Petersen (1995); Poirier (1978); K. Powers (1995); Rebel (1989); J. Robbins (1995); Roseberry (1988); A. Ross

## ASSESSING POSTMODERNISM

*Postmodernism explores the processes by which "others"—the people anthropologists study—are presented in publications. We look at two general works closely associated with Postmodernism—one edited by James Clifford and George Marcus, and the other by George Marcus and Michael Fischer. A third book by Marilyn Strathern offers an ethnographic example of the approach. The authors of* Writing Culture *consider the rhetorical devices anthropologists apply in presenting their ethnographic materials. Marcus and Fischer call for experimentation in reframing ethnographies, offering a range of possibilities that anthropologists might consider. Strathern examines how we represent others in our writing, especially the way we describe gender, exchange, and social units in Melanesian societies.*

*Once again, the three works offer much food for thought. But I am cautious about accepting that the authors' collective efforts embody significant intellectual progress as defined above. First, they don't directly build on each other, either ethnographically or analytically. Instead, they collectively emphasize a potpourri of possibilities. Second, the underlying problems facing Postmodernism are never addressed. We are left to guess how to assess the experiments and positions various authors embrace if not by normal intellectual standards. The trend strives to create an impression that it is above the rhetorical politics it analyzes, while in fact being very much a part of them. One senses the trend tries to appear new, innovative, and unburdened with the field's old baggage, while at the same time striving for the same disciplinary status rewards and validation as others.*

The final trend examined, Postmodernism, was prominent in anthropology from the mid-1980s through the 1990s. It focuses on the role of the knower (the anthropologist) in the known (ethnographic accounts). It explores the processes by which "others"—the people that anthropologists studied—are presented in publications. In exploring this trend, we look at two general works closely associated with Postmodernism—*Writing Culture* edited by James Clifford and George Marcus, and *Anthropology as a Cultural Critique* by George Marcus and Michael Fischer. A third book by Marilyn Strathern, *The Gender of the Gift*, offers an ethnographic example of the approach. For a trend that rebelled

(1995); Russell (1978); Sahlins (1988, 1989, 1993); Said (1988); J. Schneider (1999); Schneider and Rapp (1995); Scull (2007); Shankman (1986); Shelley (1979); C. Smith (1997); Trask (1985); Vincent (1986); and Wyndham (1995a, 1995b).

against broad master narratives and valued pastiche in ethnographic writing (drawing bits and pieces from here and there together into an anthropological account), the tenets of Postmodernism appear relatively coherent.[142] One repeatedly reads about "a crisis of representation" and "uncertainty about adequate means of describing social reality."[143] There is an emphasis on reflexivity—on "working into ethnographic texts a self-conscious account regarding the conditions of knowledge production as it is being produced."[144] There is a call for intellectual experimentation in ethnographic writing.[145]

Postmodernism portrays itself as superseding modernism, but it would be more accurate to suggest that it amplifies selected modernist tendencies. One anthropologist shrewdly notes that "fragmentation, pastiche, and the juxtaposition of images and genres had been used [to question certain established Western frames of reference since] . . . at least as early as Nietzsche's writings. In art, this trend was foreshadowed by French impressionism and then made explicit in cubist and surreal art."[146] A prominent literary critic notes that "incompletion is the password to modernism . . . in modernism, form is not a perfect act but process and incessant revision."[147]

142  The label that is repeatedly attached to the trend by others—Postmodernism—turns out not to necessarily be embraced by the trend's key figures in their key works. It is relatively easy to find comprehensive discussions of postmodernism in recent accounts of anthropological theory (e.g., Barnard and Spencer [1996]; M. Harris [1999]; Knauft [1996]; Layton [1997]) as well as in broad synthetic works (e.g., Barfield [1997]; Barnard and Spencer [1996]). But the term—if we judge by the pages cited in each book's index—is downplayed in both *Anthropology as Cultural Critique* and *The Predicament of Culture*. In *Writing Cultures*, Clifford intriguingly suggests, "most of us [involved in the book] were not yet thoroughly 'post-modern'" (in Clifford 1986:21)—cf. Pool (1991:318–319); Sangren (1988:425). See, e.g., Rabinow in Clifford and Marcus (1986:249–250); Knauft (1996:68).

143  Marcus and Fischer (1986:7, 8ff.). "No longer is it credible," Fischer asserts, "for a single author to pose as an omniscient source on complex cultural settings, nor to pose those settings as distanced exotic forms without direct interaction with the author's own society, time, and place" (M. Fischer 1997:370).

144  Marcus (1994:45). He continues that it involves replacing "the observational objective 'eye' of the ethnographer with his or her personal . . . 'I.'"

145  Marcus and Fischer (1986) is subtitled *An Experimental Moment in the Human Sciences.* "What motivates [these] experiments," Marcus suggests, "is the recognition of a much more complex world, which challenges the traditional modes of representing cultural difference in ethnographic writing" (Marcus and Fischer 1986:168).

146  Knauft (1996:16); cf. Marcus and Fischer (1986:122–125). Gellner (1992) points out that postmodernism parallels the Romantic Counter-Enlightenment's opposition to positivistic ideals.

147  G. Steiner (1999:3). As with the (Re)Turn to History trend, the new and old very much overlap (cf. Pool [1991:310ff.]; Marcus and Fischer [1986:67–68]).

In *Writing Culture*, editors Clifford and Marcus state that "by looking critically at one of the principal things ethnographers *do*—that is, write—. . . [they
seek] to come to terms with the politics and poetics of cultural representation."[148]
Beyond a shared concern with this theme, the book's contributors move off in a
number of directions. The best way to convey a sense of the book—in a pastiche
(postmodern) way—is to quote a few passages from it.

From Clifford: "The focus on text making and rhetoric serves to highlight
the constructed, artificial nature of cultural accounts. . . . Ethnographic truths
are . . . inherently *partial*—committed and incomplete." From Rabinow: "When
corridor talk about fieldwork becomes discourse, we learn a good deal. Moving
the conditions of production of anthropological knowledge out of the domain
of gossip—where it remains the property of those around to hear it—into that
of knowledge would be a step in the right direction." From Marcus: "More is at
stake than the mere de-mystification of past dominant conventions of representation. Rather, such a critique legitimates experimentation and a search for
options in research and writing activity."[149]

*Writing Culture* may be a "benchmark publication," to quote one reviewer,
but it has had more than its share of critics. Two criticisms are repeatedly heard.
First, while acknowledging that the book opens new possibilities for analysis,
critics wonder how to evaluate these possibilities. To emphasize the constructed
nature of ethnographies and then step outside of this framework to objectively
criticize the biases in certain ethnographic texts brings a critical question to

148   Clifford and Marcus (1986:vii–viii). "Anthropology's premier postmodernist text," Barnard (2000:169) suggests, was "Writing Culture." James, Hockey, and Dawson (1997:1) refer to it as
"a watershed in anthropological thought." Or as Nugent (1996:443) noted, it involved "a benchmark
publication indicating . . . possible trajectories for a postmodernist . . . anthropology." The volume
grew out of a 1984 School of American Research seminar.

149   Clifford in Clifford and Marcus (1986:2, 7); Rabinow in Clifford and Marcus (1986:253);
and Marcus in Clifford and Marcus (1986:263). See also Clifford: "May not the vision of a complex,
problematic, partial ethnography lead, not to its abandonment, but to more subtle, concrete ways
of writing and reading, to new conceptions of culture as interactive and historical" (25)? Rosaldo:
The pastoral mode of writing—in the work of Evans-Pritchard and Le Roy Ladurie—"permits a
polite tenderness that more direct ways of acknowledging inequality could inhibit. Its courtesy
becomes respect. . . . Yet the pastoral also licences [*sic*] patronizing attitudes of condescension, such
as reverence for a simplicity 'we' have lost . . . the pastoral mode becomes self-serving because the
shepherd symbolizes that point beyond domination where neutral ethnographic truth can collect
itself," in Clifford and Marcus (1986:97). Asad: "The ethnographer's translation/representation of
a particular culture is inevitably a textual construct, that as representation it cannot normally be
contested by the people to whom it is attributed . . . the process of 'cultural translation' is [thus]
inevitably enmeshed in conditions of power," in Clifford and Marcus (1986:163).

the fore: What allows anthropologists to emphasize the constructed nature of ethnographies while, at the same time, seeming to act as objective observers of these texts, specifying where and how they are biased? Why is a "postmodern perspective" not simply another construction, responding to another set of political structures? What makes a postmodern account objective and other accounts not? Second, despite the repeated focus on how authors construct ethnographic texts, little attention is paid to how indigenous informants construct *their* texts or assert *their* knowledge claims.

What is intriguing about Marcus and Fischer's *Anthropology as Cultural Critique*, the second key text, is that, while it is strongly criticized by those not embracing Postmodernism, it seems fairly conventional in both content and structure.[150] One might divide the book into three parts.

(1) The first two chapters frame the book. Seeking to place the present "crisis of representation" in historical perspective, Marcus and Fischer write: "The current period, like the 1920s and the 1930s, . . . [is] one of acute awareness of the limits of our conceptual systems as systems."[151]

(2) The next two chapters offer a range of illustrative experimental texts: Chapter 3 examines ways to represent "the authentic differences of other cultural subjects . . . focusing on the person, the self, and the emotions." Chapter 4 takes "account of power relations and history within the context of their subjects' lives."[152]

---

150    While described as "an important contribution to the postmodernist discussion" (Birth [1990:549]), as a "milestone" (Whitten [1988:733]), and as a companion volume to *Writing Culture* that "instigated a wider debate" (James, Hockey, and Dawson [1997:1]), one has a hard time discovering—beyond such brief snippets—extended positive commentary from reviews in major anthropological journals. It appears almost universally recognized as an important book. At the same time, it is strenuously criticized (even more so than *Writing Culture*). This holds despite the fact that several writers—including many critics—acknowledge *Anthropology as Cultural Critique* is in many ways a fairly conventional book. Pool writes: "The critics usually single out *Writing Culture* . . . and *Anthropology as Cultural Critique* . . . for criticism as the programmatic statements or the examples of postmodern ethnography. In fact, it is the latter book, which is perhaps the most 'conventional' of all the so-called postmodern anthropological texts, which receives the most attention" (Pool [1991:319]).

151    Marcus and Fischer (1986:12). "An experimental ethnography works," Marcus and Fischer suggest, "if it locates itself recognizably in the tradition of ethnographic writing and if it achieves an effect of innovation" (1986:40). What is sought "is not experimentation for its own sake, but the theoretical insight that the play with writing technique brings to consciousness" (1986:42).

152    Marcus and Fischer (1986:44–46, 77). What is most striking, in both chapters, is the range of ethnographies made reference to. Chapter 3, for example, includes not only Geertz's "Person,

(3) Chapters 5 and 6 focus on anthropology as a form of cultural critique: "The juxtaposing of alien customs to familiar ones, or the relativizing of taken-for-granted concepts . . . that lend certainty to our everyday life, has the effect of disorienting the reader and altering perception."[153]

Critical comments regarding *Anthropology as Cultural Critique* focus on the same problems highlighted in respect to *Writing Culture*. First, critics question how one evaluates the experimental ethnographies, if not in traditional ways. Marcus and Fischer list several standards for determining a "good ethnography"—a sense of fieldwork conditions, effective "translation" across cultural boundaries, and holism. But these standards don't appease critics. One critic writes: "Like Marcus and Fischer, I believe that anthropology is and ought to constitute a kind of reflexive cultural critique; unlike them, I believe that such a critique must emanate from a holistic and explicit allegiance to scientific values."[154] Critics charge that Marcus and Fischer frequently downplay the politics of their own ploys while emphasizing the political ploys of others. As the above critic phrased it, "Postmodernists feel free to mythologize, criticize, and demystify 'realist' arguments as hopelessly limited by the historical and cultural contingencies of their production while at the same time refusing to allow criticism of their own arguments on similar grounds."[155] Second, many critics view Postmodernism and the examples referred to in the book as forms of self-

---

Time and Conduct in Bali," Obeyesekere's *Medusa's Hair*, and Crapanzano's Tuhami but also Levy's *Tahitians*, Shostak's *Nisa*, Rosaldo's *Knowledge and Passion*, and Shore's *Sala'ilua*. Chapter 4 includes not only Willis's *Learning to Labour*, Taussig's *The Devil and Community Fetishism in South America*, and Price's *First Time* but also Wolf's *Europe and the People Without History* and Sahlins's *Historical Metaphors and Mythical Realities*.

153    Marcus and Fischer (1986:111) add: "The promise of anthropology as a compelling form of cultural critique has remained largely unfilled." They write: "The idea of the ethnographer's function as uncovering, reading, and making visible to others the critical perspectives and possibilities for alternatives that exist in the lives of his subjects is an attractive one. It is a function that anthropology has been performing abroad, and it should be a style of cultural criticism it could perform at home" (1986:133). Offering examples, in chapter 6, of "epistemological critique," Marcus and Fischer note Sahlins's *Culture and Practical Reason* as well as Geertz's Negara. Examples of "defamilization by cross-cultural juxtaposition" include Mauss's *The Gift* and Mead's *Coming of Age in Samoa*. The chapter ends with a call for recognizing that ethnographers, especially if they write cultural critiques, are writing for "diverse and critical readerships at home and abroad" that extend beyond the discipline itself (Marcus and Fischer 1986:164).

154    Sangren (1988:421).

155    Sangren (1988:421).

absorbed navel-gazing focused less on their informants than on the anthropologists themselves. J. C. Jarvie writes that "Postmodernism offers navel-gazing (study of texts)."[156]

To get a sense of how the trend has played out ethnographically, we turn to British anthropologist Marilyn Strathern's *The Gender of the Gift*. It brings us full circle to the gender issues that concerned Margaret Mead decades before in the same region of the world, Melanesia. A reviewer of *The Gender of the Gift* calls the book "a brilliant, subversive, anti-comparative analysis of what gender in Melanesia is not: it . . . reveals the fictions and hegemonic ethnocentrisms in our anthropological representations of the 'other,' and questions our capacity to view the world from a perspective different than our own."[157] The book focuses on three overlapping questions.

First, Strathern asks, how do Melanesian senses of gender clarify our perceptions and misperceptions of gender? (Here she emphasizes anthropology as cultural critique.) In Melanesia, she writes: "Being 'male' or being 'female' emerges as a holistic unitary state under particular circumstances. In the one-is-many

156    Jarvie (in Sangren [1988:428]). We are left with a puzzle regarding *Anthropology as Cultural Critique*. Why did a book that seems so inclusive in its praise, makes its arguments in a comparatively straightforward fashion, and affirms the need for ethnographic experimentation without demanding the dismantling of the discipline's traditions seem to arouse so many anthropologists' ire? It relates to context. Like Lowie (1937) and Harris (1968) before them, Marcus and Fischer reframe the discipline's history in terms that highlight their own orientations (cf. Hobsbawm and Ranger [1983] for this process on a nationalistic scale). Goldschmidt describes it as an "effort to recreate anthropology in their own image, to make what they have to say loom larger and more significant than it is" (Goldschmidt [1987:472]). And like Lowie and Harris, Marcus and Fischer are fairly inclusive regarding who they depict as "the good guys." Still it was a political move that most anthropologists understood. Polier and Roseberry write: "Ethnographic 'textualism' has become a formidable, and in some ways hegemonic, movement within American anthropology. . . . Institutionally, contributors to the movement are in a position to exercise extraordinary influence on the dissemination of ideas" (Polier and Roseberry [1989:245–246]). Spencer adds: "There is every chance that it has set the agenda for self-criticism in American (if not British) anthropology for the next few years" (Spencer [1989:161]). What one sees in the negative reviews is resistance to a wave that swept over the discipline in the late 1980s and into the 1990s (cf. Pool [1991:327–328]).

Since today most anthropologists accept the need for critically analyzing the construction of their texts, one might say that the trend has won out. But what is intriguing is how it won out. Essentially, it was done by a small, cohesive cadre—Pool refers to Marcus, Fischer, Clifford, and Tyler as the "central gang of four" (1991:319) with, we might say, Crapanzano, Rabinow, Taussig, and Geertz as fellow-travelers. One might well argue that the Boasians and the cultural ecologists carried out similar coups.

157    Gewertz (1990:797–798).

mode, each male or female form may be regarded as containing within it a suppressed composite identity." We might assume that breasts belong to women and phalluses to men, she continues, but "if people say that phalluses were stolen from women or if a phallus is treated like a fetus, it is not at all clear that we can be so certain in our evaluation on the Melanesians' behalf." Strathern writes: "As I have construed Melanesian ideas, . . . the person is revealed in the context of relationships . . . the relations that compose him or her [constitute] . . . an inherently multiple construct."[158]

Building on this theme, the second question asks, how do Melanesian gift-oriented economies shape notions of gender domination in ways that diverge from those created in more commodity–oriented economies like our own? "In a commodity-oriented economy," Strathern writes, people "experience their interest . . . as a desire to appropriate goods; in a gift-oriented economy, the desire is to expand social relations." She suggests, despite ethnographic data that could be interpreted as contradicting her stand, no permanent domination exists between men and women in Melanesian contexts. "Being active and passive," she writes, "are relative and momentary positions; in so far as the relevant categories of actors are 'male' and 'female' then either sex may be held to be a cause of the other's acts; and . . . vulnerable to the exploits of the other. . . . The conclusion must be that these constructions do not entail relations of permanent domination."[159]

The third question asks, how do we describe the dynamics of Melanesian sociality when they diverge from concepts Western anthropologists employ, such as society? "The argument of this book," Strathern writes, "is that however useful the concept of society may be to analysis, we are not going to justify its use by appealing to indigenous [Melanesian] counterparts." She continues: "As I understand [the] Melanesian concept of sociality, there is no indigenous supposition of a society that lies over or above or is inclusive of individual acts and unique events."[160]

*The Gender of the Gift* has been generally praised. (Positioned as a study of gender relations, it seems to have escaped the negative reaction of the books discussed above.) Still, if one looks, there are the same criticisms of it as with

158   M. Strathern (1988:14, 127, 274).
159   M. Strathern (1988:143, 333–334, see also p. 134).
160   M. Strathern (1988:3, 102).

the other books. First, it isn't clear exactly how to evaluate Strathern's assertions. She doesn't provide a detailed cognitive analysis of a few or even one Melanesian group, so we are left pondering how to interpret her interpretations. She admits: "I have not presented Melanesian ideas but an analysis from the point of view of Western anthropological and feminist preoccupations of what Melanesian ideas might look like if they were to appear in the form of those preoccupations."[161] Second, while Strathern criticizes how Westerners essentialize the concepts of gender and society, it is clear she has her own set of essentialisms. For example, drawing from various Melanesian groups, she suggests a general Melanesian form of sociality and aesthetic. But Melanesia, especially Papua New Guinea, is perhaps the most culturally diverse region in the world. What about the hundreds of Melanesian groups she does not discuss?[162] Third, in reply to a set of reviews, Strathern admitted that "the book falls down . . . in its failure to be explicit about its interpretive methods." Again, we are left uncertain as to how we should assess her claims.[163]

One final time, we may ask: How should we view this trend's major studies in terms of refining certain perspectives and/or building cumulative knowledge? In a vague sort of way, we might perceive the books discussed as perhaps vaguely building on one another. *Writing Culture* sets the stage, so to speak, for the other books by suggesting that ethnographies can be analyzed as literary constructions. *Anthropology as Cultural Critique* offers a more systematic, programmatic accounting of Postmodernism. It places Postmodernism in historical context and presents a range of "experimental" texts that readers might consider following in their own work. *The Gender of the Gift* fleshes out the postmodern agenda ethnographically. It offers an in-depth analysis of Melanesian gender relations and how we, as Westerners, tend to distort them in describing them.

However, as in previous trends, the works discussed do not directly build on each other, either ethnographically or analytically. The contributors to *Writing Culture*, for example, do not deal collectively with a specific ethnographic area in depth. They represent a potpourri of possibilities. Nor do the authors/editors of these works take particular note of each other's publications. Strathern's *The Gender of the Gift*, published two years after the others, doesn't cite either

---

161    M. Strathern (1988:309, also 244); P. Brown (1992:127).
162    M. Strathern (1988:341, also 342); note R. Keesing (1992:130) and Gewertz (1990:798).
163    M. Strathern (1988, also 1992:133–134 and 1988:153).

*Writing Culture* or *Anthropology as Cultural Critique*. While Clifford and Marcus list *Anthropology as Cultural Critique*, and Marcus and Fischer list *Writing Culture* in their bibliographies, neither lists the other work in the index (allowing us to see how they were cited). The absence of discussion (or even reference) to Clifford's well-known introductory chapter for *Writing Culture* in *Anthropology as Cultural Critique* is puzzling since Marcus obviously knows it.[164]

The three books address similar concerns. But the authors emphasize their own perspectives rather than engaging with each other's. Critical problems regarding the trend are not adequately addressed. To determine to what degree those citing the works of Clifford and Marcus, Marcus and Fischer, and Strathern intellectually engage with them, I examined citations five, ten, and fifteen years out from these three books' publication dates in some of the discipline's leading journals: the *American Anthropologist, American Ethnologist, Current Anthropology,* and *Man.* For the fifth journal, I chose one of Postmodernism's leading forums, *Cultural Anthropology* (of which George Marcus was the founding editor). If we look at to what degree (of the total articles in which these three leading figures are cited) the authors of the articles make a sustained attempt to develop one of the figures' ideas—involving at least *three* sentences of discussion of the specified author's work—we get the following percentages:

| CLIFFORD AND MARCUS (1986) | MARCUS AND FISCHER (1986) | STRATHERN (1988) |
|---|---|---|
| 0% | 0% | 7% |

---

164  While some of the contributors listed in *Writing Culture* are cited in *Anthropology as Cultural Critique*—e.g., Rosaldo, Crapanzano, Marcus, and Fischer—the ethnographic examples Marcus and Fischer cite in the latter tend to be different from those used by the contributors in the former. That is not to say there is no ethnographic overlap between the two books. Marcus considers Willis's fieldwork (Willis 1981) in both books and brief remarks regarding Rosaldo's and Crapanzano's ethnographies by Marcus in *Writing Culture* (1986:165, 192) are elaborated upon in Marcus and Fischer (1986). Fischer refers to novels by Arlen and by Kingston in both. And Pratt considers Shostak's Nisa (Shostak 1983) in *Writing Culture*, which Marcus and Fischer discuss as well in *Anthropology as Cultural Critique*. But that is essentially the degree to which the same ethnographic texts are seriously engaged with in both texts. Given the range of texts referred to in all three books, it is a fairly low percentage. Even when there is ethnographic overlap, the discussions in *Anthropology as Cultural Critique* downplay reference to the analyses in *Writing Culture* or vice versa. Obviously since Marcus and Fischer are the main source of these overlapping analyses, they know of their existence.

The specific citations for Clifford and Marcus,[165] Marcus and Fischer,[166] and Strathern[167] are listed in the footnotes.

165  CLIFFORD AND MARCUS: (a) Number of citations examined in five leading journals five, ten, and fifteen years following dates of publication: 28. (b) A sustained attempt to DEVELOP one of the three authors' work in a specific way (through reinterpreting, building on, or criticizing their respective work). Involves at least *three* sentences of discussion of the specified author's work [o percent]. (c) A sustained attempt to DISCUSS one of the three authors' work—in a review of the literature—before presenting the anthropologist's own perspective. Involves at least *three* sentences of discussion of the specified author's work [4 percent]: Poewe (2001). (d) Relevant author's work CITED ONLY IN PASSING as a way of demonstrating the anthropologist's own competence and credibility—by indicating her or his familiarity with the relevant literature. Often embedded in a list of citations but may be referred to separately in one or, on a rare occasion, two sentences in passing as the anthropologist is developing a certain point [96 percent]: Aggarwal (2001); Badone (1991); Barnard (1991); Borofsky et al. (2001); Bridgman (2001); Briggs (1996); C. Brown (1996); Carnegie (1996); Crain (1991); Crane (1991); Escobar (1991); Helmreich (2001); Howe (2001); Jean-Klein (2001); Leavitt (1996); Linnekin (1991); Lutzker and Rosenthal (2001); Lyons (2001); Murray (1991); Okely (1991); Palmer and Jankowiak (1996); Piccini (1996); Reff (1991); Samuels (1996); Sanjek (1991); Shore (1991); and Werbner (2001).

166  MARCUS AND FISCHER: (a) Number of citations examined in five leading journals five, ten, and fifteen years following dates of publication: 8. (b) A sustained attempt to DEVELOP one of the three authors' work in a specific way (through reinterpreting, building on, or criticizing their respective work). Involves at least *three* sentences of discussion of the specified author's work [o percent]. (c) A sustained attempt to DISCUSS one of the three authors' work—in a review of the literature—before presenting the anthropologist's own perspective. Involves at least *three* sentences of discussion of the specified author's work: [13 percent]: Crane (1991). (d) Relevant author's work CITED ONLY IN PASSING as a way of demonstrating the anthropologist's own competence and credibility—by indicating her or his familiarity with the relevant literature. Often embedded in a list of citations, but may be referred to separately in one or, on a rare occasion, two sentences in passing as the anthropologist is developing a certain point: [88 percent]: C. Brown (1996); Bruner (2001); Escobar (1991); Lewis (2001a); Linnekin (1991); Shore (1991); Werbner (2001).

167  STRATHERN: (a) Number of citations examined in five leading journals five, ten, and fifteen years following dates of publication [30]. (b) A sustained attempt to DEVELOP one of the three authors' work in a specific way (through reinterpreting, building on, or criticizing their respective work). Involves at least *three* sentences of discussion of the specified author's work [7 percent]: Gershon (2003); Hays (1993). (c) A sustained attempt to DISCUSS one of the three authors' work—in a review of the literature—before presenting the anthropologist's own perspective. Involves at least *three* sentences of discussion of the specified author's work: [13 percent]: Aswani and Sheppard (2003); Kingston (2003); Konrad (1998); Ouroussoff (1993). (d) Relevant author's work CITED ONLY IN PASSING as a way of demonstrating the anthropologist's own competence and credibility—by indicating her or his familiarity with the relevant literature. Often embedded in a list of citations but may be referred to separately in one or, on a rare occasion, two sentences in passing as the anthropologist is developing a certain point [80 percent]: Akin (2003); Battaglia (1993); C. Cohen (1998); Daniels (2003); Dubisch (1993); Fowler and Cummings (2003); Guyer (1993);

These data suggest that the anthropologists citing the above works appear less interested in constructively building on them than on using them to lend credence to their own work. Only in Strathern's case do some colleagues seek to seriously engage with her work at any depth. The more general tendency is to simply cite these figures in passing—the same "bump and go" pattern observed in other trends. [168]

## Taking Note of Positive Advances

*Saying there have been only limited intellectual advances in the decades examined is not to say there have been no intellectual advances. There have been advances. We also saw that cultural anthropologists ask a host of interesting questions that draw us to reflect on the world around us in insightful ways. While many anthropologists may not directly engage with the above figures, most cultural anthropologists, I suspect, would affirm those figures still constitute intellectual resources that directly or indirectly shape their ideas.*

Clearly there are fewer significant intellectual advances within cultural anthropology during the period studied than we might wish. But that is not to say there were no advances by the standards outlined in this chapter. In terms of standards, we see progress in how Service builds on the work of Sahlins and Steward in respect to levels of social integration. In addition, there is the Festschrift volume honoring Rappaport in which several authors address his work. A number of anthropologists intellectually engage with the work of Lévi-Strauss. And we see in the case of the Sahlins-Obeyesekere controversy involving Captain Cook's visit to Hawaii a clear, indisputable advance in our understanding of British-Hawaiian interactions in 1779.

We also see that anthropologists consider a range of rather interesting topics. Few disciplines ask such a breadth of questions in such interesting ways. Here are a few examples: (a) the fluid nature of gender characterizations (Mead); (b)

---

Hayden (2003); Helmreich (2003); Jean-Klein (2003); Kipnis (2003); Kockelman (2003); Kulick (1993); Li (1998); Maschio (1998); Maurer (2003); Mosko (1998); Osella and Osella (1998); Parkin (1993); Pina-Cabral (1993); Staples (2003); Stasch (2003); Verdery (1998); and Viegas (2003).

168   Readers interested in exploring this topic further might refer to Anderson (1999); Berube (2000); Biersack (1990); Birth (1990); P. Brown (1992); Fernandez (1990); Fischer (1999); Fischer and Marcus (1989); Frum (2000); Herbert (1999); Himmelfarb (1999); Jameson (1999); Jolly (1992); Leyner (1997); Marcus and Cushman (1982); Marrus (1998); Mendelsohn (1999); Munn (1994); Murray (1994); Nugent (1988); Parini (1998); Patai (1994); Rosaldo (1989); Sangren (2007); Steiner (1999); Taussig (1980); Wasserstrom (1998); and Yagoda (1998).

how ritual helps right environmental imbalances (Rappaport); (c) the mythic processes humans use to come to terms with contradictions in their social lives (Lévi-Strauss); and (d) how the interaction of ritual structures with historical events helps us understand non-Western perceptions of Europeans (Sahlins). If one talks informally to cultural anthropologists, it is clear that several of the figures cited constitute intellectual resources that cultural anthropologists draw on from time to time. This is especially true for junior professors and graduate students. Sometimes the focus on originality leads them to downplay this relationship in publications. Still, it is there. These figures' works remain in the background to be noted as needed.

## Why Has This Pattern Persisted for So Long?

*A key factor limiting intellectual advances in the field involves how accountability is framed. While refining perspectives and/or building cumulative knowledge are widely affirmed in principle as important publishing standards—if for no other reason than they fit with what the larger public expects of the field and what scholars need in order to get funded—in practice they are generally not adhered to. The focus is less on producing publications that advance knowledge than on producing publications needed for career advancement.*

It is to cultural anthropology's distinct advantage to publicly embrace the standards highlighted in this chapter. Supporting these standards conveys to the wider public and university administrators that cultural anthropologists are not simply self-serving individuals bent on their own aggrandizement. Rather, they are scholars dedicated to serving the common good and advancing knowledge. Such affirmations encourage foundations and governmental organizations to fund their research. Embracing these standards emphasizes that cultural anthropology is an intellectual endeavor worthy of financial support.

Most cultural anthropologists resist the suggestion that they produce works of fiction. They do not compose their ethnographies out of thin air. An ethnography often only sells two thousand to three thousand copies—a pittance compared to the millions of books Castaneda's *The Teachings of Don Juan* sold. While anthropologists claim they are producing professional works of scholarship that are ethnographically valid and advance knowledge, few check to ensure anthropologists produce such knowledge. Although it is critical for their funding and for their professional image within the academy to assert they are advancing knowledge, it is not critical that anthropologists actually do so for career and status advancement. To succeed at these, many lower and reframe the previously discussed set of standards. To quote Deborah Rhode's *In Pursuit of Knowledge: Scholars, Status, and Academic Culture*: "Because academic reputation and rewards are increasingly dependent on publication, faculty have incentives to churn out tomes that will advance their careers regardless of whether they will also advance knowledge."[169]

Lowering the standards—from the actual production of reliable knowledge to the appearance of producing such knowledge—achieves two important ends. It provides considerably more freedom to anthropologists regarding where and what they study. They are not tied to "building" on or "refining" earlier work in specific ways that restrict their intellectual freedom. It also increases the chances for career advancement. Lowering the standards allows them to produce more publications in a shorter time—just what they need if they are on the publishing treadmill seeking promotion. Let me offer an example of how the tension between public appearance and the politics of academic advancement plays out. As I noted in Chapter 1, the National Science Foundation (NSF) considers "the potential to advance knowledge." The Social Sciences and Humanities Research Council of Canada expects its funded research to have "broad objectives for the advancement of knowledge."[170]

In most grant proposals, applicants need to summarize the relevant literature related to their topic. They also need to explain how their proposed work will constitute a contribution to the field. But as Adam Kuper asserts: "The [grant] review process rewards people who can write good proposals even if they failed to deliver on earlier grants. Few foundations evaluate the research they fund. . . . The best credential for a fellowship is a previous fellowship. And landing a grant usually wins you more kudos than getting out the results of your research."[171] The path to success lies, in other words, in claiming to advance knowledge—not necessarily in demonstrating that you have. Without returning to a previously studied locale and conducting further research that directly relates to the publications of earlier researchers who worked there, it seems a stretch to claim you are building a body of cumulative knowledge or refining a researcher's theoretical insights related to that group. But as we have seen, anthropologists can, in a sense, have their cake (of appearing to advance knowledge) while eating it too

169   Rhode (2006:11).
170   NSF (2013); Social Science Research Council (2017).
171   Kuper (2009).

(go off and study wherever they want) because no one is really enforcing the publicly embraced standards.

What anthropologists do is quietly embrace weaker standards. These weaker standards are less effective than we might wish. But they work well for those caught up in the push to publish. A manuscript needs to be seen as an intellectual contribution to a particular topic. But this is a fairly loose criterion. As most journal and university press editors know, different anthropologists judge a manuscript in different ways. This means that, to a certain degree, the standards for publication are somewhat flexible. If an anthropologist cannot publish an article in one journal, quite likely she or he can publish it in another. As noted, one standard many reviewers emphasize involves discerning whether the research done appears credible. Cultural anthropologists often assess a manuscript's credibility by whether the author is familiar with certain references. Also, an author's research data should fit within generally depicted norms for an ethnographic region. It should involve concrete data that suggest the author conducted extensive research with real people in a real locale. Readers should not wonder whether the anthropologist made up his or her data out of thin air.

Another standard many reviewers emphasize is originality. The striving for originality isn't new. The historian William Clark dates it to the German Romantic Era of the late eighteenth and early nineteenth centuries. Michèle Lamont highlights its importance in *How Professors Think*. Originality is listed as one of the most important criteria in assessing grant applications. On the grant-assessing panels studied by Lamont, 89 percent of the panelists viewed originality as a significant factor in weighing a grant application. The panelists perceived developing a new perspective, a new approach, or a new method as affirming originality. This fits with a commonsense view of originality. If an individual "discovers" something new, it often leads in time to an intellectual advance in a field. Originality may also unleash a flood of publications by other scholars. Without new methods, new perspectives, new arguments to write about, scholars might find themselves repeating much of what they had written previously.[172]

But there is a problem. As Thomas Kuhn notes in *The Structure of Scientific Revolutions*, ideas that too openly challenge the existing consensus may be rejected or ignored. Cultural anthropologists often strive to be original in appearance but not so original as to challenge the hegemonic-like structures

---

172   Clark (2006:442); Lamont (2009:167, 171–172). The focus on originality may help explain why so many seek out different field sites from those of their mentors (Amelia Borofsky, personal communication).

supporting the status quo. Appearing original can open up publishing possibilities. Being too original can dampen them. Many trends in cultural anthropology are not necessarily "new." Remember Andrew Abbott's observation: "The young build their careers on forgetting and rediscovery, while the middle-aged are doomed to see the common sense of their graduate-school years refurbished and republished as brilliant new insights." We see this in respect to the (Re)Turn to History trend. Various anthropologists play up their originality by downplaying their predecessors' work. Anthony Wallace provides a telling image: "Theory in cultural . . . anthropology is like slash-and-burn agriculture: After cultivating a field for a while, the natives move on to a new one and let the bush take over; then they return, slash and burn, and raise crops in the old field again."[173]

James Rule suggests, in *Theory and Progress in Social Science*, that what seems original and innovative one day may seem less so another: A "manifestation of our troubled theoretical life is the . . . contested, and transitory quality of what are promoted as 'state-of-the-art' lines of inquiry. Apparently unsure of where the disciplines are headed, we are subject to a steady stream of false starts. . . . Exotic specialties arise . . . to dazzle certain sectors of the theoretical public, then abruptly lose both their novelty and their appeal."[174] But that does not necessarily matter. If the focus is on producing publications—rather than producing knowledge—such fads serve their purpose well.

The five trends discussed in this chapter have an order to them centering on the two main ways anthropologists explain cultural behavior. First, one pole of the continuum is emphasized (explaining cultural behavior in terms of mental/psychological, or idealistic, processes) and then the other pole (explaining cultural behavior in terms of external, environmental or materialistic pressures). The two modes of explanation alternate with one another through time. It is almost as if focusing on one perspective for a decade or so leads anthropologists to pay closer attention to the other perspective. The Culture and Personality trend emphasizes psychological processes, the Cultural Ecology trend the environmental or materialistic ones. The Myths, Symbols, and Rituals trend returns to psychological processes, then it's back to more materialistic ones with the (Re)Turn to History trend (especially with Foucault's and Wolf's work), and finally back to a psychological orientation with Postmodernism.

---

173    Abbott (2001:147–148); Wallace (1966:1254); also note Lévi-Strauss (1991:91–92).
174    Rule (1997:23).

For most objective observers familiar with the relevant literature, the Sahlins-Obeyesekere controversy over Captain Cook was basically resolved in favor of Sahlins. But many controversies are not resolved. They take on a life of their own. That is the case with the Yanomami, a well-known Amazonian Indian group. Are the Yanomami fierce? Have anthropologists caused the group significant harm? Are they representative of an earlier form of social organization? There have been over fifty books written on the Yanomami.[175] We might think that at

175  My thanks to Les Sponsel for providing this information on books relating to the Yanomami: 1841, Sir Robert H. Schomburgk, *Reisen im Guiana und am Orinoko wahrend der Jahre 1835–1839* (Leipzig, Germany); 1923, Theodor Koch-Grunberg, *Vom Roraima Zum Orinoco, Vol. 3 Ethnographie* (Stuttgart, Germany: Strecker and Schroder); 1953, Alain Gheerbrandt, *L'expedicion Orenoque-Amazone, 1948–1950* (Paris, France: Gallimard); 1954, Alain Gheerbrandt, *Journey into the Far Amazon* (New York: Simon and Schuster); 1956, Alfonso Vinci, *Samatari (Orinoco-Amazzoni)* (Bari, Italy: Leonardo da Vinci Editrice); 1959, Alfonso Vinci, *Red Cloth and Green Forest* (London, England: Hutchinson); 1960, Pablo Anduze, *Shailili-ko: Descubrimiento de las fuentes del Orinoco* (Caracas, Venezuela: Editor Talleres Graficas); 1960, Hans Becker, *Die Surara und Pakidai: Zwei Yanomami-Stamme in Nordwest Brasilien* (Hamburg, Germany: Mitteilunger aus dem Museum fur Volkerkunde); 1960, Georg Seitz, *Hinter dem grunen Vorhang* (Wiiesbaden, Germany: F.A. Brockhaus); 1963, Georg Seitz, *People of the Rain-Forests* (London, England: Heineman); 1963, Johannes Wilbert, *Indios de la Region Orinoco-Ventuari* (Caracas, Venezuela: Fundacion La Salle de Ciencias Naturales); 1964, Otto Zerries, *Waika: Die Kulturgeschichtliche Stellung der Waika-Indianer des Oberen Orinoco im Rahmen der Volkerkunde Sudamerikas* (Munich, Germany: Klauss Renner Verlag); 1965, Ettore Biocca, *Yanoama: The Story of Helena Valero, a Girl Kidnapped by Amazonian Indians* (New York: Kodansha America, 2nd edition 1996); 1968, Napoleon A. Chagnon, *Yanomamo: The Fierce People* (New York: Holt, Rinehart and Winston); 1969, Inga Steinvorth-Goetz, *Uriji jami! Life and Beliefs of the Forest Waika in the Upper Orinoco* (Caracas, Venezuela: Associacion Cultural Humboldt); 1970, Elizabeth Montgomery, *With the Shiriana in Brazil* (Dubuque, IA: Kendall/Hunt Publishing); 1972, Luis Cocco, *Iyewei-Teri: Quince Anos entre los Yanomamos* (Caracas, Venezuela: Libreria Editorial Salesiana); 1974, Kenneth I. Taylor, *Sanuma Fauna: Prohibitions and Classification* (Caracas, Venezuela: Fundacion La Salle de Ciencias Naturales); 1974, Otto Zerries and Meinhardt Schuster, *Mahekodotedi: Monographie eines Dorfes des Waika-Indianer (Yanoama) am oberen Orinoco (Venezuela)* (Munich, Germany: Klauss Renner Verlag); 1974, Daniel de Barandiaran, *Los Hijos de La Luna: Monografia Anthropologica Sobre los Indios Sanema-Yanoama* (Caracas, Venezuela: Editorial Arte); 1976, Jacques Lizot, *La Cercle des Feux: Faits et dits des Indiens Yanomami* (Paris, France: Editions du Seuil); 1976, William J. Smole, *The Yanoama Indians: A Cultural Geography* (Austin: University of Texas Press); 1977, Napoleon A. Chagnon, *Yanomamo: The Fierce People* (New York: Holt, Rinehart and Winston); 1977, Margaret Jank, *Culture Shock* (Chicago: Moody); 1979, Alcida Rita Ramos and Kenneth I. Taylor, *The Yanoama in Brazil 1979* (Copenhagen, Denmark: IWGIA); 1982, Florinda Donner, *Shabono* (New York: Dell Publishing Co.); 1983, Napoleon A. Chagnon, *Yanomamo: The Fierce People* (New York: Holt, Rinehart and Winston); 1983, Comite para la Creacion de la Reserve Indigena Yanomami, *Los Yanomami Venezolanos* (Caracas, Venezuela: Vollmer Fundacion, Inc.); 1984, Helena Valero, *Yo Soy Napeyoma: Relato de una mujer raptada por los Indigenas Yanomami* (Caracas, Venezuela:

least some of the controversies swirling around the group would be resolved by these publications. But the disputants do not focus on the same locale, nor do they argue with the same data or data that others can confirm—such as assessing fierceness by how many individuals were killed within a specific time period at a specific locale. Anthropologists mostly talk past one another using different material to draw different conclusions. It may seem dysfunctional to some. But resolving such arguments is not necessarily central to their careers. Producing more publications is.

---

Fundacion La Salle de Ciencias Naturales); 1984, Maria Isabel Eguillor Garcia, *Yopo, Shamanes y Hekura: Aspectos Fenomenologicos del Mundo Sagrado Yanomami* (Puerto Ayachucho, Venezuela: Editorial Salesiana); 1985, *Tales of the Yanomami: Daily Life in the Venezuelan Forest* (New York: Cambridge University Press, English translation of 1978 book); 1985, Marcus Colchester, ed., *The Health and Survival of the Venezuelan Yanoama* (Copenhagen, Denmark: IWGIA); 1986, Jean Chaffanjon, *El Orinoco y el Caura* (Caracas, Venezuela: Editorial Croquis); 1990, *The Population Dynamics of the Mucajai Yanomama* (New York: Academic Press); 1990, Johannes Wilbert and K. Simmoneau, *Folk Literature of the Yanomami Indians* (Los Angeles, CA: UCLA Latin American Center Publication); 1991, Kenneth R. Good with David Chanoff, *Into the Heart: One Man's Pursuit of Love and Knowledge Among Yanomama* (Englewood Cliffs, NJ: Prentice-Hall); 1992, Dennison Berwick, *Savages: The Life and Killing of the Yanomami* (London, England: Hodder and Stoughton); 1992, Napoleon A.Chagnon, *Yanomamo* (New York: Harcourt Brace Jovanovich); 1992, Napoleon A. Chagnon, *Yanomamo: The Last Days of Eden* (San Diego, CA: Harcourt Brace Jovanovich); 1995, R. Brian Ferguson, *Yanomami Warfare: A Political History* (Santa Fe, NM: School for American Research); 1995, Alcida Rita Ramos, *Sanuma Memories: Yanomami Ethnography in Times of Crisis* (Madison: University of Wisconsin Press); 1996, Mark Andrew Ritchie, *Spirit of the Rainforest: A Yanomamo Shaman's Story* (Island Lake, IL: Island Lake Press); 1996, Frank A. Salamone, ed., *Who Speaks for the Yanomami?* (Williamsburg, VA: Studies in Third World Societies Publication No. 57); 1997, Franke A. Salamone, ed., *The Yanomami and Their Interpreters: Fierce People or Fierce Interpreters?* (Lanham, MD: University Press of America, Inc.); 1997, Bruce Albert and Gale Goodwin Gomez, *Saude Yanomami: Un Manual Etnolinguistico* (Belem, Brasil: Musueu Paraense Emilio Goeldi); 1997, Napoleon A. Chagnon, *Yanomamo* (New York: Harcourt Brace College Publishers); 1997, Jean Chiappino and Catherine Ales, eds., *Del Microscopio a la Maraca* (Caracas, Venezuela. Editorial Ex Libris); 1997, Geoffrey O'Connor, *Amazon Journal: Dispatches from a Vanishing Frontier* (New York: E.P. Dutton); 1998, John F. Peters, *Life Among the Yanomami: The Story of Change Among the Xilixana on the Mucajai River in Brazil* (Orchard Park, NY: Broadview Press, Ltd); 1998, Linda Rabben, *Unnatural Selection: The Yanomami, the Kayapo, and the Onslaught of Civilization* (Seattle: University of Washington Press); 2000, Claudia Andujar, *Yanomami* (Curitiba, Brazil); 2000, John D. Early and John F. Peters, *The Xilixana Yanomami of the Amazon: History, Social Structure, and Population Dynamics* (Gainesville: University of Florida Press); 2000, Mark Andrew Ritchie, *Spirit of the Rainforest: A Yanomamo Shaman's Story* (Island Lake, IL: Island Lake Press, 2nd edition); 2000, Patrick Tierney, *Darkness in El Dorado: How Scientists and Journalists Devastated the Amazon* (New York: W.W. Norton); 2005, Robert Borofsky, ed., *Yanomami: The Fierce Controversy and What We Can Learn from It* (Berkeley: University of California Press); 2006, Michael Dawson, *Growing Up Yanomamo* (Enumclaw, WA: Wine Press Publishing).

If anthropologists are not committed to resolving controversies such as the ones involving the Yanomami, it is hard to see how they can resolve conceptual problems in the trends discussed in this chapter. It is not that most anthropologists are, in principle, against resolving controversies. Rather, it is that they prefer to resolve them on their own terms. They see no reason to compromise in ways that will reduce what they perceive as their intellectual integrity but more precisely might be viewed as their intellectual freedom to assert what they want when they want. A controversy becomes personalized. It extends beyond objective data. With no accepted way to resolve it—by agreeing on what data will constitute verification of one or another position and then gathering it— many controversies go on and on. We might wonder if the reason the Sahlins-Obeyesekere controversy basically got resolved is because not only were the relevant data publicly available but only a few scholars were familiar enough with the material to analyze them in detail and pronounce judgment. There were not a lot of chefs trying to stir the pot.

Often a publication's intellectual value is assessed by the degree to which others cite it. This is a flawed standard. Citing an author does not guarantee actual engagement with the author's ideas. Rhode notes: "There is no guarantee that authors have actually read the sources cited. Indeed, with technological advances, they need not even trouble to type them; entire string citations can be electronically lifted from other publications. Nor does it follow that the sources listed establish the proposition for which they are cited. Even when someone checks the notes, it is generally to determine only whether particular authorities support the text, not whether they are reliable or respected among experts."[176]

Earlier I criticized the "bump and go" citation pattern—citing other anthropologists without engaging with these anthropologists' ideas. Yet the pattern makes sense in a way. Some anthropologists are inclined—in affirming their own intellectual competence—to point out flaws in other anthropologists' work. This might antagonize those referred to. It could prove detrimental to these anthropologists' career advancement. Citing others in "bump and go" patterns is safer. No one feels challenged, just acknowledged.

I add one final point regarding the push to publish. The expectations regarding how many articles and books professors need to publish for promotion have significantly increased in recent years. I have no hard figures. But in the 1960s one might expect a person up for tenure to have published a few articles

176   Rhode (2006:38).

and ideally a book. Today, having a series of articles and at least one book is critical. Having a number of books is preferred. It would be virtually impossible to have the number of articles published in anthropology journals today published in the 1960s. There simply were not enough journals available. The American Anthropological Association's primary journal in the 1960s was the *American Anthropologist*. Today the AAA's website indicates that it publishes twenty-two journals. To keep up with the increased demand for publications, a number of new journals have been created by a number of publishers. My point is, because of the weak standards for evaluating a publication's value, the concern for originality, and the push to publish, the publications produced do not necessarily advance knowledge. They tend to produce uncertain, ambiguous knowledge claims. We see the triumph of style over substance, of quantity over quality.

## How the Focus on Publishing Fits into the Pursuit of Status

*In and of itself, the chase for status can be a positive process. It drives anthropologists to be continually productive, even after tenure. The problem is that status is often entwined with the push to publish in a way that the quality of publications—to what degree they advance knowledge by the standards specified in the chapter—is not that critical to career advancement. The chase for status works fine with weaker assessment standards. In fact, they often work better since they allow for the production of more publications in a shorter period of time. Specialized studies fit this pattern.*

The anthropological chase for status in cultural anthropology—for recognition by one's peers, for citations by colleagues, for prominent positions and/or promotions—is not bad in and of itself. It motivates anthropologists to stay productive throughout their careers. One might "fall asleep" intellectually after gaining tenure or promotion to full professor without serious consequences. Some do, but most don't. The chase for status is a powerful force that drives anthropologists to remain productive throughout their careers. In looking at this drive for status, I am reminded of Max Weber's *The Protestant Ethic and the Spirit of Capitalism*. In Calvinism, he suggests, "the question, Am I one of the elect? . . . sooner or later [arises] . . . for every believer. . . Favor in the sight of God is measured primarily . . . in terms of the importance of the goods produced." He writes: "Continuous, systematic work. . . . [was] the surest and most evident proof of rebirth and genuine faith."[177] Like Weber's self-doubters, many anthropologists remain uncertain as to their status. We only need look at the care lavished on CVs to realize the degree to which anthropologists strive to affirm status through their scholarly activities.

So how do you know when you've "made it," especially when many of your peers are competing with you for more citations, more publications, more recognition in a zero-sum pursuit of status in which your rise often means someone else's decline? With status markers (and trends) changing through time, uncertainty surrounds "making it" in the discipline. To quote Deborah Rhode: "The arms race for relative status has almost no winners and many losers. . . . Few academics will achieve true eminence as scholars, and even those who do typically find that there is always someone more distinguished."[178] I don't know if her statement is correct. I suspect it is since I have heard others make the same point. Even Clifford Geertz, one of the most recognized anthropologists in the discipline during the 1980s, is reputed to have felt undercited by colleagues. The statement surprises many. After all, Geertz had a prominent status that many anthropologists can only dream of. Success in the status chase often comes with uncertainty. Ambiguities abound as to whether you've really made it and, if you have, for how long.

The result is that anthropologists continually publish, continually strive for further recognition (and, in the junior ranks, promotion). It may not feel pleasant for the anthropologists involved. But the chase for status generates lots of publications. In navigating various possibilities and problems, anthropologists employ a number of strategies. There is a turned-inward quality to them. Andrew Abbott writes: "Professionals draw their self-esteem more from their own world than from the public's."[179] Drawing on the work of Mary Douglas, we might perceive this turned-inward tendency in terms of purity and pollution.[180] Moving beyond the academic pale makes one impure. It pollutes. The pure remain comfortably ensconced within cultural anthropology, producing work that few read.

177   Weber (1958:110, 172).
178   Rhode (2006:13).
179   Abbott (1988:119).
180   Douglas (1966).

In principle, one can move up the status ladder holding to either the stronger publicly embraced standards (discussed earlier in the chapter) or the weaker academically oriented standards (discussed here). Holding to the higher standards need not be detrimental to one's career. But it involves more effort. That is why the weaker standards are often preferred. They let you publish more in a shorter period of time. One problem anthropologists face in advancing their status is establishing a distinct intellectual identity. Many find it wise, when they are starting out, to cite senior faculty, in a manner not unlike what James Frazer articulated with his "Law of Contagion" in *The Golden Bough*. Contact with a senior faculty member allows junior faculty to gain some of the senior faculty's status.[181] It gives junior faculty a step up the status hierarchy. It also has a less mystical advantage. Though the peer-review process is reputedly blind—that is, an author doesn't know who will review a manuscript—an author often has a reasonable idea of who will review it. It is a wise person who thinks ahead to consider which senior specialists in the field are likely to review a manuscript and then suitably cites them.

But at some point, the subordination needs to stop if a faculty member is going be seen as more than a clone of a mentor. Faculty have to articulate their own vision, their own perspective backed by their own data. They need to be original. The further a junior anthropologist moves from dependence on a mentor's reference letters for career advancement, the more that anthropologist is likely to articulate perspectives that diverge from a mentor. This occurred with Franz Boas's students and the students of their students. Alfred Kroeber only explored the areas of Boas's work he found congenial to his interests, studiously rejecting others. Critiquing Boas's approach to history, Kroeber writes: "The uniqueness of all historic phenomena is . . . taken for granted. . . . No laws or near-laws are discovered. . . . there are no historical findings." In a biography of Julian Steward, Virginia Kerns writes that Steward "privately denied that his teachers—with the slight exception of Lowie—had affected his thought. His unpublished writings suggest that he saw practically no connection between his graduate training and his ideas; he considered himself a maverick and freethinker, not anyone's disciple. (Lowie declared in print that no one in his own field, including his graduate teacher, Franz Boas, had been a 'source of inspiration' for him)." Eric Wolf begins *Europe and the People Without History* with a critique of the work of his former teacher (i.e., Steward). Students may draw on their teachers' ideas when

---

181    Frazer (1922[1963]).

they are under their teachers' tutelage. But, once free and on their own, they frequently branch off in new directions as a way of establishing their intellectual independence.[182]

A second problem in the chase for status—besides establishing an independent identity—involves how to position your publications in the best possible light so others will notice them. There are two basic strategies that mark the ends of a continuum. At one end, faculty can write on a fairly broad subject. The more journals a faculty member publishes in, the more likely others will recognize and refer to her or him. The problem, however, is that this works best when one can publish more than one's peers on a subject in a shorter period of time. If a faculty member who cannot get ahead of the publishing curve may get lost in the deluge of competitors publishing their own articles and books on the topic. It becomes a numbers game. Deborah Rhode refers to a Carnegie Foundation report indicating more than a third of university faculty believed their publications were mostly assessed in terms of quantity rather than quality. (At schools with doctoral programs, the figure was over 50 percent.)[183] An alternative publishing strategy is to master a narrow specialization. The value of knowing certain material inside out and writing thoroughly on that subject is that anyone who wishes to refer to the topic needs to reference your work to be seen as well-read. The problem is that the niche you master may be too narrow to gain broad recognition.

It is relevant to note that one's status is entwined with the status of one's department. Being a member of a high-status department often increases publishing possibilities. As Rhode writes: "Researchers took twelve articles that had been published in the preceding two-and-a-half years and resubmitted them with minor changes to the same journals in which they had appeared; the authors' names were changed, they were given less prestigious institutional affiliations, and the opening paragraphs were slightly revised. Only three of the articles were recognized as resubmissions. The other nine previously published manuscripts went through the full review process, and eight were rejected, most of them for 'serious methodological flaws.'"[184]

But residing in a lower-status department can also be an advantage. This is what happened in the case of Postmodernism. Unlike many of the authors cited in this chapter, the key figures of Postmodernism—Marcus, Fischer, and

---

182    Kroeber (1935:542); Kerns (2003:5); E. Wolf (1982:14–15).

183    Rhode (2006:46).

184    Rhode (2006:58–59).

Clifford—belonged to relatively small departments. Marcus and Fischer, at the time they wrote *Anthropology as a Cultural Critique*, held positions at Rice University; Clifford was (and continues to work) in the History of Consciousness Program at the University of California–Santa Cruz. They didn't have the option of disseminating their ideas through graduate students at prestigious universities as Boas, for example, had. Instead, they applied a form of generational politics— establishing alliances with others of their approximate age set. The approach disrupted the established status system (centered in high-status departments). Economic factors enhanced the strategy. Teachers in the 1980s couldn't guarantee their graduate students university positions. As a result, many junior faculty had an incentive for embracing Postmodernism. It opened up new publishing opportunities.

What we see, in brief, is that the chase for status and promotion within cultural anthropology is closely tied to publishing. It often is not necessary to embrace the standards cited in this chapter. How much faculty members publish, who cites them, and how "original" they are, tend to be stressed. Publishing solid credible work that addresses a trend's major problems and/or builds cumulative knowledge about a particular group is not necessary for moving up the status ladder. The ephemeral, dazzling possibilities, as James Rule notes— that arise and then abruptly lose their appeal—work just as well as the more solid, steady efforts at advancing knowledge. Sometimes they work even better at advancing one's status.[185]

185  Readers interested in further exploring topics covered in the last three sections of this chapter may wish to peruse Anastas (2002); Anonymous (1919); Arnst (2007); Basken (2009a, 2009b, 2009c); Bauerlein (2009); Z. Bauman (2000); M. Bauman (2001); Beard (1939); T. Bender (1993); Berube (1997); Best (2006); Bourdieu (1988); Brainard (2005, 2008a, 2008b, 2008c); F. Brown (1954); P. Campbell (1999); Cohen (2007); Conley (2009); Corbyn (2009); Darnton (1997); Dawkins (2000); Economist (2006b, 2007e, 2008d, 2008f, 2009c); English (2005); Fawcett (1999); Florence (1940); Fontana (2004); Givier (1999); Glenn (2002, 2007c); Goldenweiser (1940); Gradgrind (2007); Grafton (1997, 2006, 2007); Gravois (2007); Guterman (2008a, 2008b, 2008c); N. Hamilton (1997); Hindo (2007); J. Howard (2008a, 2008b); Hurlbert (1976); Insole (2008); Iyer (2000); R. Jenkins (1997); Jensen (2007); June (2008a, 2008b); T. Kemper (2000); Kiernan (2004); Kirn (2001); Lamont (2009); Lariviere and Gingras (2009); Lasswell (1940); H. Lewis (1998); Lord (1960); Lundberg (1939); Lynd (1939); Mackey (2007); Magner (2000); Mark Ware Consulting (2008); McFeely (2001); McHenry (2002); Mcmillen (1997); McMurty (2001); D. W. Miller (2001); David Mills (2008); Mirsky (1998); Monaghan (2009); Monastersky (2002, 2005); Mowry (1939); Nash (1997); Nicholson (2007); Oakes and Vidich (1999); Ogle (2007); Pieters and Baumgartner (2002); Price (2018); Prospect (1998); Quiggin (2015); Read (2006, 2007a, 2007b); Reeson (2008); Schmidt (2008a); Stark (2006); Surowiecki (2007); Throsby (2007); Townsend (2005); UpFront

## THE PROBLEMATIC NATURE OF SPECIALIZATION
## UNDER THESE CONDITIONS

A focus on specialization, common throughout the biological and social sciences, proves problematic when one specialized study does not really build on another in a cumulative or refining fashion. The publications have limited credibility independent of what an author claims for them. One result of such specialization is fragmentation. A host of specialized studies could, in principle, lead to a larger insight, a larger truth. But given they do not build on one another, they draw readers off in divergent directions.

A second result is an information overload for many readers. Readers are unsure how to assess one study versus another and, moreover, what broader significance the various studies have. There is no broad framework to unite them. Normally, if a set of studies build toward a specific end and one of the studies contradicts others, that study is reexamined to see if and why it is problematic. But with little to guide readers, they are left with a number of equally meaningful or, depending on your perspective, equally meaningless studies with no way to order them. This fits with the "do no harm" paradigm of appearing to serve a broader purpose without in fact disrupting the status quo. The specialized studies mainly enhance an author's career.

Cultural anthropology has the tools to address intellectual fragmentation and information overload. It can fit specialized studies into broader frameworks through broad syntheses or comparisons. Following the pattern of Nader, Nadel, and Wolf, controlled comparisons can prove illuminating. But, as noted in Chapter 1, few anthropologists attempt them today. Similarly, few anthropologists bring together a range of specialized studies into a framework that provides a broad, insightful understanding of a subject. Instead, what many do is claim that there is a broader significance to their specialized studies without offering substantial data to support this assertion.

## The Winners and Losers in the Push to Publish Uncertain, Ambiguous Knowledge

*The system, as it currently operates, advances the interests of those within the academic community—not only individual academics but also their departments and universities. It does little to advance the interests of the field as a whole or*

(2007); Van Der Werf (2009); Veblen (1918); Walker (2003); Wasley (2007); Waters (2001); P. Weintraub (1941); Westbrook (1994); Westhoff (1995); and R. Wilson (1998).

*the broader society that frequently funds anthropology. The lack of transparency in the system is important. It means that people outside of the academy often puzzle over what is going on within it. They can't effectively evaluate what anthropologists produce. The lack of transparency allows anthropologists, if they choose, to pursue their personal interests, without being that beholden to those funding their academic pursuits.*

It is critical to note that there are clear winners to the system described here. Individuals are free to creatively strive, in an entrepreneurial way, for upward mobility. Gaining high status through one's publications across a specialization or, better yet, across a whole field benefits more than just the individual anthropologist. It adds status to the individual's department. Increasing a department's status increases its ability to attract graduate students. It also strengthens the department vis-à-vis other university departments in the competition for resources and positions. Having high-status individuals in high-status departments gives a university status relative to other universities, which in turn allows them to raise more money. In brief, the status chase can be a winning formula for all three parties.

That is why publishing trumps teaching and service in promotion and tenure reviews. Teaching is not easily drawn into the status competitions between departments or between universities. It lacks the clean, comparable markers—in contrast to publications—that departments can emphasize in their competition for funds vis-à-vis other departments. Service faces the same problem. Public service to the broader community may be deemed admirable. But it holds limited competitive value. In cultural anthropology, publishing is the dominant marker that individual faculty, departments, and universities use in their status competitions with each other. The citation system—with its breadth of references—keeps outsiders from fully understanding what is going on. Reading deeply in cultural anthropology often confuses the uninitiated. They are overwhelmed by the names, by the references, by the way the articles are written. Readers think they are supposed to understand what they read. (They don't realize that the citations are often used as a way of enhancing the author's credibility.)

The result is that the larger society rarely fully grasps the field's dynamics—how they publicly espouse strong standards but in fact often follow weaker standards in practice. Outsiders perceive the field's excitement. They see the publications. But they lack a way to assess the value of what is produced. They lack external reference points, external measurements, for ensuring cultural anthropologists are advancing knowledge and serving the common good as much as they claim.

Returning to a theme in Chapter 1, the focus on academic publishing also serves another end. Like the redefinition of objectivity within universities (to limit activism), competing over how many books are published, how many articles are cited, keeps the "powers that be" within universities comfortable, especially since few outside a field will read or understand what is published in it. Appearing to advance knowledge and seeming to serve the social good, without significantly changing the social structures in place, doesn't threaten the financial and political powers that be. It supports them.

You might think that anthropologists would offer something significant in return for others' financial support. They clearly offer a rhetoric of support. Only some offer more. As long as anthropologists publicly embrace the strong standards publicly, they continue to be funded by various groups without—as we have seen—necessarily advancing knowledge in significant ways. One might wonder if there is a parallel to nongovernmental organizations (NGOs) receiving foreign aid to address problems in Third World countries. As the 2015 Nobel laureate in economics, Angus Deaton, asserts: "One reason why today's aid does not eliminate global poverty is that it rarely tries to do so. . . . In most cases aid is guided less by the needs of the recipients than by the donor country's domestic and international interests. . . . Although there is a strong domestic constituency for global poverty reduction . . . donors must balance a number of considerations, including political alliances and maintain good relationships with ex-colonies where donors often have important [financial] interests."[186]

One sees the power of the triadic structure discussed in Chapter 1. There has been increasing funding for research (along with higher education more generally). But fitting with the "do no harm" paradigm, there often seems to be a focus on the appearance of progress rather than a system of accountability that ensures the funding does indeed benefit those beyond the academy. Hopefully this chapter makes clear the "do no harm" paradigm's basic flaw: the focus on positive appearances—claiming to serve the broader society—while in fact mostly enhancing the prestige of individual faculty and their universities. The upbeat tone of the paradigm's message disguises that its focus is mostly on supporting the political and financial status quo.[187]

---

186   Deaton (2013:274).
187   See June (2018b), Rabesandratana (2018).

# 3

## SHIFTING THE PARADIGM TOWARD
## PUBLIC ANTHROPOLOGY

**CHAPTER 3 TURNS** to an alternative paradigm, one focused on benefitting others in more substantial ways than generally manifested by the "do no harm" paradigm. The question is what to call it. Unlike the "do no harm" paradigm that is embedded in the existing structures of academia, this alternative paradigm is more of a hope, a possibility. Its depth and breadth are still being explored, still remain to be defined.

Some readers, familiar with my work, might be surprised to learn that my first choice for this alternative paradigm was not "public anthropology." My first choice was "to do good," because it provided a clear contrast with "do no harm." It emphasized a call to action. Marcia McNutt, the editor-in-chief of *Science* journals, writes: "Data, particularly those collected with public funding, should be used so that they do the most good."[1] The problem with this phrasing is its vagueness. Good can be defined in a host of ways by a host of people to the point

---

1    McNutt (2015:7).

that a call to action gets replaced by confusing rhetoric and arguments over what "good" means. My second choice for this alternative paradigm—"benefitting others"—is also vague, which is perhaps why many use it. A host of people claim their work benefits others. People being helped, however, may not perceive this "help" in the same way. Moreover, the alternative paradigm I want to emphasize calls for more than benefitting others. There are structural issues that must be addressed.

Public anthropology lacks these complex associations. It is reasonably well known in the field and several programs and projects focus on it. There is an Institute of Public Anthropology at California State University–Fresno,[2] a public anthropology area of specialty at the University of Oregon,[3] and a master's program in public anthropology at American University as well as an annual Public Anthropology Conference.[4] Public anthropology is also part of the undergraduate program at Tufts University.[5] There is a public issues anthropology master's program at the University of Guelph and the University of Waterloo.[6] In respect to the American Anthropology Association, public anthropology is a topic in the *Anthropology News*, and there is a "Public Anthropologies" section within the *American Anthropologist*.[7] There is a master's program in the Anthropology of Public Orientation (Máster en Antropología de Orientación Pública) at the Universidad Autonoma de Madrid in Spain,[8] and a public anthropology cate-

---

2    See Institute of Public Anthropology at California State University–Fresno, https://www.fresnostate.edu/socialsciences/anthropology/ipa/ (accessed October 5, 2017).

3    See the public anthropology specialty at the University of Oregon, https://anthropology.uoregon.edu/public-anthropology/ (accessed October 5, 2017).

4    See the master's in public anthropology at American University, http://www.american.edu/cas/anthropology/ma/, and Public Anthropology Conference, http://www.american.edu/cas/anthropology/public/ (accessed October 5, 2017).

5    See Tufts University, https://ase.tufts.edu/anthropology/undergraduate/public.htm (accessed October 5, 2017).

6    See the Public Issues Anthropology programs at Universities of Guelph and Waterloo, http://www.uoguelph.ca/socioanthro/masters-program-public-issues-anthropology and https://uwaterloo.ca/graduate-studies-academic-calendar/arts/department-anthropology/master-arts-ma-public-issues-anthropology (accessed October 5, 2017).

7    See both publications at http://www.anthropology-news.org/index.php/tag/public-anthropology/ and http://www.americananthropologist.org/public-anthropologies-guidelines/ (accessed October 5, 2017); see also Checker, Wali, and Vine (2009).

8    See the Universidad Autonoma de Madrid in Spain at http://www.uam.es/UAM/M%C3%A1ster-en-Antropolog%C3%ADa-de-Orientaci%C3%B3n-P%C3%BAblica/1446748489690.htm?title=M%C3%A1ster%20en%20Antropolog%C3%ADa%20de%20Orientaci%C3%B3n%20P%C3%BAblica (accessed October 5, 2017).

gory for posts on anthro{dendum} (formerly Savage Minds).[9] Courses dealing with public anthropology are taught at a number of North American schools. I myself edit the California Series in Public Anthropology.

I coined the term "public anthropology" in the late 1990s. Being relatively new, it does not have some of the associations (both positive and negative) of more established terms, such as applied anthropology. The phrase "public anthropology" provides a concrete reference point with a certain newish buzz to contextualize its significance. While the focus of public anthropology remains on engaging with broader publics beyond the academy in ways that benefit them not just ourselves, it has been defined in a variety of ways. In the master's program in public anthropology at American University, for example, students "explore the workings of culture, power, and history in everyday life and acquire skills in critical inquiry, problem solving, and public communication."[10] The website of the Anthropology Department at the University of Oregon states: "In public anthropology, we take anthropology out of the academy and into the community. Public anthropology brings the issues, concerns, and insights of anthropology as broadly understood to both an academic and non-academic audience, striving to produce materials . . . that speak to a wide range of social sectors."[11] At Tufts University, according to the university's website: "Public anthropology includes both civic engagement and public scholarship more broadly, in which we address audiences beyond academia. It is a publicly engaged anthropology at the intersection of theory and practice, of intellectual and ethical concerns, of the global and the local."[12] The Public Issue Anthropology program at University of Guelph "focuses on the interface between anthropological knowledge and on the ground practice. We work with students to address issues critical to contemporary governance, public discourse, livelihoods, and civil society and to meet the demands and concerns of our world. Our Public Issues Anthropology MA seeks to make our world a better, healthier, more equitable place to live."[13] The review section of the *American Anthropologist* highlights "anthropology of

9    See the online publications at https://savageminds.org/tag/public-anthropology/ (accessed October 5, 2017); for anthro{dendum}, see https://anthrodendum.org/.

10    See http://www.american.edu/cas/anthropology/public/upload/PAC_Program_2013.pdf (accessed October 5, 2017).

11    See https://anthropology.uoregon.edu/public-anthropology/ (accessed October 5, 2017).

12    See the Tufts Anthropology Department, https://ase.tufts.edu/anthropology/undergraduate/public.htm (accessed October 5, 2017).

13    See the Program in Public Issues Anthropology at the University of Guelph, http://www.uoguelph.ca/socioanthro/masters-program-public-issues-anthropology (accessed October 5, 2017).

general interest to a broad audience. We seek perspectives that explicitly engage with public debates taking place around the world."[14] In brief, being only partially embedded in the academic establishment and being defined in a variety of ways gives public anthropology an advantage as a paradigm name. Its future remains to be written. It is "new" without being too new.

## Placing the Public Anthropology Paradigm in Historical Contexts

*Public engagement played a valued role in early anthropology. But as anthropology departments expanded in the late 1960s, this sense of engagement diminished. It now plays a less significant role in shaping the books anthropologists write and in the status hierarchy they embrace.*

Readers should note that anthropology has not always been as isolated from the general public as it seems today. If we view public anthropology as an effort to present in nonacademic terms insights about how life is lived beyond the pale of Western societies, we might perceive it as dating back to the Early Renaissance. Marco Polo's late thirteenth-century adventures (recorded by Rustichello da Pisa and known today as *The Travels of Marco Polo*) describes his travels to the court of Kublai Khan in China. Like many accounts of the period, it remains unclear where truth leaves off and fantasy begins.

During the Enlightenment, explorers frequently took care to provide credible reports of what they experienced in their adventures to other parts of the world. Among the most famous were the journals of James Cook's three voyages published in the late 1700s. They were best sellers; first editions sold out quickly. (The first edition of Cook's third voyage—a three-volume work of over sixteen hundred pages—sold out in three days.)[15] The journals provided a reasonably empirical description of life across a broad swath of the Pacific as experienced by Cook and his crew.

During the first half of the twentieth century, James Frazer, Franz Boas, Margaret Mead, and Ruth Benedict engaged a wide range of readers outside the academy. Frazer's *The Golden Bough*, for example, was widely influential at the

---

14    See the guidelines of the *American Anthropologist*, http://www.americananthropologist.org/public-anthropologies-guidelines/ (accessed October 5, 2017).

15    See, e.g., Sean Samuels, "The Story Behind Captain James Cook's Voyages," BaumanRare Books.com, March 12, 2014, https://www.baumanrarebooks.com/blog/story-behind-captain-james-cooks-voyages/ (accessed October 5, 2017).

time—being drawn on by a host of poets (e.g., Robert Graves, T. S. Elliot, and William Butler Yeats), writers (e.g., Ernest Hemingway, James Joyce, and D. H. Lawrence), scholars (e.g., Sigmund Freud, Joseph Campbell, and Camille Paglia), and philosophers (e.g., Ludwig Wittgenstein) for commentary and inspiration.[16] Benedict's *Patterns of Culture* was in its time hugely popular. It was translated into fourteen languages. Her *Chrysanthemum and the Sword* played an important role in framing the terms of the Japanese surrender at the end of World War II and the preservation of Hirohito as the Japanese emperor.[17] As noted in Chapter 1, Boas appeared on the cover of *Time* magazine in May 1936. During the 1950s, Mead was a widely known and respected figure throughout the world.

Why did anthropology become less publicly engaged? Basically, an academic trend that had been building since the early 1900s came to dominate the discipline. By the late 1960s anthropology had very much embraced the academy (or university), and the academy had very much embraced anthropology. The founders of anthropology in the mid- to late 1800s resided outside universities, either as private scholars (e.g., Henry Lewis Morgan) or as government employees (e.g., James Mooney and John Wesley Powell). But with the rise of universities as centers of learning in the late 1800s—for anthropology, it started with Boas becoming a professor of anthropology in 1899 at Columbia University— more and more anthropologists became associated with academic settings.

What is striking about anthropology's early years is how few anthropologists there were. The American Anthropological Association had 306 members in 1910 and 666 in 1930. "Some elders of our tribe," George Stocking notes, "can recall an age when most anthropologists knew each other personally, and [conferences] could be held . . . in one meeting hall of modest size."[18] This meant that anthropologists who wrote books had to write for wider audiences if they wanted anyone to publish them. The anthropology market was too small to attract major publishers. Raymond Firth, reflecting on his ethnography of a Polynesian island in the South Pacific, phrased it this way:

> In writing *We, The Tikopia* . . . I had to cater for a nonspecialist readership . . .
> in the mid-thirties, the name Tikopia would be completely meaningless to the
> outside world. . . . I believe then as now that . . . anthropology by its very nature
> ought to have a wider appeal than its tiny specialist market indicated. I had been

16    Wikipedia, s.v. "The Golden Bough."
17    Wikipedia, s.v. "Ruth Benedict" and "The Chrysanthemum and the Sword."
18    Stocking (1976:1).

supported in this view by the enthusiastic response to my public lectures and broadcasting talks to schools. So I tried to broaden the interest of the material— opening of the book "reads like a novel" as a friend remarked—without sacrificing the scientific rigor of its exposition.[19]

A key turning point was the expansion of student enrollments at American universities in the 1960s associated with the post–World War II baby boom. This led to an expansion in the number of anthropology departments, which in turn led to considerably more anthropology majors. This meant teachers, if they wanted to be published, no longer had to write primarily for public audiences. They could write books solely for students taking anthropology courses. This trend continues today. Academically oriented publishers find it profitable to focus on classroom sales for anthropology books.

Especially striking is how anthropologists now frame their work. Today, anthropological publications often have a "turned inward" quality. Seeking a broader public is not a priority for many. As Andrew Abbott notes: "Professionals draw their self-esteem more from their own world than from the public's" today. Engagement with the public, he adds, "that is both their fundamental task and their basis for legitimacy becomes the province of low-status colleagues and para-professionals."[20] One sees this in the tendency for large introductory classes to be taught by lower-status professors and adjuncts. High-status, full professors tend to teach small courses in their specialties. Drawing on Mary Douglas, we might frame this effort to keep the broader public at bay—while accepting public funding—again in terms of purity and pollution. Moving beyond the academic pale may be perceived as making faculty impure—as "polluting" them. (Mead's failure to gain a prominent university position is a prime example.) The "pure" remain comfortably ensconced in anthropology departments producing work that few read outside the discipline.

## Is It Necessary to Differentiate Between *Public* and *Applied Anthropology?*

*While some anthropologists seek to make a clear delineation between applied and public anthropology, I personally am uneasy with this effort. The two fields overlap in some ways but not in others. They differ most prominently*

19    Firth (1975:4).
20    Abbott (1988:119).

*in how they developed. Applied anthropology, which originated in the 1940s, focuses on addressing social problems through the lens of anthropology. Public anthropology, started as a book series in the late 1990s, seeks to address broad public problems in public ways that lessen other people's suffering (as well as exposing the structures causing it).*

After I coined the term "public anthropology," I was under pressure to demarcate how the field differed from "applied anthropology." I wondered why various academics felt a need to make a clear delineation between ambiguously defined fields as if they could differentiate between them as between cars or football teams. I personally feel uneasy making precise delineations between overlapping fields, especially when there are bigger issues at stake: helping people. What follows is a suggestive sense of how the two fields differ, no more.

Let me start with how the two overlapping fields developed. Applied anthropology has its roots in late nineteenth-century American and British colonialism. The focus was on understanding how various indigenous groups lived in order to administer them more effectively. E. E. Evans-Pritchard's famous studies of the Nuer, for example, were financed by the British government of Anglo-Egyptian Sudan to understand why the Nuer were opposing colonial rule. The American Bureau of Ethnology had a similar aim. It sponsored precedent-setting studies by Frank H. Cushing, George A. Dorsey, Matilda C. Stevenson, and James Mooney to understand the dynamics of how certain North American Indian tribes were changing under American domination.

In 1941 a group of anthropologists formally established the Society for Applied Anthropology "to promote the investigation of the principles of human behavior and the application of these principles to contemporary issues and problems." The society's opening statement in its journal notes that "*Applied Anthropology* is designed not only for scientists, but even more for those concerned with putting plans into operation, administrators, psychiatrists, social workers, and all those who as part of their responsibility have to take action on problems of human relations."[21] Today, the Society's website repeats the first sentence ("to promote the investigation of") and then continues: "The society is unique among professional associations in membership and purpose, representing the interests of professionals in a wide range of settings—academia, business, law, health and medicine, government, etc. The unifying factor is a commitment to making an

---

21    Applied Anthropology (1941:2).

impact on the quality of life in the world."[22] In a recent review of the field, Trotter, Schensul, and Kostick write that applied anthropology tends to have a pragmatic, practical orientation focused on direct interventions and policy changes as well as improving anthropological theory as it relates to such interventions.[23]

Public anthropology grew out of a different context. I coined the term to give an upbeat, positive name to the California book series I was developing in the late 1990s (though, as just noted, its basic idea is much older). Why did I not use "applied anthropology" in the series title? I wanted something new that could catch people's attention. "Applied anthropology" no longer had the same innovative buzz that it had in the 1940s-1960s. This chapter, and more broadly this book, provides my sense of what public anthropology entails.

Personally, I feel uncomfortable getting caught up in what Sigmund Freund called the "narcissism of small differences" – related groups arguing over small differences to differentiate their identities? There are too many serious problems for anthropology to address.

Take, as an example, the anthropologist Ben Finney. Challenging Sharp's assertion that Polynesia was settled accidentally by unskilled navigators, Finney became a leading advocate that Polynesia was intentionally settled by Polynesians highly skilled in the art of open-ocean navigation, able to travel across thousands of miles guided by the stars and waves. In 1973, he co-founded the Polynesian Voyaging Society and served as its first president. The Polynesian Voyaging Society became the lead organization in building the Hokule'a, a 62-foot-long double hull canoe. He was a part of the initial crew that sailed the Hokule'a by celestial navigation to Tahiti in 1976. Later he helped crew the trips to New Zealand (Aotearoa) in 1985 and Rarotonga in 1992. Quoting Nainoa Thompson, the Polynesian Voyaging Society's current president and a prominent figure in the Hawaiian Cultural Renaissance movement, the voyage of the Hokule'a "changed the whole identity of the Hawaiian people. We went from being castaways . . . to being children of the world's greatest navigators, . . . We owe it to our visionaries . . . and Ben was the first."[24]

I do not see what is gained by trying to attach applied or public to Ben Finney's work. What he did was impressive. He played a leading role in the resurrection of Hawaiian voyaging and, through that, the Hawaiian Cultural Renaissance.

22    See the Society for Applied Anthropology, https://www.sfaa.net/ (accessed October 5, 2017).
23    Trotter, Schensul, and Kostick (2015:661).
24    Kubota (2018).

# Why a More Socially Engaged Public Anthropology Has Not Taken Root

*A focus on public engagement, on benefitting others, is not new to the discipline. But it has fluctuated in importance. It might be seen as an anti-structure in Turner's terms—as periodically arising as an alternative mode of stressing anthropology's value. In charting a way forward, the public anthropology paradigm must be careful to not get drawn too deeply into the hegemonic-like structures that limit anthropology's potential benefit to others. Four public anthropology strategies suggest its paradigm-shifting intent.*

Since at least the founding of the Bureau of Ethnology in 1879 under John Wesley Powell, American anthropologists have sought to address problems faced by various groups of people. Prominent in those early years was the work of James Mooney, who described the Ghost Dance, a religion sweeping Indian tribes of the American West in 1889 and 1890 in response to American domination. He provided vivid details regarding a cavalry massacre of more than two hundred Sioux at Wounded Knee on December 29, 1890. The commitment to social engagement continued into the twentieth century, even as anthropology became institutionalized as an academic field within universities. As noted, Boas was very much an activist. He opposed racist theories popular in the United States and Europe during the 1930s. Anthropologists, moreover, were actively involved in the Allied war effort during World War II. Cora Du Bois, discussed in Chapter 2, served with the Office of Strategic Services. She was awarded the Army's Exceptional Civilian Award as well as the Order of the Crown by Thailand.[25]

Mead noted that anthropologists coming out of the war years realized "their skills could be applied fruitfully to problems affecting modern societies and the deliberations of national governments and nation states."[26] In the 1960s anthropologists such as Marvin Harris and Marshall Sahlins played prominent roles in establishing the first "teach-ins"—activist public discussions held at universities—opposing the Vietnam War. They wrote pieces in widely read publications such as *The Nation* and *Dissent*.[27]

25    Fowler (1991).
26    Mead (1973:1–2).
27    See, e.g., Sahlins (2005:229–260).

In the late 1980s public engagement was once again popular in the discipline. In 1972, 88 percent of new PhDs were employed in academic settings, and just 12 percent were employed in nonacademic ones. But in 1988, 54 percent were employed in nonacademic settings.[28] This change in the job market both symbolized and encouraged increased engagement with those outside the discipline. In 1997, 71 percent of new PhDs were hired for academically related positions and 29 percent for nonacademic positions.[29] In 2016, roughly 80 percent held academic positions. The other 20 percent worked in nonacademic research, nonprofits, for-profits, or the government or were self-employed.[30] As we see, efforts at wider engagement often languish over time. The efforts of Boas, Harris, and Sahlins are still remembered, but only some emulate their efforts today.

In considering why a more engaged anthropology has not fully taken root in cultural anthropology, let me suggest three points. First, despite the institutionalized structures and hegemonic-like frameworks limiting public outreach (discussed in Chapter 1), public engagement seems to repeatedly return to excite the discipline. Why? Victor Turner's concept of anti-structure offers an answer. As previously noted, Turner highlights "two alternative 'models' for human relations. One involves society as a structured, differentiated, and often hierarchical system of politico-legal-economic positions."[31] The other, termed "anti-structure," opposes society's formal structures, emphasizing instead alternative, less conforming orientations. He writes that "there would seem to be—if one can use such a controversial term—a human 'need' to participate in both modalities."[32] Public engagement is not precisely the same as Turner's anti-structure. Still, it emphasizes a different form of accountability from standard academic practice. It reaches out to others beyond the discipline. It supports a different style of prose. It focuses on actively addressing the world's problems.

Since many anthropologists tend to be ensconced in departmental structures, one might suspect many periodically long for greater social engagement and public recognition. They tire of the narrow, inward-looking academic structures that pervade the field. They reach out, seeking to engage the public on its own terms, not theirs. But their efforts usually do not last—they lack the structural support that would allow these efforts to be more than momentary bursts of

28   Givens and Jablonski (2000).
29   Givens and Jablonski (2000).
30   Ginsberg (2016).
31   Turner (1969:96).
32   Turner (1969:203).

enthusiasm against the hegemonic-like structures of the academy. In this context, anthropologists' attempts at stronger social engagement are momentary defiances of the established academic order. With time, most anthropologists are drawn back into the professional grind centered on academic standards of accountability and pursuing their separate interests in their separate ways.

Second, applied anthropology has an ambiguous relationship with mainstream academic anthropology. On the one hand, applied anthropologists should feel proud that they have resisted the academic structures of the discipline better than any other well-established group in the discipline's history. They have their own formal association (the Society for Applied Anthropology), annual meeting, and journal (*Human Organization*). Applied anthropology is often described as a major disciplinary subfield (along with cultural anthropology, archaeology, biological anthropology, and linguistics). On the other hand, applied anthropology has succeeded by adopting certain academic structures. Despite a determined effort to engage those outside the academy, a sizable number of applied anthropologists hold university positions. There are a few reasons for this. To become a certified applied anthropologist, one needs a graduate degree. The field can only reproduce itself if a number of applied anthropologists remain in universities to train new generations of applied anthropologists. Also, given that applied anthropology is now very much a part of the discipline, anthropology departments are a prime source of paid positions. Many of the applied anthropologists who attend the Society's annual meeting and publish in its journal are academics. They give the meeting and journal an academic feel while, at the same time, claiming to be distinct from mainstream anthropology.

Third, if the public anthropology paradigm is to avoid the fate of earlier efforts—that is, to not get drawn back into the university-based hegemonic-like structures it is resisting—it must reflect on how to shift the discipline's paradigmatic focus. It needs to reframe the underlying hegemonic-like structures that repeatedly limit public engagement. This means rethinking what cultural anthropology does and how it does it. I suggest four strategies that emphasize the paradigm-shifting intent of the public anthropology paradigm.

## Benefitting Others

*The public anthropology paradigm seeks to move beyond "doing no harm"—demonstrating how anthropology actually benefits other people in ways that they recognize and appreciate. Early anthropology was frequently associated with colonialism. Even today there is a sense that First World researchers often study those less powerful than themselves in Third/Fourth World societies. In seeking guidelines for differentiating between the rhetoric and reality of helping others, this section compares the Vicos Project of highland Peru with the CIMA/ SIM project in Micronesia.*

This section's focus on benefitting others matches the National Science Foundation's concern with "the potential to benefit society and contribute to the achievement of specific, desired, societal outcomes."[33] It also fits with the National Institutes of Health's (NIH) emphasis on "proposals of high scientific caliber that are relevant to public health needs."[34] In addition, it corresponds to the "common rule" of beneficence applied by fourteen US federal departments and agencies. Fitting with the Belmont Report of 1974, "beneficence" includes making efforts to secure people's well-being and maximizing possible research benefits for them.[35]

The focus on benefitting others needs to be placed in historical context. Since its disciplinary beginnings, cultural anthropology has tended to be the study of less powerful groups by scholars from more powerful groups. Whether you phrase it as the First World studying the Third World, "us" studying "them," or the richer studying the poorer, there is usually a power differential involved. Those with more power are studying those with less. Anthropologists do not return empty-handed from their research. They return with knowledge that they then systematically circulate to others in the form of publications and lectures. In most cases, this knowledge circulation enhances their careers. Few anthropologists make thousands of dollars from their publications and lectures. But most anthropologists make hundreds of thousands of dollars over their careers. The publications constitute critical stepping-stones for professional advancement.

The less powerful, then, give something of value to the more powerful who are studying them. Anthropologists—out of respect, kindness, guilt, or a combination of all three—tend to provide a host of compensating gifts. But rarely do these gifts add up to the monetary value anthropologists earn as they advance through their academic careers based on visiting and writing about the less

33    See NSF (2013).

34    NIH (2017). Paralleling these perspectives, the United Kingdom's Research Councils (RCUK) stresses a commitment "to supporting and rewarding researchers to engage with the public" (n.d.)

35    See the Belmont Report, https://www.hhs.gov/ohrp/regulations-and-policy/belmont -report/read-the-belmont-report/index.html#xbenefit.

powerful. This is not to say the power differential goes unnoticed. It is widely perceived by all the parties involved. The indigenous filmmaker Vilsoni Hereniko asks, for example: "Do outsiders have the right to speak for and about Pacific Islanders? . . . Westerners seem to think they have the right to express opinions (sometimes labeled truths) about cultures that are not their own in such a way that they appear to know it from the inside out. . . . The least that outsiders can do . . . is to invite indigenous Pacific Islanders, whenever possible, to share the space with them, either as co-presenters or as discussants or respondents. Not to do so is to perpetuate unequal power relations between colonizer and colonized."[36] Prins notes that "the image made in Accra to commemorate the achievement of political independence by Ghana shows the fleeing agents of colonialism. Along with the [administrative] District Officer is the anthropologist, clutching under his arm a copy of Fortes and Evans-Pritchard's *African Political Systems*."[37]

Some cultural anthropologists acknowledge the problem in their writings. Claude Lévi-Strauss observes: "It is an historical fact that anthropology was born and developed in the shadow of colonialism."[38] Talal Asad writes: "It is not a matter of dispute that social anthropology emerged as a distinctive discipline at the beginning of the colonial era, that it became a flourishing academic profession towards its close, or that throughout this period its efforts were devoted to a description and analysis—carried out by Europeans, for a European audience—of non-European societies dominated by European power." Anthropology is, he continues, "rooted in an unequal power encounter . . . that gives the West access to cultural and historical information about the societies it has progressively dominated."[39]

We should be cautious. The broad outline is clear, but there are shades of gray that also need to be taken into account. James Clifford notes that while colonial domination framed most early anthropological accounts, cultural anthropologists "adopted a range of liberal positions within it. Seldom 'colonists' in any direct instrumental sense, ethnographers accepted certain constraints while, in varying degrees, questioning them."[40] What concerns me here is how cultural anthropologists, once they acknowledge this power differential, respond to it.

36  Hereniko in Borofsky, ed. (2000:86).
37  Prins as quoted in Kuper and Kuper (1985:870).
38  Lévi-Strauss (1994:425).
39  Asad (1973:14–15, 16–17).
40  Clifford (1983:142).

Many offer forms of appreciation to informants: gifts, money, and/or help. A decent percentage of anthropologists, moreover, continue contact with informants long after they, the anthropologists, have left the field. Interestingly, pre–World War II issues of *American Anthropologist* published obituaries of key informants. This suggests that many informants held honorable, publicly acknowledged places within the discipline during this period.[41] But at a broader level, the abstract formulations anthropologists offer for addressing this power differential, while frequently sounding nice, tend to perpetuate the power structures.

We see this in a 1967 report by Ralph Beals titled "International Research Problems in Anthropology: A Report from the USA." Beals takes note of certain problems that have come before the Committee on Research Problems and Ethics. He writes: "Visiting anthropologists collect data in order to make money from books or to get degrees; they 'mine' the host country and give nothing in return. . . . Visiting anthropologists do not cooperate with their colleagues in the host country or contribute to the development of anthropology in the host count."[42]

Contrary to popular belief, the Hippocratic Oath that medical students affirm on becoming doctors does not primarily focus on "do no harm." The original phrasing of the oath in Epidemics, book I, section II is: "As to disease make a habit of two things—help, or at least, to do no harm." As noted in Chapter 1, the phrase "first, do no harm" is attributed to Thomas Sydenham, a seventeenth-century English physician.[43] When things are falling apart politically and economically in a society, I would question whether doing no harm is a reasonable standard to follow. There is self-absorption in the "do no harm" framing: the injunction implies that we—the outsiders, the Westerners, the powerful—are the major source of other people's troubles. If we leave others alone, everything should be fine. In the case discussed below, the troubles of the Ik people in Uganda did not stem from actions by the West but from specific actions by the Ugandan government.

What does "do no harm" mean when informants have been suffering—perhaps for decades—before you arrive? Do you try to help lessen their pain, help address their problems? Or do you sidestep them, believing that since you did

---

41    While this happens less often today, it still does occur (see Casagrande [1960] and McIlwraith [2017]).

42    Beals (1967:473).

43    See Bartleby.com, http://www.bartleby.com/73/847.html (accessed October 5, 2017); also see Sydenham referred to in Wikipedia, s.v. "Primum non nocere".

not cause them, they are not *your* problem? The Ik offer an example of the issues at stake. Bordering on starvation, the Ik were falling apart as a society when Colin Turnbull studied them. The back cover of the 1987 paperback edition of Turnbull's book explains: "In *The Mountain People*, Colin M. Turnbull . . . describes the dehumanization of the Ik, African tribesmen who in less than three generations have deteriorated from being once-prosperous hunters to scattered bands of hostile, starving people whose only goal is individual survival. . . . Drought and starvation have made them a strange, heartless people, . . . their days occupied with constant competition and the search for food."[44]

How does one respond to a situation such as this? K. Anthony Appiah ponders why "the former general secretary of Racial Unity [i.e., Turnbull] had done so little to intervene? Why had he not handed over more of his own rations? Taken more children to the clinic in his Land Rover? Gone to the government authorities and told them that they needed to allow the Ik back into their hunting grounds or give them more food?"[45] Turnbull took a group-dictated letter to government authorities at Moroto concerning the Ik's plight. "I delivered the letter and a report of my own, without much conviction that either would carry any weight."[46] And when they apparently did not, he went off to the capital, Kampala, to stock up with fresh supplies for himself. That was it: no insistence, no pleading, no seeking to bring pressure on local authorities from those higher up, no public exposé with the hope of helping the Ik.[47]

What Turnbull did, instead, is offer a general reflection on the state of humanity: "Most of us are unlikely to admit readily that we can sink as low as the Ik, but many of us do, and with far less cause. . . . Although the experience was far from pleasant, and involved both physical and mental suffering, I am grateful for it. In spite of it all, . . . the Ik teach us that our much vaunted human values are not inherent in humanity at all, but are associated only with a particular form of survival called society, and that all, even society itself, are luxuries that can be dispensed with."[48] Keeping the issue at an abstract level—reflecting on what the Ik teach us about ourselves—means the power differential is never addressed. The anthropologist remains an observer of other people's suffering and, in Turnbull's case, deaths.

---

44 Turnbull (1987).
45 Appiah (2000:58).
46 Turnbull (1987:109).
47 See also Grinker (2000:166).
48 Turnbull (1987:12, 294); see also Grinker (2000:156, 163).

The American Anthropological Association's statements on ethics for 1998, 2009, and 2012 offer a study in how it has sought to navigate through this issue over time. With each succeeding statement, the focus on research benefitting those one works with and "doing no harm" to their communities becomes less assertive. The 1998 code states: "Anthropological researchers have primary ethical obligations to the people, species, and materials they study and to the people with whom they work. . . . To consult actively with the affected individuals or group(s), with *the goal of establishing a working relationship that can be beneficial to all parties involved. . . . Anthropological researchers must do everything in their power to ensure that their research does not harm the safety, dignity, or privacy of the people with whom they work,* conduct research, or perform other professional activities."[49]

The 2009 code repeats the first part of the 1998 code but then, in the final section, offers a slightly different emphasis: "In conducting and publishing their research, or otherwise disseminating their research results, anthropological *researchers must ensure that they do not harm the safety, dignity, or privacy of the people with whom they work,* conduct research, or perform other professional activities, or who might reasonably be thought to be affected by their research."[50] Instead of emphasizing "guidelines for making ethical choices" (as the 1998 and 2009 do), the 2012 Principles of Professional Responsibility refers to "resources to assist anthropologists in tackling difficult ethical issues." It continues:

> A primary ethical obligation shared by anthropologists is to do no harm . . . *each researcher think through the possible ways that the research might cause harm. Among the most serious harms that anthropologists should seek to avoid are harm to dignity, and to bodily and material well-being,* especially when research is conducted among vulnerable populations. . . . Anthropologists may choose to link their research to the promotion of well-being, social critique or advocacy. As with all anthropological work, *determinations regarding what is in the best interests of others or what kinds of efforts are appropriate to increase well-being are value-laden and should reflect sustained discussion with others concerned.*[51]

49    American Anthropological Association (1998), emphasis added.
50    American Anthropological Association (2009), emphasis added.
51    American Anthropological Association (2012), emphasis added. Compensation for another person's help is mentioned in the 1998 and 2009 codes but only in reference to students and trainees, not informants. The 2012 code affirms that "anthropologists should appropriately acknowledge all contributions to their research, writing, and other related activities, and compensate contributors justly for any assistance they provide." Presumably, this includes informants.

There is no simple answer to resolving the power differential embedded in the ethnographic endeavor. It is not from want of caring that the problem remains the uninvited guest in many anthropological publications and at many anthropological meetings. Most anthropologists care about helping those who so caringly helped them. The problem is embedded in contexts of power that shape this relationship.

## A CAUTION

A note of caution is in order. Neither "do no harm" nor "benefitting others" is easily defined in any all-encompassing way. The two terms seem best delineated as contrasts with one another. But there are shades of meaning and complications in the way the two paradigms approach the problem. We can see this through a case study, the Yanomami fieldwork of Napoleon Chagnon and James Neel.

The Yanomami are an Amazonian group living on the border of Venezuela and Brazil. Chagnon's accounts of the group, especially an article published in *Science,* were used by Brazilian politicians wanting to cut up a planned large Yanomami reserve into several smaller ones.[52] They justified their plan, they said, on Chagnon's ethnographic research that implied the Yanomami were too violent to interact with one another. In fact, however, what the Brazilian politicians really wanted was more land for gold mining. (A large reserve was established in 1992.) Chagnon spoke out against the politicians' abuse of his work. But he did so only in the English-speaking press, not in Brazil's Portuguese-speaking press. For the Yanomami and their Brazilian and international supporters, the negative consequences of Chagnon not speaking out in the Brazilian press seemed clear. We might, in fairness to Chagnon, ask: Given the gold resources in the Yanomami reserve, would the Brazilian politicians have been less vociferous in their opposition to the large reserve if Chagnon had never written about the Yanomami?[53]

The difficulty in resolving to what degree Chagnon "did harm" became clear when the American Anthropological Association (AAA) sought to reprimand him. A formal AAA-constituted body, the El Dorado Task Force, sanctioned Chagnon for various actions among the Yanomami. Later in protest over the sanction, the issue was put before the whole association in a referendum. Despite

---

52    Chagnon (1988).
53    See Borofsky et al. (2005:80–82).

considerable publicity to encourage voting, roughly 11 percent of the member-ship participated.[54] While the vote overturned the sanction, the matter today remains hotly disputed.

Turning to the work of James Neel among the Yanomami, we perceive some of the complications in "benefitting others." Neel, viewed by some as the father of modern human genetics, began his research among the Yanomami in 1966. One may infer from his actions and writings that he felt doing research among the Yanomami—specifically collecting their blood samples for analysis—involved an obligation to provide something in return for their assistance. When Neel learned the Yanomami were susceptible to measles, he brought over two thousand doses of the Edmonson B vaccine (that he obtained at minimal cost from the Centers for Disease Control) to vaccinate the group against a potential deadly measles epidemic. Half of this supply he gave to the Venezuelan govern-ment to distribute. (What happened to that vaccine is not known.) Neel planned to hand the rest over to missionaries for an inoculation campaign. But when a measles epidemic unexpectedly broke out, he scrapped this plan and began a vaccination campaign himself to minimize the epidemic's impact. Neel was only partially successful. He inoculated many Yanomami. A number, however, had adverse reactions to the vaccine because he failed to include immune gamma globulin (MIG). (He had given much of his gamma globulin to the Venezuelan authorities.) Regretfully, a number of Yanomami died.[55]

Some praised Neel's attempt to save Yanomami lives. Others have suggested that he helped spread the epidemic through his research or at least aggravated the problem by using the Edmonson B vaccine, without immune gamma glob-ulin. If he had purchased a more expensive measles vaccine, they suggest, the Yanomami would have had fewer adverse reactions. Today, the Yanomami rarely mention Neel's assistance.

Despite these complications, there are guidelines both Chagnon and Neel might have followed that would have made things less muddled. Much of the discussion surrounding Chagnon's work centers on whether he harmed the Yanomami. There is little discussion of to what degree the Yanomami benefitted from his research. Chagnon mostly helped the Yanomami by providing them with trade goods. However, the royalties from Chagnon's Yanomami books amounted to well over a million dollars. There is no indication that he ever

54    See Darkness in El Dorado; see also Borofsky et al. (2005:289–313) "The Eldorado Task Force Reports."

55    Borofsky et al. (2005:84–86).

shared a portion of this money with them. Might they have been more positively disposed to Chagnon—despite what he did or did not write—if he had?

In Neel's case, it is clear that the Yanomami were barely consulted regarding his research. Neel decided to conduct his research without first gaining Yanomami permission. And he decided, on his own, what the reciprocal benefit of his research would be. Might his efforts to help the Yanomami—then and now—be perceived more positively if he had seriously consulted them regarding what he planned to do and how he hoped to help them? It certainly would have made for a better working relationship between Neel and the Yanomami during the measles epidemic.

## SOME POINTS TO PONDER

Let me suggest some points to ponder to help readers sort through the complications of trying to help others. Despite "do no harm" being central to the American Anthropological Association's code of ethics, it is both out of date and somewhat self-serving. The basic concept is drawn from the early 1900s, when anthropologists tended to differentiate themselves from missionaries and colonial administrators who sought to reshape indigenous societies. Anthropologists did not want to be part of that effort. But this early context no longer holds. The "do no harm" ethic is now self-serving in that it allows anthropologists to skirt certain moral dilemmas and obligations. When you ask people for help—such as in your research—you are usually expected to return the favor in some form at some time. Reciprocity is a key principle of social relations (articulated by Marcel Mauss in the anthropological classic *The Gift*).[56]

One clear priority is providing benefits back to those who helped in one's research. Tad McIlwraith emphasizes that, as anthropologists, we should be sure our work benefits "the groups of people who have shared with us their lives and entrusted us with their stories."[57] The key question is not whether you, the researcher, feel you have benefitted them through your research. The question is whether they perceive concrete benefits from your research and appreciate them. In consulting with those you are trying to help and sharing the accrued benefits gained from research with them, it is perhaps wisest to work with socially constituted groups, especially those respected by most of your informants. Consulting with a group, rather than a few select individuals, means there will be

56    Mauss (1954).
57    McIlwraith (2018).

broader structural support for your research and your efforts to help. Working with respected socially constituted groups also means your efforts to provide something in return for their help will be more effective, more enduring, and more widely distributed. There will be more collective appreciation, less individual jealousy. Even if your efforts are less than successful than you'd hoped, working with these groups acknowledges and empowers them.

Philippe Bourgois suggests, in cultural anthropology, "the power relations that create the worlds of the people they study and cause them to suffer disproportionately . . . are usually glaringly absent from . . . ethnographies." He continues: "[In] focusing our discussion of ethnography onto fascinating, hypertextual topics we do not threaten significant power structures. Our debates over the politics of representation are of little real consequence to the blood, sweat and tears of everyday life that ethnographers by definition encounter on the ground and even in discourse, but usually fail to write against." He suggests, as Nancy Scheper-Hughes does, that anthropologists should "conduct ethnographies of actually existing social suffering."[58] It makes their suffering real to others and, hopefully, through making such suffering more public, offers paths—through explicit action by those with power—to alleviate it. This may sound idealistic. But it certainly happens, as we saw in the summer of 2018 with the Trump administration's separation of immigrant parents and infants along the southern US border being overturned through public pressure.

### A COMPARISON

Given the complications of sorting through seeking to benefit others, it might be best if we consider a contrast between two prominent anthropological projects—the Coordinated Investigation of Micronesian Anthropology (CIMA) and the Vicos Project. In the post–World War II period, CIMA represented "the largest research project in the history of American anthropology." It involved roughly 10 percent of the American anthropological profession in fieldwork for the US Navy, who at the time administered Micronesia for the United States. The goal was to help decision makers make better decisions. On the one hand, both CIMA and the Scientific Investigation of Micronesia (SIM) that followed it had a profound impact on the profession. Mac Marshall concluded that roughly 6 percent of all anthropology PhDs granted from 1948 to 1994 derive directly or indirectly from CIMA and the Scientific Investigation of Micronesia (SIM) proj-

---

58    Bourgois (2002:217, 219); see also Scheper-Hughes (1993).

ect that followed it. Marshall observes: "The CIMA, SIM, and other programs in Micronesia in the decade following World War II . . . created a splash of such magnitude that the ripples continue to move across the discipline today. Those who participated . . . had a major hand in redirecting postwar anthropology in America, contributed importantly to anthropological theory and method, trained subsequent generations of Oceanists . . . and assumed major leadership positions that have helped shape the course of American anthropology over the past half century." On the other hand, CIMA and SIM had much less impact on Micronesia and Micronesians. Robert Kiste notes "that anthropology had little influence on the development of health care and legal systems in the trust territory."[59]

The reason derives from a disconnect between anthropologists and administrators. Whatever overtures one or the other group made, the relationship between the two ultimately revolved around each doing their own tasks without seriously engaging with the other's perspectives, the other's modus operandi. Important decisions regarding Micronesia were, by and large, made in Washington—in some cases, these were initiated before the anthropological research that was supposed to inform such decisions. While anthropologists might be subsequently consulted, particularly in relation to education where funding was limited, they were significantly less involved in questions of health, medicine, or the judiciary. Citing Judge King, Kiste comments: "There was never any dialogue between anthropologists and the judiciary in regard to fundamental questions about the nature and role of the courts in Micronesia."[60] Elsewhere, Kiste and Falgout write: "Mutual animosity frequently characterized the relations between anthropologists and administrators . . . [and] anthropologists' suggestions about administrative practices were often disliked."[61] In summary, CIMA and SIM seemed to have ended up benefitting American anthropology far more than the Micronesians for a fairly simply reason—a political disconnect existed between the anthropologists and the administrators. Neither really took the other's perspectives seriously into account, or seriously enough, to adjust their ways of operating.

The Vicos Project in the highlands of Peru was more successful in helping the indigenous population. In 1952, guided by Alan Holmberg, Cornell University leased Vicos, a Peruvian highland hacienda (farm) with roughly eighteen

59   Kiste and Marshall (1999: front cover, 427, see also 404, 449).
60   Kiste and Marshall (1999:450).
61   Kiste and Falgout in Kiste and Marshall (1999:36).

hundred Quechua-speaking residents, to help improve their condition. According to Paul Doughty, who participated in the project and revisited Vicos years later: "In the decades since the end of the project [officially in 1966], the community experienced numerous successes as well as failures as an independent community. Its attempts to diversify the economic base were often thwarted [by others] and the farming enterprise was affected by plant diseases [and] bad market prices. . . . For several years from 1974–80, self-serving government manipulations left the people in the community confused, corrupted their leadership, and eroded their confidence."[62] Still, Doughty concluded that the Vicosinos had "altered their society from one of denigrated serfdom and subordination to become an autonomous community of Quechua highlanders fending for themselves on a par with others in Peru's complex and uncertain milieu."[63]

A pivotal step in this success was the Vicosinos' purchasing of their land in 1962. A study found that "between 1952 and 1957 Holmberg, with colleagues and students, initiated a set of social, economic, and agrarian changes. . . . By the end of a second lease in 1962, sufficient political pressure had been brought to bear . . . to force the sale of Vicos to its people."[64] In 1962, Edward Kennedy visited Vicos and because the Peruvian president, Pedro Beltrán, was attempting to obtain funding under the "Alliance for Progress" from the US government, Kennedy was able to end the roadblock that was preventing the sale of land to the Vicosinos.[65]

The difference between Vicos and CIMA/SIM was that the anthropologists involved in the Vicos Project helped the Vicosinos connect with larger political processes that helped facilitate significant change. The Vicos Project is not without its critics. Still, it has had clear positive effects. Quoting Barbara Lynch: "The project was a highly qualified success. The terms of Vicos integration into Peruvian society became somewhat less exploitative as a result of project activities. In general, Vicosinos became better fed. Housing and education improved for some. Increasing command of Spanish allowed a larger segment of the population to engage in economic transactions with Huaraz and Marcara merchants on

---

62   Doughty (2002:238).

63   Doughty (2002:239). See also Lynch (1982: especially pp. ii–iv, 86ff).

64   Greaves, Bolton, and Zapata (2011:viii).

65   "Edward Kennedy who was planning to run for the senate, along with faculty and students from Harvard, visited Vicos and he was moved by the stories told by Vicosinos about their efforts to buy the hacienda. He intervened and the government finally facilitated the sale" (Vicos [n.d.]). See also Doughty (1987:433–459).

more equal terms. The standard of living in Vicos rose faster than that of neighboring communities and towns, and Vicosinos became less diffident and more confident about expressing their needs and demanding their due."[66] CIMA and SIM ultimately benefitted American anthropology and American anthropologists more than it did the Micronesians. But, in Vicos, anthropologists assisted the Vicosinos to alter established social structures, and these changes, despite various setbacks, helped improve the standard of living for the Vicosinos. Whatever the project's limitations, it clearly proved beneficial to the Vicosinos. It helped them as much, if not more, than the anthropologists who worked with them and published books about them.

## Fostering Alternative Forms of Faculty Accountability

*Academic accountability can be defined in various ways. This section moves beyond the treadmill of publications discussed in Chapter 2 and the metrics frequently used today to assess faculty "productivity" to focus on outcomes—the degree to which a research project benefits others beyond the academy. We might ask: How significant is the problem being addressed? To what degree does the author successfully address it? Does it improve other people's lives? This section makes its point through three examples: Jeffrey Sachs's Millennium Villages Project, Gerald F. Murray and M. E. Bannister's reforestation project in Haiti, and Abhijit Banerjee, Esther Duflo, Dean Karlan, and Jacob Appel's work on randomized controlled trials.*

It is important to understand what is at stake with accountability standards. They are not innocent suggestions. They constitute hegemonic-like structures that universities use to shape faculty behavior. They could be used to maintain the "do no harm" paradigm, or they could be used to help move faculty toward an alternative set of standards embraced by the public anthropology paradigm. The "benefitting others" strategy is a suggestive ideology, but it is not grounded in concrete, enforceable social structures. The accountability standards are. They shape faculty careers—what faculty need to do to progress from junior to senior professor. There is no escaping them in academia.

Instead of emphasizing quantitative calculations—publishing X articles or books per year—the public anthropology paradigm encourages academic administrators to use standards framed in more pragmatic terms—not how

---

66    Lynch (1982:98). See also Greaves, Bolton, and Zapata (2011).

many publications faculty have produced but how effective they have been in addressing problems of broader social concern. Administrators might ask: How significant is the problem being addressed in a publication or project? To what degree does the author (or authors) successfully address it? What impact does this effort have on those beyond the academy? Does it improve other people's lives in large and/or small ways?

The paradigm's standards offer a way to escape the pull of the metric standards (a point discussed in Chapter 5). The paradigm's standards emphasize more qualitative studies. Marcia McNutt, the editor-in-chief of *Science* journals, stresses that "data, particularly those collected with public funding, should be used so that they do the most good."[67] Robert J. Jones, the president of the University of Albany, suggests: "Public research universities in particular have a responsibility to work with communities . . . to solve some of the complex problems that face society. . . . [How could this be fostered?] You have to send that message to your faculty and staff, particularly the faculty on the tenure track, that the work they do in public engagement is not at the margins of the academic discipline but is at the core. It's very much valued, and it will count in consideration for advancement in the university."[68]

The alternative assessments of faculty productivity discussed below are not perfect. But neither are the current standards. These alternative standards, however, have an added benefit: Instead of focusing primarily on advancing individuals' careers and internal institutional agendas, they encourage faculty to focus on benefitting others beyond the academy—just what their institutions promise to do. The paradigm's focusing on impact, especially social impact, also subverts the fragmenting tendencies of specialized studies. It draws cultural anthropologists together toward a broader purpose. The downside of focusing on impact is that it takes time. Faculty cannot be assessed simply by how many publications they produce in a short period of time. But faculty can present progress reports that provide a sense of what a research project seeks to do and how successful it has been to date. It requires patience from administrators. There are alternative standards of faculty accountability than those mostly used today, ones that fit better with the hopes of both funders and universities. Given the ambiguities and complications that arise in generalizing across a range of cases, I focus on a few examples to clarify what is possible in assessing projects that strive for social impact.

---

67    McNutt (2015:7).
68    Quoted in Hebel (2016).

## JEFFREY SACHS

In considering Sachs's efforts to end extreme poverty, we might start with a question: Why, despite good intentions displayed by many Western donors in spending trillions of dollars to assist development in Third World countries, have the results been mixed at best? Why has such aid not proved more effective? Sachs, in his 2005 book *The End of Poverty*, writes that given the resources at our command, "the wealth of the rich world, the power of today's vast storehouses of knowledge, and the declining fraction of the world that needs help to escape from poverty all make the end of poverty a realistic possibility by the year 2025." Wikipedia offers a summary of the book: "Sachs argues that extreme poverty—defined by the World Bank as incomes of less than one dollar per day—can be eliminated globally by the year 2025, through carefully planned development aid. He presents the problem as an inability of very poor countries to reach the 'bottom rung' of the ladder of economic development; once the bottom rung is reached, a country can pull itself up into the global market economy, and the need for outside aid will be greatly diminished or eliminated."[69]

The book has attracted considerable attention. Nina Munk notes in her 2013 work, *The Idealist*, that Sachs's book "had been excerpted on the cover of *Time* magazine. It . . . made the *New York Times* best-seller list . . . [and has also been] translated into eighteen languages."[70] It became the basis for the 2008 movie *The End of Poverty?* To his credit, Sachs sought to do more than publish a plan for ending extreme poverty. He developed a plan to actually end it. He proved masterful at raising money. With the help of George Soros and other sources, Sachs raised close to the $120 million he thought was needed to launch a five-year project across Africa. A second stage of the project collected an additional $72 million in pledges.[71]

Did Sachs's Millennium Villages Project succeed in its stated goals? That is a matter of dispute as an article in the *Economist* explains. The article's subtitle is "Evidence that the millennium villages project is making a decisive impact is elusive." To continue:

> For something designed to improve lives in some of the poorest parts of the world, the Millennium Villages Project certainly stirs up a lot of bad blood. The project, the brain child of Jeffrey Sachs of Columbia University in New York, takes 14

---

69   Wikipedia, s.v. "The End of Poverty"

70   Munk (2013:1).

71   Munk (2013:40–41).

"villages" (mostly small areas) with around 500,000 people, and scales up aid to them in the hope of springing the poverty trap in which they are caught. Late in 2011, there was a flurry of accusation and rebuttal at the time of the first independent evaluation of one of the villages, Sauri in Kenya, which challenged some of the claims made on behalf of the villages. The *Economist* reviewed the dispute here and Mr. Sachs criticised our account. Now debate has erupted again, producing yet another round of criticism online, as well as duelling editorials in two leading British scientific journals. . . . The *Economist* concluded [a] previous article by saying that the evidence does not yet support the claim that the millennium villages project is making a decisive impact. That still seems about right.[72]

*Foreign Policy* reports in a 2013 review of Sachs's work: "In May 2012, shortly after an editorial in *Nature*, the influential science journal, scolded Sachs and his colleagues for unreliable analysis, Sachs and his team were forced to admit they had committed a basic error in an academic paper intended to prove their project's effectiveness. 'The project's approach has potential, but little can be said for sure yet about its true impact,' *Nature* stated." Later in the same article, author Paul Starobin observers: "As critics see it, Sachs botched his project by not putting in place a system by which progress (or lack thereof) at the Millennium Villages could be objectively measured, evaluated, and compared with trends in surrounding rural communities. 'The idea that it is a demonstration project has failed because we're seeing that the evaluation wasn't thought through enough,' says Jonathan Morduch, a prominent development economist at New York University's Wagner Graduate School of Public Service. 'It was a mistake and a real loss—a real loss for the world community.'"[73]

Munk helps clarify Sachs's position: "To focus on metrics—on 'sustainability' and 'scalability' . . .—is in Sachs' opinion, to reduce the lives of human beings to crude economic terms, to abstractions. 'We are not waiting fifteen years for results—we are trying to move as fast as possible to help people who are suffering.' In effect, he wanted us to trust him, to accept without question his approach to ending poverty, to participate in a kind of collective magical thinking."[74]

Despite the complexity of Sachs's project, assessing its benefits is not necessarily that hard. One only need conduct a Google search to discover a range of

72   Economist (2012).
73   Starobin (2013).
74   Munk (2013:217).

respectable sources that assess it. Certainly these sources are as valid and reliable as those currently employed to assess faculty publications—especially given many faculty feel their publications are mainly counted, not read. We might ask why Sachs did not pay closer attention to early failed efforts at development, to learn from their mistakes. A *Washington Post* review of his book states:

> Sachs pays surprisingly little attention to the history of aid approaches and results. He seems unaware that his . . . plan is strikingly similar to the early ideas that inspired foreign aid in the 1950s and '60s. Just like Sachs, development planners then identified countries caught in a "poverty trap," did an assessment of how much they would need to make a "big push" out of poverty and into growth, and called upon foreign aid to fill the "financing gap" between countries' own resources and needs. . . . Spending $2.3 trillion (measured in today's dollars) in aid over the past five decades has left the most aid-intensive regions, like Africa, wallowing in continued stagnation; it's fair to say this approach has not been a great success.[75]

We might also ask why, when things got difficult, did Sachs seem to lose interest in the project instead of redoubling his efforts, seeking new ways to address the problems faced? Munk reports:

> Officially, the Millennium Villages Project wasn't scheduled to end until 2015, yet it seemed to me that Sachs had distanced himself from his ongoing African experiment. His impassioned articles and speeches and interviews and tweets now centered on income equality in the United States, climate change, the collapse of Greece, tax reforms, greed on Wall Street, the decline of moral standards, chaos in the euro zone, gun control, and the political vacuum in Washington. He was all over the place. . . . Sachs was like a sawed-off shotgun, scattering ammunition in all directions, and the result was a watering down of his message, whatever the message happened to be.[76]

If, as suggested in Chapter 1, cultural anthropology can be an antidote to despair, we should acknowledge one result of the project, especially among those who deeply cared about it, was a sense of despair. Many people in the Millennium Villages felt despondent when, despite their best efforts, things mostly fell apart. Quoting Lia Haro, whose research focused on Sauri (one of Sachs's first

75  Easterly (2005).
76  Munk (2013:229, 231).

Millennium Villages): "People in Sauri consistently expressed dismay that the Project 'destroyed the community.'"[77] Near the end of Munk's book, she quotes a member of Sachs's inner circle: "In hindsight it's like we were set up to fail. . . . It's not that Jeff's ideas are wrong—he is a big, inspiring thinker. It's that the project's ambition moved more quickly than the capacity. It makes me feel like a chump. It makes me feel totally hollow."[78]

The pattern we see in the Millennium Villages Project is not unlike the trends discussed in Chapter 2. There is a hot flash of excitement, past work is dismissed, and the focus is on asserting a new and different future. But with time, the enthusiasm fades as initial hopes fail to be realized. The "advances" seem, in retrospect, to have less to do with intellectual progress—in which perspectives are refined and cumulative knowledge is built—than to do with the advancement of individual careers. Ultimately, Sachs did not come out better from the Millennium Project. As the above quotes suggest, there has been considerable criticism of the project. But, for a time at least, the project did enhance his status. He made a movie with Angelina Jolie, he counted Bono and Kofi Annan among his friends, and he was special advisor to Ban Ki-moon, the United Nations secretary-general. When a vacancy became available, Sachs nominated himself for the World Bank. There was even a campaign to encourage him to run for the US presidency.

### GERALD F. MURRAY

Murray is best known for initiating an anthropological-focused reforestation program in Haiti. Haiti's limited forest cover is widely publicized, often specified as covering only 2 percent of the country. Through the US AID program Agroforestry Outreach Project that Murray worked with, "more than 300,000 Haitian peasant households—over a third of the entire rural population of Haiti . . . [were able] to plant wood trees as a domesticated, income-generating crop on their holdings." The project has been widely recognized in anthropological circles. "Two years after its onset [in 1981], it won the international Anthropological Praxis Award, a competitive annual prize for applied anthropology. The project is now one of the most frequently cited cases of applied anthropology in recent college cultural anthropology textbooks (e.g., Robbins 1993, Nanda and

77    Haro (2017:8).
78    Haro (2017:8); Munk (2013:203).

Warms 1998, Peoples and Bailey 1997, Ferraro 1998, Harris and Johnson 2000). A description of the project has been reprinted in several editions of a widely circulated reader in applied anthropology (Podolefsky, Brown, and Lacy)."[79]

What is striking about the project is the number of studies confirming its success. From Murray and Bannister's 2004 article:

> The research scrutiny given to one project has been quite unusual. Pre-project feasibility investigations include Murray (1979i; 1981) and Smucker (1981). Two years after the project started Murray published the first description of the project (Murray 1984), followed by an analysis focusing on anthropological issues (Murray 1987). A project agroforester returned to villages where he had delivered trees three years earlier to examine their fate (Buffum 1985; Buffum and King 1985). One anthropologist wrote his doctoral dissertation on the project (Balzano 1989). Another anthropologist examined decision-making processes in a community of early tree planters (Conway 1986a) and synthesized the results of five additional studies of tree-planting communities done under the auspices of either PADF [Pan-American Development Foundation] or the University of Maine, a project research partner (Conway 1986b; Lauwerysen 1985). An economist calculated monetary returns to tree planters and documented higher-than-predicted internal rates of return (Grosenick 1986). Another economist examined the charcoal and pole markets (McGowan 1986), and Smucker (1988) analyzed six years of tree planting in several communities. In the early 1990s, Bannister and Nair (1990) discussed the soon-to-be expanded hedgerow component of the project, and Bannister and Josiah (1993) examined extension and training issues. An anthropologist/forester team (Smucker and Timyan 1995) did case studies that included harvest information. The following year Timyan (1996) published a volume on the trees of Haiti. Land-tenure issues were analyzed by Smucker et al. (2002). Most recently Bannister and Nair (2003) analyzed data from 1540 households and 2295 plots that had received project interventions.[80]

The Agroforestry Outreach Program involved the donation of funds to non-governmental organizations that distributed seedlings to interested peasants. In return for providing land (to plant the trees) and labor (in growing the trees),

79    Murray and Bannister (2004:383, 385); see Murray and Bannister (2004) for the referenced texts.
80    Murray and Bannister (2004:384–385); see Murray and Bannister (2004) for the referenced texts.

the peasants gained total control over the trees' ownership. It was not the first effort at reforesting Haiti. But with its anthropological focus—on giving peasants control over the donated trees—it was certainly the most successful. Quoting Murray and Bannister:

> The 65 million [donated] seedling figure for two decades, all voluntarily planted in small lots of several hundred or fewer by over 300,000 peasants on their own holdings, leaves absolutely no doubt as to the enthusiasm generated by the project for the planting of wood trees in a country where they were formerly extracted from nature.... With the project reaching a minimum of 350,000 households ... more than 40% and perhaps nearly 50% of the households of rural Haiti may have received seedlings or otherwise participated in the project at one point or another during the two decades. Even if these national participation figures are dropped by 10 or even 20 percentage points for "safety's sake," the level of nationwide involvement in and enthusiasm for a tree planting project must still be seen as unprecedented in the annals of agroforestry.[81]

Let me make two points. First, in contrast to Sachs, one cannot assess the benefits of Murray's (and Bannister's) project simply through a quick Google search for information. There are not that many references, certainly compared to Sachs. But as the above quotes make clear, there are considerable confirming data indicating the project's success. There is little doubt that the project was a significant success and brought considerable benefit to Haitians who grew the trees. But, and this is my second point, one might not realize the reforestation project was successful if one just read certain news sources. The *Guardian* reported in 2013: "Haiti aims to plant 50m trees a year in a pioneering reforestation campaign to address one of the primary causes of the country's poverty and ecological vulnerability. President Michel Martelly will launch the drive to double forest cover by 2016 from the perilous level of 2%—one of the lowest rates in the world.... The Dominican Republic, Haiti's neighbour on the Caribbean island of Hispaniola, has lush forests but satellite photos show Haiti is all but bare."[82] Laurent Dubois in the *New York Times* notes: "Foreign descriptions of the country frequently claim it is almost completely deforested."[83] Andrew Tarter reports in *EnviroSociety* that "virtually every single popular media description, development narrative, and academic account addressing deforestation in Haiti

---

81  Murray and Bannister (2004:387, 392).
82  Lall (2013).
83  Dubois (2016).

over the past five decades opens with the cliché citation of a grim and staggering statistic: only 2 percent of Haiti is forested."[84]

Yet Dubois goes on: "In fact, about a third of Haiti is covered in trees." Tarter observes, despite these negative reports, that "a recent analysis of high-resolution satellite imagery from 2010, triangulated through the ground truthing of hundreds of randomly selected locations throughout the country—suggest[s] a contemporary tree cover of approximately a third of the surface of Haiti."[85] What gives? Dubois suggests: "The country does have a deforestation problem—it's just more complicated than the world imagines." For the government and the NGOs seeking to help Haiti, the 2 percent figure has considerable value. It emphasizes the need for foreign aid to address the problem. As Murray reported in 2012 (relating to the Haitian earthquake of 2010): "Quite apart from the dilemma of a country with a non-functioning State, the NGOs themselves can be (and many big ones currently are) as predatory as any government. . . . There are hordes of NGOs, U.S. universities, and for-profit companies rubbing their hands in anticipation of a 'piece of the action' in the 'development' of post-earthquake Haiti. Billions of dollars have been pledged into what appears to be a lose-lose situation in which the principle beneficiaries will be the institutions and individuals contracted to manage the money and in which the people of Haiti themselves will see only a small fraction of the funds."[86]

This fits with what some others have reported about development projects. As Muhammad Yunus, the 2006 Nobel Peace Prize winner, noted in *Creating a World Without Poverty*: "Many antipoverty efforts are funded by well-intentioned people in the developed countries, either through NGOs, government grants, or international aid agencies. It's sad to see much of this money being invested in ways that are wasteful. In many cases money that is supposed to help the poor ends up creating business for companies and organizations in the developed world—training firms, suppliers of equipment and materials, consultants, advisers, and the like."[87]

So yes, despite Murray and Bannister's impressive work, much remains to be done in Haiti, especially after Hurricane Mathew in 2016. But all one has to do, to uncover both the benefits of Murray and Bannister's work and the distortions of it, is to compare the scientific documentation available (cited above) with

84   Dubois (2016); Tarter (2016).
85   Dubois (2016); Tarter (2016).
86   Murray (2012).
87   Yunus (2007:112–113).

various media references discovered through Google searches. In other words, the assessing of benefits produced and how others distort them for their own ends can be readily uncovered with a little research.

## ABHIJIT BANERJEE, ESTHER DUFLO, AND DEAN KARLAN

Banerjee and Duflo helped found MIT's J-PAL (or Abudul Latif Jameel Poverty Action Lab) and play prominent roles in its work. Karlan founded IPA (Innovations for Poverty Action). What is intriguing about their collective methodology—focusing on randomized controlled trials—is how few researchers had employed this methodology prior to their work. Given the money spent, one might think that researchers and funders would want to know which approaches work to what degree and in which contexts prior to spending millions on aid. Before J-PAL and IPA, such studies were comparatively rare. According to Munk, Sachs once asked Duflo for advice on how to measure the results of the Millennium Villages Project.[88] Sachs dismissed her randomized controlled trials approach, stating in an interview with the *New York Times*: "Millennium villages don't advance the way that one tests a new pill." Duflo was outraged, Munk reports. "He adopts this completely anti-scientific attitude. . . . I am not really asking for a crazy standard of proof, just comparing."

Banerjee and Duflo's methodology is well illustrated in *Poor Economics*.[89] The authors systematically explore what approaches work best for which aid problems in which contexts. For example, they asked: Which has a better chance of being used in a set of Indian villages—a malaria fighting net that is given away free to villagers, or a malaria fighting net that villagers have to partly pay for (and hence have an investment in using properly)? To learn the answer, they compared randomized groups in various locales involving different levels of financial support for the nets. With this information they were able to draw a conclusion regarding what is the best way to distribute nets in a range of Indian villages to fight malaria. The answer is that (a) everyone accepts free nets, but as the price goes up, fewer do, and (b) there is no difference in usage between those who obtain the nets free and those who have to pay for them. People value the nets—no matter how they get them—because they help fight malaria. The Nobel-winning author Robert Solow writes of *Poor Economics*: "Abhijit Banerjee and Esther Duflo are allergic to grand generalizations about the secret of eco-

---

88   Munk (2013:216–217).
89   Banerjee and Duflo (2011).

nomic development. Instead they appeal to many local observations and experiments to explore how poor people in poor countries actually cope with their poverty."[90]

We perceive the same focus in Dean Karlan and Jacob Appel's *More Than Good Intentions: Improving the Ways the World's Poor Borrow, Save, Farm, Learn, and Stay Healthy.*[91] They discuss a project to increase attendance in Kenyan primary schools through deworming. They note deworming "generated an additional year of attendance for about $3.50; the next best solution, providing free uniform, cost about twenty-five times that much. And that doesn't even consider the simple health benefits of being worm-free." Regarding combatting diarrhea, Karlan and Appel write: "Two million people do not need to die of diarrhea each year. . . . Treating drinking water with chlorine is a cheap and highly effective preventative measure" if people use it. "Despite the benefits of protection, distributing chlorine to households, even if free, has not proved effective enough. Yet providing free chlorine in an easy-to-use dispense at water collection points . . . has."[92]

Again, let me make two points. First, assessing who benefits and how from these individuals' work is fairly straightforward. They specify which approaches work well, which do not. Both J-PAL and IPA work with aid funders and governmental organizations. One can examine which governments implement J-PAL's and IPA's research with what results. Both organizations' websites carry details of the projects they have conducted in which contexts with what results as well as what various media report about them. For those who wish to explore the details further, they can read the media, funders, and government agencies' reports on these projects—using the links provided on the websites as a starting place and then conducting Google searches from there. Second, Chapter 2 noted that anthropologists assert they seek to refine earlier perspectives and/or build cumulative knowledge in their research. It is less than clear that many in fact do. One sees in Sachs's work, for example, the same rush for "trendiness" discussed in Chapter 2. It is unclear what his work achieved. He has neither refined earlier perspectives nor built a body of cumulative knowledge to any significant degree, especially given the millions of dollars spent.

I am impressed by Murray and Bannister's work, however. There is considerable confirming evidence for Murray's successful effort at reforestation in Haiti.

90   Banerjee and Duflo (2011:49–50, 57–58, back cover).

91   Karlan and Appel (2012).

92   Karlan and Appel (2012:273–275).

But, as is common in cultural anthropology, it remains unclear how to tie this research project to others operating in other contexts, with other problems and other funders. What Banerjee, Duflo, and Karlan do is refine the best way to approach a range of problems across a range of contexts. They build cumulative knowledge as one randomized controlled trial builds on another. By comparing the effectiveness of various approaches in different settings involving the people directly concerned with the problem being studied, they are able to develop a comprehensive, objective understanding of how best to address a particular issue. The benefits they provide others are both considerable and confirmable.

## Transparency

*Given the call for greater accountability in research, the need for transparency is clear. This section highlights two broad concerns. It touches on anthropology's undercover work for governmental counterinsurgency agencies. It also discusses the complications of trusting an ethnographer's account based solely on the data the author presents. Trusting another's ethnography often boils down to whether there is a potential to restudying the group with an understanding of how the initial data were collected. This allows others, when appropriate, to draw alternative conclusions. Transparency is important because it fosters trust in what others write.*

Transparency is key to ensuring the two strategies discussed above move beyond nice words and kind intentions. As we saw in Chapter 2, cultural anthropologists make a host of claims. We need to have a clear understanding of the data that support these claims to vouchsafe their validity. When different ethnographers study the same group, we gain a bifocal view of the group. The bifocal view is not perfect. But it lets us see the interplay of various contextual factors to make better sense of each researcher's claims. Keeping the public mystified as to the basis for a study's conclusions makes life easier for the researcher. She or he is relieved of being held publicly accountable. But it dodges an important question: Why should the broader public fund anthropological research if it doesn't understand what this research involves or how trustworthy the researcher's data are? We need to know how a particular research project is conducted, what its full results are (not just the published ones), and why readers should trust the researcher's assertions.

In Chapter 1, I noted *The Lancet* reported that perhaps $200 billion—which constitutes about 85 percent of all global medical research spending—is likely wasted on poorly designed and reported research studies.[93] Since this is a rather shocking figure, let me offer the actual quote. Malcolm Macleod et al. report: "Global biomedical and public health research involves billions of dollars and millions of people. . . . Although this vast enterprise has led to substantial health improvements, many more gains are possible if the waste and inefficiency in the ways that biomedical research is chosen, designed, done, analysed, regulated, managed, disseminated, and reported can be addressed. In 2009, Chalmers and Glasziou . . . estimated that the cumulative effect was that about 85% of research investment—equating to $200 billion of the investment in 2010—is wasted." In a related article, Paul Glasziou states: "Research publication can both communicate and miscommunicate. Unless research is adequately reported, the time and resources invested in the conduct of research is wasted. . . . Adequate reports of research should clearly describe which questions were addressed and why, what was done, what was shown, and what the findings mean. However, substantial failures occur in each of these elements."[94]

Ben Goldacre, in *Bad Pharma: How Drug Companies Mislead Doctors and Harm Patients*, discusses transparency in relation to the pharmaceutical industry. He reports:

> Missing data is key to the whole story . . . because it poisons the well for everybody. If proper trials are never done, if trials with negative results are withheld, then we simply cannot know the true effects of the treatments that we use. Nobody can work around this, and there is no expert doctor with special access to a secret stash of evidence. With missing data, we are all in it together, and we are all misled . . . evidence in medicine is not an abstract academic preoccupation. Evidence is used to make real-world decisions and when we are fed bad data, we make the wrong decision, inflicting unnecessary pain and suffering, and death, on people just like us.[95]

In suggesting what might be done, Goldacre writes: "We need full disclosure, and I don't say this out of some waffly notion of truth and reconciliation. Medicine today is practiced using drugs that have come onto the market over several decades, supported by evidence that has been gathered since at least the 1970s. We now know that this entire evidence base has been systematically distorted

---

93    *The Lancet*, for those unfamiliar with the life sciences, is one of the world's leading medical journals.

94    Macleod et al. (2014:101); Glasziou et al. (2014:267).

95    Goldacre (2012:341–342).

by the pharmaceutical industry, which has deliberately and selectively withheld the results of trials whose results it didn't like, while publishing the ones with good results."[96] As Goldacre stresses, transparency in research facilitates effective reviewing, assessing, and confirming of important studies. In the life sciences the stakes are high since they involve human lives. In the social sciences they involve our ability to refine perspectives and build cumulative knowledge. Without transparency, we cannot tell what are "alternative facts" and what are real facts or how to distinguish "fake news" from real news.

Equally important, we gain little sense of the false leads that did not pan out. Brian Nosek observes there is a "publication bias" in many publications. "Positive results get reported, negative results ignored." Reading an article in which the author argues for a particular position, the reader does not know what data were collected that might lead to a different position than that argued for by the author. Someone reading a journal article may never know about all the suggestive experiments that came to naught.[97] In an essay titled *Other People's Money and How Bankers Use It*, Justice Louis Brandeis famously states: "Publicity is justly commended as a remedy for social and industrial diseases. Sunlight is said to be the best of disinfectants; electric light the most efficient policeman."[98]

### IN ANTHROPOLOGY

Besides helping accountability standards work in ways that lessen the focus on metrics (emphasized in Chapter 5), transparency plays two critical roles in anthropology. First, anthropology has a long tradition of exposing anthropological participation in clandestine government work. In a letter by Franz Boas to the *Nation* in 1919, Boas accused four American anthropologists of spying for the US government in Central America.[99] (Boas was censured by the American Anthropological Association for his letter.) Ralph Beals, in "International Research Problems in Anthropology," writes: "Academic institutions and individual members of the academic community, including students, should scrupulously avoid both involvement in clandestine intelligence activities and the use of the name of anthropology, or the title of anthropologists, as a cover for intelligence activities."[100] Still, as Eric Wolf and Joseph Jorgensen wrote in the

---

96   Goldacre (2012:349).
97   Nosek as quoted in Achenbach (2015).
98   Brandeis (1914:92).
99   D. Rice (2005).
100  Beals (1967:475).

*New York Review of Books* in 1970, anthropologists were involved, especially in Thailand, in Project Camelot. The project sought "to enhance the Army's ability to predict and influence social developments in foreign countries. This motive was described by an internal memo on December 5, 1964: 'If the U.S. Army is to perform effectively its part in the U.S. mission of counterinsurgency it must recognize that insurgency represents a breakdown of social order and that the social processes involved must be understood.'"[101]

The American Anthropological Association's 2012 Principles of Professional Responsibility states: "Anthropologists should be clear and open regarding the purpose, methods, outcomes, and sponsors of their work. Anthropologists must also be prepared to acknowledge and disclose to participants and collaborators all tangible and intangible interests that have, or may reasonably be perceived to have, an impact on their work. Transparency, like informed consent, is a process that involves both making principled decisions prior to beginning the research and encouraging participation, engagement, and open debate throughout its course."[102]

Second, a degree of transparency is essential for establishing reliable ethnographies. Anthropologists in their publications often provide considerable ethnographic data and, based on them, offer insightful, provocative conclusions. But when the ethnography is the account of a single author with limited supporting data from other sources, we are forced to accept the author's conclusions on trust. If an author explains the contexts that shaped her or his data collection, if the author provides a sense of how pervasive the patterns illuminated are, we feel on more solid ground. The key is whether the ethnographer provides enough contextual data to allow others to return to her or his field site and, in collecting new information, gain a sense of how and why this ethnographer collected the data and drew the conclusions she or he did. It is the possibility of a new ethnographer revisiting a field site and building on earlier work—as Annette Weiner did on Bronislaw Malinowski's Trobriand work—that makes the original account more credible.

In Chapter 1, I offered two examples from my fieldwork on Pukapuka, an atoll five anthropologists had visited before me. The first example, illustrating status rivalry, focused on the competition between Molingi and Nimeti regarding string figures. In the book *Making History*, from which the example was taken,

---

101  Wolf and Jorgensen (1970); Wikipedia, s.v. "Project Camelot."
102  American Anthropological Association (2012).

I noted that status rivalry was pervasive on the atoll. My daughter Amelia, who lived on the atoll for two years starting in 2011, perceived the same pervasive status rivalry. But, with the second example focusing on whether Waletiale or Malangaatiale had an enlarged penis, Amelia did not find many Pukapukans deferring to elders as authorities on traditional matters. I thought this would certainly be an enduring pattern as it had been with key anthropologists working on the atoll before me. Why the difference? Cyclone Percy (a category-four cyclone) devastated the atoll in 2005, causing considerable damage.[103] When the government provided an opportunity for Pukapukans to migrate, a considerable number—especially older people knowledgeable in traditional matters—did. The elderly population on the atoll now includes many who spent much, if not most, of their time in New Zealand. Today, many Pukapukans are hesitant to trust these people's views on traditional matters given their limited time on the atoll.

Still, and this is the important point, what I wrote in *Making History* could be openly questioned. I had provided the contexts under which I had gathered my information and drawn certain conclusions. Neither the data nor the conclusions were obscured by an ambiguous fog preventing others from revisiting the atoll, interviewing the same or similar people, and drawing different conclusions. It is the same pattern described in Chapter 2—regarding Redfield/Lewis, Beaglehole/Borofsky, and Sahlins/Obeyesekere. The problem with *The Teaching of Don Juan* is that there is no way Castaneda's data can be directly confirmed or challenged. Others had no idea where to visit or whom to talk to in order to corroborate Castaneda's account. There is no transparency in *The Teachings of Don Juan*.

I have already discussed the heated debate concerning Yanomami violence. A key article in the debate involves a well-cited 1988 article by Chagnon in *Science*. The problem is that the data, on which Chagnon bases his dramatic conclusions regarding Yanomami violence, have never been made public. Chagnon writes: "I have never published data that would enable someone to determine who specifically was a 'killer,' his name, his village, his age, how many wives he had, and how many offspring. In short, the data needed to make the criticism that Fry makes [regarding the limited violence of Yanomami] cannot be gleaned from my published data."[104] If Chagnon will not release his data so others can visit the locales

---

103   New Zealand Herald (2005); Wikipedia, s.v. "Pukapuka."
104   Chagnon (1988); Chagnon in Miklikowska and Fry (2012:61).

he visited and interview various informants who would likely be knowledgeable about who killed whom in earlier times, we are basically stuck. Despite the various statistics Chagnon presents, it would be unwise to put too much faith in them. Still, in fairness to Chagnon, we should not simply dismiss his data. We are left, once again, with unsubstantiated assertions of uncertain, ambiguous value.

In a widely discussed 1994 book titled *The Bell Curve*, coauthors Richard Herrnstein and Charles Murray suggest racial differences in intelligence exist because different "races" (as they defined them) perform differently on certain IQ tests. The book implies the reason "whites" appear more economically successful than "blacks" is because "whites" are more intelligent. Needless to say, the book caused considerable stir in the public media. Initially many reviewers—trusting the statistical analyses of the authors—gave positive reviews of the book. Nicholas Lemann notes a key reason for the positive reviews was because "the ordinary routine of neutral reviewers having a month or two to go over the book with care did not occur. . . . The [initial] debate . . . was conducted in the mass media by people with no independent ability to assess the book." They had to base their reviews on the statistics and analyses Herrnstein and Murray provided. "It was not until late 1995 that the most damaging criticism of *The Bell Curve* began to appear. . . . *The Bell Curve*, it turns out, is full of mistakes ranging from sloppy reasoning to miscitations of sources to outright mathematical errors."[105] What the authors had done was quickly push the book out to the media before negative reviews could appear. It was a clever strategy to attract attention. But ultimately it failed because scholars familiar with the subject were eventually able to carefully go through their data to see how they had drawn their fallacious conclusions.

## Collaborating with Others

*Given the difficulties in trying to "make a difference" on one's own, collaborating with others becomes a crucial way to enhance one's ability to produce positive impacts that benefit others. But in emphasizing this point, it is clear one should not become overly dependent on a single collaborator—as Man: A Course of Study (MACOS) did with the National Science Foundation (NSF). Ideally, one should gain broad support and, moreover, embed the project in social structures that will continue the project with or without you—as*

---

105   Lemann (1997).

*Partners in Health (PIH) has done. The Yanomami campaign indicates that
even when the collaboration is informal, persistence and publicity can over
time wear down opposition.*

Collaboration has much to offer as a strategy for change. True, we can list prominent individuals who led the charge for change, such as Nelson Mandela, Martin Luther King, Jody Williams, Wangari Maathai, or, from an earlier era, Jane
Adams. But they did not facilitate change on their own. Their efforts proved successful because others collaborated with them. Many anthropologists harbor a
secret hope that their publications will break through the hegemonic-like structures of the academy and bring change. They may. But if you look carefully—
as we will in the next chapter—readers will see that most examples of seminal
publications leading to change involve an author's publications being taken up
by powerful groups beyond the academy. These groups embrace the author's
message not because of the power of the author's prose but because it fits with
their own agenda. The author's success depends on willing collaborators.

I would not suggest that collaboration is always easy. It can be complicated.
Anthropologists need to be careful about subordinating their goals to the goals
of collaborators. Anthropologists should be cautious about becoming "private
contractors," hired out as researchers and educators to people who will use their
knowledge to their own ends, for good or ill. To have credibility—to really speak
truth to power—cultural anthropologists can't be pawns of the powerful. With
their academic appointments and tenured positions, anthropologists can maintain a certain independence while working with these groups. In this regard,
we might take note of a prominent debate in the 1920s between the journalist
Walter Lippmann and the philosopher-educator John Dewey.

In 1922, Lippmann suggested that given the complexity of the problems that
afflicted America, the general public was incapable of coming to reasoned, effective solutions. Lippmann preferred instead a class of special experts—a group of
professionals—who could sort through and order the mass of data relevant to a
problem. They would present their analyses to decision makers who would then
act on these professionals' advice. Dewey questioned Lippmann's dependence on
experts to order knowledge for others. For Dewey, professional social scientists
should educate the broader public—not just the decision makers—about social
issues. Building democratic communities, Dewey asserted, entailed the active
involvement of citizens. "The union of social science, access to facts, and the art
of literary presentation," Dewey wrote, "is not an easy thing to achieve. But its

attainment seems to me the only genuine solution of the problem of an intelligent direction of social life."[106] Under Lippmann's scenario, anthropologists may be bureaucrats (or *apparatchiks*) of the system. Cultural anthropologists should not be mere technicians, hired guns, or patrons of the powerful. They should be independent voices that challenge accepted "wisdom." Their responsibility is to those who make their roles as intellectuals, as academics, possible—the broader democratic society. Their role is to speak truth to power.

Before moving on to three examples of the power—and complications— involved in collaborating with those beyond the academy, let me add a few additional notes. First, reaching out to nonacademic groups and making one's research public helps anthropologists soften the hegemonic-like hold the academic system has on their careers. Collaboration in democratic settings draws in other players that, depending on the contexts and parties involved, need be listened to by university administrators. Second, there are hundreds of examples of collaborative efforts by academics reaching beyond the academy to explore different possibilities in various ways. The examples provided here are only suggestive. Readers can certainly find others.[107]

Third, it might sound obvious, but it is not always carried out in practice. As emphasized earlier in the section titled "Benefitting Others," collaborating with others with the resources to facilitate a project's success is valuable. But it is critical to collaborate with those you wish to help so they are active not passive participants, so they are committed to the projects that seek to benefit them.

---

106    Lippmann (1922:236); Dewey (1922[1983]:343, 158). See also Dewey (1916, 1927); Hickman and Alexander (1998). Professionals, the prominent sociologist Eliot Freidson writes, should use their knowledge for the public good. They have "the duty to appraise what they do in light of . . . [the] larger good, a duty which licenses them to be more than passive servants of the state, of capital, of the firm, of the client. . . . [They should not be] mere technicians . . . [who] serve their patrons as . . . hired guns . . . [who] advise their patrons . . . but . . . don't . . . violate their wishes" (Freidson 2001:122, 217). Readers interested in further exploring this topic might consider: Aboulafia (1992); Alterman (1999); Barros (1970); Brandeis (1914); Champlin and Knoedler (2006); Cmiel (1993); Conklin (1992); Creighton (1916); Damico (1978); Dewey (1916); Hickman and Alexander (1998); Diggins (1993); Hocking (1929); Hook (1939); I. King (1917); Kloppenberg (1992); A. Moore (1916); E. Moore (1917); Myers and Myers (2001); Otto (1920); Pepper (1928); Rueschemeyer (1995); T. V. Smith (1929); Steiner (1992); Westbrook (1991); Westhoff (1995); and Whipple (2005).

107    See, e.g., the Community Engaged Scholarship Institute at Guelph University, http://www .cesinstitute.ca/. The Institute fosters "collaborative and mutually beneficial community-university partnerships and build mechanisms for universities and communities to work together in innovative and strategic ways." Also, one should note Bennett and Whiteford (2013).

And fourth, collaboration takes time. It can push academics off the standard schedule of producing so many publications within a set period of time. But researchers can show steps of progress. They can explain to academic oversight committees how they are progressing in what ways with what complications. Having a successful collaborative project, many might agree, counts for a slew of publications—especially when it is unclear what the broader public value of these publications is.

## MAN: A COURSE OF STUDY (MACOS)

MACOS was perhaps anthropology's most successful effort at embedding the discipline's values in elementary school programs. At its height, in the early 1970s, MACOS involved seventeen hundred elementary schools in forty-seven states (with approximately four hundred thousand students). It grew out of the educational reform movement, following the Sputnik era. Quoting Peter Dow, who became MACOS's director: "Never before had university research scholars taken such a deep interest in the improvement of instruction in the public schools. . . . The role of the National Science Foundation in providing funding for the new reforms was especially significant. . . . [It] supplied the principle supports of curriculum innovation."[108]

Douglas Oliver was seminal in its formulation. Quoting Harry Wolcott: "At the beginning, the idea of 'turning all students into little anthropologists' had . . . been central to the program. The idea originated with Douglas Oliver, a Harvard anthropologist whose earliest vision was to make anthropology the unifying core of the *entire* social science program to begin in the first grade."[109] After Oliver dropped out, for personal reasons relating to his wife's death, Jerome Bruner took over. Bruner narrowed the focus of the course to one grade and deepened its conceptual framework while, at the same time, making it more interdisciplinary. Dow wrote: "The overriding objective of the course was [now] to help children understand what it means to be human. [Quoting Bruner:] 'We seek exercises and materials . . . through which our pupils can learn wherein man is distinctive in his adaption to the world, and wherein there is a discernible continuity between him and his animal forbears.' "[110]

The program initially functioned under the auspices of Educational Services Incorporated (ESI), an organization founded by Jerrold Zacharias of MIT to

108   Dow (1991:216); Ruby (2005:685, 28–29).
109   Wolcott (2007:202–203).
110   Bruner as quoted in Dow (1991:79).

support his revision of the high school physics curriculum (PSSC). In the 1960s ESI became the Educational Development Center (EDC). EDC constituted the structural umbrella under which MACOS functioned, providing guidance and support, through NSF funding, for its development. Dow's formal position, in guiding the program, was director of EDC's School and Society Programs. His 1991 book *Schoolhouse Politics* is the most detailed account of MACOS's rise and fall. What made MACOS so successful was, in the end, what also undid it. Through its formation, overcoming of various problems (such as the initial rejection of the project by textbook publishers), and the establishment of regional training centers (to address problems of training teachers), MACOS persisted because of NSF support. In the mid-1970s various parents and politicians protested against MACOS, believing the program threatened the religious values of American children. This pushback eventually caused the termination of NSF funding. Because it was unable to fund itself at that point, MACOS collapsed.

As summarized in the 2003 film *Through These Eyes*, MACOS's failure appeared to derive from a clash of cultural values. Dow writes: "What became increasingly plain as we worked with teacher educators was that MACOS was more than an unusual set of materials about animals and Eskimos. It represented a different point of view about children, learning, and society. More important than the specific units . . . was the way the course confronted conventional assumptions about how children learn and about the kind of subject matter that is appropriate for the young." Dow notes that the "reluctance on the part of Congress to support social science research reflected a belief on the part of many conservative congressmen that social science research fosters social change. As Roberta Miller, the current NSF social science chief, puts it, '[They] felt that untrammeled social science research might undo the existing social order.' "[111]

One might presume the framers of MACOS would be aware of this problem. To an extent, they were. In discussing why MACOS dropped the use of the Kalahari Bushmen, Dow indicates: "Despite great success in our classroom tryouts . . . by 1967 it had become politically unacceptable to use materials that showed partially naked, dark-skinned 'primitives' in a public school classroom." But they were less politically sensitive than they might have been, especially regarding various aspects of Eskimo life that differed from our own. Quoting Dow: "The authors of MACOS . . . were insufficiently aware of the extent to which political considerations shape the content of instruction. We saw ourselves engaged in

111   Dow (1991:150, 236).

the task of closing the gap between the research laboratory and the classroom, and we assumed that the social value of this enterprise was self-evident. We did not foresee that in devising an anthropologically based program for elementary students we were challenging beliefs, deeply held in some parts of the country, about what children should learn."[112]

I would not discount the clash of values generated by MACOS, but it is also true that the project had, and still has, numerous supporters. It might well have persisted with the training centers that constituted a key part of the program if the project had freed itself from NSF funding and become financially self-supporting. In my opinion the fact that the project was disrupting cultural values in certain parts of the country was not the central factor in its demise. It was that the project was disrupting cultural values *and* it was dependent on federal funding. It could not do both. EDC and MACOS agreed, in principle, that MACOS should end its NSF funding and become commercially viable on its own. MACOS simply took its time going about this. It thought its funding would last longer than it did. Why did MACOS not respond quicker to outside demands and its own commitment to become commercially viable without federal funding? This goes back to the selection of a publisher/distributor—Curriculum Development Associates (CDA) over Westinghouse Learning. Dow writes:

> The choice between CDA and Westinghouse Learning was far from easy. Westinghouse had money, organizational strength, marketing expertise, and a need for success in the educational market-place. . . . Wirtz [the president of CDA] . . . was a man of enormous eloquence and persuasiveness, and his impeccable reputation in academic circles . . . might be just what we needed to gain the support of the educational establishment. On the other hand, the Westinghouse proposal was clearly superior from a business point of view. Wirtz's academic and political clout were hardly a match for the economic power of the Westinghouse organization . . . in the end the lure of an educator's collaborative outweighed hard-headed business considerations.[113]

MACOS decided to work with CDA. Dow continues: "We expected to be able to raise new funds . . . the NSF was allocating a growing percentage of its precollege educational funding to support teacher training activities, and we

112    Dow (1991:122, 268).
113    Dow (1991:174).

questioned the wisdom of 'selling out' to the commercial marketplace."[114] Unfortunately, "the partnership between EDC and CDA proved to be an imperfect marriage. Ironically, we were too much alike, too similar in our goals, to be able to help each other very much."[115] Neither EDC nor CDA was able to raise the funds needed when NSF terminated its support.

In reflecting on whether he had made the right decision, Dow notes that there were "compelling reasons why we should have chosen a bona fide commercial partner for the widespread distribution of MACOS. . . . The establishment of the regional center network demonstrated . . . that a new kind of marketing program for a new kind of product might make sense. Having done so, however, it was now time to invent the commercial alternative to the NSF-sponsored network that would facilitate implementation on a scale that was beyond the resources of the NSF. This required the skills and financial resources of an organization experienced in dealing with the commercial marketplace. Neither EDC nor CDA had that experience. The ultimate test of an educational innovation like MACOS is its ability to survive in the profit-making sector."[116]

The MACOS project represents a wonderful example of collaboration. It involved a range of disciplines, academics, and educators collaborating with the National Science Foundation. But MACOS overestimated how long its NSF collaboration would continue. While in principle, embracing the marketplace, it felt more comfortable selecting CDA as its publisher because CDA's values corresponded to its own. As a result, MACOS lacked the financial independence needed when the going got rough. If it had made the jump into the commercial marketplace earlier, the project might have survived, despite the testy political climate and pushback received from various areas of the country. It absolutely needed NSF funding to develop the project. The problem was that the project became overly dependent on this collaboration rather than freeing itself from it and moving on.

## PARTNERS IN HEALTH (PIH)

The medical nonprofit Partners in Health (PIH) offers an alternative model for collaborating with others. It establishes collaborative relationships not only

114   Dow (1991:175).
115   Dow (1991:176).
116   Dow (1991:175–176).

with local communities but with national governments and multimillion-dollar funders. In respect to the former, PIH embeds key aspects of health care—especially patient home care—in community personnel. (The two medical doctors who helped found PIH, Paul Farmer and Jim Kim, have PhDs in anthropology.) The *Catalogue for Philanthropy* reports that PIH involves "community members at all levels of assessment, design, implementation, and evaluation. Community health workers may be family members, friends, or even patients who provide health education, refer people who are ill to a clinic, or deliver medicines and social support to patients in their homes. Community health workers do not supplant the work of doctors or nurses; rather, they are a vital interface between the clinic and the community. . . . [As PIH states, it] 'doesn't tell the communities we serve what they need—they tell us.' "[117] Quoting from PIH's website:

> For nearly three decades, PIH has hired and trained community health workers to help patients faced with [various] . . . challenges receive care. Our 12,000 community health workers around the world visit patients at home, assess their health, and link them with clinics and hospitals.
>
> In Haiti, where PIH's community health worker program originated, they are called *accompagnateurs* to emphasize the importance of accompanying people in their journey through sickness and back to health.
>
> Living in the communities where they work, community health workers are trusted and welcomed into patients' homes to provide high-quality services for a wide range of health problems. A patient beginning treatment for tuberculosis, for example, is paired with a health worker who visits every day to supervise treatment and ensure the patient takes medications regularly and correctly. For people living with HIV or other chronic diseases, this support enables them to live longer and healthier lives.[118]

In Haiti, Partners in Health (or Zanmi Lasante) serves an area of roughly 4.5 million people and has "recorded more than 1.6 million patient visits, provided educational assistance to 9,400 children, delivered prenatal care to 30,000 pregnant women, and started 1,700 patients on treatment of tuberculosis."[119] Importantly, PIH has sought to ensure that its health program will continue over time without it. To do this in Haiti, PIH (Zanmi Lasante) has helped construct and,

117    Catalogue for Philanthropy (2011).

118    Partners in Health, Community Health Workers, http://www.pih.org/priority-programs/community-health-workers (accessed October 5, 2017).

119    Partners in Health, Haiti, http://www.pih.org/country/haiti (accessed October 5, 2017).

for now, runs Hôpital Universitaire de Mirebalais, a three-hundred-bed teaching hospital. "At a time when . . . [Haiti] desperately needs skilled professionals, [PIH is] providing high-quality education for the next generation of nurses, medical students, and residents."[120] Regarding Rwanda, "in 2015, Partners in Health took the first steps in realizing a long-sought aspiration, to create a university that would advance the science of health care delivery and create a cadre of global changemakers. University of Global Health Equity (UGHE) is reimagining health sciences education by rethinking every aspect of a university in the 21st century—from what we teach to how we teach, from our values to our research priorities, from the location and design of our campus to our local and global impact."[121]

In Haiti and Rwanda, PIH has collaborated with the national governments. But, importantly, PIH has not become totally dependent on them. The web pages for Hôpital Universitaire de Mirebalais include a list of contributors who have donated funds to design, build, and outfit the hospital and residences. The list includes the Haitian Ministry of Public Health and Population. But it also includes more than 170 additional supporters.[122] While the Haitian government was the largest contributor to the running of the university hospital during its first year, it has not been the only one. (The Haitian support constitutes less than 15 percent of the health ministry's budget.)[123] In the case of the University of Global Health Equity, the Rwandan government donated $43 million in land and infrastructure support.[124] But the Bill and Melinda Gates Foundation and the Cummings Foundation have also been key supporters of the project.

My point, in comparing MACOS with PIH, is that (a) collaboration is often essential in developing effective projects. But (b) one also has to maintain a degree of independence, especially after the initial development phase, from the organization (or organizations) that one is collaborating with—so as not to be subject to the stresses and strains that can result if a particular collaborator drops out. One needs a network of collaborators to ensure a project's viability in good times and bad.

---

120    Partners in Health, Haiti, http://www.pih.org/country/haiti (accessed October 5, 2017).

121    University of Global Health Equity, http://ughe.org/vision/support-our-mission/ (accessed October 5, 2017).

122    Partners in Health, Hôpital Universitaire de Mirebalais, http://www.pih.org/pages/mirebalais (accessed October 5, 2017).

123    Farmer (2015).

124    Fairbanks (2017).

## CAMPAIGN TO RETURN THE YANOMAMI BLOOD

A less formal collaboration involved the campaign to return Yanomami blood samples, stored in American research institutions, to the Brazilian Yanomami.[125] It grew out of a relationship between Bruce Albert, a French-trained anthropologist who had spent years working with the Brazilian Yanomami, and myself as I prepared *Yanomami: The Fierce Controversy and What We Can Learn From It.*[126] Two things were clear to me as I gathered material for the book. A number of American anthropologists had clearly benefitted from their research among the Yanomami—in terms of faculty positions, promotions, and, in Napoleon Chagnon's case, royalties. But it was less clear that the Yanomami had particularly benefitted from assisting these anthropologists. They remained deeply troubled by the intrusion of gold miners into their nationally protected reserve and by the spread of various diseases. In truth, there was relatively little American anthropologists could do on their own to address either of these concerns. The one thing done, that I know of, was the producing of a bilingual Portuguese-Yanomami health manual to facilitate the work of health-care providers.[127]

During one of our telephone conversations, Bruce Albert indicated that both the Yanomami and various prominent deputy attorneys of Brazil had repeatedly asked Pennsylvania State University (Penn State)—where the largest number of blood samples from James Neel's research were stored—to return the blood samples which held religious significance for the Yanomami. Penn State refused. Albert asked if the Center for a Public Anthropology might, in some way, be able to help. To a certain degree, the Center could. In February 2006, working with volunteer students from the Center's Community Action Project, we were able to obtain written agreement from Penn State's provost, Rodney Erickson, to return its stored Yanomami blood samples. His letter suggested the samples could be sent back with those from the National Cancer Institute (NCI). Dr. Joseph Fraumenini, the Institute's director, had already agreed to return the samples stored at NCI.

But despite working together with Dr. Pitt, Dr. Fraumenini's assistant, to facilitate the Institute's return of the samples, a lawyer at the Institute—who refused to give her name or even talk with me—complicated the process. She insisted the National Cancer Institute would only return the blood samples if

---

125    For a more detailed account with the relevant documentation, refer to Borofsky (2017:26ff) or "Returning Blood Samples to the Yanomami," 2015, http://center-yanomami.publicanthropology .org/ (accessed October 5, 2017).

126    Borofsky et al. (2005).

127    Albert and Gomez (1997).

the Brazilian government formally signed an agreement that waived all legal liability for the condition of the blood samples stored at the Institute. (Since the blood samples appeared in good shape and, when returned to the Yanomami, would be immediately destroyed, this did not make a great deal of sense to most outside observers. Still, she insisted.)

The Brazilian officials in charge of the blood transfers were at first puzzled and suspicious of her demand. There was one delay after another, as Brazilian officials tried to make sense of the lawyer's demand and ensure that something was not amiss. For the next several years, there was a standoff. On one side, Penn State and NCI insisted they wanted to return the blood samples; on the other, the Brazilian government insisted it wanted the samples returned. The problem was they could not agree on how this would be done.

The indigenous Hutukara Yanomami Association, partnering with Instituto Socioambiental (a supportive NGO to which Bruce Albert belonged), got involved and repeatedly stressed the importance of the blood transfer to various Brazilian officials. As a result, there was an accumulation of publicity regarding the need to return the blood samples—mostly sponsored by the Instituto Socioambiental but also by the Center. At this point the Foreign Ministry, ANVISA (Brazil's FDA equivalent), and the AGU (the attorney general of Brazil) weighed in on the issue. Only after many discussions among the Brazilian parties, followed by conversations with NCI's American lawyer, was the matter resolved. In April 2015, Penn State returned the blood samples to the Yanomami. The National Cancer Institute returned them in September 2015—more than ten years after our campaign had started.

The collaboration was informal, a makeshift alliance centering on Bruce Albert and myself calling and emailing each other through time. The Center for a Public Anthropology and the volunteer students working through the Center's Community Action Project were able to soften the resistance of US research institutions to returning the blood—something the Hutukara and the Brazilian deputy attorneys had not been able to do. But the NCI lawyer stopped us cold. It was only over a period of several years, as a collaboration of the Hutukara Yanomami Association, Instituto Socioambiental, and various Brazilian governmental officials coalesced, that the push to return the blood samples succeeded.[128]

---

128  Penn State returned 2,693 vials (these included vials that had been stored at Binghamton University [SUNY]). The National Cancer Institute returned 474 vials.

In foreshadowing Chapter 4's focus on targeted transparency, we might ask: Why did Penn State sidestep various requests by Brazilian authorities to return the blood samples but then agree to do so when the Center and students made a similar request? Only weeks after a Penn State dean threw up roadblocks with the Brazilian officials to returning the samples, Penn State's provost agreed to return them. Why the different response? I do not know. But I can guess. The letter sent by the Center to Penn State's president and provost included the possibility of a massive student letter-writing campaign to the Pennsylvania governor and the General Assembly. At that time Penn State was undergoing a review by the General Assembly of its funding for the coming year. Because Penn State already was enduring negative publicity regarding another matter at the time that might well have affected its budget request, perhaps the president and provost thought it best to avoid further negative publicity. I doubt either the students' or my prose proved that convincing to them. But I suspect that the threat of a massive letter-writing campaign to the governor and the General Assembly when the university's budget was under consideration might have.

# 4

## MAKING YOUR VOICE COUNT

### Exploring Why, Despite Considerable Effort, Few Anthropologists Succeed in Changing Public Policy

*Many anthropologists hope to speak to broader audiences in captivating ways that facilitate change. Unfortunately, few anthropologists succeed. Often interactions with various politicians and policy makers are one-off events with limited follow-up. What is needed, to make their messages more effective, are structures that push their messages consistently and persistently with relevant audiences.*

Cultural anthropology possesses a valuable analytical tool kit that combines close observation often stretched over many years, the ability to place behaviors and beliefs, different from our own, in meaningful contexts that make them understandable, and a comparative framework that lets researchers explore the broader dynamics at work. Few fields have such powerful analytical tools for analyzing social problems and suggesting solutions. A number of anthropologists have delineated thoughtful, significant solutions to important social concerns.

Take the work of Norwegian anthropologist Fredrik Barth on ethnic conflict and coauthors Philippe Bourgois and Jeff Schonberg on opiate addiction.

Based on comparative work in Pakistan and Norway, Barth writes that "contrary to what is still a widely shared view, I [have] argued that ethnic groups are not groups formed on the basis of shared culture, but rather the formation of groups on the basis of differences of culture. . . . The contrast between 'us' and 'others' is what is embedded in the organization of ethnicity." He asserts that there are few clear, distinct cultural boundaries. Rather, a range of continuous variation exists across a geographic area. Oppositions make cultural distinctions come alive. Barth suggests that behind many cultural conflicts—such as the bitter tensions between Arabs and Christians, Serbs and Croats, Sunni and Shiite Arabs—are "ethnic entrepreneurs." He continues: "The conflicts we see today are the work mainly of middle echelon politicians who use the politics of cultural difference to further their ambitions for leadership. This is tempting to them because in ethnic identities they see a potential constituency, so to speak, waiting for them, and all they need to find is the key to set the process in motion. Leaders seek these constituencies and mobilize them by making select, contrastive cultural differences more salient, and . . . by linking them to grievances and injustices. . . . They engage in confrontational politics."[1]

To reduce ethnic conflict, Barth suggests bringing into the open how these political entrepreneurs operate. Rather than letting these entrepreneurs emphasize group differences to mobilize political followings, we should focus on people's interrelated ties. "We need to reduce the saliency of . . . particular differences," he writes, "and draw [people's] attention to all the other crisscrossing differences and the joint interests they have. We want to create arenas, specifically for negotiations, where one can work from common interests and move outward. . . . You don't start with opposed constituencies and try to bring them together. You start with the common ground. You ask what the shared interests between the parties are. Then you negotiate to expand that common ground."[2]

In their 2009 book *Righteous Dopefiend*, Bourgois and Schonberg studied a number of heroin injectors over a twelve-year period in a semiderelict warehouse and shipyard district of San Francisco they term Edgewater. In their conclusion the coauthors "propose short-term pragmatic policy recommendations and discuss the structural, political and economic changes necessary for

---

1    Barth (1995:1, 7).
2    Barth (1995:8).

the longer-term improvement of the lives of the indigent poor in the United States."[3] In respect to short-term solutions, Bourgois and Schonberg suggest: "Opiate withdrawal symptoms are indisputably painful, and they merit medical treatment without stigma. A heroin prescription program delivered through pain clinics and treatment programs would immediately reduce the everyday torments of the Edgewater homeless. Arguably, a simple prescription constitutes the short-term magic-bullet solution for much of the embodied suffering presented in [this ethnography]. . . . [T]he Swiss opiate prescription program reduces pain.[4] It also benefits the larger society by decreasing crime, violence, and family disruption, and it is less expensive than incarceration."[5]

In respect to a longer-term problem regarding housing the homeless, they write: "In the mid-2000s, progressive cities such as San Francisco and Seattle bypassed federal zero-tolerance regulations by building and rehabilitating SRO [single room occupancy]-style apartments for the homeless using municipal funds. This allowed them to develop a flexible harm reduction approach to housing the homeless and to tolerate nondisruptive drug users and alcoholics. Cities that cannot afford to finance the building of public housing without federal aid can increase access to affordable housing for the homeless by enforcing laws that protect low-income SROs and providing incentives for the construction of new low-income rental units for transients."[6]

Bourgois and Schonberg conclude their study with the following aspiration: "We hope this photo-ethnography of the everyday lives of the Edgewater homeless in San Francisco motivates readers to care about the phenomena of homelessness and income inequality in the United States. During the 1990s and the 2000s, the United States was the wealthiest and most military powerful nation in the world yet a larger proportion of its population lived in abject destitution than that of any other industrialized nation."[7]

I chose these anthropologists because they are prominent in the academy and also have reputations that extend beyond anthropology to the larger public. Their prominence has led to numerous public talks and conversations with policy makers. And yet, as far as I know, their ideas have only had limited impact on policy makers and politicians. Perhaps these audiences are overwhelmed by

3    Bourgois and Schonberg (2009:23).
4    Bourgois (2000), cited in Bourgois and Schonberg (2009).
5    Bourgois and Schonberg (2009:23, 298–299).
6    Bourgois and Schonberg (2009:310).
7    Bourgois and Schonberg (2009:319).

a mass of information from a range of sources. They are not always sure how to separate the wheat from the chaff in addressing problems that concern them. But more is involved. Their talks and interactions tend to be one-off events. They are not embedded in structures that push their messages through time—with persistence and consistency.

Didier Fassin's suggestion that we track the "public afterlife of ethnography" and his personal experiences with his books on French police (*Enforcing Order*) and French prisons (*Prison Worlds*) reinforce this point. In discussing a potential review of *Prison Worlds* in the French newspaper *Libération*, Fassin writes: "Even if *Libération* had [published the review as intended] . . . and had discussed the questions raised about the prison system at length, this would not have changed the carceral condition and would probably not even have significantly modified the terms of the debate about the politics of retribution."[8] In respect to *Enforcing Order*, he notes, the police union's representatives either used points in his book to reinforce their own demands or, when he made critical comments about the police, dismissed them, suggesting they were the exception rather than the rule.

At first glance, official reaction to *Prison Worlds* was more positive.[9] Fassin writes: "I was invited by the central as well as local administration to present my work. . . . At the national level, I was asked to give a talk at a seminar for Department of Corrections officials and to lecture at the Correctional Officer Academy, and I had private conversations with the minister of justice." But even here little concrete change occurred. "The reaction of the national director of the Department of Corrections was angry and dismissive," Fassin writes. "She disqualified my reflections as pure activism and refused to enter the discussion [relating to a talk she attended]. . . . I was . . . told by one of her deputies that she had thoroughly read the six hundred pages of my book with a mixture of interest and irritation. My modest [proposals] . . . were definitely not timely suggestions."[10]

That does not mean they have not had some effect. Fassin writes: "My work on the police and the many public interventions I have done have contributed with others' interventions to modifying the terms of the debate about police violence and discrimination. My work on prison and punishment is used by lawyers,

8    Fassin (2017:314).
9    Fassin (2016).
10   Fassin (2017: 337).

activists, politicians in their combat for more justice and less severity."[11] Still, what is needed for changing the social structures—to make the effort more enduring, to help more people—is strong, consistent political support over time, from French unions, political figures, and/or the general public. Otherwise, the efforts, though important, do not move beyond individual cases, do not persist through time to help change the structures of French policing and French prisons.

There are times, certainly, when presenting a particular message resonates with public audiences and makes a host of people take the message seriously. Margaret Mead's *Coming of Age in Samoa*, a comparison of Samoan and American sexual practices, became quite popular after it was published in 1928.[12] It stirred public debate. But such cases are relatively rare. For most anthropologists, publishing an important book with important ideas is often a bit like "waiting for Godot." They wait for their ideas to "take off," to be seriously discussed by policy makers and politicians. Unfortunately, for many anthropologists Godot never comes—despite the relevance and significance of their ideas.

No doubt it is partly a matter of timing, partly a matter of relevance. Mead's book, for example, came out at the end of the Roaring Twenties, when loosening American sexual mores was a hot topic. Certainly a message can catch on by itself because it provides new insight into a continuing problem that concerns important people. But, more likely than not, it is a matter of having one's message embedded in structures that persistently and consistently push that message with relevant audiences. People need to repeatedly "hear" the message, see its relevance, in the overload of information that swamps them day after day. Trying to get a message successfully out on one's own can prove difficult. The odds are against you. This problem is certainly not limited to cultural anthropology. A recent "Focus" supplement in the *Chronicle of Higher Education* suggests many fields share the same problem: "In short, university scientists have shown they're good at turning research into products, and they're getting better by the day. But are researchers, and their funders, making the same effort to translate the work of greatest benefit to society? . . . Why have research universities become really good places for analyzing the world's major problems, but perhaps not the best places for solving them?"[13]

---

11    Fassin, personal communication (2018).

12    Mead (1928).

13    Basken (2016a:4, 14).

## Structures That Enhance Anthropological Messages

*Having structural support to push forward a plan for change is critical to being heard in public arenas. J-PAL and PIH offer suggestive possibilities as does BRAC. While few projects possess such structural support on their own, it does not mean they cannot explore establishing support structures that over time could enhance their projects.*

There is no precise set of rules for fostering public impact. Still, I offer two examples that focus on a common theme: the structures need to be enduring, need to be more than individual efforts, to prove effective.[14] The first example is J-PAL (or Abudul Latif Jameel Poverty Action Lab). It was founded in 2003 at MIT by Abhijit Banerjee, Esther Duflo, and Sendhil Mullainathan. The J-PAL website states: "Our mission is to reduce poverty by ensuring that policy is informed by scientific evidence. We do this through research, policy outreach, and training across six regional offices worldwide."[15] J-PAL is university based and appears to be funded by a combination of donations, endowments, university funding, and payments for its research. What gives Banerjee and Duflo's book, *Poor Economics,* political and public heft is that it involves key players beyond their own lab.[16] The J-PAL website states: "Our affiliates are 145 professors at 49 universities."[17] In respect to "Partners," the website indicates:

> We work closely with Innovations for Poverty Action (IPA), an non-profit research organization with programs and offices around the world. Other partners are: Implementing organizations like governments, NGOs, multilateral organizations, and businesses who run programs that our affiliated professors evaluate, use our policy lessons from research, and scale up programs that are proven effective. Donors including foundations and bilateral organizations who provide funding

14    Barney Frank, the astute and politically powerful liberal former US Congressman, writes in his memoir (see Bruni [2015]:13): "If you care deeply about an issue and are engaged in group activity on its behalf that is fun and inspiring and heightens your sense of solidarity with others . . . you are most certainly not doing your cause any good." Frank's point is that one needs to do more than protest; you also need grassroots organizing.

15    "About Us," J-PAL, https://www.povertyactionlab.org/about-j-pal (accessed October 5, 2017).

16    Banerjee and Duflo (2011).

17    "Affiliated Professors," J-PAL, https://www.povertyactionlab.org/affiliated-researchers (accessed October 5, 2017).

for evaluations, scale-ups, and research initiatives. Research centers and organizations that run the randomized evaluations of our affiliated professors, including the Center for Effective Global Action (CEGA) at the University of California, Berkeley, the Center for Economic Research in Pakistan (CERP), the Crime Lab at the University of Chicago, Evidence for Policy Design (EPoD) at Harvard Kennedy School, and IFMR Lead.[18]

*Poor Economics* is more than a book by two MIT researchers. It is supported by a broad array of partners and organizations that repeat its message regarding the importance of careful scientific methods based on randomized trials. Their message has to compete with the messages of other researchers who have their own suggestions. But, with such a broad support network, the coauthors are able to not only highlight their message but also, importantly, facilitate concrete projects that make a difference in the lives of people around the world. They convince by example.

Since its founding in 1987, Partners in Health has involved a combination of university-affiliated doctors and private donors. The original founders are Dr. Paul Farmer (a professor at Harvard Medical School), Dr. Jim Yong Kim (president of the World Bank), Ophelia Dahl (chair of Dahl and Dahl LLP), Todd McCormack (senior corporate vice president of IMG Media), and Tom White (owner and president of J. F. White Construction Co.). White helped fund the early work of PIH with a million-dollar donation and, following that, tens of million dollars more. Today, PIH has ties to Harvard Medical School. Clinical and research fellows and associates in the Harvard Global Health and Social Medicine Department provide technical support at the Hôpital Universitaire de Mirebalais in Haiti as well as, with other US academic medical centers and universities, the Rwanda Human Resources for Health Program.[19]

Paul Farmer's ideas—as espoused in such books as *Pathologies of Power*, *To Repair the World*, and *Partner to the Poor*—have considerable structural support behind them. Audiences can read about his ideas in action in Haiti and Rwanda. They can learn about them from a range of prominent individuals and diverse groups who support PIH's work. Tracy Kidder, a Pulitzer Prize–winning author,

---

18    "Our Partners," J-PAL, https://www.povertyactionlab.org/partners (accessed October 5, 2017).

19    See, e.g., "Featured Initiatives," Department of Global Health and Social Medicine, Harvard Medical School, http://ghsm.hms.harvard.edu/programs/surgery/featured-initiatives.

wrote a biography of Farmer, *Mountains Beyond Mountains*, and a new documentary, *Bending the Arc*, has just been released.[20]

As we see in these examples, various structural arrangements can support an author's publications, an author's ideas. There is a positive feedback loop between the books and the institutions associated with them. The organizations provide concrete demonstrations of each book's message. Each book in turn provides an intellectual legitimization of the organizations. It proves them with a coherent vision that adds to their credibility. Many anthropologists likely find such associations a "bridge too far." Still, they need not give up. They might explore BRAC's "social business" model.[21] BRAC mostly funds its activism through its own outreach activities. According to its 2015 *Bangladesh Annual Report*, BRAC generates roughly 75 percent of its $726 million budget through its own entrepreneurial enterprises. Again, perhaps a self-funding nongovernmental organization may be a "bridge too far." Few anthropologists strive to establish NGOs given the effort involved in maintaining them.

But that does not mean that anthropologists cannot explore some more limited versions of such groups. Setting up a nonprofit is fairly straightforward. Universities are often open to establishing research centers (such as J-PAL), especially if financial arrangements can be resolved. Taking a step in this direction is certainly not a bridge too far. My point is: Ideas espoused by anthropologists—no matter how insightful, how valuable—are unlikely to become part of a larger, public debate, are unlikely to affect public policy, without social structures that persistently and consistently support their message. In the absence of outside structural support, few anthropological ideas tend to shape public debates or directly facilitate significant social change.

## Targeted Transparency as a Means for Enhancing Public Attention

*At first glance, targeted transparency may simply seem a way to push one's ideas out into the public arena. Several examples indicate that targeted transparency is more complicated, however: Edward Snowden and the NSA, Nancy Scheper-Hughes and the FBI, the NSF's Project Outcome Reports, and Westmoreland's "Search and Destroy" strategy during the Vietnam War. A set of reflections emphasize (a) the importance of properly framing one's message*

---

20    Farmer (2004, 2010, 2013); Kidder (2004).
21    See http://www.brac.net/.

*for the intended audience, (b) timing, and (c) the danger in disengaging from important political events. In the case of the Vietnam War, this disengagement, in an effort to "do no harm," may have facilitated considerable harm—in terms of Vietnamese and American lives lost.*

Disclosing the unpublicized secrets of others—as Ben Goldacre does in *Bad Pharma* regarding the pharmaceutical industry—by itself is not always effective in facilitating change. People are often deluged with information. They do not necessarily focus on one particular point or, if they do, they do so for only a limited time. Still, there are clear cases when making particular information public *does* make a significant difference.

The key to getting readers to take note often lies less in *what* one discloses than in *whom* one discloses that information to. Anthropologists must target their information to those most interested in it while being sure to present it in a form these parties can readily use. The value of targeted transparency— providing institutions with truthful, public information they need to enhance themselves and/or discredit their competitors—is that there is a ready group of individuals committed to publicizing it. Archon Fung, Mary Graham, and David Weil in *Full Disclosure: The Perils and Promise of Transparency* write that "the availability of more information does not always produce markets that are more efficient or fair, or collective action that advances public priorities. Transparency policies are likely to be effective when the new information they generate can be easily embedded into the routines of information users."[22] Or, phrased more specifically, anthropologists in their writings should target audiences who have a keen interest in the information they are presenting.

Targeted transparency makes clear why anthropologists need to reach out beyond policy makers to other constituencies in presenting their information. Providing information solely to a few policy makers (who then use it at their discretion) can be a dangerous tango. To have credibility—to really speak truth to power—cultural anthropologists should not be pawns of the powerful. Facilitating change through exposés might at first glance seem pretty straightforward. We do see examples of this. The *Chronicle of Higher Education* reported that the "University of California will no longer pay for Regent's dinners and parties."[23] The change came just after the *San Francisco Chronicle* reported: "The night before the University of California Board of Regents voted to raise student

---

22    Fung, Graham, Weil (2007:173–174).
23    A. Harris (2017).

tuition to help cash-strapped campuses, they threw themselves a party at the luxury Intercontinental Hotel in San Francisco and billed the university. The tab for the Jan. 25 banquet: $17,600 for 65 people, or $270 a head."[24] The *San Francisco Chronicle* included, in the same article, a list of other lavish parties that the university reimbursed the regents for, totaling $225,000 since 2012.

Or take the firing of Michael Flynn as President Trump's national security advisor. In her role as acting attorney general, Sally Yates had informed the White House counsel that Vice President Pence was making false public statements based on misinformation Flynn had given Pence. But no action was taken. In an article reporting on Yates's public testimony on the topic before a Senate subcommittee, the *Washington Post* asked and answered the following question: "Would Trump have ever acted [to fire Flynn] if the *Washington Post* hadn't broken the story that Flynn was not telling the truth? It appears no meaningful action was taken until the *Post* reported details on Feb. 9 of the Flynn-Kislyak conversation that contradicted what he had told his West Wing colleagues. Even then, it took four more days for Flynn to go. . . . Who knows how long Trump would have tried to sit on what Yates had said if the truth had never come out via the press?"[25]

Usually, however, it is not that simple. Two cautions need be noted. First, you tend to lose control over your message when you share it. It becomes part of someone else's project as well. Still, it constitutes an effective way to have your message heard. And, if you feel it is being seriously distorted, there is nothing stopping you from targeting other prominent groups that might distort your message less. Second, you need to carefully select the group or groups you wish to work with. It is not only a matter of a group being interested in your information. You need to ask what is the relationship of the group you are targeting with those you want to assist? Will sharing your information over time benefit those you seek to help, or will it mainly enhance the group itself? Below are some examples for consideration.

## EDWARD SNOWDEN AND THE NSA

Snowden's leaking classified government documents about the activities of the US National Security Agency (NSA) made world news for many months. Wikipedia summarizes the case:

---

24    Gutierrez and Asimov (2017).
25    Hohmann (2017).

On May 20, 2013, Snowden flew to Hong Kong after leaving his job at an NSA facility in Hawaii and in early June he revealed thousands of classified NSA documents to journalists Glenn Greenwald, Laura Poitras, and Ewen MacAskill. Snowden came to international attention after stories based on the material appeared in *The Guardian* and the *Washington Post*. Further disclosures were made by other newspapers, including *Der Spiegel* and the *New York Times*. . . .

It was revealed that the NSA was harvesting millions of email and instant messaging contact lists, searching email content, tracking and mapping the location of cell phones, and undermining attempts at encryption via Bullrun and that the agency was using cookies to "piggyback" on the same tools used by internet advertisers "to pinpoint targets for government hacking and to bolster surveillance." The NSA was shown to be secretly tapping into Yahoo and Google data centers to collect information from hundreds of millions of account holders worldwide by tapping undersea cables using the MUSCULAR surveillance program.[26]

It might seem obvious that Snowden's whistleblowing would garner wide public attention since it involves explosive documentation on the degree to which the NSA was collecting information most people around the world thought was private. The two journalists who reported on Snowden's revelations for the *Washington Post*, Martin Baron and Barton Gellman, won the 2014 Pulitzer Prize for the "revelation of widespread secret surveillance by the National Security Agency, marked by authoritative and insightful reports that helped the public understand how the disclosures fit into the larger framework of national security."[27] The documentary *Citizen Four*, based on Greenwald's initial revelations, won the American Academy Award (or Oscar) for best documentary in 2015.[28]

It seems obvious. But what is intriguing is that another, related story published in 2010 by the *Washington Post*, by Dana Priest and William Arkin, received considerably less recognition. They reported: "Nine years after the terrorist attacks of 2001, the United States is assembling a vast domestic intelligence apparatus to collect information about Americans using the FBI, local police, state homeland security offices, and military criminal investigators. The system, by far the largest and most technologically sophisticated in the nation's history, collects, stores, and analyzes information about thousands of U.S. citizens and

26   Wikipedia, s.v. "Edward Snowden."

27   See the 2014 Pulitzer Prize winners at http://www.pulitzer.org/winners/washington-post-1.

28   See *Citizenfour*, https://www.youtube.com/watch?v=AeERpE-S7fs (accessed October 5, 2017).

residents, many of whom have not been accused of any wrongdoing."[29] Priest and Arkin's disclosures did not make worldwide news for months on end. It made headline news in the United States for a short time and appeared on *Frontline*. But it was soon set aside as fresh news stories made new headlines.

Why the difference? In part, it was a matter of audience. The disclosures by Snowden and those by Priest and Arkin differ in their focus. Priest and Arkin's exposé only examined data collected in the United States about Americans. Presumably much of their reporting had been cleared prior to publication by the relevant intelligence agencies—otherwise they might have been criminally charged, as Snowden was, with exposing national secrets.[30] While Priest and Arkin's exposé may have made a number of NSA officials uncomfortable, the coauthors also noted that much of the secret information being collected was not that useful. In contrast, the European Union, given its greater concern for individual privacy, was upset by the depth of the National Security Agency's penetration of its citizens' and governments' privacy. The NSA even hacked into the cell phone of Angela Merkel, the German prime minister—a key ally who was on cordial terms with President Obama. Once the Europeans expressed their shock, the Americans became more upset. From my perspective, Snowden was smart in revealing his information to reporters from the British *Guardian* before the NSA knew the degree to which its secret operation had been compromised. Snowden was able to get his information out to a wider and more attentive audience than Priest and Arkin and, as a result, his exposé had a greater impact.

Reinforcing this perspective is a *New York Times* report that questions the degree to which the NSA, post-Snowden, has taken steps to improve the security of its highly classified data:

> The government's efforts to tighten access to its most sensitive surveillance and hacking data after the leaks of National Security Agency files by Edward J. Snowden fell short, according to a newly declassified report.
>
> The NSA failed to consistently lock racks of servers storing highly classified data and to secure data center machine rooms, according to the report, an investigation by the Defense Department's inspector general completed in 2016. The

---

29    Priest and Arkin (2010).

30    See "A note on this project. Top Secret in America: A Washington Post Investigation," http://projects.washingtonpost.com/top-secret-america/articles/editors-note/ (accessed October 5, 2017).

report was classified at the time and made public in redacted form this week in response to a Freedom of Information Act lawsuit by the *New York Times*.

The agency also failed to meaningfully reduce the number of officials and contractors who were empowered to download and transfer data classified as top secret, as well as the number of "privileged" users, who have greater power to access the NSA's most sensitive computer systems. And it did not fully implement software to monitor what those users were doing.[31]

What is clear is that other countries, especially in Europe, became very upset at the NSA's covert surveillance and put legal restrictions on it. I suggest that is why the Snowden incident became worldwide news that persisted for months and made Snowden an international criminal/hero—depending on one's perspective. The contrast with Dana Priest is interesting. After her exposé she became the Knight Chair in Public Affairs Journalism at the University of Maryland. Snowden became a criminal hounded by the US government.

## NANCY SCHEPER-HUGHES AND THE FBI

We see a related pattern with Scheper-Hughes's work on illegal organ donations. Through her ethnographic research she was able to facilitate the trial of the first person ever convicted for organ trafficking in the United States. The following report appeared in *Bloomberg Business*: "A New York man admitted to brokering black-market sales of human kidneys to three Americans, becoming the first person convicted in the U.S. of organ trafficking. Levy Izhak Rosenbaum, 60, pleaded guilty today to three counts of organ trafficking and one count of conspiracy in federal court in Trenton, New Jersey. He said three ailing people in New Jersey paid him a total of $410,000 to arrange the sale of kidneys from healthy donors and an undercover FBI agent paid him $10,000. A 1984 U.S. law bans the sale of human organs."[32]

Most news reports on the conviction did not mention the role Scheper-Hughes played. However, Wikipedia in its description of Operation Bid Rig, a well-known New Jersey political corruption scandal, noted that "anthropologist and organ trade expert Nancy Scheper-Hughes claimed that she had informed

31    See Savage (2017). Also note that Shane, Perltoth, and Sanger (2017), which in some ways was a more serious breach than Snowden's, has attracted significantly less worldwide publicity compared to Snowden.

32    Bloomberg Business (2011).

the FBI that Rosenbaum was 'a major figure' in international organ smuggling."[33] Quoting Scheper-Hughes: "I went to the media, to CBS, to *60 Minutes*, and then to *48 Hours*, which did send an investigative reporter, Avi Cohan, to meet me in Israel where we spoke to patients who had had 'undercover' transplants at hospitals in NYC, Philadelphia, the Bay Area, and Los Angeles. CBS decided not to do the exposé. I was stumped. No one wanted to accuse surgeons, or prevent a suffering patient from getting a transplant, even with an illegally procured kidney from a displaced person from abroad."[34]

It took several years for the New Jersey FBI office to arrest Rosenbaum. He was eventually arrested in 2009 as part of a larger organized crime sting. It was because Rosenbaum was involved in another case—one more important to the FBI—that the agents finally followed up on Scheper-Hughes's information. As Scheper-Hughes explains: "The FBI finally came to me for help in 2009 when Rosenbaum was ... arrested. From then on, I worked closely with the Federal Prosecutor, Mark McCarren, and with the FBI, one in particular, FBI Agent Waldie, was terrific."[35] What made the FBI become interested in Scheper-Hughes's information, in brief, was the Bureau's arrest of Rosenbaum on a different charge and their trying to find out more information about him.

## THE NATIONAL SCIENCE FOUNDATION

Since January 4, 2010, the NSF has in theory required all grantees to submit Project Outcome Reports within ninety days of their grants' expiration. (Since 2016, it has been 120 days.) Quoting from a Research.gov fact sheet: "The Project Outcomes Report for the General Public is a required report, written by Principal Investigators (PIs) specifically for the public, to provide insight into the outcomes of National Science Foundation (NSF)-funded research. The America COMPETES Act (ACA) of 2007, Section 7010, requires that research outcomes and citations of published documents resulting from research funded, in whole or in part, by NSF be made available to the public in a timely manner and electronic format. . . . [It is] required for new awards made or existing awards that receive funding amendments on or after January 4, 2010."[36]

---

33    Wikipedia, s.v. "Operation Bid Rig."
34    Scheper-Hughes (2011).
35    Scheper-Hughes, personal communication (2018).
36    The fact sheet is available at https://www.purdue.edu/business/sps/pdf/ProjectOutcomes ReportFactSheet.pdf (accessed October 5, 2017).

The NSF's "Proposal and Award Policies and Procedures Guide" for 2016 states:

No later than 120 days following expiration of the grant [the 2010, 2013, and 2014 editions of the guide specify 90 days], a project outcomes report for the general public must be submitted electronically. This report serves as a brief summary, prepared specifically for the public, of the nature and outcomes of the project. This report will ... describe the project outcomes or findings that address the intellectual merit and broader impacts of the work as defined in the NSF merit review criteria. This description should be a brief (generally, two to three paragraphs) summary of the project's results that is written for the lay reader. Principal Investigators are strongly encouraged to avoid use of jargon, terms of art, or acronyms.[37]

Examining data at Research.gov, however, shows only a limited number of grantees submitted reports from 2010 through 2013.[38] Few anthropologists are willing to challenge the NSF given it is a key source of much anthropological funding. Fortunately, the Center for a Public Anthropology does not receive NSF funding. When writing directly to the NSF director did not elicit a response, the Center and a number of student volunteers (using their home addresses) wrote letters to members of the US House Subcommittee on Research and Technology

---

37    "Proposals and Award Policies and Procedure Guide," NSF, effective January 2016, https://www.nsf.gov/pubs/policydocs/pappguide/nsf16001/nsf16_1.pdf. Please note the guides for 2010 (https://www.nsf.gov/pubs/policydocs/pappguide/nsf10_1/nsf10_1.pdf), 2013 (https://www.nsf.gov/pubs/policydocs/pappguide/nsf13001/nsf13_1.pdf), and 2014 (https://www.nsf.gov/pubs/policydocs/pappguide/nsf14001/nsf14_1.pdf) follow the same or similar phrasings.

38    See http://www.research.gov/research-portal/appmanager/base/desktop?_nfpb=true&_event Name=viewQuickSearchFormEvent_so_rsr. After recent correspondence with the NSF and further investigation, there is a more accurate compilation of those who have submitted their Project Outcome Reports based on Faculty Award Numbers. Reviewing these and related data, four important points stand out: (1) Data collected with the Faculty Award Numbers, while higher than that publicly displayed at the above website, still indicate compliance is comparatively low. (2) While the NSF asserts it has a high compliance rate in respect to Project Outcome Report submissions, from the data I have available, I believe the NSF has in fact not done a systematic study of compliance rates using the Faculty Award Numbers and hence is uncertain as to what the actual compliance rate is for Project Outcome Report submissions. (3) Nor is it certain, from a limited examination of related data, that the NSF software, contrary to what is claimed, always bars those who have failed to submit Project Outcomes Reports from obtaining new grants. (4) The overall impression gained is that, while the NSF acts quite professional in its grant approval process, it is, at times, less than professional in insuring grantees actually carry out their research in the manner promised and provide a Project Outcomes Reports as promised when they received their funding—the point suggested in Chapter 1, pp. 33–34.

and the US Senate Subcommittee on Science and Space, who jointly control the NSF's budget. The budget, it should be noted, was up for renewal in 2014. As the campaign started, various media (e.g., the *Chronicle of Higher Education*, October 24, 2014) reported on the House Subcommittee's attempt to review NSF grants, especially in the social sciences. However, the Subcommittee ran into various problems and was unsuccessful. Still, the NSF felt threatened.

In assessing the campaign's effectiveness, it is interesting to compare how many additional Project Outcome Reports were submitted during the three months of the campaign compared to the number of the reports submitted prior to its start. The table below reveals Project Outcome Reports from grants awarded as a percentage of total awarded grants in 2010, 2011, 2012, and 2013:

Grants Awarded as Percent of Total Awarded Grants[39]

|  | BEFORE THE CAMPAIGN | AFTER THE CAMPAIGN |
|---|---|---|
| 2010 | 6% | 85% |
| 2011 | 11% | 82% |
| 2012 | 3% | 82% |
| 2013 | 23% | 84% |

What I hypothesize occurred is this: When the House Subcommittee ran into resistance in seeking to review NSF grants, the students' "snail mail" letters—over two thousand in all—attracted the Subcommittee's interest and offered an alternative means for it to assert authority over the NSF. (Copies of the letters were also sent to the NSF director.) Given the NSF's failure to enforce its own requirement in relation to federal law, the NSF had little choice but to address the problem regarding the Project Outcomes Reports. It could not push back against the Subcommittee as it did with the Subcommittee's inquiry into NSF grants. What we see again is how targeted transparency fosters greater account-ability. Clearly, the Center and students, working together, could not have influenced the NSF on their own. But they could provide the House Subcommittee with information it needed to push back against the NSF—information it apparently did not previously have. The House Subcommittee, given its control over the NSF's budget, had to be listened to. The Center and students did not.

---

39    If requested, I can provide data relevant to this campaign. The data here are drawn from the readily available public date referred to in footnote 38. While I hypothesize below regarding the pressures involved in fostering the change, I leave others to speculate as to how the data change was actually managed in a relatively short period of time.

## VIETNAM

The Vietnam Veterans Memorial on the Mall in Washington, DC, is one of the world's great memorials. When you visit it, you frequently see people—perhaps a woman holding a child or an elderly couple—lovingly running their hands over one of the 58,256 names inscribed on the wall. A number of the three million people who visit the memorial each year leave sentimental items relating to the loved ones inscribed there. As you look at the names of the dead, you see your own reflection, creating a space that brings the past and the present together. I know of no other memorial that generates such emotion or draws people to interact with it with such love and respect.

With insight gained from the passage of time, many people have reflected on what "went wrong" in Vietnam. Might I suggest, the tragedy of Vietnam resulted from key American statesmen and the US public failing to understand important dynamics of Vietnamese society? Here is how the anthropologist Neil Jamieson phrases this point in his 1993 book, *Understanding Vietnam*: "Over two and a half million Americans went to Vietnam, and over 55,000 thousand . . . died there. . . . Yet our understanding of this tragic episode remains . . . I believe, in many respects simply wrong. We have failed to understand our experience [in Vietnam] because, then and now, we have ignored the perspectives of the people most deeply concerned with the war in which we became involved: The Vietnamese. . . . The images of Vietnam about which the controversy swirled in the United States arose from our own culture not from Vietnamese realities or perceptions."[40]

David Halberstam, in his acclaimed 1972 book *The Best and the Brightest*, asks how so many intellectually astute individuals in the upper levels of the Kennedy and Johnson administrations could have gotten things so wrong. The short answer, he suggests, is that they were arrogant: "An administration which flaunted its intellectual superiority and superior academic credentials made the most critical of decisions with virtually no input from anyone who had any expertise on the recent history of that part of the world, and it in no way factored in the entire experience of the French Indochina War."[41] As Halberstam writes in *The Making of a Quagmire*, it was "a classic example of seeing the world the way we wanted to, instead of the way it was."[42] The tragedy is that so many—Americans and Vietnamese—lost their lives as a result.

---

40    Jamieson (1993:ix); see also Sheehan (1988:131).
41    Halberstam (1993:xv); see also Sheehan (1988:42).
42    Halberstam (1964:339); see also Karnow (1983:362).

The United States failed to grasp North Vietnam's strategy for fighting the war. The US military assumed it could carry out a conventional war of attrition against North Vietnam. Stanley Karnow states: "Official U.S. communiqués and press reports . . . conveyed the idea that U.S. air strikes were devastating North Vietnam. . . . On my initial trip to the region, I expected to see it in ruins. Yet Hanoi, Haiphong, and the nearby countryside were almost totally unscathed. I remembered General Curtis LeMay's thunderous cry to 'Bomb them back into the Stone Age'—but, scanning the north, I concluded that it had been in the Stone Age for decades."[43] What the United States failed to grasp was the dedication the North Vietnamese brought to their cause. They played the same game of attrition as the United States. But they were able to play it longer and harder. Quoting Karnow:

> American strategists went astray by ascribing their own values to the communists. [General William] Westmoreland, for one, was sure that he knew the threshold of their endurance. . . . Even after the war, he still seemed to have misunderstood the dimensions of their determination. "Any American commander who took the same vast losses as General Giap," he said, "would have been sacked overnight."
>
> But Giap, the brilliant North Vietnamese general, was not an American confronted by a strange people in a faraway land. His troops and their civilian supporters, fighting on their own soil, were convinced that their protracted struggle would ultimately wear away the patience of their foes.
>
> "We were not strong enough to drive a half million American troops out of Vietnam, but that wasn't our aim," Giap explained to me. "We sought to break the will of the American government to continue the conflict. Westmoreland was wrong to count on his superior firepower to grind us down. Our Soviet and Chinese comrades also failed to grasp our approach when they asked how many divisions we had in relation to the Americans, how we would cope with their technology, their artillery, their air attacks. We were waging a people's war [in the Vietnamese manner] . . . a total war in which every man, every woman, every unit, big or small, is sustained by a mobilized population. So America's sophisticated weapons, electronic devices, and the rest were to no avail. Despite its military power, America misgauged the limits of its power. In war there are two factors—human beings and weapons. Ultimately, though, human beings are the decisive factor."
>
> Ironically, many U.S. officers concurred. "The American army and its South Vietnamese allies," General Bruce Palmer writes after the war, "demonstrated a

tendency to rely on superior firepower and technology rather than on professional skill and soldierly qualities. . . . [The Viet Cong] had an extraordinary ability to recuperate," Palmer notes, "absorbing casualties in numbers unthinkable to us, replacing people, retraining and reindoctrinating them, and then bouncing back."[44]

One of the striking points of the Vietnam War is how few academics actually studied Vietnam during this period. Fox Butterfield, in a review article for the *New York Times Magazine*, notes that a "black hole" existed in the American academy with respect to Vietnam during the war. The *New York Times* conducted a survey in 1970 and found not a single scholar focusing on North Vietnam; fewer than thirty students were studying Vietnamese.[45] One might argue that key political decision makers were not inclined to trust academic writings during this period. But even if they had wanted to, there were few to guide them. In *The Best and the Brightest*, Halberstam notes that key government experts on Asia had been pushed out of government service during the anti-Communist campaigns of the 1950s and were never replaced. As a result, few officials in key administrative positions understood Vietnam or the Vietnamese.

Not having on-the-ground information meant that more than money was lost; so were thousands of lives. In the spring of 1965, General William Westmoreland was eager to gain combat troops to conduct extensive search-and-destroy missions against the Viet Cong. As a precaution, Westmoreland and the Military Assistance Command, Vietnam (MACV) decided to do a study of the enemy's capacity to replace its losses. Halberstam writes:

> When Colonel William Crossen, one of the top intelligence officers, put . . . [the report] together he was appalled: the number of men that Hanoi could send down the trails [into South Vietnam] without seriously damaging its defense at home was quite astonishing. . . . When Crossen came up with his final figure he could not believe it, so he checked it again, being even more conservative . . . and still he was staggered by what he found; the other side had an amazing capacity and capability of reinforcing. When he brought the study to Westmoreland's staff and showed the figure to a general there . . . "Jesus," said the general, "if we tell this to the people in Washington we'll be out of the war tomorrow. We'll have to revise [the figures] downward." So Crossen's figures were duly scaled down considerably . . . the staff intuitively protecting the commander from things he didn't want

44    Karnow (1983:20–21); see also Butterfield (1983:11); Hastings (2018).
45    Butterfield (1983); see also Halberstam (1969:xviii).

to see and didn't want to hear, never coming up with information which might challenge what a commander wanted to do at a given moment.[46]

The information Crossen collected was not top-secret intelligence. To collect it, you could simply examine Vietnamese birth records gathered by the colonial French administration from the 1930s and 1940s.

One might criticize Crossen for not reporting his figures to the US Congress when the surge in troop strength was being debated. He was a soldier follow-ing orders and could conceivably have been court-martialed for disobeying the chain of command. But a few tenured anthropologists could have investigated Vietnamese birthrates in French colonial archives and, without any threat of being fired, made their data widely available to the US Congress and to world media. They could have made clear to all that Westmoreland's strategy was likely to not only fail but, in allowing the war to escalate as it did, cause untold misery and destruction.

## SOME REFLECTIONS

By widening the scope of analysis beyond the normal confines of anthropol-ogy, there are clear lessons regarding how individuals might make a significant difference, might have a significant impact, outside the academy. I offer three observations. First, it is critical to put much thought into how you prepare your message for your intended audience. It must appeal to their concerns, their interests. It does seem, for example, that despite Snowden's reported "crime" of stealing classified NSA documents, his bigger crime was divulging the NSA's operation to the wider world, especially to those belonging to the European Union who took serious affront at the NSA's secret surveillance. If Snowden's crime was simply stealing data—not exposing the breadth of the surveillance to other countries—then why, following the *New York Times* report, is the NSA not taking more care in protecting its data now?

Second, timing is important, which is why it is critical to persist until an oppor-tune moment arises. The FBI only became interested in Scheper-Hughes's data on Rosenbaum when it began investigating him for a different crime. The US House Subcommittee on Research and Technology might not have paid attention to the students' letters if the Subcommittee had not been in a tense stand-off with the NSF. One might also wonder what impact the students' and the Center's letters to Penn State's President Spanier, regarding returning the Yanomami blood samples,

---

46   Halberstam (1969:545).

would have had if the university had not been in a tense relationship with the Pennsylvania General Assembly regarding budgetary matters.

Third, we might reflect on the protests that anthropologists helped lead regarding the Vietnam War. They certainly had a cathartic effect and gradually, over several years, helped in ending the war. But one might wonder whether other efforts might have proven effective as well—if, for example, various academics had seriously investigated the Vietnamese and how they were able to overcome their high death toll in battle. I referred to Butterfield's article regarding the "black hole" that existed in the American academy with respect to Vietnam during the war. This lack of academic guidance was significant given Halberstam's point that key government experts on Asia had been pushed out of government service during the anti-Communist campaigns of the 1950s and never replaced. True, key politicians might not have listened to academic advice. But, even if they had not, going public with their information might have helped changed the tenor of the public debate, especially if it had been aimed at members of the US Congress when they were discussing an expansion of the Vietnam War.

Speaking truth to power, when one has important data that others are critically interested in, can be an important role for anthropologists. In presenting their observations and analyses to a wide public audience at critical historical moments, anthropologists can make a real difference. For Vietnam it is only hypothetical. But perhaps if anthropologists had understood the Vietnamese far better, they might have helped prevent the US military from trying to destroy the Vietnamese opposition by way of attrition. Despite clear military defeats on the ground and an enormous loss of lives during the Tet Offensive, the North Vietnamese persisted. They were less engaged in a war of attrition than the United States was. Rather, they were focused on a longer game for which they possessed the manpower to endure repeated US military "victories" until Americans' political support for the war withered.[47]

47    Readers interested in exploring this topic further might refer to: American Experience (n.d.); Anonymous (n.d.); Appy (2006); Atwood (2008); Bissell (2006); Burk (2008); Church (2001); Clarke (2007); CNN.com (2007); Economist (2007d, 2009b); Fall (1965); Francis (2008); Frankel (1995); Glenn (2007a, 2007c, 2008c); Hastings (2018); Jamieson, Nguyen, and Rambo (1992); Klein (2007); Marr (1994); Mass (2004); McLeod (1994); Mitgang (1991, 1993); Moyar (2006); Nagl (2002, 2008); Navasky (1972); Packer (2007); Pike (1983); T. Powers (1999); Schwenkel (2009); W. Scott (1994); Steel (1988); Wikipedia, s.v. "Vietnam War"; and Wright (2009).

# 5

## TWO ROADS DIVERGED . . .

**CHAPTER 1 SET** the stage for the book's themes by suggesting the field's ethnographic tools be applied to studying the field itself. Chapter 2 discussed a key question hanging over the dominant "do no harm" paradigm—the degree to which it advances knowledge for the broader community versus serves the career interests of anthropologists. Chapters 3 and 4 outlined an alternative paradigm, one centered on public anthropology, that seeks to address problems with the "do no harm" paradigm. By emphasizing concerns beyond the field, the paradigm strives to broaden support for cultural anthropology in the wider society. Chapter 5 addresses the question in the book's subtitle: Is it time to shift paradigms?

It is best to start with Thomas Kuhn. As previously noted, Kuhn writes: "Paradigms gain their status because they are more successful than their competitors in solving a few problems that the group of practitioners has recognized as acute." He continues: "Probably the single most prevalent claim advanced by the proponents of a new paradigm is that they can solve the problems that have led the old one to a crisis."[1] In answering the question, we need ask: Do the field's practitioners, operating within the "do no harm" paradigm, feel in a crisis? And, critically, could the public anthropology paradigm help them address it? There is also another question: Even with the crisis, even with the problems faced, are the field's practitioners open to shifting away from their current paradigm to a new one?

Kuhn describes how scientific communities in other times resisted shifting paradigms:

> How, then, are scientists brought to make this transposition? Part of the answer is that they are very often not. Copernicanism made few converts for almost a century after Copernicus' death. Newton's work was not generally accepted, particularly on the Continent, for more than half a century after the *Principia* appeared. Priestly never accepted the oxygen theory, nor Lord Kelvin the electromagnetic theory and so on . . . Darwin, in a particularly perceptive passage at the end of his *Origin of Species* wrote: "Although I am fully convinced of the truth of the views given in this volume . . . I by no means expect to convince experienced naturalists whose mind are stocked with a multitude of facts all viewed, during a long course of years . . . [But] I look forward . . . to young and rising naturalists, who will be able to view both sides of the question with impartiality."[2]

Kuhn writes: "Max Planck, surveying his career, . . . sadly remarked that 'a new scientific truth does not triumph by convincing its opponents and making them see the light, but rather because its opponents eventually die, and a new generation grows up that is familiar with it.'" But Kuhn adds: "In the past [resistance to shifting paradigms has] most often been taken to indicate that scientists being only human cannot always admit their errors, even when confronted with strict proof. I would argue, rather, that in these matters neither proof nor error is at issue. The transfer of allegiance for [sic] paradigm to paradigm is a conversion experience that cannot be forced."[3] The question comes down to: How great is the paradigmatic crisis cultural anthropologists feel they are in, and how many are willing to explore an alternative that might soften the crisis and over time help address it?

1    Kuhn (1970:23, 153).
2    Kuhn (1970:150–151).
3    Kuhn (1970:151).

## Is This Enough of a Crisis?

*This section explores (1) how the assessment of intellectual productivity has become dominated by a series of metric measurements of ambiguous value, (2) the negative reactions many faculty have to this development, and (3) the dynamics behind this change. Based on Kuhn's assertion about crises in old paradigms leading to new paradigms, this section asks if the quantification of faculty productivity—with the frustrations and distortions it generates—is enough of a crisis to foster a paradigm shift among cultural anthropologists.*

As William Clark notes in Chapter 1, faculty accountability has been phrased in terms of publications for centuries. But recently, as funding for faculty research has increased, there has been a growing concern, by outside funding sources, for increased faculty accountability—often framed in quantitative or metric terms focused on the number of publications produced and who cites them. This movement is exemplified by Academic Analytics in the United States and the Research Excellence Framework (REF) in the UK. The UK's REF provides a succinct statement of its purpose: "To provide accountability for public investment in research and produce evidence of the benefits of this investment."[4] The push for quantification fits with the current concern regarding international academic rankings, such as provided by Times Higher Education (THE), QS, and the Shanghai Academic Ranking of World Universities. The *Economist* observes: "Highly cited papers provide an easily available measure of success [for these rankings], and, lacking any other reliable metric, that is what the league tables are based on."[5]

The following report from Elsevier for the British government offers an example of how such metrics are phrased: "While the UK represents just 0.9% of global population, 3.2% of R&D expenditure, and 4.1% of researchers, it accounts for 9.5% of downloads, 11.6% of citations and 15.9% of the world's most highly-cited articles. Amongst its comparator countries, the UK has overtaken the US to rank 1st by field-weighted citation impact (an indicator of research quality). Moreover, with just 2.4% of global patent applications, the UK's share of citations from patents (both applications and granted) to journal articles is 10.9%."[6] Pushing faculty to attain a set of metric scores has proved stressful for some. To enhance their metric scores, roughly 30 percent of UK academic insti-

---

4    REF 2021 (2017).
5    Economist (2018a).
6    El Aisati et al. (n.d.).

tutions set faculty funding targets. The target for an Imperial College professor reputedly led to his suicide when he was unable to reach it.[7]

There has been considerable faculty pushback against framing intellectual productivity in metric terms. Marc Edwards, the civil engineer who exposed the dangerously high lead levels in the water in Flint, Michigan, states: "I am concerned about the culture of academia in this country [the United States] and the perverse incentives that are given to young faculty. The pressures to get funding are just extraordinary. We're all on this hedonistic treadmill—pursuing funding, pursuing fame, pursuing h-index [a type of citation count]—and the idea of science as a public good is being lost."[8]

In a critique of Academic Analytics, David Hughes, an anthropologist who is president of the Rutgers faculty union, writes:

> Academic Analytics crawls the Internet and, it says, has assembled profiles of more than 270,000 scholars at more than 385 colleges in the United States and abroad. The database enumerates "scholarly productivity" in a handful of categories: books, journal articles, citations, published conference proceedings, federal funding, and honorific awards. In the world of Academic Analytics, nothing else counts. . . . Under this logic, the strategically minded professor or department might then stop engaging in less conventional and less measurable activities, such as public scholarship, community engagement, software, patents, films, book chapters, articles in less-well-known journals, and nonfederal grants—not to mention teaching and service. The database even discourages book publishing, by conflating edited and single-author works. . . . Even within the narrow range it measures, the firm makes unpredictable mistakes. I obtained my profile after a freedom-of-information request. I learned that I had published two books and three articles in the given time windows. In fact, I had published two books and one article. Where did Academic Analytics find the two . . . [additional] texts I didn't write? Because of such errors, the database is losing legitimacy. None of the many deans with whom I have spoken actually trust the spreadsheet. Still, they consider Academic Analytics useful for . . . [university] branding. With metrics, an administration can claim to have the best [XXX department] in the country.[9]

---

7    Jump (2015a).
8    Kolowich (2016:26).
9    Hughes (2016).

The Rutgers faculty of Arts and Sciences voted overwhelmingly to exclude Academic Analytics from faculty assessments.[10]

James Wilsdon et al., in the "Report of the Independent Review of the Role of Metrics in Research Assessment and Management," assert that "within the REF [the UK's assessment framework], it is not currently feasible to assess the quality of UOAs [units of assessment, such as departments] using quantitative indicators alone . . . no set of numbers, however broad, is likely to be able to capture the multifaceted and nuanced judgements on the quality of research outputs that the REF process currently provides."[11]

Paul Jump, quoting other sources, writes: "Research managers can become 'over-reliant on indicators that are widely felt to be problematic or not properly understood . . . or on indicators that may be used insensitively or inappropriately,' and do not 'fully recognize the diverse contributions of individual researchers to the overall institutional mission or the wider public good.'"[12] A report by the American Association of University Professors (AAUP) regarding Academic Analytics cautions that "measuring faculty 'productivity' with an exclusive or excessive emphasis on quantitative measures of research output must inevitably fail to take adequate account of the variety and totality of scholarly accomplishments."[13] Cris Shore and Susan Wright observe that "a key aspect of this process has been its effect in changing the identity of professionals and the way they conceptualize themselves. The audited subject is recast as a depersonalized unit of economic resource whose productivity and performance must constantly be measured and enhanced."[14]

David Graeber writes:

In most universities nowadays—and this seems to be true almost everywhere—academic staff find themselves spending less and less time studying, teaching, and writing about things, and more and more time measuring, assessing, discussing, and quantifying the way in which they study, teach, and write about things (or the way in which they propose to do so in the future). European universities,

---

10    But Rutgers did not cancel its subscription to Academic Analytics. Instead, the administration allowed faculty to check what was reported on them—to ensure it was correct—and the chancellor formed a committee to assess how Academic Analytics would be used on campus (see Flaherty [2016]).

11    Wilsdon et al. (2015).

12    Jump (2015b).

13    AAUP (2016); see also Stein (2017).

14    Shore and Wright (2000:62).

reportedly, now spend at least 1.4 billion euros [roughly $1.6 billion] a year on failed grant applications.). It's gotten to the point where "admin" now takes up so much of most professors' time that complaining about it is the default mode of socializing among academic colleagues; indeed, insisting on talking instead about one's latest research project or course idea is considered somewhat rude. . . . One might be tempted to lay all this down to the peculiarities of the British academy . . . but in the United States the problem is just as bad.[15]

Scholars have offered various reasons for the rise of metric assessments of faculty productivity. Sally Engle Merry suggests it is part of a wider trend—"the dissemination of the corporate form of thinking and governance into broader social spheres."[16] Marilyn Strathern terms this trend an audit culture "in which the twinned precepts of economic efficiency and good practice are . . . pursued."[17] Paul Jump, in an article titled "Metrics: How To Handle Them Responsibly," comes closest to the dynamic involved, in my opinion. While writing about the turn to metrics in the UK, what he states is equally relevant to the United States. He notes the focus on quantification

is being whipped up by "powerful currents" arising from, inter alia, "growing pressures for audit and evaluation of public spending on higher education and research; demands by policymakers for more strategic intelligence on research quality and impact; [and] competition within and between institutions for prestige, students, staff and resources."

Metrics—numbers—give at least the impression of objectivity, and they have become increasingly important in the management and assessment of research ever since citation databases such as the Science Citation Index, Scopus and Google Scholar became available online in the early 2000s. Metrics are particularly popular in political circles. . . . Within universities, too, metrics have been widely adopted, not merely for institutional benchmarking but also, increasingly, for managing the performance of academics. . . . The Metric Tide [a report produced by the Higher Education Funding Council of England as part of the REF] . . . attributes this state of affairs to the increasing pressure on universities to be "more accountable to government and public funders of research," and also

15    Graeber (2018).
16    Merry (2011:S83).
17    M. Strathern (2000).

to the financial pressures imposed on institutions by constrained funding and globalisation.[18]

To understand the transformation taking place, we need to step back and see the bigger picture. Since I am most familiar with the United States, let me focus on that. During the first half of the twentieth century, American universities were relatively self-contained communities with limited direction from the government. But starting with the establishment of the National Science Foundation in 1950 (to promote science as well as national health and welfare), the National Defense Education Act in 1958 (in response to the Soviet launch of Sputnik), followed by the Higher Education Act (HEA) of 1965 (part of President Johnson's Great Society), a considerable amount of federal money has poured into universities.[19] HEA has been repeatedly reauthorized by the US Congress. In 1953 the federal government provided $14.03 billion for research and development. By 2017 the amount had increased to $117.46 billion.[20] The federal government now represents a critical source of funding for most universities. Following the baby boom of the 1960s, government funding supported large influxes of students, which has led in turn to more anthropology departments and more students taking anthropology courses.

In terms of the federal government's funding focused specifically on research (vs. research and development), it went from $7.6 billion in 1976 to $83.5 billion in 2018.[21] Unfortunately, federal funding for the social sciences for 1970 to 2017 went only from $1.09 to $1.17 billion (though in 1978, 1979, and 2014, federal spending topped $1.5 billion).[22] Understandably, the federal government (as well as state governments, which also provide significant funding) wants assurances

18    Jump (2015b); see also Wilsdon et al. (2015). In the United States, the state of Wisconsin has passed a law that requires universities "to track how much time each faculty member spends in the classroom, make the information public, and then reward those who teach more than the standard workload" (June 2018). The problem is that less quantifiable tasks faculty carry—from research to mentoring students to committee meetings—are ignored in their workload.

19    The HEA's mission was "to strengthen the educational resources of our colleges and universities and to provide financial assistance for students in postsecondary and higher education" (Public Law No. 89-329, https://www.govtrack.us/congress/bills/89/hr9567/summary).

20    See "Historical Trends in Federal R&D," https://www.aaas.org/page/historical-trends-fed eral-rd (accessed August 11, 2018).

21    See "Federal R&D as a Percent of GDP, 1976–2018," https://www.aaas.org/page/historical -trends-federal-rd.

22    See "Federal Research Funding by Discipline, 1970–2017," https://www.aaas.org/page/ historical-trends-federal-rd.

that the funding is not being wasted. They want something in return. This has resulted in increased demands for accountability, which, over time, has evolved into the use of metrics to judge accountability. Given the limited research funding for the social sciences in comparison to the life sciences (which gained $26.18 billion in 2017), the framing of accountability in metric terms makes some sense. Similar to the Institutional Research Boards (IRBs), the life sciences tend to be the point of reference for framing accountability.

As stressed below, faculty productivity need not be measured primarily in metric terms. But they are often convenient to use. Metrics facilitate comparisons across disciplines. Moreover, they are understandable by both high-level academic administrators and key government officials. They also can seem impressive (as the above Elsevier example suggests). Referring to an interview with Robert Berdahl, the former president of the Association of American Universities, Basken writes: "As a dean, a provost, and an historian, Mr. Berdahl said, he knew his department. But he was also responsible for departments in physics, chemistry, and economics. To assess them, he said, it would be invaluable to have comparable data from other institutions."[23]

The "do no harm" paradigm initially helped universities address the problem of outside funders demanding more accountability. Universities simply doubled down on their focus of appearing to "do good," offering, as they had in the past, anecdotal examples, while still focusing on their self-interest. The images conveyed implied universities were centers of intellectual insights and advancing knowledge. With time, however, the pronouncements and anecdotes started to grow stale. Various parts of the government demanded more substantive confirmation of what skills students were gaining from these studies and what researchers were producing of value to the broader society. The hegemonic-like triadic infrastructures (discussed in Chapter 1) readily adapted to the change in accountability standards—presumably because of the financial awards in doing so. Funding agencies have not objected since they can now offer considerably more funding to researchers. As noted in Chapter 1, they have made some effort at holding grantees and their universities accountable for how they use government funds.[24] University administrators also have taken the govern-

---

23    Basken (2016c). Mr. Berdahl, it should be noted, is now an adviser to Academic Analytics.

24    In a study of the impact statements written by fifty senior scholars in applying for research grants in the UK and Australia, Chubb and Watermeyer (2017) report that applicants tended to exaggerate the future impact of their research to gain funding. In the authors' words: "Interviewees were united in identifying that funding applicants may exaggerate the impact claims of prospective

ment's increased demands for accountability seriously. They have revised faculty accountability to focus on metrics that they and government officials can readily understand.

The one group that has noticeably suffered from the locus of accountability being shifted to funders outside the academy is the faculty. Few want to go back to the salary levels before the increase in funding. Few want to return to when research funding was far more limited. But the metrics used to assess their intellectual productivity frequently seem to be arbitrary and often counter to their intellectual mission. Until recently, as indicated in Chapter 2, faculty were able to define advancing knowledge in their own terms, for their own benefit. That is no longer the case.

I noted in Chapter 1 how the NIH is now enforcing greater restrictions on research. As Francis Collins, the NIH's director states: "We can't afford to waste resources and produce non-reproducible conclusions."[25] We also see this in the recent demand for federal funding agencies to focus research funding on national priorities. The *Chronicle of Higher Education* reports the US House of Representatives wants to "require the National Science Foundation to award grants only for research projects that the agency can certify as being in the national interest."[26] Though "national interest" is vaguely defined, the intent is clear. Governmental funding should serve the broader society's interests, not the interests of academics. The distinguished journal *Science* observes, even "the agency's friends—both the NSF officials who testified and Democratic legislators who have staunchly defended the agency's grantmaking practices—appear to have accepted [the US House Committee's chair's] premise that NSF has lost sight of its obligation to fund research 'in the national interest' and agree that Congress needs to keep NSF on a short leash."[27]

---

research where the impact was not immediately obvious in order to acquire research funding. . . . Success in competitive funding processes was perceived by interviewees as the primary motivator for academics adopting a sensationalist approach to marketing the future impact of their prospective research. The importance associated with the acquisition of research funds was thus also seen to instill a moral permissiveness and/or elasticity in the authoring of PIS [Pathways to Impact Statements] and a sense among funding applicants that to overstate impact claims was an inevitable means to an end in the acquisition of research funds" (Chubb and Watermeyer 2017:2364).

25   Voosen (2015:A12); See, for example, the significant restrictions NIH placed on Duke researchers (McCook (2018a)). Also note McCook (2018b). Also note McCook (2018b) in respect to Ohio State, although intriguingly Ohio State did not stop the work of Dr. Carlo Croce, perhaps because of his status and substantial funding (see Glanz and Armendariz [2017]).

26   Basken (2016b).

27   Mervis (2018).

There is no easy way to escape this changing control over accountability standards. Faculty cannot, as in the past, turn inward to various specialties (and subspecialties) and simply ignore these broader pressures for one simple reason: They lack the personal funds to be masters of their own fate. They are dependent on others for financial support. The "do no harm" paradigm has not changed in its basic orientation—the self-serving focus on appearances is still there. But it now pays less attention to faculty interests vis-à-vis the interests of other key players. It parallels the pattern described by Mary Furner during the early 1900s.

None of this means the current push to assess faculty value in quantitative terms makes sense. As Chapter 2 affirms, certain metrics—such as citation counts—are highly problematic. They have caused much faculty frustration without necessarily increasing faculty productivity. Who would want, in quest of a promotion, to produce serious professional publications as examples of one's intellectual competence only to have them counted rather than read—often because departmental reviewers are too distracted with their own publications?

## Problems

*This section explores why to date faculty have not been more effective in pushing back against the quantification of intellectual productivity. It emphasizes two factors: (1) the diminished role of anthropology as a discipline, and (2) the hesitancy of faculty to challenge the status quo, especially before they have tenure. It then asks: Is the current crisis motivating enough to draw faculty to explore an alternative paradigm?*

Many faculty would like to change the metric standards for accountability. Some hold out hope that through collective resistance, such as at Rutgers, they can change the standards. Shore and Wright write: "Given the individualizing and totalizing nature of governing by numbers . . . the most successful antidote probably lies in collective action and a reassertion of academic and professional values. If there is power in numbers, there is also strength in numbers."[28] Graeber calls for a universal guaranteed income that would free academics up to pursue their intellectual interests independent of the university. Few, however, seriously expect that to happen soon in the United States.[29] One might also

---

28    Shore and Wright (2015:431).
29    Graeber (2016).

interpret Sherry Ortner's "anthropology of resistance" as implying a challenge to the current metrics regime: "The anthropology of resistance, at least as I am defining it here, includes both 'cultural critique'—that is, the critical study of the existing order—and studies that emphasize thinking about alternative political and economic futures."[30]

The problem for cultural anthropologists is they currently lack the political, social, and financial "muscle" to effectively confront, in a direct manner, the political and financial powers that foster the metric assessment standards. Let me explain.

## CULTURAL ANTHROPOLOGY'S DIMINISHED ROLE

Today anthropology lacks the broad social support it once had. The continual push to publish has helped foster a fairly fragmented field. There are some vague trends that attract field-wide attention. But field-wide trends, discussed in Chapter 2, no longer prevail. Instead, scholars now tend to stress fairly narrow subjects. George Marcus observes: "One of the characteristics of the [current] period is the relative absence of focusing discussions and debates among anthropologists. . . . There are many specialized discussions and debates within the discipline arising from the multiplicity of subfields and specialties, but no longer any discourse at the center that self-consciously engages the identity of the discipline as such."[31]

There is, at times, the momentary excitement that James Rule referred to in Chapter 2: "the . . . transitory quality of what are promoted as 'state-of-the-art' lines of inquiry . . . to dazzle certain sectors . . . [and] then abruptly lose . . . their . . . appeal."[32] But there are few riveting problems that most cultural anthropologists attend to today for any length of time—in contrast to earlier times. Cultural anthropologists are now addressing all sorts of problems in all sorts of ways and publishing them in all sorts of places (as a perusal of the metrics. publicanthropology.org site affirms).

Also, cultural anthropology possesses an uncertain public status today. While the National Science Foundation breaks out funding for psychology, economics, political science, and sociology, for example, anthropology is listed under "social

---

30   Ortner (2016:66).
31   Marcus (1998:248–249).
32   Rule (1997:23).

sciences, nec" (or "not elsewhere classified").[33] In Chapter 3, I touched on the ambivalence many indigenous groups feel toward anthropologists. Some indigenous groups appreciate the work anthropologists have done; others clearly do not. For many anthropologists, seeking a broader public audience for their work is not a priority. Andrew Abbott observes: "Professionals draw their self-esteem more from their own world than from the public's today."[34] As a result, while some praise cultural anthropology, others seem neutral or negative toward it—wondering what cultural anthropology does for others.

Reflecting this, world media give more attention to archaeology and physical anthropology than to cultural anthropology.[35] The cultural anthropology article receiving the most attention in world media since 2011, according to data provided by Altmetric.com, is "Natural Sleep and Its Seasonal Variations in Three Pre-Industrial Societies" published in *Current Biology*.[36] Cultural anthropology articles published by the American Anthropological Association's journals are rarely cited in world media. Based on data from departmental websites regarding full-time faculty for the 2012–2013 academic year—focusing on 94 research-oriented schools—I collected the following departmental faculty averages: anthropology (20.63), economics (27.4), political science (28.46), psychology (38.07), and sociology (21.56). Although these data are a bit dated, they provide a sense of the full-time faculty positions university administrators feel comfortable with per field.

Membership in the American Anthropological Association (AAA) is declining, likely a result of the field's fragmentation and limited focus on publicly relevant questions. In the 1990s, AAA membership ranged between 11,000 and 12,000 members.[37] In 2015 the Association had approximately 9,500 members. In 2016 membership was down to around 8,600.[38] Daniel Ginsberg, reporting on "Trends in Anthropology Bachelor's Degrees" for the AAA, observes: "Anthropology degree completions peaked in 2013 and have decreased sharply

33    "Table 8. Higher education R&D expenditures, by source of funds and R&D field: FY 2015," https://ncsesdata.nsf.gov/herd/2015/html/HERD2015_DST_08.html (accessed October 5, 2017).

34    Abbott (1988:119).

35    See Public Anthropology's Metrics Project list of the world's top anthropology articles published since 2011, http://metrics.publicanthropology.org/results.php?step1-get=anthropology &step2-get=bytime&step3-get=all-time.

36    Yetish et al. (2015).

37    David Givens, personal communication (2017).

38    AAA Membership Department, personal communication (2017).

since then. 2016 saw the fewest anthropology degrees granted since 2009."[39] The disciplinary and abstract language common to cultural anthropology publications has historically proven a political advantage. It puts a boundary around cultural anthropology, demarcating its special, purified value. Only those within the field can really understand it. By claiming privileged knowledge, they defend the field's significance from outsiders.

But the ploy at purity—to keep outsiders at bay—falls apart in the present context. Unable to reach out to centers of power outside the academy, cultural anthropologists are drawn into the hegemonic-like structures that helped create the current crisis. As noted, the desire to wall off the field from outside assessments is one reason metric assessments are popular today with administrators. They allow administrators to avoid deferring to disciplinary-framed assessments. It provides them with readily obtainable statistics above and beyond what those in the field choose to provide.

The result of cultural anthropology's diminished role is that the field lacks the political heft to effectively resist the assessing of faculty productivity in metric terms. It has few outside supporters—especially in the halls of political and financial power beyond the academy. Cultural anthropologists can heatedly voice their disapproval. But that rarely changes the metric framework except perhaps around the edges. The metric assessment of faculty seems comfortably ensconced in the academic and governmental halls of power.

## HESITANCY TO CHALLENGE THE STATUS QUO

There is another reason why the metric assessment of faculty is unlikely to disappear anytime soon. Despite the oppressive nature of these assessments, despite the increased pressure to repeatedly publish (or "perish"), despite the stresses these assessments cause, many anthropologists seem hesitant to change. We see the power of the hegemonic-like structures. For Antonio Gramsci (as previously noted), hegemony involves "the 'spontaneous' consent given by the great masses of the population to the general direction imposed on social life by the dominant fundamental group." [40] In this case, the dominant group is key university administrators.

In discussing the "turned inward" quality of many anthropological publications, I cited Mary Douglas's work regarding purity and pollution. When

---

39   Ginsberg (2017).
40   Gramsci (1971:12).

faculty move beyond the academic pale, other faculty may perceive their work as "impure." In Douglas's terms, it pollutes—it confuses the intellectual boundary separating "us" from "them." In cultural anthropology the pure remain comfortably ensconced within disciplinary boundaries producing work that few read. Most faculty understand they will be judged by their departments on the degree to which they publish "pure" cultural anthropology, not "impure" work that engages and benefits the broader public.

Take the example of Jared Diamond. Barbara King, a senior professor at the College of William and Mary, in her review of Diamond's book *The World Until Yesterday*, asks: "Why does Jared Diamond make anthropologists so mad?" Quoting King:

> Wade Davis says that Diamond's "shallowness" is what "drives anthropologists to distraction." For Davis, geographer Diamond doesn't grasp that "cultures reside in the realm of ideas, and are not simply or exclusively the consequences of climatic and environmental imperatives."
>
> Rex Golub at *Savage Minds* slams the book for "a profound lack of thought about what it would mean to study human diversity and how to make sense of cultural phenomena." In a fit of vexed humor, the Wenner-Gren Foundation for anthropological research tweeted Golub's post along with this comment: "@savageminds once again does the yeoman's work of exploring Jared Diamond's new book so the rest of us don't have to."
>
> This biting response isn't new; see Jason Antrosio's post from last year in which he calls Diamond's Pulitzer Prize–winning *Guns, Germs, and Steel* a "one-note riff," even "academic porn" that should not be taught in introductory anthropology courses.

And yet, King continues: "Readers eager to learn about practices considerably different from their own will come away from the book with significant rewards. . . . Even if Diamond makes mistakes — and he does — might his taking on big questions for large numbers of readers do more good than harm?" King asks: "Where, at least since 1982 and Eric Wolf's *Europe and the People Without History*, are the 'big books' in which we anthropologists do a better job than Diamond?"[41]

Reading various anthropological reviews of Diamond's book, one sees anthropologists trying to defend their field from an outsider rather than doing

---

41    King (2013); see also Carse (2014) and Wilk (2013).

what they claim to do best—engaging with different perspectives in productive ways. How can cultural anthropologists live in distant lands, extol the value of different lifestyles, and then seek to shut down Diamond when he engages with anthropological matters—often successfully, many reviewers suggest—just because he presents his material differently?

Nor should one necessarily expect the American Anthropological Association to spearhead the charge for change. I noted the referendum to rescind the AAA's "El Dorado Task Force Report" (regarding Chagnon's treatment of the Yanomami), despite a joint campaign by those both for and against the referendum to get out the vote, only drew around 11 percent participation. According to David Givens, who worked for the AAA's Information Services between 1985 and 1997, most Association referenda during his tenure drew less than 20 percent participation.[42] There is a recent exception to this pattern: the 2016 referendum on boycotting Israeli academic institutions. After a massive publicity push by the supporters of the boycott—a publicity campaign that went beyond anything ever attempted in the Association's history—roughly 51 percent participated in the voting. That might seem impressive. But one might also ask: Why, despite the most massive publicity campaign for a referendum in the Association's history, did only half the members vote? And, one might observe, fewer than half of these members (2,384) voted for a change in the Association's policy. The majority either abstained or voted to maintain the status quo. Generally speaking, many anthropologists prefer to stay on the sidelines regarding AAA's affairs unless it affects them directly.

In a way, you cannot really blame many faculty, especially junior faculty, for embracing the status quo. There are prominent cases of well-recognized scholars being denied tenure or not having their contracts renewed because—as best as can be determined from the information available—they did not "fit in" to their departments. There is the case of Paul Starr, who was denied tenure at Harvard despite winning the first Pulitzer Prize ever awarded to a sociologist. (He also won the prestigious Bancroft Prize in American history.) A prominent anthropological case involves David Graeber. Quoting the *New York Times* on Yale's failure to renew Graeber's contract:

> Battles with the police are a fact of life for Dr. Graeber, an associate professor of
> anthropology at Yale and a self-proclaimed anarchist. It was his battle with Yale
> that surprised him. The university notified him in the spring of 2005 that it would

42   Author's personal communication with David Givens, October 25, 2017.

not renew his contract next year. Yale gave no reason, and officials said they could not discuss the dismissal because personnel matters were confidential.

But to Dr. Graeber the reason was obvious: his politics. He appealed, and supporters around the world wrote letters on his behalf, some calling him one of the most brilliant anthropologists of his generation. . . . "So many academics lead such frightened lives," he said. "The whole system sometimes seems designed to encourage paranoia and timidity. I wasn't willing to live like that."[43]

Many junior anthropologists reasonably assume if some of the leading anthropologists in the field could not protect Graeber at Yale, why should they be politically active in ways that might "ruffle the feathers" of their institution's political and financial backers?[44] Starr and Graeber were able to eventually land on their feet, with new positions at equally prominent institutions—Starr at Princeton, Graeber at the London School of Economics. But few junior faculty assume they will be able to do that. If they challenge the hegemonic-like structures in a way their institutions find threatening, they may be left without a position, perhaps even forced to seek a new career. While some may challenge the hegemonic-like structures in small ways that may perhaps feel empowering, many perceive it better to pretty much stay within the prescribed boundaries— publishing away with articles that likely will not advance knowledge, that likely will not noticeably benefit others, and that may even go unread by those who are assessing their work for promotion and tenure. To get along (in a career), as the famous saying goes, you need to go along. Why take unnecessary risks, especially before tenure?

### THE KEY QUESTION

*The key question is whether the current crisis surrounding metric assessments is enough to encourage faculty to explore an alternative paradigm, given the "do no harm" paradigm no longer seems to protect faculty interests. Furthermore, there is limited support for directly challenging the metric standards both within the academy and from government officials outside the academy who provide research funding. These problems limit the ability of faculty to push for a return to pre-*

---

43    Arenson (2005).

44    In fact, it was worse than this. Graeber (2017) reports that, after his firing, he failed "to win a position despite 20+ attempts. . . . In fact, in 20+ attempts, I failed even once to be considered for a job. Not only did I not make any short lists, I failed to make any long lists. Not a single university asked me for my letters of recommendation." Despite having an impressive academic record, he was essentially blackballed by many American anthropology departments.

*metric standards. The question becomes: Are faculty open to moving to new faculty assessment standards, given it is unlikely they can return to the old ones?*

I noted in Chapter 1 that hegemonic-like structures, despite their ability to enforce conformity, are also flexible. Gramsci wrote: "Common sense [the 'spontaneous consent' provided to hegemonic-like structures] is not something rigid and immobile, but is continually transforming itself, enriching itself with scientific ideas and with philosophical opinions which have entered ordinary life."[45] There is no reason to believe the academic hegemonic-like structures that support the "do no harm" paradigm would not also support the alternative public anthropology paradigm. In fact, there is substantial reason to believe these structures would embrace it over time since it fits with their own agenda.

There is a desire, by many in centers of power, for the social sciences to be more involved in addressing serious social problems beyond the academy. We see this in an Obama-era presidential Executive Order dated September 15, 2015, that states: "By the authority vested in me as President by the Constitution and the laws of the United States, I hereby direct . . . [Executive departments and agencies to] develop strategies for applying behavioral science insights to programs and, where possible, rigorously test and evaluate the impact of these insights."[46] I noted in Chapter 3 the suggestion by Robert J. Jones, president of the University of Albany, that "public research universities in particular have a responsibility to work with communities. . . . It's very much valued [work], and it will count in consideration for advancement in the university."[47] University public relations departments repeatedly emphasize that their universities are serving the public good. This message is prominently displayed in alumni magazines and press releases.

Edward Tenner, in *The Efficiency Paradox: What Big Data Can't Do,* calls into question the pseudo-precision of metric standards. Creating efficient services and products involves false starts and failures—"creative waste" in his terms. It is how innovations are born. Relying solely "on the algorithms of digital platforms [such as those used in assessment metrics] can . . . lead to wasted efforts, missed opportunities, and above all an inability to break out of established

45   Gramsci (1971:326).

46   "Executive Order—Using Behavioral Science Insights to Better Serve the American People," September 15, 2015, https://obamawhitehouse.archives.gov/the-press-office/2015/09/15/execu tive-order-using-behavioral-science-insights-better-serve-american (accessed August 11, 2018).

47   Quoted in Hebel (2016).

patterns."[48] Metric standards should not overwhelm more qualitative and less arbitrary ones. As Tenner observes, efficiency is not the same as the appearance of efficiency. Still, no one should expect to wake up tomorrow and have the field undergo a shift toward the public anthropology paradigm. Paradigm shifts take time—as we saw with Copernicus, Darwin, and Planck.

Anthropology departments are central to faculty assessments. They adapt abstract standards to concrete cases. That makes them ground zero for paradigm shifts. The hegemonic-like structures do not allow departments to create their own standards. But as Gramsci observed, there is flexibility in how "common sense" is used to interpret these hegemonic-like structures. There is no reason anthropology departments cannot ask higher-level administrators for flexibility in applying tenure and promotion standards—making the case, as Tenner has, that metric standards can at times be inefficient. They may foster conformity more than innovation. Anthropology departments, following the UK's REFs, might add additional assessment criteria focusing on the social impact of faculty work. A REF report on social impacts concludes: "The societal impact of research from UK Higher Education Institutions (HEIs) is considerable, diverse and fascinating." It continues: "The stories that are told in the impact case studies capture what is great about academic research in the UK: the range of interests, the expertise and experience, the commitment of individuals and the benefits to communities across the world. The case studies make an inspiring read that demonstrate the value of research to today's society, and to the future."[49] Why should deans and provosts in the United States not say the same about the work cultural anthropologists do?

What is important about focusing on impacts is that they are frequently framed in nonmetric terms. They often tell stories. Phrased another way, they subvert metric assessment standards of faculty productivity. There is no reason individual departments could not begin the shift now—one by one or perhaps in coordination with other departments. It will be a slow process . Still, there are guidelines they might follow. The American Anthropological Association has updated guidelines regarding "communicating public scholarship in anthropology."[50] With this perspective in mind, let us return to the public anthropology

---

48    Tenner (2018: jacket blurb).

49    King's College and Digital Science (2015:71, 73).

50    AAA (2017:8–9).

paradigm and review some of the key themes suggested in earlier chapters. They offer a path forward. Rather than trying to directly confront the hegemonic-like structures that currently embrace metric standards, departments can work around these standards, can subvert them, by focusing on the social impact of anthropological work. Administrators and government officials embracing metric standards today often seem to do so by default. The metrics represent an awkward shorthand for accountability. Outsider funders and school administrators are more interested in the social impacts of the research they support. (It has greater PR value.)

## Seeing the Bigger Picture

*This section emphasizes two points. First, it asserts the public anthropology paradigm moves us beyond the details of specialization to remind us of the broader contexts cultural anthropologists operate in—especially in relation to the hegemonic-like structures surrounding publications. Second, it suggests flexibility exists in how publications are judged in respect to their quality. Faculty and administrative standards for assessing intellectual productivity may well overlap, especially if they focus on outcomes.*

### UNDERSTANDING THE HEGEMONIC-LIKE STRUCTURES THAT SHAPE CULTURAL ANTHROPOLOGY

No one should doubt the pull of the existing hegemonic-like structures. Marx famously stated: "Men make their own history, but they do not make it as they please; they do not make it under self-selected circumstances, but under circumstances existing already, given and transmitted from the past. The tradition of all dead generations weighs like a nightmare on the brains of the living."[51] Many anthropologists go along with the existing hegemonic-like standards of accountability to get along with their careers. Caught up in narrow, focused research they want to publish, many may have a hard time conceptualizing alternative standards for accountability.

No doubt, some individuals resist the push to publish. But true to the nature of hegemonic-like structures, the resistance often seems ineffective and, moreover, tends to reinforce the status quo by emphasizing these individuals' deviancy.

---

51   Marx in Smelser (1973:165).

Such scholars as Paul Farmer, Nancy Scheper-Hughes, and Philippe Bourgois are honored for the way they engage with the world and, through that engagement, seek to transform it. They are well respected by colleagues—not only for their publications but for their activism. But their example has not pushed the rest of the field to transform itself. They mainly highlight unfulfilled disciplinary possibilities. They represent a safety valve, so to speak, for those disheartened by the academic focus on publications not being widely circulated or read. For those who resist more strongly—without the disciplinary recognition of Farmer, Scheper-Hughes, or Bourgois—there are the coercive structures surrounding hiring, promotion, and tenure. Professors have to jump through these academic hoops to survive. Few escape them.

I have discussed how these structures shape the dynamics of cultural anthropology and the careers of cultural anthropologists. There is no need to repeat that here. But I hope readers agree that these hegemonic-like structures exist and indeed affect both the field and its practitioners. What intrigues me is why more people have not written about the structure of anthropology within the academy. There is Pierre Bourdieu's *Homo Academicus*, a study of French academic life and power.[52] It examines the intellectual capital many of France's leading intellectuals accrue through time and how they display their power and capital (the preface to the English edition contains critiques of both Foucault and Lévi-Strauss). But I know of only a few American studies, such as R. G. D'Andrade et al., that examine the discipline, and most of these do not touch on the hegemonic-like structures shaping anthropology.[53]

The reason I began the book with a discussion of cultural anthropology's central tools—participant-observation, context, and comparison—is to emphasize their importance. Context is pervasively used by anthropologists to make sense of people's behavior. Why more have not explored the contexts that shape anthropology, especially cultural anthropology, is puzzling. The Postmodernist trend focused on the role of the knower in the known. There are scores of publications that discuss the role anthropologists play in framing ethnographic

---

52    Bourdieu (1988), for a general statement regarding his thesis; see, e.g., Bourdieu (1988:40–41).

53    D'Andrade et al. (1975); see also Nelson et al. (2017) for an analysis of how sexual harassment during fieldwork and responses to it shape academic career advancement today. Also see Brenneis (2009); Brenneis, Shore, and Wright (2005); Couzin-Frankel (2018); and Sangren (2007). Biruk's *Cooking Data* (2018) is a thoughtful analysis on the social construction of data.

descriptions of others. But Postmodernism never extended its frame of reference to itself and the field at large in any substantial way. I have offered some generalities in Chapters 1, 2, and 5. But it would be valuable to examine in more detail how specific anthropology departments and the anthropologists within them adjust to the hegemonic-like structures discussed.

## HOW THE FLEXIBILITY IN ACCOUNTABILITY STANDARDS CAN BE USED TO FACILITATE CHANGE

In Chapter 2, I highlighted the problematic way many publications are assessed in cultural anthropology. It is questionable whether the host of publications produced between the 1930s and 2000s—as exemplified by the five trends discussed—have significantly advanced knowledge within the field. What is intriguing is that the administrators enforcing the hegemonic-like standards seem not to mind. The publications provide the appearance of advancing knowledge, and academic institutions can publicly broadcast this appearance of knowledge to others. Few in the broader public likely know the difference, few seem to question the results—especially in contrast to what I described for the life sciences.

Since the hegemonic-like structures—tied to assessing faculty through their publications—seem well established, dating back at least two hundred years, they are not going to go away soon. But, as noted, there is flexibility in interpreting them. This flexibility opens up important possibilities for how a department's faculty's work is assessed. Based on what I have already stated, I hope it is reasonably clear what administrators, who set a university's assessment standards, want (and do not want): (a) they want their institution to be respected and appreciated by the broader public; (b) they do not want faculty threatening the support their institution receives from its political and financial backers; and (c) they want easy, clear assessments that reduce complications in respect to how faculty are judged as intellectually productive. Three goals a department's faculty might hope for are:

(1) Being assessed on the quality of their work, especially the degree to which they advance knowledge and/or produce positive outcomes beyond the academy, not just have their publications counted.

(2) Reduce the stress felt, especially by junior faculty, regarding the number of publications they must produce between each review period.

(3) If they receive recognition from outside organizations, recognition that adds to the credibility of their institutions, it is not seen as a detriment within the department—especially since it strengthens a department's position vis-à-vis the administration and makes it less subject to the bureaucratic whims of particular administrators.

What we see, in brief, are the possibilities for addressing the concerns of both parties. The public anthropology paradigm's focus on outcomes allows faculty to produce work that administrators can highlight to the public. It adds to their university's prestige relative to other educational institutions. Rather than focusing on citation counts, which often offer a distorted sense of quality and impact, faculty might highlight citations in Altmetric.com—regarding how the world's media react to their publications. Equally valuable would be if faculty gave clear, credible statements in their departmental reviews of how their work advances knowledge rather than relying on a plethora of publications to make the point. Faculty could select two or three publications for review. Those evaluating a faculty member would then be able to read them and assess to what degree these publications do indeed advance knowledge. The flash, the buzz, of an exciting new approach would be set aside, and reviewers could assess to what degree a publication (or set of publications) actually refines a perspective and/or builds cumulative knowledge. They could evaluate to what degree the claim made in a grant application that a particular research project will enhance the common good actually produces work that does.

For departments that find administrators locked into the flaws and faults of the current system, there is the "traditional" work-around. The effort to judge faculty by alternative standards might be deemed a three- to five-year "experiment"—to see (a) if they are workable, and (b) if they fit the academic institution's goals. Many administrators might be open to the experiment. It certainly would not hurt to ask, to try.

## Building a Broader Constituency of Support

*This section outlines four steps for building broader support for cultural anthropology as a valued field of study. (1) It emphasizes the importance of moving beyond the dictum of "do no harm" to helping people—either by directly improving certain people's lives or by advancing knowledge that in time will benefit others. (2) It stresses the power of storytelling for conveying ideas and meaning. (3) It suggests that cultural anthropologists ask broader*

*questions, especially questions centered around comparisons. And (4) it*
*stresses the importance of working with structured entities beyond the*
*academy, such as NGOs, to have greater impact.*

## MOVING BEYOND "DO NO HARM" TO HELPING IMPROVE OTHER PEOPLE'S LIVES

In principle, some doctors may abstractly affirm the ethic of "first do no harm."
But few doctors actually embrace it in their work. Most doctors, most of the
time, view their primary responsibility as helping patients—treating them—not
trying to avoid harming them. They seek to heal what ails their patients even if
they cannot always guarantee the process will be pain-free. Focusing on "do no
harm" as an ethics code allows cultural anthropologists to sidestep important
power and moral imbalances in field research. It encourages them to continue
on, as they did in the Micronesian CIMA project, to produce publications primarily for anthropological audiences.

Ward Goodenough's *Property, Kin, and Community on Truk*—the first major
book published by Yale related to CIMA—was instrumental in developing
the New Ethnography (or Ethnoscience) that was popular during the 1960s.
In terms of the practical use of his research for the US Naval Administration,
which financed the research, Goodenough writes: "The problem of rendering an
ethnographic account that can be of practical use to administrators boils down,
we feel, to trying to give the reader a basis for learning to operate in terms of the
culture described in somewhat the same manner that a grammar would provide
him with a basis for learning to speak a language. To seek to do this implies that
a culture is as susceptible to rigorous analysis and description as is any language.
The demonstration of this proposition is, in fact, a long-range objective towards
which the present study was undertaken as an exploratory step."[54] This long-
range project was never accomplished nor was an incomplete cultural analysis
of Chuk (or Truk), in Goodenough's terms, ever produced that would prove
relevant to administrators. In striving to do no harm, it is not clear the CIMA
project did much good for the Micronesians or those administering them. As
Kiste and Falgout write: "Mutual animosity frequently characterized the relations between anthropologists and administrators."[55]

---

54   Goodenough (1951 [1966]:10).
55   Kiste and Falgout in Kiste and Marshall (1999:36).

Contrast this with Alan Holmberg's work with Vicos and Gerald Murray's work in Haiti. No, Holmberg et al. did not accomplish all their goals. No, the Vicos Project was not a perfect success any more than Murray's reforestation program was. They both encountered obstacles, only some of which they could overcome. But they did succeed to a certain extent. The Vicosinos' and the Haitians' standards of living improved because of their efforts. To reinvigorate cultural anthropology, the public anthropology paradigm suggests we need to reach out to others, beyond the field, beyond the academy, to help them address their concerns, their problems. We need to address problems that benefit others, not just ourselves. It is true the funders of anthropological research do not seem overly disturbed by the gap between the benefits applicants claim will result from their research and the actual benefits that result from their work. (I presume the Naval funding for CIMA fit this pattern.)

In seeking to benefit others, cultural anthropologists can simultaneously advance knowledge. There is no reason the two need be separate. Producing thousands of publications of ambiguous, uncertain value may not hurt many people. But neither does it particularly help them. *Advancing knowledge—in respect to refining perspectives and building cumulative knowledge (in fact, not just appearance)—is certainly a form of benefitting others when it enriches our broader understanding of the world in which we live in concrete, substantive ways.* We come to understand how others differ from us and why they behave as they do.

Cultural anthropology suffers when it does not reach out to others. It is similar to what both Taylor and Lévi-Strauss suggest about exogamy. We might call it *cultural anthropology's exogamy problem*. Cultural anthropology needs to reach out to others or die out in respect to having diminished public importance. Cultural anthropology loses it potential to be recognized as more than a small field represented by an association with a declining membership. Not reaching out beyond the discipline diminishes the power of the field's ethnographic tools. It sells short cultural anthropology's potential to prove of wider benefit in understanding the world around us. In reporting on the fluid nature of group and individual identities through time and space, cultural anthropology helps people avoid the easy polarizations between "us" and "them." In emphasizing the ways context shapes behavior, it encourages people to reshape the contexts needed to reshape their lives—medically, economically, socially—so as to find new meaning, opportunity, and hope. At its best, cultural anthropology represents an antidote to hate, provincialism, and despair.

Looking at two popular ethnographies, we might ask: Why aren't cultural anthropologists publishing works like these that provide insight and provoke thought among a host of readers. These ethnographies of other people in other places, away from our everyday experiences, help readers make sense of the rise of populism in America, especially in rural settings. The first ethnography is J. D. Vance's *Hillbilly Elegy*. As Jennifer Senior writes in the *New York Times*, Vance offers "a compassionate, discerning sociological analysis of the white underclass that has helped drive the politics of rebellion, particularly the ascent of Donald J. Trump. Combining thoughtful inquiry with firsthand experience, Mr. Vance has inadvertently provided a civilized reference guide for an uncivilized election, and he's done so in a vocabulary intelligible to both Democrats and Republicans."[56] On Vance and his book, Wikipedia reports:

> Alongside his personal history, Vance raises questions such as the responsibility of his family and people for their own misfortune. Vance blames hillbilly culture and its supposed encouragement of social rot. Comparatively, he feels that economic insecurity plays a much lesser role. To lend credence to his argument, Vance regularly relies on personal experience. As a grocery store checkout cashier, he watched people on welfare talk on cell phones while Vance himself could not afford one. This resentment towards those who apparently profited from misdeeds while he struggled, especially combined with his values of personal responsibility and tough love, is presented as a microcosm of Appalachia's overall political swing from strong Democratic Party to strong Republican affiliations.[57]

For reactions to the book—from the political left and the political right—refer to Wikipedia. But, whatever your take on the book, it is a wonderful example of participant-observation combined with contextual analysis to present a clear vision of what growing up in enduring poverty with low-paying jobs is like in Middletown, Ohio. The book has been on the *New York Times* bestseller list for more than sixty-two weeks. David Brooks, in a *New York Times* opinion piece, calls it "essential reading for this moment in history." When was the last time someone suggested that for an anthropological ethnography—to a nonanthropological audience in a nonanthropological publication?

The second ethnography is Arlie Hochschild's *Strangers in Their Own Land*. Hochschild is a sociologist at UC Berkeley. In talking about books such as Hoch-

---

56   Senior (2016).

57   Wikipedia, s.v. "Hillbilly Elegy."

schild's and Vance's, Nathaniel Rich writes in the *New York Review of Books*: "These books are written not by historians but by sociologists, anthropologists, and reporters. . . . These are studies of political groups, but they are not chiefly political in nature; they tend to be written in the manner of *Coming of Age in Samoa* or *Notes on the Balinese Cockfight*."[58] What is intriguing is that none of the books listed by Rich as dealing with the politics of the poor and resentment today are actually written by anthropologists. Rich points to anthropologists as models. But the books he discusses are written by sociologists and reporters.

Hochschild made ten trips to southwestern Louisiana over a six-year period to interview sixty people, "visiting their homes, communities and workplaces." She deals with what we might view as a baffling paradox: People seem to be working against their own self-interest. "Even the most ideologically driven zealots don't want to drink poisoned water, inhale toxic gas, or become susceptible to record flooding. Yet southwestern Louisiana combines some of the nation's most fervently antiregulatory voters with its most toxic environmental conditions. It is a center of climate change denial despite the fact that its coast faces the highest rate of sea-level rise on the planet." What Hochschild calls the Great Paradox involves "virtually every Tea Party advocate I interviewed . . . [they] personally benefited from a major government service or has close family who have . . . many were ashamed [of using these services]. But shame didn't stop those who disapproved of public services from using them."[59] Hochschild's book was nominated for the National Book Award in 2016. You may well ask: Why are anthropologists not receiving the recognition these authors receive? It is puzzling, especially if you believe, as I do, in cultural anthropology's ethnographic power to reach beyond the everyday worlds of readers to convey the lives of people who live beyond their experiences.

If cultural anthropologists "circle the wagons" around their field emphasizing its distinctiveness—regarding its scholarship and standards—it is only shutting itself off from the broader currents and ideas that can refresh it, that can invigorate it. Cultural anthropology needs to reach out to others, to help them understand their problems, their concerns, and, when possible, help them solve their problems. That is the reason this book has such a wide range of references that go well beyond the discipline. Holding an abstract sense of professional purity is self-destructive for a small field with a declining association membership. The

---

58    Rich (2016).

59    Hochschild (2016, E-book version, Chapter 1, "The Great Paradox").

field closes in on itself—much as those studied by Hochschild and Vance do—without realizing it or perhaps caring about the negative consequences involved.

## THE POWER OF STORYTELLING

In Chapter 1, I quoted Victoria Clayton, suggesting that for academics "their intended audience is always their peers. That's who they have to impress to get tenure."[60] In Chapter 2, I noted that the citation system—with its breadth of references—keeps outsiders from fully following what is being communicated. Reading deeply in cultural anthropology often confuses the uninitiated. In demarcating their work in this manner, cultural anthropologists reinforce their professional credentials, their distinctiveness, from the broader society. Only the "initiated" can understand what is being said. To understand key works in cultural anthropology, one often needs a cultural anthropologist to interpret them.

But with the increased quantification of assessment standards—and the diminished faculty control over these standards—it makes sense to be less exclusive, to demonstrate cultural anthropology's value to wider audiences. It broadens the constituency supporting the field's work and funding. In respect to the UK's Research Excellence Framework that has frustrated faculty, I noted the positive assessment made of impact stories. The impact reports in anthropology entwine case studies with quotes and stories. Quoting from the assessment of the cultural anthropology and development studies: "Most of the submissions returned outputs that were judged by the panel to be world-leading and the majority of outputs submitted were of at least internationally recognised quality, confirming the excellent research being carried out by UK development studies and anthropology departments." It continues: "The impact case studies were themselves of extremely high quality overall, and provided strong evidence of productive engagement with publics, users and policy makers from all subfields of anthropology and development studies. The most convincing case studies gave a clear and coherent account of the relationship between the underpinning research and the impact claimed, what the impact involved and who were the beneficiaries."[61]

There is every reason to believe that stories about impact—without the obscuring language and references—will be well received by those beyond the academy. Humans frequently understand the world through stories. In our

---

60    Clayton (2015). In relation to Clayton's statements, Derek Hawkins (2018) presents an interesting piece on "What Made Hawking's 'A Brief History of Time' So Immensely Popular?"
61    Research Excellence Frame (2015:97, 99).

fieldwork we frequently rely on the informants' stories to make sense of the group we are studying. Emotional, powerful anecdotes may count more with public audiences than a mass of statistics. As Michael Jones and Deserai Crow suggest, scientists "would do well to recognize themselves as storytellers—not to distort the truth, but to help people to connect with problems and issues on a more human level in terms of what matters to them."[62] Carolyn O'Hara, writing in the *Harvard Business Review*, states: "In our information-saturated age, business leaders 'won't be heard unless they're telling stories,' [according to] . . . Nick Morgan . . . founder of Public Words. . . . 'Facts and figures and all the rational things that we think are important in the business world actually don't stick in our minds at all.' But stories create 'sticky' memories by attaching emotions to things that happen."[63]

If cultural anthropologists wish to build a wider constituency so they are less vulnerable to the dictates of administrators and government officials regarding accountability standards, then it would be wise to let the broader public understand the impact cultural anthropology has on others—not in standard academic language but in stories. For example, Sally Engle Merry's *The Seductions of Quantification: Measuring Human Rights, Gender Violence, and Sex Trafficking* and Virginia Eubanks's *Automating Inequality: How High-Tech Tools Profile, Police, and Punish the Poor* are excellent books with a similar message. Both have been well reviewed. But only Eubanks's book has received a glowing review in the *New York Times Book Review*. The reviewer writes: "*Automating Inequality* is riveting (an accomplishment for a book on technology and policy). Its argument should be widely circulated, to poor people, social service workers and policymakers, but also throughout the professional classes. Everyone needs to understand that technology is no substitute for justice."[64] The difference between the two books? Eubanks's book is full of powerful stories that make her points in a way that captures readers both intellectually and emotionally.

*In brief, focusing on impacts offers a means for escaping the frustrations of the metric standards. First, administrators and government officials seem to readily understand impacts despite their being from across diverse fields outside their specialties, especially when they are embedded in stories. Stories vacate the need for phrasing everything in metric terms. Second, given much of the push for increased accountability comes from outside institutions, focusing on impacts builds bridges*

62    Jones and Crow (2017).
63    O'Hara (2014).
64    Featherstone (2018:19).

*to those beyond the academy. The value of research (and the need to keep funding it) is made clear to everyone in concrete terms by results that benefit others. Third, given the time it takes to build impacts, there will be fewer of them when faculty are reviewed for promotion and tenure. Faculty reviews become less of a numbers game—quality will count.*

## USING COMPARISONS, ESPECIALLY CONTROLLED COMPARISONS, TO ASK BIG QUESTIONS

Barbara King, in her review of Diamond's book discussed earlier, asserted that whatever Diamond's mistakes were, he was asking big questions that interested a range of readers. She asks: "Where, at least since 1982 and Eric Wolf's *Europe and the People Without History*, are the 'big books' in which we anthropologists do a better job than Diamond?"[65] Comparisons, especially controlled comparisons, have lost the popularity they once had. There are still comparisons. But an examination of recent articles in the *American Anthropologist* suggests they are now relatively narrow or relatively brief. "The sheer number of comparative articles and books published" in the early 1950s, Laura Nader observed in 1994, reminds us "that energetic debates about the intellectual place of comparison are missing among today's anthropological agendas."[66] Adam Kuper adds: "Comparison is no longer the central interest of many field anthropologists."[67] And Ladislav Holy in 1987, in a book titled *Comparative Anthropology*, observes: "These days, a great proportion of empirical research is distinctly non-comparative" and "comparisons aimed specifically at generating cross-culturally valid generalizations seem to be conspicuous by their absence."[68]

These statements contrast with those of earlier times, when Oscar Lewis wrote: "Within the past five years there have appeared an unusually large number of theoretical writings dealing with comparative method in anthropology." Fred Eggan, furthermore, observed: "In the last decade there has been an unusually large number of theoretical writings in anthropology concerned with comparative method."[69] Part of the reason I started this book with cultural anthropology's tools is to highlight the importance of comparison—using the insightful

65   B. King (2013). Note should be taken of the thoughtful and widely popular *Sapiens: A Brief History of Mankind* by Yuval Noah Hariri, published after King's comments (see Hariri [1915]).

66   Nader in Borofsky, ed. (1994:85).

67   A. Kuper in Borofsky, ed. (1994:116).

68   Holy (1987:8, 13); cf. Candea (2019).

69   O. Lewis (1956:260); Eggan (1965:357).

analyses of Nader, Nadel, and Wolf. In reflecting on times past, for example, do readers remember Eggan's comparison of kinship terminologies and subsistence patterns among North American Plains Indians? He divided North American Plains Indian kinship into two major types: one stressing lineage unity, the other generational unity. Indians in the eastern portion of the Great Plains were primarily horticulturalists and lived in permanent villages organized as unilineal descent groups (e.g., the Omaha, Iowa, Illinois, Hidatsa, and Pawnee). The Indians of the High Plains were seminomadic hunters in bilateral bands centering around a camp circle (e.g., the Cheyenne, Kiowa, and Dakota). Their classificatory kinship system emphasized generation and sex, drawing in a wide range of other relationships with (unlike the lineage system of the horticulturalists) only a vague sense of outer limits.

Eggan suggested the principle of lineage unity—as manifested in unilineal descent organization—provided the settled horticulturalists of the Eastern Plains with a sense of stability and continuity through time. The concern with generational unity among the Indians of the High Plains, in contrast, stimulated ties of wide-ranging extension, but shallow depth—a pattern fitting with the flexible forms of solidarity needed among seminomadic hunters adapting to a variable set of ecological conditions. Eggan noted that Indian groups, such as the Crow, altered their kinship system as they moved from one region of the Plains to another.[70]

The problem with today's comparisons is that they frequently involve the *comparative fallacy* (noted earlier). In seeking to enlarge their research's relevance, anthropologists relate their work to research on the same topic by prominent figures—often emphasizing how their work compares to or challenges these figures' conclusions. The implication often is that since both field sites deal with human beings and humans share certain traits, the new research can act as a test of a prominent figure's work. To draw effective comparisons, we need detailed knowledge of how the groups involved overlap—in what ways, to what degree—to understand, as we did with Nadel, Nader, and Wolf, the value of the comparisons being drawn.

Fredrik Barth's comparison of Pakistani and Norwegian groups offers a suggestive possibility for comparative study. Focusing on "ethnic entrepreneurs" could lead to a reframing of how we view ethnic conflict and, equally important, how we might address it. Comparisons do that. They can lead us to see old problems in new ways. We might note that comparison is alive and well in

---

70    Eggan (1954, 1968).

other disciplines such as political science. Take Jean-Pierre Filiu's *From Deep State to Islamic State* as an example. In examining responses to the Arab Spring across the Middle East, Filiu uses a comparative perspective to make sense of the region's current tensions, conflicts, and brutalities. Prominent dictatorships, he suggests, fostered religious radicalism to provide them with a mission of stamping the radicals out. The Arab Spring's democratic revolution was followed by a counterrevolution in which not only did various dictatorships increase their power (e.g., Egypt) but so did certain religious radicals (e.g., ISIS). This counterrevolution created the present standoff between authoritarian "deep states" and religiously fervent "Islamic states." In placing the current conflicts in a comparative perspective, Filiu helps us make sense of the puzzling dynamics now at work across the region. Again, we might ask: Why are anthropologists not producing work like this?

A renewed focus on controlled comparison opens up possibilities. One might compare at the local level, for example, how democratic hopes are corrupted by political ploys in Nigeria, Hungary, and the United States. Or how, again at the local level, democratic hopes have been rekindled in France and Indonesia. Or why do populist ideologies take hold in local communities in Australia (with One Nation), in Germany (with Alternative für Deutschland), and in South Africa (with the Economic Freedom Fighters)? Such questions represent traditional, comparative anthropology. But they also represent cutting-edge research about current political problems that have implications far beyond the local communities involved—as anthropology should have.

What is lost in the focused, specific studies common today is the broader meaning that public audiences desire. If cultural anthropologists did not have to worry about producing so many publications per year, might they take the time to synthesize an array of ethnographic data to address important questions involving, for example, inequality, terrorism, and the positive and negative impacts of globalization? The list of comparative possibilities anthropologists could address is almost endless and, I suggest, exciting. Rather than turning inward and facing the *exogamy problem*, they could revitalize the field by enriching public discussions and advancing knowledge.

## USING COLLABORATION TO BRING IDEAS TO LIFE BEYOND THE ACADEMY

As I suggested in Chapter 3, collaboration has much to offer as a strategy for facilitating change and implementing innovative solutions to problems. Some cultural anthropologists collaborate with others within their discipline and, more broadly, with other faculty in the social sciences.[71] I suggest reaching out to groups beyond the academy and collaborating with them. There are a host of topics cultural anthropologists might work with others on that are of critical importance and, in contrast to simply writing papers, might bring concrete, positive results. Since many of these topics attract public attention, there should be funding for them.

As I noted in Chapter 2, cultural anthropologists often have an entrepreneurial flair—finding all sorts of topics to explore in all sorts of creative ways. There is no reason these entrepreneurial skills could not be harnessed to establish important connections to those outside the academy—working with NGOs (such as PIH), university-based centers working with development organizations (such as J-PAL), think tanks, or governmental agencies that address specific social problems. How they collaborate, of course, needs to be negotiated. I have emphasized that anthropologists should be cautious about becoming "private contractors," hired out as researchers and educators to people who will use their knowledge to their own ends, for good or ill. To have credibility—to speak truth to power—cultural anthropologists cannot be pawns of the powerful.

Reaching out to nonacademic groups and making one's research public not only draws in important structural support often lacking in academic settings but, also allows anthropologists to soften the hegemonic-like hold the academic system has over their careers. Collaboration draws in other players with voices that, depending on the contexts and parties involved, need be listened to by university administrators. The examples of Partners in Health and J-PAL are instructive in this respect. Their outside support adds heft to their books, with scholars attracting more attention than they would otherwise receive. As I emphasized in Chapter 4, ideas espoused by cultural anthropologists—no matter how powerful, how insightful, how valuable—are unlikely to become part of a larger, public debate without outside social structures that persistently and

71 Because of its broad synthetic approach, anthropologists are often schooled, I suggest, in collaboration with others from different backgrounds and different experiences. Wolf describes anthropology as: "the most scientific of the humanities, the most humanist of the sciences" (E. Wolf 1964:88). Lévi-Strauss, with a touch of poetry, suggests that anthropology nourishes "a secret dream: it belongs to the human sciences, as its name [anthropo- (human) and -logy (study of)] adequately proclaims; but while it resigns itself to making its purgatory beside the social sciences, it surely does not despair of awakening among the natural sciences at the hour of the last judgement" (Lévi-Strauss 1966:118).

consistently support them. Collaborations with groups beyond the academy can bring new excitement to individual careers. It can create more credibility for anthropology departments with administrations as their work resonates with university supporters and enhances a university's public status. It also brings vitality to cultural anthropology as it reaches beyond the field's traditional borders to help others in significant ways.

## Explaining the Chapter's Title: Two Roads Diverged

*The hegemonic-like structures and paradigmatic frames of reference that shape cultural anthropologists' intellectual lives are not likely to be reframed in a day or even a year. But that need not stop cultural anthropologists from finding their own center of gravity. The chapter's title, "Two Roads Diverged," taken from Robert Frost's poem, suggests cultural anthropologists have a choice. In terms of the field, they can turn inward to "protect" the field's intellectual "purity," or they can reach out to others beyond the academy as well, which will help revitalize the field. On an individual level, cultural anthropologists have a choice in how they navigate their careers. Will they be able to look back years hence with pride, knowing they have helped others, not just themselves?*

Let me explain the chapter's title in two ways—one relating to the field of cultural anthropology and the other relating to cultural anthropologists in a more personal way. Some readers will recognize the reference to "two roads diverged." It comes from Robert Frost's poem "The Road Not Taken":

> Two roads diverged in a yellow wood,
> And sorry I could not travel both
> And be one traveler, long I stood
> And looked down one as far as I could
> To where it bent in the undergrowth;
>
> Then took the other, as just as fair,
> And having perhaps the better claim,
> Because it was grassy and wanted wear;
> Though as for that the passing there
> Had worn them really about the same,
>
> And both that morning equally lay
> In leaves no step had trodden black.
> Oh, I kept the first for another day!

> Yet knowing how way leads on to way,
> I doubted if I should ever come back.

> I shall be telling this with a sigh
> Somewhere ages and ages hence:
> Two roads diverged in a wood, and I—
> I took the one less traveled by,
> And that has made all the difference.[72]

## IN TERMS OF THE FIELD

Cultural anthropology, as a field of study, faces a choice. It may turn inward, seeking strength in past successes—hoping that, despite the changing times, what worked well in the past will work well today. This road draws the field into more metrics—counting publications and funding—because administrators do not accept cultural anthropologists' affirmations of quality on trust, especially given the piles of publications produced of uncertain, ambiguous value. More than likely, it involves more fragmentation as cultural anthropologists, in trying to keep to the required number of publications per review period, explore a host of diverse topics in a host of diverse ways. Since this plethora of possibilities rarely gain public attention, the field faces the noted exogamy problem—failing to reach out to those outside the academy it diminishes in intellectual importance. It may feel "pure," in Douglas's terms, to those within the field but few others will appreciate this purity. *In isolating itself from others, cultural anthropology, I suggest, is harming itself.*

The alternative road involves producing publications that draw public attention and praise without threating their universities' political and financial supporters. With outside recognition, administrators are less likely to fall back on metrics. Instead, they may well be open to alternative standards for assessing intellectual productivity based on outcomes, since the publications produced for such projects often increase their university's status. Encouraging cultural anthropologists to focus on bigger questions of broader relevance to a range of audiences helps soften the field's fragmentation. Being relevant to others—not just claiming to be—facilitates more funding for anthropological research and the hiring of additional faculty.

---

72    Frost (1949:131).

## ON A MORE PERSONAL LEVEL

Paradigm shifts take time. Quoting Thomas Kuhn: "Conversions will occur a few at a time until after the last holdouts have died, the whole profession will again be practicing under a single, but now different, paradigm."[73] Given the slow pace of structural change, it is relevant to ask what steps individuals can take to help shift the paradigm. Frost's poem, as various critics emphasize, is not a paean to American individualism—taking the road less traveled by. (Frost admits that "the passing there had worn them really about the same.") Rather, it is reflecting, in hindsight, on earlier choices made and the implications these have had on one's life—how one way has led to another way from these earlier decisions.

It is clear the academy shapes anthropology's intellectual agenda and that individuals must navigate their careers through hegemonic-like structures in various ways. Many know colleagues self-absorbed in their work and self-aggrandizing in a continuing chase for status. If we accept Erik Erikson's daughter's reflections on her father, "success" in the chase for status does not necessarily reduce the vulnerability, the uncertainty, many intellectuals feel vis-à-vis their colleagues. Here is what Sue Erikson Bloland writes about her father:

> To those close to him my father was—and continued to be—a life-size human being, suffering from all the same difficulties in living that had plagued him in the years before his celebrity. Despite his brilliance as an analyst and writer, and his great charisma, he was an insecure man, described as "exceedingly vulnerable" by his friend the analyst Margaret Brenman-Gibson in a reminiscence about him after his death. He evoked in those closest to him a wish to comfort and reassure him: to make him feel that he was worthy and lovable; to help him wrestle with his lifelong feelings of personal inadequacy, his punishing self-doubt.[74]

At first glance, it might seem difficult to believe. A person so honored, of such high status, so widely appreciated, would possess such self-doubt. That happens to some people, but it need not dominate your life.

There is no reason individual anthropologists need pursue their careers lock-step with the specifications and goals of the current publishing treadmill and metric assessment standards. As many are drawn to produce publication after

---

73   Kuhn (1970:151–152).
74   Bloland (1999:52).

publication of ambiguous value, there is no reason you cannot—perhaps subversively—also produce work that does indeed refine perspectives, does indeed build cumulative knowledge and, most important, does indeed benefit others. Though few departments presently emphasize pragmatic standards in assessing faculty publications—what problems are solved, what benefits accrue to others through these solutions—there is no reason you cannot hold yourself personally to such standards. You have a choice regarding how tightly you embrace the current hegemonic-like system. It is not an all-or-nothing proposition. While adhering to it, you can also subvert it.

Cultural anthropologists may ponder, "somewhere ages and ages hence," regarding the decisions they now make concerning the unfolding of their careers. Will they take pride in asserting with the thousands of research dollars provided by public and private foundations to facilitate their work that they have "done no harm"? Might they, instead, feel proud that their research was more than a self-indulgent exercise in status seeking, that they sought to make a positive difference—somewhere, somehow—in the lives of others with these funds? They may have only partially succeeded. Life is like that. But did they at least try?

*An Anthropology of Anthropology*, in fostering the public anthropology paradigm, seeks to enlarge our sense of moral community—broadening who we are concerned with, who we care about. With time, there may indeed be a paradigm shift—especially given the crisis with metric assessment standards. But for now, individual anthropologists can embrace the public anthropology paradigm on a personal and departmental level—hoping that when they look back in later life, they can take pride in the choice made.

# REFERENCES

Abbott, Andrew

    1988    The System of Professions: An Essay on the Division of Expert Labor. Chicago: University of Chicago Press.

    2001    Chaos of Disciplines. Chicago: University of Chicago Press.

Abeles, Marc

    1988    Modern Political Ritual. Current Anthropology 29(3):391–404.

Aboulafia, Mitchell

    1992    The Ideal of Democracy (Review: *John Dewey and American Democracy* by R. Westbrook). American Quarterly 44:284–291.

Abruzzi, William S.

    1982    Ecological Theory and Ethnic Differentiation among Human Populations. Current Anthropology 23(1):13–35.

Achenbach, Joel

    2015    The New Scientific Revolution: Reproducibility at Last. Washington Post, January 27. https://www.washingtonpost.com/national/health-science/the-new-scientific-revolution-reproducibility-at-last/2015/01/27/ed5f2076-9546-11e4-927a-4fa2638cd1b0_story.html?utm_term=.e1997635e997 (accessed August 6, 2018).

    2018    Researchers Replicate Just 13 of 21 Social Science Experiments Published in Top Journals. Washington Post, August 27. https://www.washingtonpost.com/news/speaking-of-science/wp/2018/08/27/researchers-replicate-just-13-of-21-social-science-experiments-published-in-top-journals/?utm_term=.79bf004377b5 (accessed August 6, 2018).

Adams, Richard Newbold

    1978    Man, Energy, and Anthropology: I Can Feel the Heat, but Where's the Light? American Anthropologist 80:297–309.

Aggarwal, Ravina

    2001    At the Margins of Death: Ritual Space and the Politics of Location in an Indo-Himalayan Border Village. American Ethnologist 28(3):549–573.

Aguilar, John

1984    Trust and Exchange: Expressive and Instrumental Dimensions of Reciprocity in a Peasant Community. Ethos 21(1):3–53.

Akin, David

2003    Concealment, Confession, and Innovation in Kwaio Women's Taboos. American Ethnologist 30(3):381–400.

Albert, Bruce, and Gale Goodwin Gomez

1997    Saude Yanomami: Un Manual Etnolinguistico. Belem, Brasil: Musueu Paraense Emilio Goeldi.

Alexander, Bobby

1991    Victor Turner Revisited: Ritual as Social Change. Atlanta, GA: Scholars Press.

Allende, Isabel

1993    The Infinite Plan. New York: HarperCollins.

Altbach, Philip G.

2001    The American Academic Model in Comparative Perspective. *In* In Defense of American Higher Education. P. G. Altbach, P. J. Gumport, and D. B. Johnstone, eds. Pp. 11–37. Baltimore, MD: Johns Hopkins University Press.

Alterman, Eric

1999    Can Democracy Work? http://facstaff.uwww.edu/mohanp/357week4.html.

American Anthropological Association (AAA)

1998    Code of Ethics of the American Anthropological Association. http://s3.amazonaws.com/rdcms-aaa/files/production/public/FileDownloads/pdfs/issues/policy-advocacy/upload/ethicscode.pdf (accessed August 6, 2018).

2002    El Dorado Task Force Final Report. 2 vols. and preface. http://s3.amazonaws.com/rdcms-aaa/files/production/public/FileDownloads/pdfs/issues/policy-advocacy/upload/AAA-Ethics-Code-2009.pdf (accessed August 6, 2018).

2009    Code of Ethics of the American Anthropological Association. http://www.aaanet.org/committees/ethics/ethcode.htm (accessed August 6, 2018).

2012    Ethics Blog. Principles of Professional Responsibility. http://ethics.americananthro.org/category/statement/ (accessed August 6, 2018).

2017    American Anthropological Association Guidelines for Tenure and Promotion Review: Communicating Public Scholarship in Anthropology. http://s3.amazonaws.com/rdcms-aaa/files/production/public/AAA%20Guidelines%20TP%20Communicating%20Forms%20of%20Public%20Anthropology.pdf (accessed August 6, 2018).

n.d.    Final Report of the Commission to Review the AAA Statements on Ethics. http://www.americananthro.org/ParticipateAndAdvocate/Content.aspx

?ItemNumber=1911&RDtoken=3371&userID=6944 (accessed August 6, 2018).

American Anthropologist

2009    List of Editors (Associate Editor for Public Anthropology). American Anthropologist 111(March 1).

American Association of University Professors (AAUP)

2016    Statement on "Academic Analytics" and Research Metrics. https://www .aaup.org/file/AcademicAnalytics_statement.pdf (accessed August 6, 2018).

American Experience

n.d.    Vietnam Online (An Online Companion to Vietnam: A Television History). PBS. http://www.pbs.org/wgbh/amex/vietnam/ (accessed August 6, 2018).

Ammerman, Albert

1987    A Reply to Meiklejohn's Review of *The Neolithic Transition and the Genetics of Populations in Europe*. American Anthropologist 89:449–450.

Anastas, Benjamin

2002    The Invisible Made Audible. New York Times Book Review, March 24, p. 19.

Anderson, Perry

1999    The Origins of Postmodernity. New York: Verso.

Angell, Marcia

1996    Science on Trial: The Clash of Medical Evidence and the Law in the Breast Implant Case. New York: Norton.

Anonymous

1919    Review: *The Higher Learning in America* by T. Veblen. American Historical Review 24(4):714–715.

n.d.    The Vietnam Veterans Memorial: The Wall-USA. http://thewall-usa.com/ mboard.asp?searchtext=guestbook (accessed August 6, 2018).

Anonymous (Thury?)

n.d.    Introduction (Victor Turner). http://showme.physics.drexel.edu/thury/ Myth/Turner2.html (accessed August 6, 2018).

Appiah, K. Anthony

2000    Dancing with the Moon. New York Review of Books, November 16, pp. 55–60.

Applebome, Peter

1994    Word for Word / Anthropology Abstracts: A Trans-Narrating, Ethnographic Good Time Was Had by All. New York Times, December 11.

Applied Anthropology
  1941    Editorial Statement. Applied Anthropology 1(October–December):
          1–2.

Appy, Christian
  2006    Vietnam: The Definitive Oral History Told from All Sides. London: Ebury
          Press.

Arenson, Karen
  2005    When Scholarship and Politics Collided at Yale. New York Times, Decem-
          ber 28. http://www.nytimes.com/2005/12/28/nyregion/when-scholarship
          -and-politics-collided-at-yale.html?_r=0 (accessed October 5, 2017).

Arnst, Catherine
  2006    Health as a Birthright. BusinessWeek, May 29, p. 20.
  2007    SciTech: Bad Science. BusinessWeek, December 31, 2007–January 7, 2008,
          p. 93.

Asad, Talal
  1973    Introduction. In Anthropology and the Colonial Encounter. T. Asad, ed.
          Pp. 9–19. Atlantic Highlands, NJ: Humanities Press.
  1983    Anthropological Conceptions of Religion: Reflections on Geertz. Man
          18(2):237–259.
  1987    Are There Histories of Peoples Without Europe? A Review Article. Com-
          parative Studies in Society and History 29(3):594–607.

———, et al.
  1997    Provocations of European Ethnology. American Anthropologist 99(4):713–
          730.

Asch, Timothy, and Napoleon Chagnon
  1974    A Man Called "Bee": Documentary Educational Resources.
  1975    The Axe Fight. Documentary Educational Resources.

Astuti, Rita
  1995    "The Vezo Are Not a Kind of People." American Ethnologist 22(3):464–
          482.

Aswani, Shankar, and Peter Sheppard
  2003    The Archaeology and Ethnohistory of Exchange in Precolonial and Colo-
          nial Roviana. Current Anthropology 44(Supplement):S51–S78.

Atkinson, Jane Monnig
  1983    Religions in Dialogue: The Construction of an Indonesian Minority Reli-
          gion. American Ethnologist 10(4):684–696.

Atwood, Paul
  2008    Vietnam War. Encarta (Online Encyclopedia).

Bacon, Francis
1605    The Advancement of Learning. London: Athlone Press.
[1975]

Badone, Ellen
1991    Ethnography, Fiction, and the Meanings of the Past in Brittany. American
Ethnologist 18(3):518–545.

Baker, Lee
2004    Franz Boas out of the Ivory Tower. Anthropological Theory 4(1):29–51.

Banerjee, Abhijit, and Esther Duflo
2011    Poor Economics: A Radical Rethinking of the Way to Fight Global Poverty. New York: Public Affairs.

Bannister, Robert C.
1976    Review: *Advocacy and Objectivity: A Crisis in the Professionalization of
American Social Science, 1865–1905* by Mary O. Furner. Isis 67(December
4):362–264.

Barber, Bernard
1941    Acculturation and Messianic Movements. American Sociological Review
6:663–669.
1979    Review: *The Rise of Professionalism* by M. Sarfatti. Political Science Quarterly 94(1):155–156.

Barber, Ian
1996    Loss, Change, and Monumental Landscaping: Towards a New Interpretation of the "Classic" Maaori Emergence. Current Anthropology 37(5):868–
880.

Barfield, Thomas
1997    The Dictionary of Anthropology. Malden, MA: Blackwell.

Barnard, Alan
1991    Writing Regional Traditions. Current Anthropology 32(2):218–219.
2000    History and Theory in Anthropology. Cambridge, UK: Cambridge University Press.

Barnard, Alan, and Jonathan Spencer, eds.
1996    Encyclopedia of Social and Cultural Anthropology. New York: Routledge.

Barnett, H. G.
1940    Culture Process. American Anthropologist 42:21–48.

Barnouw, Victor
1963    Culture and Personality. Homewood, IL: Dorsey Press.

Barrett, Stanley
1984    The Rebirth of Anthropological Theory. Toronto: University of Toronto
Press.

Barros, Francis

1970 Review: *The Academic Revolution* by C. Jencks and D. Riesman. Journal of Negro Education 39(1):86–88.

Barth, Fredrick

1995 Ethnicity and the Concept of Culture. Program on Nonviolent Sanctions and Cultural Survival Seminar Synopses Paper presented to the Conference "Rethinking Culture," Harvard University.

Bartlett, Tom

2017 Spoiled Science. The Chronicle Review (March 31):B6–B9.

Basken, Paul

2009a "JAMA" Orders Whistle-Blowers to Blow Their Whistles in Private. Chronicle of Higher Education, March 23. https://www.chronicle.com/article/JAMA-Orders-Whistle-Blowers/42609 (accessed August 6, 2018).

2009b Medical "Ghostwriting" Is Still a Common Practice, Study Shows. Chronicle of Higher Education, September 10. https://www.chronicle.com/article/Medical-Ghostwriting-Is-a/48347 (accessed August 6, 2018).

2009c Professor at Canada's McGill U. Admits Signing Research Generated by Drug Maker. Chronicle of Higher Education, August 24. https://www.chronicle.com/article/McGill-U-Professor-Admits/48164 (accessed August 6, 2018).

2016a Applying Research to Real World Problems. Chronicle of Higher Education, Focus (October).

2016b US House Backs New Bid to Require "National Interest" Certification for NSF Grants. Chronicle of Higher Education, February 11. http://www.chronicle.com/article/US-House-Backs-New-Bid-to/235275 (accessed August 6, 2018).

2016c As Concerns Grow About Using Data to Measure Faculty, a Company Changes Its Message. Chronicle of Higher Education, October 11. https://www.chronicle.com/article/As-Concerns-Grow-About-Using/238034 (accessed August 6, 2018).

2018 Peer Review in Flux. Chronicle of Higher Education, March 9, pp. B16–18.

Basso, Ellen

1989 Kalapalo Biography: Psychology and Language in a South American Oral History. American Anthropologist 91:551–569.

Bates, Daniel G., and Ellito M. Fratkin

2003 Cultural Anthropology, third edition. Boston: Allyn and Bacon.

Battaglia, Debbora

1993 At Play in the Fields (and Borders) of the Imaginary: Melanesian Transformations of Forgetting. Cultural Anthropology 8(4):430–442.

Bauer, Brian

1996    Legitimatization of the State in Inca Myth and Ritual. American Anthropologist 98(2):327–337.

Bauerlein, Mark

2009    Diminishing Returns in Humanities Research. Chronicle of Higher Education, July 20. https://www.chronicle.com/article/Diminishing-Returns-in/47107 (accessed August 6, 2018).

Bauman, M. Garrett

2001    The Devilments of Style. Chronicle of Higher Education, November 9, p. B5.

Bauman, Zygmunt

2000    The Man from Waco. Times Literary Supplement, July 7, pp. 6–7.

Beaglehole, J. C., ed.

1964    The Death of Captain Cook. Historical Studies, Australia and New Zealand 11(43):289–305.

Beals, Ralph

1967    International Research Problems in Anthropology: A Report from the USA. Current Anthropology 8(5)(December):470–475.

Beard, Charles

1939    Review: *Knowledge for What* by R. Lynd. American Political Science Review 33(4):711–712.

Begler, Elsie B.

1978    Sex, Status, and Authority in Egalitarian Society. American Anthropologist 80(3):571–588.

Bellah, Robert, et al.

1985    Habits of the Heart: Individualism and Commitment in American Life. New York: Harper and Row.

Belluz, Julia

2017    Most Research Spending Is Wasted on Bad Studies. These Billionaires Want to Change That. Vox, October 4. https://www.vox.com/2015/10/4/9440931/arnold-foundation-meta-research (accessed August 6, 2018).

Bender, Barbara

1992    Theorising Landscapes and the Prehistoric Landscapes of Stonehenge. Man 27(4):735–755.

Bender, Thomas

1993    Intellect and Public Life: Essays on the Social History of Academic Intellectuals in the United States. Baltimore, MD: Johns Hopkins University Press.

Benedict, Ruth
  1934      Patterns of Culture. New York: Houghton Mifflin.

Bennet, John
  1998      Classic Anthropology. New Brunswick, NJ: Transaction.

Bennett, Linda, and Linda Whiteford
  2013      Anthropology and the Engaged University: New Vision for the Discipline within Higher Education. Annals of Anthropological Practice 37(1) (May):1–204.

Bentley, G. Carter
  1984      Hermeneutics and World Construction in Maranao Disputing. American Ethnologist 11(4):642–655.
  1987      Ethnicity and Practice. Comparative Studies in Society and History 29(1):24–55.

Bercovitch, Eytan
  1994      The Agent in the Gift: Hidden Exchange in Inner New Guinea. Cultural Anthropology 9(4):498–536.

Bergendorff, Steen, Ulla Hasager, and Peter Henriques
  1988      Mythopraxis and History: On the Interpretation of the Makahiki. Journal of the Polynesian Society 97(4):391–408.

Bernstein, Richard
  1995      Cook Was (a) God or (b) Not a God. New York Times, May 24, p. C22.

Berube, Michael
  1997      The Contradictions of the Job Market in English. Chronicle of Higher Education, December 19, p. B7.
  2000      Teaching Postmodern Fiction Without Being Sure That the Genre Exists. Chronicle of Higher Education, May 19, pp. B4–B5.

Best, Joel
  2006      Flavor of the Month: Why Smart People Fall for Fads. Berkeley: University of California Press.

Besteman, Catherine
  1996      Violent Politics and the Politics of Violence: The Dissolution of the Somali Nation–State. American Ethnologist 23(3):579–596.

Bettinger, Robert L.
  1977      Aboriginal Human Ecology in Owens Valley: Prehistoric Change in the Great Basin. American Antiquity 41(1):3–17.

Bidwell, Charles
  1969      Review: *The Academic Revolution* by C. Jencks and D. Riesman. American Sociological Review 34(4):590–591.

Biersack, Aletta

1989    Local Knowledge, Local History: Geertz and Beyond. *In* The New Cultural History. A. Biersack and L. Hunt, eds. Pp. 72–96. Berkeley: University of California Press.

1990    Review: *The Gender of the Gift* by M. Strathern. Man 25(3):559–561.

1999a   Introduction: From the "New Ecology" to the New Ecologies. American Anthropologist 101(1):5–18.

1999b   The Mount Kare Python and His Gold: Totemism and Ecology in the Papua New Guinea Highlands. American Anthropologist 101(1):68–87.

Birth, Kevin K.

1990    Reading and the Righting of Writing Ethnographies. American Ethnologist 17(3):549–557.

Biruk, Crystal

2018    Cooking Data: Culture and Politics in an African Research World. Durham, NC: Duke University Press.

Bissell, Tom

2006    Destination Vietnam. Salon.com, June 15. https://www.salon.com/2006/06/15/vietnam_15/ (accessed August 6, 2018).

Bledsoe, Caroline

1984    The Political Use of Sande Ideology and Symbolism. American Ethnologist 11(3):455–472.

Bledstein, Burton

1976    The Culture of Professionalism. New York: Norton.

1995    Review: *The "True Professional Ideal" in America.* Journal of Interdisciplinary History 25(4):747–750.

Bloland, Sue Erikson

1999    Fame: The Power and Cost of Fantasy. Atlantic Monthly (November): 51–62.

Bloomberg Business

2011    Kidney Broker Pleads Guilty in First US Organ Trafficking Prosecution. Bloomberg Business, October 27. http://www.bloomberg.com/news/articles/2011-10-27/kidney-broker-pleads-guilty-in-first-u-s-organ-trafficking-prosecution (accessed October 5, 2017).

Boas, Franz

1912    Changes in Bodily Form of Descendants of Immigrants. New York: Columbia University Press.

1911    The Mind of Primitive Man. New York: Macmillan Company.
[1938]

1896    The Limitations of the Comparative Method. *In* Race, Language and
[1940]   Culture. F. Boas, ed. Pp. 270–280. New York: Macmillan Company.

1945       Race and Democratic Society. New York: J. J. Augustin.

Boddy, Janice
   1988       Spirits and Selves in Northern Sudan: The Cultural Therapeutics of Posses-
               sion and Trance. American Ethnologist 15(1):4–27.

Boeck, Filip de
   1994       "When Hunger Goes Around the Land": Hunger and Food Among the
               Aluund of Zaire. Man 29(2):257–282.

Boehm, Christopher
   1978       Rational Preselection from Hamadryas to *Homo Sapiens*: The Place of De-
               cisions in Adaptive Process. American Anthropologist 80:265–296.

Boettke, Peter
   2002       Review: *Chaos of Disciplines* by A. Abbott. Journal of Economic Literature
               40(4):1230–1231.

Bohannan, Paul
   1992       We, the Alien: An Introduction to Cultural Anthropology. Prospect
               Heights, IL: Waveland Press.

Bolton, Giles
   2007       Poor Story: An Insider Uncovers How Globalisation and Good Intentions
               Have Failed the World's Poor. London: Ebury.

Bolton, Ralph
   1984       The Hypoglycemia-Aggression Hypothesis: Debate versus Research. Cur-
               rent Anthropology 25(1):1–53.

Borofsky, Robert
   1987       Making History: Pukapukan and Anthropological Constructions of
               Knowledge. New York: Cambridge University Press.
   1997       Cook, Lono, Obeyesekere, and Sahlins. Current Anthropology 38(3):255–
               282.
   2000       To Laugh or Cry? Anthropology News, February 2000, pp. 9–10.
   2002       The Four Subfields: Anthropologists as Mythmakers. American Anthro-
               pologist 104(2):463–480.
   2017       Public Anthropology. *In* Perspectives: An Open Invitation to Cultural
               Anthropology. Nina Brown, Laura Tubelle de González, and Thomas
               McIlwraith, eds. Pp. 1–33. American Anthropological Association. http://
               perspectives.americananthro.org/Chapters/Public_Anthropology.pdf (ac-
               cessed October 5, 2017).

———, ed.
   1994       Assessing Cultural Anthropology. New York: McGraw-Hill.
   2000       Remembrance of Pacific Pasts: An Invitation to Remake History. Hono-
               lulu: University of Hawaii Press.

————, et al.

2001    WHEN: A Conversation about Culture. American Anthropologist 103(2):432–446.

2005    Yanomami: The Fierce Controversy and What We Can Learn from It. Berkeley: University of California Press.

Bosk, Charles

2006    Review Essay: Avoiding Conventional Understandings: The Enduring Legacy of Eliot Friedson. Sociology of Health and Illness 28(5):637–653.

Bourdieu, Pierre

1975    The Specificity of the Scientific Field and the Social Conditions of the Progress of Reason (Richard Nice, trans.). Sociology of Science 14(6):19–47.

1988    Homo Academicus. Stanford, CA: Stanford University Press.

Bourgois, Philippe

2000    Disciplining Addictions: The Bio-Politics of Methadone and Heroin in the United States. Culture, Medicine and Psychiatry 24(2):165–195.

2002    Ethnography's Troubles and the Reproduction of Academic Habitus. Qualitative Studies in Education 15(4):417–410.

Bourgois, Philippe, and Jeff Schonberg

2009    Righteous Dopefiend. California Series in Public Anthropology 21. Berkeley: University of California Press.

Bourguignon, Erika

1996    American Anthropology: A Personal View. General Anthropology 3(1):1, 7–9.

Bousquet, Marc

2002    The Waste Product of Graduate Education: Toward a Dictatorship of the Flexible. Social Text 20(1):81–104.

Boyer, Pascal

1996    Symbolism. *In* The Social Science Encyclopedia. A. Kuper and J. Kuper, eds. Pp. 860–861. New York: Routledge.

Brainard, Jeffrey

2005    A Makeover for the NIH's Peer-Review Process. Chronicle of Higher Education, March 18, pp. A22–24.

2008a   Incompetence Tops List of Complaints About Peer Reviewers. Chronicle of Higher Education, August 27. https://www.chronicle.com/article/Incompetence-Tops-List-of/1101 (accessed August 6, 2018).

2008b   NIH Turns Blind Eye to Academics' Financial Conflicts, Audit Says. Chronicle of Higher Education, February 1, p. A8.

2008c   Sen. Grassley Pressures Universities on Science Conflicts and Financial Aid. Chronicle of Higher Education, July 25. https://www.chronicle.com/article/Sen-Grassley-Speaks-on/1011 (accessed August 6, 2018).

2008d    Too Many Secretive Strings Are Attached to Federally Financed Projects, Universities Complain. Chronicle of Higher Education, July 18.

Brandeis, Louis
2014    Other People's Money and How the Bankers Use It. New York: Frederick A. Stokes.

Brenneis, Don
2009    Anthropology in and of the Academy: Globalization, Assessment and Our Field's Future. Social Anthropology 17:261–275.

Brenneis, Don, Cris Shore, and Susan Wright, eds.
2005    Universities and the Politics of Accountability. Anthropology in Action 12(1):1–10.

Briggs, Charles
1996    The Politics of Discursive Authority in Research on the "Invention of Tradition." Cultural Anthropology 11(4):435–469.

Brock, William
1994    Review: *The State and Social Investigation in Britain and the United States* by M. Lacey and M. Furner. Journal of American History 81(3):1280.

Brooks, David
2016    Revolt of the Masses. New York Times, June 28. https://www.nytimes.com/2016/06/28/opinion/revolt-of-the-masses.html (accessed October 5, 2017).

Brosius, J. Peter
1999a    Analyses and Interventions. Current Anthropology 40(3):277–309.
1999b    Green Dots, Pink Hearts: Displacing Politics from the Malaysian Rain Forest. American Anthropologist 101(1):36–57.

Brown, Carolyn Henning
1996    Contested Meanings: Tantra and the Poetics of Mithila Art. American Ethnologist 23(4):717–737.

Brown, Francis
1954    Review: *The Higher Learning in America*. Journal of American Education 25(8):453.

Brown, Michael F.
1984    The Role of Words in Aguaruna Hunting Magic. American Ethnologist 11(3):545–558.

Brown, Paula
1992    Review: *The Gender of the Gift*. Pacific Studies 15(1):123–129.

Brown, Robert
1976    The Idea of Punishment (Review: *Discipline and Punish* by M. Foucault). Times Literary Supplement, June 16, p. 658.

Browne, Malcolm W.
   1989    Physicists Debunk Claim of a New Kind of Fusion. New York Times, May 3, section A, p. 1.

Brumfiel, Elizabeth
   1992    Breaking and Entering the Ecosystem—Gender, Class, and Fraction Steal the Show. American Anthropologist 94(3):551–567.

Bruner, Edward
   2001    The Maasai and the Lion King: Authenticity, Nationalism, and Globalization in African Tourism. American Ethnologist 28(4):881–908.

Bruni, Frank
   2015    House Proud: Former Representative Barney Frank, a Liberal Mainstay, Offers His Views on the Political Process and His Role in It. New York Times Book Review, March 15, p. 13. https://www.nytimes.com/2015/03/15/books/review/frank-barney-franks-memoir.html (accessed August 6, 2018).

Bulmer, Martin
   2001    Review: *Chaos of Disciplines* by A. Abbott. American Journal of Sociology 107(3):818–819.

Burger, Henry
   1974    Review: *The Rise of Anthropological Theory* by M. Harris. American Anthropologist 76:576–578.

Burk, Kathleen
   2008    The History of the Political Summit. Times Literary Supplement (online), April 23.

Burke, Peter
   2000    A Social History of Knowledge: From Gutenberg to Diderot. Malden, MA: Polity Press.

———, ed.
   1992    Critical Essays on Michel Foucault. Hants, UK: Scolar Press.

Burton, John
   1992    On "First Contact" and Mythical Aborigines. American Anthropologist 94(3):696–697.

BusinessWeek
   1997    Everyone Knows E=MC2—Now Who Can Explain It? A Science Guru Wants Students to Interpret Data, Not Parrot It. BusinessWeek, October 6, pp. 66–68.
   2005    It Takes a Global Village (Review: *The End of Poverty* by J. Sachs). BusinessWeek, April 11.

Butterfield, Fox

    1983    The New Vietnam Scholarship. New York Times, February 13. http://part ners.nytimes.com/library/world/asia/021383vietnam-school.html (accessed October 5, 2017).

Butterworth, Douglas

    1972    Oscar Lewis 1914–1970. American Anthropologist 74:747–757.

Calderisi, Robert

    2006    The Trouble with Africa: Why Foreign Aid Isn't Working. New York: Palgrave Macmillan.

Calhoun, Daniel H.

    1976    Review: *Advocacy and Objectivity: A Crisis in the Professionalization of American Social Science, 1865–1905* by Mary O. Furner. Journal of Interdisciplinary History 7(2):362–364.

Camerer, Colin, et al.

    2018    Evaluating the Replicability of Social Science Experiments. Nature and Science. August 27. https://www.nature.com/articles/S41562-018-0399-Z (accessed August 6, 2018).

Campbell, Duncan

    2005    Chomsky Is Voted World's Top Public Intellectual. Guardian, October 18. https://www.theguardian.com/world/2005/oct/18/books.highereducation (accessed August 6, 2018).

Campbell, Paulette

    1999    NEH Official Calls for Broader Research into US Humanities Policy. Chronicle of Higher Education, June 25, p. A42.

Candea, Matei

    2019    Comparison in Anthropology: The Impossible Method. New York: Cambridge University Press.

Carey, Benedict

    2015a    Many Psychology Findings Not as Strong as Claimed, Study Says. New York Times, August 27. http://www.nytimes.com/2015/08/28/science/many -social-science-findings-not-as-strong-as-claimed-study-says.html?_r=0 (accessed October 5, 2017).

    2015b    Study Using Gay Canvassers Erred in Methods, Not Results, Author Says. New York Times, May 29. https://www.nytimes.com/2015/05/30/science/ michael-lacour-gay-marriage-science-study-retraction.html (accessed October 5, 2017).

Carmack, Robert

    1972    Ethnohistory: A Review of Its Development, Definitions, Methods, and Aims. Annual Review of Anthropology (1):227–246.

Carnegie, Charles

1996    The Dundus and the Nation. Cultural Anthropology 11(4):470–509.

Carneiro, Robert L.

1968    Cultural Adaptation. *In* International Encyclopedia of the Social Sciences, vol. 3. D. Sills, ed. Pp. 551–554. New York: Macmillan.

1979    White, Leslie Alvin. *In* International Encyclopedia of the Social Sciences: Biographical Supplement, vol. 18. D. Sills, ed. Pp. 803–807. New York: Macmillan.

2003    Evolutionism in Cultural Anthropology: A Critical History. Boulder, CO: Westview.

Carrier, James

1992    Occidentalism: The World Turned Upside-Down. American Ethnologist 19(2):195–212.

Carrithers, Michael

1990    Is Anthropology Art or Science? Current Anthropology 31(3):263–282.

Carroll, Michael P.

1978    Lévi-Strauss on the Oedipus Myth: A Reconsideration. American Anthropologist 80(4):805–814.

1979    A New Look at Freud on Myth. Ethos 7(3):189–205.

Carse, Ashley

2014    The Year 2013 in Sociocultural Anthropology: Cultures of Circulation and Anthropological Facts. American Anthropologist (May 26).

Casagrande, Joseph, ed.

1960    In the Company of Man. New York: Harper and Row.

Cassidy, John

2005    Always with Us? Jeffrey Sachs's Plan to Eradicate World Poverty (Review: *The End of Poverty* by J. Sachs). The New Yorker, April 11. https://www.newyorker.com/magazine/2005/04/11/always-with-us (accessed August 6, 2018).

Castaneda, Carlos

1968    The Teachings of Don Juan: A Yaqui Way of Knowledge. Berkeley: University of California Press.

Catalogue for Philanthropy

2011    Partners in Health: A Non Profit Corporation – 2011. http://www.philanthropydirectory.org/charity/partners-health-nonprofit-corporation (accessed October 5, 2017).

Chagnon, Napoleon

1968    Yanomamö: The Fierce People. New York: Holt, Rinehart and Winston.

1974    Studying the Yanomamö. New York: Holt, Rinehart and Winston.

1988      Life Histories, Blood Revenge, and Warfare in a Tribal Population. Science
          239(4843):985–992.

Chalmers, Iain, and Paul Glaziou
2009      Avoidable Waste in the Production and Reporting of Research Evidence.
          Lancet 374:86–89.

Champlin, Dell P., and Janet T. Knoedler
2006      The Media, the News, and Democracy: Revisiting the Dewey–Lippmann
          Debate. Journal of Economic Issues 40(1):135–152.

Chandrasekaran, Rajiv
2006      Imperial Life in the Emerald City: Inside Iraq's Green Zone. New York:
          Random House.

Chaney, Richard Paul
1978a     Polythematic Expansion: Remarks on Needham's Polythetic Classification.
          Current Anthropology 19(1):139–143.
1978b     Structures, Realities, and Blind Spots. American Anthropologist 80:589–
          596.
1993      Review: *Unthinking Social Science* by I. Wallerstein. American Anthropol-
          ogist 95(1):193–194.

Checker, Melissa, Alaka Wali, and David Vine
2009      American Anthropologist Launches Public Anthropology Reviews—
          Request for Submission of Review Materials. Email received June 15, 2009,
          publicanthreviews@gmail.com.

Chilungu, Simeon W.
1976      Issues in the Ethics of Research Method: An Interpretation of the Anglo-
          American Perspective. Current Anthropology 17(3):457–481.

Christian, William
1987      Tapping and Defining New Power. American Ethnologist 14:140–166.

Chubb, Jennifer, and Richard Watermeyer
2017      Artifice or Integrity in the Marketization of Research Impact? Investigating
          the Moral Economy of (Pathways to) Impact Statements Within Research
          Funding Proposals in the UK and Australia. Studies in Higher Education
          42(12):2360–2372.

Church, George
2001      Lessons from a Lost War. Time, June 24. http://content.time.com/time/
          magazine/article/0,9171,141574,00.html (accessed August 6, 2018).

Ciano, Stephany
2001      Margaret Mead. https://pabook.libraries.psu.edu/literary-cultural-heritage
          -map-pa/bios/Mead__Margaret.

Clark, William
　2006　Academic Charisma and the Origins of the Research University. Chicago: University of Chicago Press.

Clarke, Lee
　1989　New Ideas on the Division of Labor. Sociological Forum 4(2):281–289.

Clarke, Peter
　2007　The Last Thousand Days of the British Empire. London: Allen Lane.

Clayton, Victoria
　2015　The Needless Complexity of Academic Writing. The Atlantic, October 26. https://www.theatlantic.com/education/archive/2015/10/complex-academic-writing/412255/ (accessed August 6, 2018).

Clemmer, Richard O., L. Daniel Myers, and Mary Leizabeth Rudden, eds.
　1999　Julian Steward and the Great Basin: The Making of an Anthropologist. Salt Lake City: University of Utah Press.

Clemons, Walter
　1978　Men Behind Walls (Review: *Discipline and Punish* by M. Foucault). Newsweek, January 2, p. 61.

Clifford, James
　1983　Power and Dialogue in Ethnography: Marcel Griaule's Initiation. *In* Observers Observed, George Stocking, ed. Pp. 121–156. Madison: University of Wisconsin Press.

Clifford, James, and George E. Marcus, eds.
　1986　Writing Culture. Berkeley: University of California Press.

Clifton, James
　1976　Cultural Evolution. *In* Encyclopedia of Anthropology. D. Hunter and N. Whitten, eds. Pp. 99–101. New York: Harper and Row.

Cmiel, Kenneth
　1993　Destiny and Amnesia: The Vision of Modernity in Robert Wiege's *The Search for Order*. Reviews in American History 21(2):352–368.

CNN.com
　2007　Bush to Invoke Vietnam in Arguing Against Iraq Pullout. CNN.com. August 22. http://www.cnn.com/2007/POLITICS/08/21/bush.iraq.speech/ (accessed August 6, 2018).

Cocks, Geoffrey, and Knorad Jarausch
　1990　German Professions, 1800–1950. New York: Oxford University Press.

Cohen, Colleen Ballerino
　1998　"This is De Test": Festival and the Cultural Politics of National Building in the British Virgin Islands. American Ethnologist 25(2):189–214.

Cohen, Noam

    2007    After False Claim, Wikipedia to Check Degrees. New York Times, March 12. https://www.nytimes.com/2007/03/12/technology/12iht-wiki.4880906.html (accessed August 6, 2018).

Cohen, Patricia

    2003    Healing Humanity on His Own Terms (Book of the Times: *Mountains Beyond Mountains*). New York Times, September 10.

Cohen, Yehudi A.

    1969    Ends and Means in Political Control: State Organization and the Punishment of Adultery, Incest, and Violation of Celibacy. American Anthropologist 71:658–687.

Colby, Benjamin

    1987    Well-Being: A Theoretical Program. American Anthropologist 89:879–905.

Cole, Johnetta

    1995    Human Rights and the Rights of Anthropologists. American Anthropologist 97(3):445–456.

Colley, Linda

    1992    Britons: Forging the Nation 1707–1837. New Haven: Yale University Press.

Collier, Paul

    2007    The Bottom Billion: Why the Poorest Countries Are Failing and What Can Be Done About It. New York: Oxford University Press.

Collins, Randall

    2002    Review: *Chaos of Disciplines* by A. Abbott. Contemporary Sociology 31(2):230–233.

Colson, Elizabeth

    1989    Overview. Annual Review of Anthropology 18:1–16.

    1992    Social/Cultural Anthropology. *In* Wenner-Gren Foundation Report for 1990 and 1991. Pp. 49–61. New York: Wenner-Gren Foundation.

Comaroff, John, and Jean Comaroff

    1987    The Madman and the Migrant: Work and Labor in the Historical Consciousness of a South African People. American Ethnologist 14:191–209.

Communications and Public Affairs, University of Waterloo

    2006    Romantic Passion Is Topic of Public Anthropology Lecture, delivered February 23. http://newsrelease.uwaterloo.ca/news.php?id=4687 (accessed August 6, 2018).

Conklin, Beth

    1997    Body Paint, Feathers, and VCRS: Aesthetics and Authenticity in Amazonian Activism. American Ethnologist 24(4):711–737.

Conklin, Paul K.

1992 Review: *John Dewey and American Democracy* by R. Westbrook. Journal of American History 79(1):297.

Conley, Dalton

2009 Elsewhere, USA. New York: Pantheon.

Content, Robin

1976 Review: *Advocacy and Objectivity: A Crisis in the Professionalization of American Social Science, 1865–1905* by Mary O. Furner. Contemporary Sociology 5(September 5):684–685.

Cooper, George, and Gavan Daws

1990 Land and Power in Hawaii. Honolulu: University of Hawaii Press.

Cooper, Richard N.

2005 Review: *The End of Poverty* by J. Sachs. Foreign Affairs, May–June. https://www.foreignaffairs.com/reviews/capsule-review/2005-05-01/end-poverty-economic-possibilities-our-time (accessed August 6, 2018).

Corbyn, Zoe

2009 Retractions Up Tenfold. Times Higher Education, August 20. https://www.timeshighereducation.com/news/retractions-up-tenfold/407838.article (accessed August 6, 2018).

Corwin, Ronald

1979 Review: *The Culture of Professionalism* by B. Bledstein. Contemporary Sociology 8(3):377–381.

Couzin-Frankel, Jennifer

2018 'Journalologists' Use Scientific Methods to Study Academic Publishing. Is Their Work Improving Science? Science, September 19. https://www.sciencemag.org/news/2018/09/journalologists-use-scientific-methods-study-academic-publishing-their-work-improving (accessed December 31, 2018).

Cowen, Tyler

2007 A Way for Resource-Rich Countries to Audit Their Way out of Corruption. New York Times, July 12. https://www.nytimes.com/2007/07/12/business/worldbusiness/12scene.html (accessed August 6, 2018).

Cowlishaw, Gillian

1987 Colour, Culture and the Aboriginalists. Man 22:221–237.

Crain, Mary

1991 Poetics and Politics in the Ecuadorean Andes: Women's Narratives of Death and Devil Possession. American Ethnologist 18(1):67–89.

Crane, Gregory
    1991    Composing Culture: The Authority of an Electronic Text. Current Anthropology 32(3):293–311.

Crapanzano, Vincent
    1995    Dances with Myths. Review: *The Story of the Lynx* by C. Lévi-Strauss. New York Times, August 20. https://www.nytimes.com/1995/08/20/books/dances-with-myths.html (accessed August 6, 2018).

Crehan, Kate
    2002    Gramsci, Culture and Anthropology. Berkeley: University of California Press.

Creighton, J. E.
    1916    Review: *Democracy and Education* by J. Dewey. Philosophical Review 25(5):735–741.

Crick, Malcom
    1982    Anthropology of Knowledge. Annual Review of Anthropology (11):287–313.

Critser, Greg
    2003    I Say It's . . . Broccoli? New York Times Book Review, August 17, p. 22.

Da Matta, Roberto
    1979    Ritual in Complex and Tribal Societies. Current Anthropology 20(3):589–590.

Dahl, Ophelia
    2008    Director's Statement. Partners in Health, August 14.

Damico, Alfonso
    1978    Individuality and Community: The Social and Political Thought of John Dewey. Gainesville: University of Florida Press.

D'Andrade, R. G., et al.
    1975    Academic Opportunity in Anthropology, 1974–90. American Anthropologist 77:753–773.

Daniels, Inge Maria
    2003    Scooping , Raking, Beckoning Luck: Luck, Agency and the Interdependence of People and Things in Japan. Journal of the Royal Anthropological Institute 9:619–638.

Darkness in El Dorado
    n.d.    Archived Document. http://anthroniche.com/darkness_documents/0440.htm (accessed August 6, 2018).

Darnell, Regna
    1977    History of Anthropology in Historical Perspective. Annual Review of Anthropology 6:399–417.

2001    Invisible Genealogies: A History of Americanist Anthropology. Lincoln: University of Nebraska Press.

Darnton, Robert

1997    George Washington's False Teeth. New York Review of Books, March 27, pp. 34–38.

Daubenmier, Judith

2008    The Meskwaki and Anthropologists: Action Anthropology Reconsidered. Chicago: University of Chicago Press.

Davison, Kenneth

1969    Review: *The Academic Revolution* by C. Jencks and D. Riesman. American Quarterly 21(2):378.

Dawkins, Richard

2000    Branching Out. New York Times Book Review, August 6, pp. 18–19.

Daws, Gavan

1968    Kealakekua Bay Revisited: A Note on the Death of Captain Cook. Journal of Pacific History 3:21–23.

Deaton, Angus

2013    The Great Escape: Health, Wealth, and the Origins of Inequality. Princeton, NJ: Princeton University Press.

Deflem, Mathieu

1991    Ritual, Anti-Structure, and Religion: A Discussion of Victor Turner's Processual Symbolic Analysis. Journal for the Scientific Study of Religion 30(1):1–25.

De Munck, Victor

1996    Love and Marriage in a Sri Lankan Muslim Community. American Ethnologist 23(4):698–716.

Department of Anthropology, American University

n.d.    Master of Arts in Public Anthropology. http://www1.american.edu/academic.depts/cas/anthro/degree_programs.html#MAPA (accessed August 9, 2009).

Department of Anthropology, CSU–Fresno

n.d.    Institute of Public Anthropology. http://www.csufresno.edu/anthropology/ipa/ (accessed August 9, 2009).

Department of Anthropology, Tufts University

n.d.    Public Anthropology. http://ase.tufts.edu/anthropology/public.html (accessed August 9, 2009).

Department of Anthropology, University of Waterloo

n.d.    Guelph-Waterloo MA Program in Public Issues Anthropology. http://anthropology.uwaterloo.ca/MAprogram.html (accessed August 9, 2009).

Deresiewicz, William

2008     The Disadvantages of an Elite Education. American Scholar. June 1. https://
         theamericanscholar.org/the-disadvantages-of-an-elite-education/#.W4tN
         vJNKiDM (accessed August 6, 2018).

Desjarlais, Robert

1994     Struggling Along: The Possibilities for Experience among the Homeless
         Mentally Ill. American Anthropologist 96(4):886–901.

1996     The Office of Reason: On the Politics of Language and Agency in a Shelter
         for "The Homeless Mentally Ill." American Ethnologist 23(4):880–900.

de Waal, Alex

1997     Famine Crimes: Politics and the Disaster Relief Industry in Africa. Bloom-
         ington: Indiana University Press.

2002     For This Relief (Review: *The Selfish Altruist* by T. Vaux). Times Literary
         Supplement, January 2, pp. 5–6.

2007     Plan after Plan after Plan (Reviews: *Poor Story* by G. Bolton, *The Trouble
         with Africa* by R. Calderisi, and *Does Foreign Aid Really Work* by R. Rid-
         del). Times Literary Supplement, September 21, pp. 8–9.

Dewey, John

1916     Democracy and Education. New York: Macmillan.

1927     The Public and Its Problems: An Essay in Political Inquiry. New York:
         Henry Holt and Company.

1922     Public Opinion (Review: *Public Opinion* by W. Lippmann, originally
[1983]   published in New Republic 30: 286–288). *In* John Dewey: The Middle
         Works, 1899–1924. J. A. Boydston, ed. Carbondale: Southern Illinois Uni-
         versity Press.

Diamond, Jared

1997     Guns, Germs, and Steel: The Fates of Human Societies. New York: W. W.
         Norton & Co.

Diener, Paul, and Eugene E. Robkin

1978     Ecology, Evolution, and the Search for Cultural Origins: The Question of
         the Islamic Pig Prohibition. Current Anthropology 19(3):493–540.

Dietze, Erich von

2001     Paradigms Explained: Rethinking Thomas Kuhn's Philosophy of Science.
         Westport, CT: Praeger.

Diggins, John

1993     Review: *John Dewey and American Democracy* by R. Westbrook. Reviews
         in American History 21(1):116–120.

Di Leonardo, Micaela

1998     Exotics at Home: Anthropologies, Others, American Modernity. Chicago:
         University of Chicago Press.

Dillon, Wilton
    1980    Margaret Mead and Government. American Anthropologist 82:319–339.

DiMaggio, Paul
    1989    Review: *The System of Professions* by A. Abbott. American Journal of Sociology 95(2):534–535.

Dixon, P. J.
    1991    "Uneasy Lies the Head": Politics, Economics, and the Continuity of Belief among Yoruba of Nigeria. Comparative Studies in Society and History 33(1):56–85.

Donham, Donald
    1994    An Archaeology of Work Among the Maale of Ethiopia. Man 29:147–159.

Doughty, Paul
    1987    Vicos: Success, Rejection and Rediscovery of a Classic Program. *In* Applied Anthropology in America, second edition. E. Eddy and W. Partridge, eds. Pp. 433–459. New York: Columbia University Press.
    2002    Ending Serfdom in Peru: The Struggle for Land and Freedom in Vicos. *In* Contemporary Cultures and Societies of Latin America. Dwight B. Heath, ed. Pp. 222–243. Prospect Heights, IL: Waveland Press.

Douglas, Mary
    1966    Purity and Danger: An Analysis of Concepts of Pollution and Taboo. London: Routlege & Kegan Paul.

Dow, Peter
    1991    Schoolhouse Politics: Lessons from the Sputnik Era. Cambridge, MA: Harvard University Press.

Doyle, William R.
    2006    Running: Twice as Fast, Just to Keep Up (Playing the Numbers). Change (March–April):57–58.

Drezner, Daniel W.
    2005    "The End of Poverty": Brother, Can You Spare $195 Billion? (Review: *The End of Poverty* by J. Sachs). New York Times, April 24. https://www.nytimes.com/2005/04/24/books/review/the-end-of-poverty-brother-can-you-spare-195-billion.html (accessed August 6, 2018).

Drummond, Lee
    1977    Structure and Process in the Interpretation of South American Myth: The Arawak Dog Spirit People. American Anthropologist 79:842–868.

Dubisch, Jill
    1993    "Foreign Chickens" and Other Outsiders: Gender and Community in Greece. American Ethnologist 20(2):272–287.

Du Bois, Cora

1944   The People of Alor: A Social-psychological Study of an East Indian Island.
[1961]   With analyses by Abram Kardiner and Emil Oberholzer. New York:
Harper and Row.

Dubois, Laurent

2016   Who Will Speak for Haiti's Trees? New York Times, October 17. https://
www.nytimes.com/2016/10/18/opinion/who-will-speak-for-haitis-trees.
html?mcubz=3&_r=2 (accessed October 2017).

Duman, Daniel

1979   The Creation and Diffusion of a Professional Ideology in Nineteenth Century England. Sociological Review 27:113–138.

Dunnell, Robert C.

1978   Style and Function: A Fundamental Dichotomy. American Antiquity
43(2):192–202.

Durham, William

1990   Advances in Evolutionary Culture Theory. Annual Review of Anthropology 19:187–210.

1992   Applications of Evolutionary Culture Theory. Annual Review of Anthropology 21:331–355.

Durkheim, Emile, and Marcel Mauss

1963   Primitive Classification. Rodney Needham, ed. Chicago: University of
Chicago.

Durrenberger, Paul, and Gisli Palsson

1987   Ownership at Sea: Fishing Territories and Access to Sea Resources. American Ethnologist 14:508–522.

Durrenberger, Paul, and Nicola Tannenbaum

1992   Household Economy, Political Economy, and Ideology: Peasants and the
State in Southeast Asia. American Anthropologist 94(1):74–89.

Dykstra, Robert R.

1976   Review: *Advocacy and Objectivity: A Crisis in the Professionalization of
American Social Science, 1865–1905* by Mary O. Furner. Journal of American History 63(June 1):142–143.

Dzuback, Mary

1993   Review: *The Culture of Professionalism* by B. Bledstein. History of Education Quarterly 33(3):375–385.

Earle, Timothy K.

1987   Chiefdoms in Archaeological and Ethnological Perspective. Annual Review of Anthropology 16:279–308.

Earle, Timothy K., and Robert Preucel

1987    Processual Archaeology and the Radical Critique. Current Anthropology 28(4):501–538.

Easterly, William

2005    A Modest Proposal (Review: *The End of Poverty* by J. Sachs). Washington Post, March 13. http://www.washingtonpost.com/wp-dyn/articles/A25562 -2005Mar10.html (accessed August 6, 2018).

2006    The White Man's Burden: Why the West's Efforts to Aid the Rest Have Done So Much Ill and So Little Good. New York: Penguin Press.

Economist

2000    Survey: Nigeria; A Tale of Two Giants. The Economist, January 13. https:// www.economist.com/special-report/2000/01/13/a-tale-of-two-giants (accessed August 6, 2018).

2002    The Poll That Bob Stole. The Economist, March 14. https://www.economist. com/special-report/2002/03/14/the-poll-that-bob-stole (accessed August 6, 2018).

2003    The Right To Be Well. The Economist, December 30. https://www.econo mist.com/books-and-arts/2003/12/30/the-right-to-be-well (accessed August 6, 2018).

2004a   How to Save the World: Jeffrey Sachs Has Some Good Ideas, But Also Some Iffy Ones. The Economist, October 28 https://www.economist.com/ finance-and-economics/2004/10/28/how-to-save-the-world (accessed August 6, 2018).

2005a   Aid to Africa: The $25 Billion Question. The Economist, June 30. https:// www.economist.com/special-report/2005/06/30/the-25-billion-question (accessed August 6, 2018).

2005b   Development: Recasting the Case for Aid. The Economist, January 20. https://www.economist.com/finance-and-economics/2005/01/20/recasting -the-case-for-aid (accessed August 6, 2018).

2005c   Looking for a Sign. The Economist, November 12, p. 86.

2005d   The Paperless Library: Free Access To Scientific Results Changing Re- search Practices, September 22. https://www.economist.com/science-and -technology/2005/09/22/the-paperless-library (accessed August 6, 2018).

2005e   Rebuilding Failed States: From Chaos, Order. The Economist, March 3. https://www.economist.com/middle-east-and-africa/2005/03/03/from -chaos-order (accessed August 6, 2018).

2005f   Thinking Big. The Economist, March 17. https://www.economist.com/ books-and-arts/2005/03/17/thinking-big (accessed August 6, 2018).

2006a   Development Aid: In Praise of Small Things. The Economist, April 1, pp. 68–69.

2006b   Mind the Gap. The Economist, September 9, p. 76.

2007a   The Face of Oppression. The Economist, March 15. https://www.economist.

com/middle-east-and-africa/2007/03/15/the-face-of-oppression (accessed August 6, 2018).

2007b How to Help the Poorest; Springing the Traps (Review: *The Bottom Billion* by P. Collier). The Economist, July 2, pp. 71–72.

2007c Humanitarian Aid: Weighed and Found Wanting. The Economist, May 26, pp. 64–65.

2007d Intervention and Peacekeeping: Paddy's Passion (Review: *Swords and Ploughshares* by P. Ashdown). The Economist, June 30, p. 94.

2007e Money Isn't Everything. The Economist, July 7, p. 78.

2008a Asia's Other Miracle. The Economist, April 24. https://www.economist .com/leaders/2008/04/24/asias-other-miracle (accessed August 6, 2018).

2008b Failed States: Nation-Building for Dummies. The Economist, June 28, pp. 91–92.

2008c Getting Away with Murder. The Economist, July 1. https://www.economist .com/middle-east-and-africa/2008/07/01/getting-away-with-murder (accessed August 6, 2018).

2008d Going by the Book. The Economist, January 12, p. 71.

2008e Grappling with Success. The Economist, January 31. https://www.econo mist.com/asia/2008/01/31/grappling-with-success (accessed August 6, 2018).

2008f Great Minds Think (Too Much) Alike. The Economist, July 19, p. 89.

2008g Half-Way from Rags to Riches. The Economist, April 24. https://www .economist.com/special-report/2008/04/24/half-way-from-rags-to-riches (accessed August 6, 2018).

2008h How to Get Him Out. The Economist, June 26. https://www.economist .com/leaders/2008/06/26/how-to-get-him-out (accessed August 6, 2018).

2008i Microfinance: Doing Good by Doing Very Nicely. The Economist, June 26. https://www.economist.com/leaders/2008/06/26/doing-good-by-doing -very-nicely-indeed (accessed August 6, 2018).

2008j Remittances: Follow the Money. The Economist, June 23. https://www .economist.com/news/2008/06/23/follow-the-money (accessed August 6, 2018).

2008k Sachs Appeal. The Economist, March 27. https://www.economist.com/ books-and-arts/2008/03/27/sachs-appeal (accessed August 6, 2018).

2008l Target Acquired. The Economist, May 31, p. 86.

2009a Liar! Liar! Fraud in Science. Scientists Are Not Quite as Honest as Might Be Hoped. June 4. http://www.economist.com/node/13776974 (accessed August 6, 2018).

2009b Robert McNamara. The Economist, July 11, p. 88.

2009c Science and Technology: The Beast That Will Not Die. The Economist, March 26, pp. 89–90.

2009d What's the Score? The Economist, March 14, p. 83.

2012  Millennium Bugs: Jeffrey Sachs and the Millennium Villages. The Econo-
      mist, May 14. https://www.economist.com/blogs/feastandfamine/2012/05/
      jeffrey-sachs-and-millennium-villages (accessed October 5, 2017).

2013a Trouble in the Lab. Unreliable Research. The Economist, October 18.
      https://www.economist.com/news/briefing/21588057-scientists-think-sci
      ence-self-correcting-alarming-degree-it-not-trouble (accessed October 5,
      2017).

2013b Economic Inequality: In Sickness and Health (Review of Deaton's *The
      Great Escape*). The Economist, October 12, pp. 100–101.

2014a Combatting Bad Science. Metaphysicians. The Economist. March 15.
      https://www.economist.com/science-and-technology/2014/03/15/metaphy
      sicians (accessed August 6, 2018).

2014b When Science Gets It Wrong. Let the Light Shine In. The Economist, June
      14, pp. 72–73.

2016a Tested, and Found Wanting: Tracking Down Missing Clinical Trials.
      The Economist, November 5. https://www.economist.com/news/science
      -and-technology/21709525-tested-and-found-wanting (accessed August 6,
      2018).

2016b Why Research Papers Have So Many Authors. The Economist, November
      24. http://www.economist.com/news/science-and-technology/21710792
      -scientific-publications-are-getting-more-and-more-names-attached-them
      -why (accessed August 6, 2018).

2018a How Global University Rankings Are Changing Higher Education. The
      Economist, May 19. https://www.economist.com/international/2018/05/19/
      how-global-university-rankings-are-changing-higher-education (accessed
      August 6, 2018).

2018b No GUTs, No Glory: Fundamental Physics Is Frustrating Physicists. The
      Economist, January 13, pp. 71–73.

2018c Some Science Journals That Claim to Peer Review Papers Do Not Do So.
      The Economist, June 23. https://www.economist.com/science-and-technol
      ogy/2018/06/23/some-science-journals-that-claim-to-peer-review-papers
      -do-not-do-so (accessed August 6, 2018).

Edens, Christopher
1992  Dynamics of Trade in the Ancient Mesopotamian "World System." Ameri-
      can Anthropologist 94(1):118–139.

Edgerton, Robert
1995  Review: How *"Natives" Think* by M. Sahlins. National Review, May 15, p. 73.

Edmunds, Mary, and Monique Skidmore
2004  Australian Anthropologists and Public Anthropology. Anthropological
      Forum 17(2):107–125.

Edwards, David
  1989    Mad Mullahs and Englishmen: Discourse in the Colonial Encounter.
          Comparative Studies in Society and History 31(4): 649–670.

Eggan, Fred
  1954    Social Anthropology and the Method of Controlled Comparison. Ameri-
          can Anthropologist 56:743–763.
  1965    Some Reflections on Comparative Method in Anthropology. *In* Context
          and Meaning in Cultural Anthropology. Melford Spiro, ed. Pp. 357–372.
          New York: Free Press.
  1968    Kinship. *In* International Encyclopedia of the Social Sciences, vol. 8. David
          Sills, ed. Pp. 390–401. New York: Macmillan.

Ehrenreich, Barbara
  2001    Nickel and Dimed: On (Not) Getting By in America. New York: Metropol-
          itan Books.

El Aisati, M'hamed, et al.
  n.d.    International Comparative Performance of the UK Research Base 2016.
          Prepared by Elsevier. https://www.elsevier.com/research-intelligence?a
          =507321 (accessed August 6, 2018).

Ellen, Roy F.
  1978    Problems and Progress in the Ethnographic Analysis of Small Scale Hu-
          man Ecosystems. Man 13(2):290–303.

Ember, Carol, and Melvin Ember
  2002    Cultural Anthropology, tenth edition. Upper Saddle River, NJ: Prentice
          Hall.
  2007    Cultural Anthropology, twelfth edition. Upper Saddle River, NJ: Pearson /
          Prentice Hall.

Ember, Carol, Melvin Ember, and Peter Peregrine
  2007    Anthropology, twelfth edition. Upper Saddle River, NJ: Pearson / Prentice
          Hall.

Engardio, Pete
  2006    Ideas Books: Throwing Money—and Missing. BusinessWeek, April 3,
          p. 132.

English, James
  2005    The Economy of Prestige: Prizes, Awards, and the Circulation of Cultural
          Value. Cambridge, MA: Harvard University Press.

Englund, Harri
  2006    Prisoners of Freedom: Human Rights and the African Poor. Berkeley: Uni-
          versity of California Press.

Epstein, David G.

1973    Review: *Town and Country in Brazil* by M. Harris. American Anthropologist 75:988–990.

Erickson, Paul A., and Liam D. Murphy

1998    A History of Anthropological Theory. Orchard Park, NY: Broadview Press.

Eriksen, Thomas Hylland

1992    Review: *Unthinking Social Science* by I. Wallerstein. Journal of Peace Research 29(2):236.

2006    Engaging Anthropology: The Case of a Public Presence. New York: Berg.

Eriksen, Thomas Hylland, and Finn Sivert Nielsen

2001    A History of Anthropology. Sterling, VA: Pluto.

Ernest, Waltraud

1997    Idioms of Madness and Colonial Boundaries. Comparative Studies in Society and History 39:153–181.

Ernst, Thomas M.

1999    Land, Stories, and Resources: Discourse and Entification in Onabasulu Modernity. American Anthropologist 101(1):88–97.

Escobar, Arturo

1991    Anthropology and the Development Encounter: The Marking and Marketing of Development Anthropology. American Ethnologist 18(4):658–682.

Eubanks, Virginia

2017    Automating Inequality: How High-Tech Tools Profile, Police, and Punish the Poor. New York: St. Martin's Press.

Evens, T. M. S.

1983    Mind, Logic, and the Efficacy of the Nuer Incest Prohibition. Man 18(1):111–133.

Ewers, John

1960    Review: *Lewis Henry Morgan: The Indian Journals 1859–1962* by Lewis Henry Morgan. American Anthropologist 62(4):701–703.

Fadiman, Anne

1997    The Spirit Catches You and You Fall Down: A Hmong Child, Her American Doctors, and the Collision of Two Cultures. New York: Farrar, Straus, and Giroux.

Fagan, Brian

1995    The Captain Cook Debate, Cont'd. Washington Post, August 3, p. C3.

Fairbanks, Michael

2017    The Heart of Africa's New Medical School. Project Syndicate, February 1. https://www.project-syndicate.org/commentary/rwanda-universal-health -care-ughe-by-michael-fairbanks-2017-02 (accessed October 5, 2017).

Fall, Bernard

    1965    Errors Escalated Too. New York Times, May 16. https://archive.nytimes.com/www.nytimes.com/books/98/03/15/home/halberstam-quagmire.html?_r=1&oref=slogin (accessed August 6, 2018).

Farago, John

    1982    Review: *On Higher Education* by D. Reisman. Journal of Higher Education 53(6):701–715.

Farmer, Paul

    2004    Pathologies of Power: Health, Human Rights, and the New War on the Poor. Berkeley: University of California Press.

    2010    Partner to the Poor: A Paul Farmer Reader. California Series in Public Anthropology 23. Haun Saussy, ed. Berkeley: University of California Press.

    2013    To Repair the World. California Series in Public Anthropology 29. Jonathan Weigel, ed. Berkeley: University of California Press.

    2015    Who Lives and Who Dies. London Review of Books 37(3):17–20. https://www.lrb.co.uk/v37/n03/paul-farmer/who-lives-and-who-dies (accessed October 5, 2017).

Farnell, Brenda

    1994    Ethno-Graphics and the Moving Body. Man 29(4):929–974.

Fassin, Didier

    2013    Enforcing Order: An Ethnography of Urban Policing. Cambridge, UK: Polity Press.

    2016    Prison Worlds: An Ethnography of the Carceral Condition. Cambridge, UK: Polity Press.

    2017    Epilogue: The Public Afterlife of Ethnography in If Truth Be Told. Didier Fassin, ed. Durham, NC: Duke University Press.

Faubion, James

    1993    History in Anthropology. Annual Review of Anthropology 22:35–54.

Fawcett, Peter

    1999    The Image of a Free Man: Andre Gide and the Quest for Human Truth. Times Literary Supplement, November 12, pp. 4–6.

FDA (US Food and Drug Administration)

    2011    FDA Update on the Safety of Silicone Gel-Filled Breast Implants. Center for Devices and Radiological Health, US Food and Drug Administration. https://www.fda.gov/downloads/medicaldevices/productsandmedicalprocedures/implantsandprosthetics/breastimplants/ucm260090.pdf (accessed August 6, 2018).

Featherstone, Liza

    2018    Programmed to Fail: Rather Than Helping the Poor, Technology Has Created More Obstacles to Getting Help. New York Times Book Review, May

6, p. 19. https://www.nytimes.com/2018/05/04/books/review/automating
-inequality-virginia-eubanks.html (accessed August 6, 2018).

Feil, D. K.

1978    "Straightening the Way": An Enga Kinship Conundrum. Man 13(3):380–
401.

Feld, Steven

1982    Sound and Sentiment. Philadelphia: University of Pennsylvania Press.

Fenton, William

1941    Masked Medicine Societies of the Iroquois. Washington, DC: Smithsonian
Institution Press.

1957    American Indian and White Relations to 1830. New York: Russell & Russell.

1962    Introduction. *In* Morgan, Henry Lewis. League of the Iroquois. New York:
Corinth Books.

1987    The False Faces of the Iroquois. Norman: University of Oklahoma Press.

1998    The Great Law and the Longhouse: A Political History of the Iroquois
Confederacy. Norman: University of Oklahoma Press.

Ferguson, Niall

2007    The Least Among Us (Review: *The Bottom Billion* by P. Collier). New York
Times Book Review, July 1, pp. 10–11.

Fernandez, James

1974    The Mission of Metaphor in Expressive Culture. Current Anthropology
15(2):119–145.

1990    Review: *The Predicament of Culture* by J. Clifford. American Anthropologist 92:823–824.

Ferraro, Gary

2004    Cultural Anthropology: An Applied Perspective, fifth edition. Belmont,
CA: Thomson/Wadsworth.

Field Museum

1999    Public Anthropology Post-Doctoral Anthropology News, October, p. 54.

Filiu, Jean-Pierre

2015    From Deep State to Islamic State: The Arab Counter-Revolution and Its
Jihadi Legacy. New York: Oxford University Press.

Finney, Ben

1991    Myth, Experiment and the Reinvention of Polynesian Voyaging. American
Anthropologist 93(2):383–404.

Firestone, Melvin

1978    Christmas Mumming and Symbolic Interactionism. Ethos 6(2):92–113.

Firth, Raymond
   1975    An Appraisal of Modern Social Anthropology. Annual Review of Anthropology (4):4.

Fischer, J. L.
   1965    Psychology and Anthropology. *In* Biennial Review of Anthropology. B. Siegal, ed. Pp. 211–261. Stanford, CA: Stanford University Press.

Fischer, Michael M. J.
   1997    Postmodern, Postmodernisms. *In* The Dictionary of Anthropology. T. Barfield, ed. Pp. 368–372. Malden, MA: Blackwell.
   1999    Emergent Forms of Life: Anthropologies of Late or Postmodernities. Annual Review of Anthropology 28:455–478.

Fischer, Michael M. J., and George Marcus
   1989    Response to Whitten. American Ethnologist 16(3):570.

Flaherty, Colleen
   2016    Refusing to Be Measured. Inside Higher Ed, May 11. https://www.inside highered.com/news/2016/05/11/rutgers-graduate-school-faculty-takes -stand-against-academic-analytics (accessed August 6, 2018).

Florence, Sargant
   1940    Review: *Knowledge for What* by R. Lynd. The Economic Journal 50(197):105–107.

Floridi, Luciano
   2001    Honesty Must Come First. Times Literary Supplement, June 15, pp. 34–35.

Fluehr-Lobban, Carolyn
   1979    A Marxist Reappraisal of the Matriarchate. Current Anthropology 20(2):341–359.

Foley, Douglas
   1999    The Fox Project: A Reappraisal. Current Anthropology 40(2):171–191.

Fontana, Biancamaria
   2004    Old World for New. Times Literary Supplement, July 2, pp. 3–4.

Foster, Stephen
   1985    Review: *Local Knowledge* by C. Geertz. American Anthropologist 87:164–165.

Foucault, Michel
   1979    Discipline and Punish: The Birth of the Prison. New York: Random House (Vintage Books).

Fowler, Chris, and Vicki Cummings
   2003    Places of Transformation: Building Monuments from Water and Stone in the Neolithic of the Irish Sea. Journal of the Royal Anthropological Institute 9:1–20.

Fowler, Glenn
1991    Cora DuBois, Harvard Professor of Anthropology, Is Dead at 87 (Obituary). New York Times, April 11. http://www.nytimes.com/1991/04/11/obituaries/cora-dubois-harvard-professor-of-anthropology-is-dead-at-87.html?scp=1&sq=cora+dubois&st=nyt (accessed October 5, 2017).

Francis, David
2008    Iraq War Cost Estimates Run into the Trillions. Christian Science Monitor, March 10. https://www.csmonitor.com/Business/2008/0310/p16s01-wmgn.html (accessed August 6, 2018).

Frank, Andre Gunder
1970    Latin America: Underdevelopment or Revolution. New York: Modern Reader.
1998    ReOrient: Global Economy in the Asian Age. Berkeley: University of California Press.

Frankel, Max
1995    McNamara's Retreat (Review: *In Retrospect: The Tragedy and Lessons of Vietnam* by R. McNamara). New York Times, April 16. https://www.nytimes.com/1995/04/16/books/mcnamara-s-retreat.html (accessed August 6, 2018).

Frazer, James
1922    The Golden Bough. New York: Macmillan.
[1963]

Freed, Stanley A., and Ruth S. Freed
1983    Clark Wissler and the Development of Anthropology in the United States. American Anthropologist 85(4):800–825.

Freidson, Eliot
1986    Professional Powers. Chicago: University of Chicago Press.
1999    Theory of Professionalism. International Review of Sociology 9(1):117–129.
2001    Professionalism, the Third Logic: On the Practice of Knowledge. Chicago: University of Chicago Press.

Friedman, Jonathan
1974    Marxism, Structuralism, and Vulgar Materialism. Man 9:444–469.
1988    No History Is an Island (Review: *Islands of History*). Critique of Anthropology 8(3):7–39.
1992    The Past in the Future: History and the Politics of Identity. American Anthropologist 94(4):837–859.

Frost, Robert
1949    Complete Poems of Robert Frost. New York: Holt, Rinehart and Winston.

Frum, David
> 2000 How We Got Here: The 1970s—The Decade That Brought You Modern Life (For Better or Worse). New York: Basic Books.

Fuchs, Lawrence
> 1961 Hawaii Pono: A Social History. New York: Harcourt Brace Jovanovich.

Fund for Peace
> 2009 Failed State Index. http://www.fundforpeace.org (accessed August 6, 2018).

Fung, Archon, Mary Graham, and David Weil
> 2007 Full Disclosure: The Perils and Promise of Transparency. New York: Cambridge University Press.

Furner, Mary
> 1975 Advocacy and Objectivity: A Crisis in the Professionalization of American Social Science, 1865–1905. Lexington: University of Kentucky Press.
> 1999 Review: *The Making of the Modern University: Intellectual Transformation and the Marginalization of Morality* by Julie A. Reuben. History of Education Quarterly 39(3):360–363.

Gabriel, Sherine, et al.
> 1994 Risk of Connective-Tissue Diseases and Other Disorders After Breast Implantation. New England Journal of Medicine 330(24):1697–1702. http://www.nejm.org/doi/pdf/10.1056/NEJM199406163302401 (accessed August 6, 2018).

Galaty, John
> 1983 Ceremony and Society: The Poetics of Maasai Ritual. Man 18(2):361–382.

Geertz, Clifford
> 1968 Religion, Anthropological Study. *In* International Encyclopedia of the Social Sciences, vol. 13. D. Sills, ed. Pp. 398–406. New York: Macmillan.
> 1973 The Interpretation of Cultures. New York: Basic Books.
> 1978 Stir Crazy (Review: *Discipline and Punish* by M. Foucault). New York Review of Books, January 26, pp. 3–6.
> 1982 Review: *Historical Metaphors and Mythical Realities* by M. Sahlins. American Ethnologist 9(3):583–584.
> 1983 Local Knowledge: Further Essays in Interpretive Anthropology. New York: Basic Books.
> 1985 Waddling In. Times Literary Supplement, June 7, pp. 623–624.
> 1995a The Culture War. New York Review of Books, November 30, pp. 4–6.
> 1995b Personal communication regarding my reviewing Geertz's *The Culture War* for errors prior to its publication in the New York Review of Books.

Gellner, Ernest
> 1992 Postmodernism, Reason and Religion. New York: Routledge.

Gennep, Arnold van
1909    Rites of Passage. Chicago: University of Chicago Press.
[1960]

Gerber, Larry
1991    Review: *The State and Economic Knowledge* by M. Furner and B. Supple. Journal of Economic History 51(3):759–760.

Gershon, Ilana
2003    Knowing Adoption and Adopting Knowledge. American Ethnologist 30(3):439–446.

Gewertz, Deborah
1990    Review: *The Gender of the Gift*. American Anthropologist 92:797–798.

Gewertz, Deborah, and Frederick Errington
1987    Cultural Alternatives and a Feminist Anthropology: An Analysis of Culturally Constructed Gender Interests in Papua New Guinea. New York: Cambridge University Press.

Gezon, Lida L.
1999    Of Shrimps and Spirit Possession: Toward a Political Economy of Resource Management in Northern Madagascar. American Anthropologist 101(1):58–67.

Gibbon, Guy E.
1972    Cultural Dynamics and the Development of the Oneonta Life-Way in Wisconsin. American Antiquity 37(2):166–185.

Gillespie, Susan
2000    Rethinking Ancient Maya Social Organization. American Anthropologist 102(3):467–484.

Gilman, Antonio
1981    The Development of Social Stratification in Bronze Age Europe. Current Anthropology 22(1):1–23.

Ginsberg, Daniel
2016    Anthropologists in and out of the Academy. Anthropology News (November–December):19.
2017    Trends in Anthropology Bachelor's Degrees. AAA 2017 Year in Review. http://s3.amazonaws.com/rdcms-aaa/files/production/public/FileDownloads/pdfs/IPEDS%20anthro%20bachelor%27s%20degrees.pdf (accessed August 6, 2018).

Givens, David, Patsy Evans, and Timothy Jablonski
1997    AAA Survey of Anthropology PhDs (personal copy of data provided by D. Givens). http://www.aaanet.org/surveys/97survey.htm (accessed October 18, 2000).

Givens, David, and Timothy Jablonski

2000    American Anthropological Association Survey of Anthropology PhDs.
http://www.americananthro.org/LearnAndTeach/ResourceDetail.aspx
?ItemNumber=1499 (accessed October 5, 2017).

Givier, Peter

1999    Scholars Books: The Coin of the Realm of Knowledge. Chronicle of Higher
Education, November 12, p. A76.

Glanz, James, and Agustin Armendariz

2017    Years of Ethics Charges, but Star Cancer Research Gets a Pass. New York
Times, March 8. https://www.nytimes.com/2017/03/08/science/cancer
-carlo-croce.html (accessed August 6, 2018).

Glasziou, Paul, et al.

2014    Reducing Waste from Incomplete or Unusable Reports of Biomedical Research. Lancet 383(9913):267–276.

Gledhill, John

1999    Eric R. Wolf: An Appreciation. Critique of Anthropology 19(2):202–208.

Glenn, David

2002    Hot Type. Chronicle of Higher Education, July 26, p. A18.

2007a    Anthropologists in a War Zone: Scholars Debate Their Role. Chronicle of
Higher Education, November 30. https://www.chronicle.com/article/An
thropologists-in-a-War-Zone-/34710 (accessed August 6, 2018).

2007b    Federal Judge Allows Defamation Lawsuit Against Best-Selling Economist to Proceed. Chronicle of Higher Education, January 16. https://www
.chronicle.com/article/Federal-Judge-Allows/122752 (accessed August 6,
2018).

2007c    Report on Anthropologists' Work with the Military Discourages Secrecy.
Chronicle of Higher Education, December 7. https://www.chronicle.com/
article/Report-on-Anthropologists/4835 (accessed August 6, 2018).

2008a    Bottom Lines Cause Unease at Societies of Scholars. Chronicle of Higher
Education, December 19. https://www.chronicle.com/article/Bottom-Lines
-Cause-Unease-at/27475 (accessed August 6, 2018).

2008b    Keep Adjuncts Away from Intro Courses, Report Says. Chronicle of
Higher Education, April 4. https://www.chronicle.com/article/Keep
-Adjuncts-Away-From-Intro/29236 (accessed August 6, 2018).

2008c    Old Fears Haunt New Social Science. Chronicle of Higher Education, July
11, p. A3.

Gluckman, Mary, and Max Gluckman

1977    On Drama and Games and Athletic Contests. In Secular Ritual. S. F. Moore
and B. Myerhoff, eds. Pp. 191–209. Assen, Netherlands: Van Gorcum.

Godelier, Maurice
    1978    Infrastructures, Societies, and History. Current Anthropology 19(4):763–771.

Gold, Ann Grodzins, and Bhoju Ram Gujar
    1997    Wild Pigs and Kings: Remembered Landscapes in Rajasthan. American Anthropologist 99(1):70–84.

Goldacre, Ben
    2012    Bad Pharma: How Drug Companies Mislead Doctors and Harm Patients. New York: Faber and Faber.

Goldenweiser, Alexander
    1940    Review: *Knowledge for What* by R. Lynd. American Anthropologist 42(1):164–166.

Goldschmidt, Walter
    1987    Review: *Anthropology as a Cultural Critique*. American Anthropologist 89:472–473.

Goldstein, Jan
    1979    Review: *Discipline and Punish*. Journal of Modern History 51(1):116–118.

Goodenough, Ward
    1951    Property, Kin and Community on Truk. Hamden, CT: Archon.
    [1966]
    1989    Cultural Anthropology: Science and Humanity. Crosscurrents 3:78–82.

Gould, Nathan
    1978    The Structure of Dialectical Reason. Ethos 6(4):187–211.

Gradgrind, Lagretta
    2007    Too Many Bad Apples. Chronicle of Higher Education, October 12. https://www.chronicle.com/article/Too-Many-Bad-Apples/46514 (accessed August 6, 2018).

Graeber, David
    2017    It Wasn't a Tenure Case: A Personal Testimony, with Reflections. Public Anthropologist, Journal Blog, October 11. http://publicanthropologist.cmi.no/2017/10/11/academic-politics-of-silencing/#david-graeber (accessed August 6, 2018).
    2018    Are You in a BS Job? In Academe, You're Hardly Alone. Chronicle of Higher Education, May 6. https://www.chronicle.com/article/Are-You-in-a-BS-Job-In/243318 (accessed August 6, 2018).

Graebner, Fritz
    1911    Methode der Ethnologie. Heidelberg, Germany: C. Winter.

Grafton, Anthony

    1997    The Footnote: A Curious History. Cambridge, MA: Harvard University Press.

    2006    The Nutty Professors. The New Yorker, October 23, pp. 82–87.

    2007    What Is History? New York: Cambridge University Press.

Gramsci, Antonio

    1971    Selections from the Prison Notebooks of Antonio Gramsci. Quintin Hoare and Geoffrey Nowell Smith, eds. New York: International Publishers.

    1985    Antonio Gramsci: Selections from Cultural Writings. David Forgacs and Geoffrey Nowell-Smith, eds. Cambridge, MA: Harvard University Press.

    2000    The Antonio Gramsci Reader. D. Forgacs, ed. New York: New York University Press.

Gravois, John

    2006    Tracking the Invisible Faculty. Chronicle of Higher Education, December 15. https://www.chronicle.com/article/Tracking-the-Invisible-Faculty/35173 (accessed August 6, 2018).

    2007    You're Not Fooling Anyone. Chronicle of Higher Education, November 9. https://www.chronicle.com/article/Youre-Not-Fooling-Anyone/28069 (accessed August 6, 2018).

Greaves, Tom, Ralph Bolton, and Florencia Zapata

    2011    Vicos and Beyond: A Half Century of Applying Anthropology in Peru. Lanham, MD: AltaMira Press.

Gregor, Thomas, and Daniel Gross

    2002    Anthropology and the Search for the Enemy Within. Chronicle of Higher Education, July 26, p. B11.

    2004    Guilt by Association: The Culture of Accusation and the American Anthropological Association's Investigation of Darkness in El Dorado. American Anthropologist 106(4):687–698.

Griffith, David

    1987    Nonmarket Labor Processes in an Advanced Capitalist Economy. American Anthropologist 89:838–852.

Griffith, David, Manuel Valdes Pizzini, and Jeffrey Johnson

    1992    Injury and Therapy: Proletarianization in Puerto Rico's Fisheries. American Ethnologist 19(1):53–74.

Grinker, Roy Richard

    2000    In the Arms of Africa: The Life of Colin M. Turnbull. New York: St. Martin's Press.

Guindi, Fadwa El, and Dwight W. Read

    1979    Mathematics in Structural Theory. Current Anthropology 20(4):761–790.

Gulbenkian Commission

1996    Open the Social Sciences: Report of the Gulbenkian Commission on the Restructuring of the Social Sciences. Stanford, CA: Stanford University Press.

Gulbrandsen, Ornulf

1995    The King by the Grace of the People. Comparative Studies in Society and History 37(3):415–444.

Guterman, Lila

2008a    Access to Online Journals Reduces Breadth of Citations, Study Finds. Chronicle of Higher Education, July 18. https://www.chronicle.com/article/Access-to-Online-Journals-Is/993 (accessed August 6, 2018).

2008b    Better Than the Impact Factor. Chronicle of Higher Education, February 27. https://www.chronicle.com/article/Better-Than-the-Impact-Factor-/40553 (accessed August 6, 2018).

2008c    Free Access to Science Papers Found Not to Increase Citations. Chronicle of Higher Education, August 1. https://www.chronicle.com/article/Free-Access-to-Science-Papers/1028 (accessed August 6, 2018).

Gutierrez, Melody, and Nanette Asimov

2017    Regents Throw Parties at UC's expense. San Francisco Chronicle, May 28. http://www.sfchronicle.com/bayarea/article/Regents-throw-parties-at-UC-s-expense-11178628.php (accessed August 6, 2018).

Guyer, Jane I.

1984    Naturalism in Models of African Production. Man 19:371–388.

1993    Wealth in People and Self-Realization in Equatorial Africa. Man 28(2):243–265.

Habe, Per, Frank Harary, and Bojka Milicic

1996    Tattooing, Gender and Social Stratification in Micro-Polynesia. Journal of the Royal Anthropological Institute 2(2):335–350.

Habermas, Jurgen

1989    The Structural Transformation of the Public Sphere. Boston: MIT Press.

Hacking, Ian

1995    Aloha, Aloha. London Review of Books, September 7, pp. 6–9.

Hadas, Edward

2007    Still with Us (Review: *The Bottom Billion* by P. Collier). Times Literary Supplement, August 24 and 31, p. 33.

Haddon, Alfred

1934    History of Anthropology. London: Watts.

Hage, Per

1977    The Atom of Kinship as a Directed Graph. Man 11:558–568.

1979 Symbolic Culinary Mediation: A Group Model. Man 14(1):81–92.

Halberstam, David

1964 The Making of a Quagmire. New York: Ballantine Books.

1969 The Best and the Brightest. New York: Ballantine Books.

1993 The Best and the Brightest (with a new introduction). New York: Ballantine Books.

Hale, Charles R.

2001 What Is Activist Research? Social Science Research Council 2(1–2):13–15. http://www.utexas.edu/cola/anthropology/_files/PDF/Hale.pdf (accessed October 5, 2017).

Hallowell, Irving

1954 Culture and Experience. Philadelphia: University of Pennsylvania Press.

Hallpike, C. R.

1973 Functionalist Interpretations of Primitive Warfare. Man 8(3):451–470.

Hamilton, Clive

2005 A Review of *The End of Poverty* by Jeffrey Sachs (Penguin). The Age 2(July). https://www.theage.com.au/entertainment/books/the-end-of-poverty-20050702-geofu2.html (accessed August 6, 2018).

Hamilton, Neil

1997 Peer Review: The Linchpin of Academic Freedom and Tenure. Academe (May–June):15–19.

Hanna, Judith Lynne

1979 Movements toward Understanding Humans through the Anthropological Study of Dance. Current Anthropology 20(2):313–339.

Hansch, Steven

n.d. Review: *The Road to Hell* by M. Maren. Hunger Notes. https://www.worldhunger.org/the-road-to-hell-the-ravaging-effects-of-foreign-aid-international-charity/ (accessed August 6, 2018).

Hanson, F. Allan

1982 Review: *Historical Metaphors and Mythical Realities* by M. Sahlins. Journal of the Polynesian Society 91(4):595–596.

Hantman, Jeffrey

1990 Between Powhatan and Quirank: Reconstructing Monacan Culture and History in the Context of Jamestown. American Anthropologist 92:676–690.

Harari, Yuval Noah

2015 Sapiens: A Brief History of Humankind. New York: Harper.

Harayda, Janice

1997 Charities in Feeding Frenzy: 2 Authors Say We Never Know Where Gifts

Go. The Plain Dealer, December 21. https://michaelmaren.com/1997/12/cleveland-plain-dealer/ (accessed August 6, 2018).

Harkin, Michael

1994    Contested Bodies: Affliction and Power in Heiltsuk Culture and History. American Ethnologist 21(3):586–605.

Haro, Lia

2017    Village at the End of Poverty: Dreams and Discontents of Millennial Development and Globalization. Unpublished Ms.

Harris, Adam

2017    University of California Will No Longer Pay for Regents' Dinners and Parties. Chronicle of Higher Education, May 30. http://www.chronicle.com/blogs/ticker/university-of-california-will-no-longer-pay-for-regents-dinners-and-parties/118702 (accessed August 6, 2018).

Harris, Gardiner

2010    Journal Retracts 1998 Paper Linking Autism to Vaccines. New York Times, February 2. http://www.nytimes.com/2010/02/03/health/research/03lancet.html (accessed October 5, 2017).

Harris, Marvin

1968    The Rise of Anthropological Theory. New York: Thomas Y. Crowell.

1974    Cows, Pigs, Wars, and Witches: The Riddles of Culture. New York: Random House.

1977    Cannibals and Kings: The Origins of Cultures. New York: Random House.

1993    Culture, People, Nature: An Introduction to General Anthropology, sixth edition. New York: HarperCollins.

1994    Cultural Materialism Is Alive and Well and Won't Go Away Until Something Better Comes Along. In Assessing Cultural Anthropology. R. Borofsky, ed. Pp.62–75. New York: McGraw-Hill.

1999    Theories of Culture in Postmodern Times. Walnut Creek, CA: AltaMira.

Harris, Marvin, and Orna Johnson

2007    Cultural Anthropology. Boston: Pearson / Allyn and Bacon.

Harris, Marvin, et al.

1968    The Rise of Anthropological Theory: A CA Book Review. Current Anthropology (9):519–533.

Hartwig, Lydia

2006    Funding Systems and Their Effects on Higher Education—Germany. Bavarian State Institute for Higher Education Research and Planning.

Hartzler, Omar Lee

1974    Review: *Pourquoi L'epouser? et autres essais*. American Anthropologist 76:375–376.

Harvey, Campbell, and Yan Liu

2014 Evaluating Trading Strategies. SSRN, August 3. https://poseidon01.ssrn
.com/delivery.php?ID=014117064098127092069099029067000
069057020066018053053081100103094126121075125002093100057
062011027030018070005014104013088007051035011087029122099107111119
073040048043085078091117001124078067087019027023081099120025084
0310311220760650250090661111&EXT=pdf (accessed August 6, 2018).

Haskell, Thomas

1977 The Emergence of Professional Social Science. Baltimore, MD: Johns Hopkins University Press.

1998 Objectivity Is Not Neutrality. Baltimore, MD: Johns Hopkins University
Press.

Hastings, Max

2018 Vietnam: An Epic Tragedy, 1945-1975. New York: Harper.

Hastrup, Kirsten, and Peter Elsass

1990 Anthropological Advocacy: A Contradiction in Term? Current Anthropology 31(3):301–311.

Hatch, Elvin

1973 Theories of Man and Culture. New York: Columbia University Press.

Haviland, William A.

1977 Dynastic Genealogies from Tikal, Guatemala: Implications for Descent
and Political Organization. American Antiquity 42(1):61–67.

1996 Cultural Anthropology, eighth edition. Fort Worth, TX: Harcourt Brace.

Hawkes, Kristen

1977 Co-operation in Binumarien: Evidence for Sahlins's Model. Man 12(3–
4):459–483.

Hawkins, Derek

2018 What Made Hawking's "A Brief History of Time" So Immensely Popular?
Washington Post, March 14. https://www.washingtonpost.com/news/
morning-mix/wp/2018/03/14/what-made-hawkings-a-brief-history-of
-time-so-immensely-popular/?utm_term=.f47da8b9106c (accessed August
6, 2018).

Hayden, Cori

2003 From Market to Market: Bioprospecting's Idioms of Inclusion. American
Ethnologist 30(1):359–371.

Hays, H. R.

1964 From Ape to Angel: An Informal History of Social Anthropology. New
York: Capricorn Books.

Hays, Terence
    1993    "The New Guinea Highlands": Region, Culture Area, or Fuzzy Set? Current Anthropology 34(2):141–164.

Hazan, Haim
    1984    Continuity and Transformation among the Aged: A Study in the Anthropology of Time. Current Anthropology 25(5):567–578.

Headland, Thomas
    1997    Revisionism in Ecological Anthropology. Current Anthropology 18(4):605–630.

Heald, Suzette
    1991    Tobacco, Time, and the Household Economy in Two Kenyan Societies: The Teso and the Kuria. Comparative Studies in Society and History 33(1):130–157.

Heath, Douglas
    1971    Review: *The Academic Revolution* by C. Jencks and D. Riesman. Political Science Quarterly 86(2):308–310.

Hebel, Sara
    2016    How to Make Public Engagement a Priority at Research Universities. Robert J. Jones. Chronicle of Higher Education, February 3. https://www.chronicle.com/article/Video-How-to-Make-Public/235150?cid=cp29 (accessed August 6, 2018).

Hefner, Robert
    1983a    The Problem of Preference: Economic and Ritual Change in Highlands Java. Man 18(4):669–689.
    1983b    Ritual and Cultural Reproduction in Non-Islamic Java. American Ethnologist 10(4):665–683.

Heider, Karl
    1972    Environment, Subsistence, and Society. Annual Review of Anthropology 1:207–226.
    2007    Seeing Anthropology: Cultural Anthropology Through Film. Boston: Pearson / Allyn and Bacon.

Helmreich, Stefan
    2001    After Culture: Reflections on the Apparition of Anthropology in Artificial Life, a Science of Simulation. Cultural Anthropology 16(4):612–627.
    2003    Trees and Seas of Information: Alien Kinship and the Biopolitics of Gene Transfer in Marine Biology and Biotechnology. American Ethnologist 30(3):340–358.

Hendricks, Janet Wall
    1988    Power and Knowledge: Discourse and Ideological Transformation among the Shuar. American Ethnologist 15(2):216–238.

Henson, Kevin

2002 Review: *Professional Work* by K. Leich and M. Fennell. Contemporary Sociology 31(5):552–553.

Herbert, Robert

1999 Goodbye to All That. New York Review of Books, November 4, p. 28.

Herszenhorn, David

2008 Estimates of Iraq War Cost Were Not Close to Ballpark. New York Times, March 19. https://www.nytimes.com/2008/03/19/washington/19cost.html (accessed August 6, 2018).

Hickman, Larry, and Thomas Alexander, eds.

1998 The Essential Dewey. Bloomington: Indiana University Press.

Hicks, David, and Margaret A. Gwynne

1994 Cultural Anthropology. New York: HarperCollins.

Hill, Jonathan D.

1984 Social Equality and Ritual Hierarchy: The Arawakan Wakuenai of Venezuela. American Ethnologist 11(3):528–544.

Hill, W. W.

1944 The Navaho Indians and the Ghost Dance of 1890. American Anthropologist 46:523–527.

Himmelfarb, Gertrude

1999 Who Wants to Be an Amateur. Times Literary Supplement, January 22, p. 10.

Hindo, Brian

2007 Mapping the Crowd. BusinessWeek, November 17, pp. IN 19–22.

Hines, Philip

1977 On Social Organization in the Middle Mississippian: States or Chiefdoms? Current Anthropology 18(2):337–338.

Hinton, Alex

2004 Why Did They Kill? Cambodia in the Shadow of Genocide. Berkeley: University of California Press.

Hobsbawm, Eric, and Terence Ranger, eds.

1983 The Invention of Tradition. New York: Cambridge University Press.

Hochschild, Arlie

2016 Strangers in Their Own Land: Anger and Mourning on the American Right. New York: New Press.

Hocking, William

1929 Review: *The Public and Its Problems* by J. Dewey. Journal of Philosophy 26(12):329–335.

Hoffman, Michael A.

1973    The History of Anthropology Revisited—A Byzantine Viewpoint. American Anthropologist 75:1347–1357.

Hohmann, James

2017    The Daily 202: 10 Important Questions Raised by Sally Yates's Testimony on the "Compromised" Michael Flynn. Washington Post, May 9. https://www.washingtonpost.com/news/powerpost/paloma/daily-202/2017/05/09/daily-202-10-important-questions-raised-by-sally-yates-s-testimony-on-the-compromised-michael-flynn/59110598e9b69b209cf2b7df/?utm_term=.0bdac68d2db8 (accessed August 6, 2018).

Hollan, Douglas

1988    Staying "Cool" in Toraja. Ethos 16:52–72.

Holloman, Regina E.

1974    Ritual Opening and Individual Transformation: Rites of Passage at Esalen. American Anthropologist 76:265–280.

Holloway, Marguerite

1997    The Paradoxical Legacy of Franz Boas—Father of American Anthropology. Natural History November—obtained from BNET.com (accessed May 20, 2008).

Holmes, Richard

2006(?)    The THES University Rankings: Are They Really World Class. Asian Journal of University Education 1(1):1–14.

Holy, Ladislav

1987    Introduction. Description, Generalization and Comparison: Two Paradigms. *In* Comparative Anthropology. L. Holy, ed. Pp. 1–21. Oxford: Blackwell.

Honigmann, John

1959    Psychocultural Studies. *In* Biennial Review of Anthropology. B. Siegal, ed. Pp. 67–106. Stanford, CA: Stanford University Press.

Hook, Sydney

1939    John Dewey: An Intellectual Portrait. New York: John Day.

Hooper, Anthony

1983    Why Tikopia Has Four Clans. Man 18(4):789–791.

1996    Review: *How "Natives" Think* by M. Sahlins. Contemporary Pacific (Fall):460–462.

Horne, Alistair

2009    Kissinger: 1973. New York: Simon & Schuster.

Howard, Alan

1982      Review: *Historical Metaphors and Mythical Realities*. American Anthropologist 84:413–414.

Howard, Jennifer

2008a     New Ratings of Humanities Journals Do More Than Rank—They Rankle. Chronicle of Higher Education, October 10. https://www.chronicle.com/article/New-Ratings-of-Humanities/29072 (accessed August 6, 2018).

2008b     News Analysis: US Librarians, Authors, and Publishers Weigh the Chilling Effects of "Libel Tourism." Chronicle of Higher Education, June 25. https://www.chronicle.com/article/News-Analysis-US/114661 (accessed August 6, 2018).

2008c     Scholarly Association Settles "Libel Tourism." Chronicle of Higher Education, June 18. https://www.chronicle.com/article/Scholarly-Association-Settles/907 (accessed August 6, 2018).

Howe, Alyssa Cymene

2001      Queer Pilgrimage: The San Francisco Homeland and Identity Tourism. Cultural Anthropology 16(1):35–61.

Howe, Kerry

1995      The Death of Cook: Exercises in Explanation. Eighteenth-Century Life 18(November):198–211.

Howsam, Leslie

2009      Past into Print. Toronto: University of Toronto Press.

Hsu, Francis L. K.

1973      Prejudice and Its Intellectual Effect in American Anthropology: An Ethnographic Report. American Anthropologist 75:1–19.

Hublin, Jean-Jacques, et al.

2017      New Fossils from Jebel Irhoud, Morocco and the Pan-African Origin of Homo Sapiens. Nature 546:289–292. https://publicanthropology.altmetric.com/details/20883775/news (accessed August 6, 2018).

Hughes, David

2016      Commentary: Academic Analytics: Buyer Beware. Chronicle of Higher Education, February 29. https://www.chronicle.com/article/Commentary-Academic/235435 (accessed August 6, 2018).

Hurlbert, Beverly

1976      Status and Exchange in the Profession of Anthropology. American Anthropologist 78:272–284.

Hyatt, Marshall

1990      Franz Boas Social Activist: The Dynamics of Ethnicity. Westport, CT: Greenwood Press.

Ingold, Tim
    1983a    The Architect and the Bee: Reflections on the Work of Animals and Men. Man 18:1–20.
    1983b    The Significance of Storage in Hunting Societies. Man 18(3):553–571.

Insole, Christopher
    2008    Informed Tolerance. Times Literary Supplement, February 1, pp. 3–4.

Ioannidis, John
    2005a    Contradicted and Initially Stronger Effects in Highly Cited Clinical Research. JAMA 294(2):218–228. https://jamanetwork.com/journals/jama/fullarticle/201218 (accessed October 5, 2017).
    2005b    Why Most Published Research Findings Are False. PLOS—Medicine 2(8):e124. https://www.ncbi.nlm.nih.gov/pmc/articles/PMC1182327/ (accessed October 5, 2017).

Irons, William
    1977    Comment on Chapple's Review of Wilson. American Anthropologist 79(4):896–898.

Iyer, Pico
    2000    The Global Soul. New York: Knopf.

Jackson, Bruce
    1978    The Machineries of Control (Review: *Discipline and Punish* by M. Foucault). The Nation, March 4, pp. 250–251.

Jacquemet, Marco
    1992    Namechasers. American Ethnologist 19(4):733–748.

James, Allison, Jenny Hockey, and Andrew Dawson, eds.
    1997    After Writing Culture: Epistemology and Praxis in Contemporary Anthropology. New York: Routledge.

Jameson, Fredric
    1999    The Cultural Turn: Selected Writings on the Postmodern, 1983–1998. New York: Verso.

Jamieson, Neil
    1993    Understanding Vietnam. Berkeley: University of California Press.

Jamieson, Neil, Manh Nguyen, and Terry Rambo
    1992    The Challenges of Vietnam's Reconstruction. Fairfax, VA: Indochina Institute of George Mason University.

Janes, Robert R.
    1977    More on Culture Contact in the Mackenzie Basin. Current Anthropology 18(3):554–558.

Jarausch, Konrad
    1990    The Unfree Professions. New York: Oxford University Press.

Jarvie, J. C.

  1983    The Problem of the Ethnographic Real. Current Anthropology 24(3):313–325.

Jean-Klein, Iris

  2001    Nationalism and Resistance: The Two Faces of Everyday Activism in Palestine during the Intifada. Cultural Anthropology 16(1):83–126.

  2003    Into Committees, out of the House? Familiar Forms in the Organization of Palestinian Committee Activism During the First Intifada. American Ethnologist 30(4):556–577.

Jencks, Christopher, and David Riesman

  1968    The Academic Revolution. Garden City, NY: Doubleday.

Jenkins, Carol L.

  1983    Ritual and Resource flow: The Garifuna *Dugu*. American Ethnologist 10(3):429–442.

Jenkins, Richard

  1997    Rethinking Ethnicity. Thousand Oaks, CA: Sage.

Jensen, Michael

  2007    The New Metrics of Scholarly Authority. Chronicle of Higher Education, June 15, pp. B6–B8.

Johnson, George

  2002    At Lawrence Berkeley, Physicists Say a Colleague Took Them for a Ride. New York Times, October 15. http://www.nytimes.com/2002/10/15/science/at-lawrence-berkeley-physicists-say-a-colleague-took-them-for-a-ride.html (accessed October 5, 2017).

Jolly, Margaret

  1992    Review: *The Gender in the Gift*. Pacific Studies 15(1):137–149.

Jones, Michael, and Deserai Crow

  2017    How Can We Use the "Science of Stories" to Produce Persuasive Scientific Stories? Palgrave Communications 3(1):1–9. https://ideas.repec.org/a/pal/palcom/v3y2017i1d10.1057_s41599-017-0047-7.html (accessed August 6, 2018).

Jones, Steve

  2006    Antonio Gramsci. New York: Routledge.

Jordanova, Ludmilla

  2000    History in Practice. New York: Arnold.

Josselin de Jong, P. E.

  1996    Structuralism. *In* The Social Science Encyclopedia. A. Kuper and J. Kuper, eds. Pp. 852–854. New York: Routledge.

Judis, John
2000      The Spiritual Wobbly. New York Times Book Review, July 9, p. 9.

Jump, Paul
2015a     Grant Income Targets Set at One in Six Universities, THE Poll Suggests.
          Times Literary Supplement, June 12. https://www.timeshighereducation.
          com/news/grant-income-targets-set-one-six-universities-poll-suggests
          (accessed August 6, 2018).
2015b     Metrics: How to Handle Them Responsibly. Times Literary Supplement,
          July 9. https://www.timeshighereducation.com/features/metrics-how-to
          -handle-them-responsibly (accessed August 6, 2018).

June, Audrey Williams
2008a     Colleges Should Change Policies to Encourage Scholarship Devoted to the
          Public Good, Report Says. Chronicle of Higher Education, June 26. https://
          www.chronicle.com/article/Colleges-Should-Change/937 (accessed August
          6, 2018).
2008b     Nearly Half of Undergraduate Courses Are Taught by Non-Tenure-Track
          Instructors. Chronicle of Higher Education, December 3. https://www
          .chronicle.com/article/Non-Tenure-Track-Instructors/1380 (accessed Au-
          gust 6, 2018).
2009      Who's Teaching at American Colleges? Increasingly, Instructors off the
          Tenure Track. Chronicle of Higher Education, May 12. https://www.chron
          icle.com/article/Whos-Teaching-at-American/117210 (accessed August 6,
          2018).
2018a     Can Faculty Workload Be Captured in a Database? Chronicle of Higher
          Education, July 20. https://www.chronicle.com/article/Can-Faculty-Work
          load-Be/243890 (accessed August 6, 2018).
2018b     Do Universities Value Public Engagement? Not Much, Their Policies Sug-
          gest Chronicle of Higher Education. October 8. https://www.chronicle.
          com/article/Do-Universities-Value-Public/244748 (accessed Dec. 31, 2018).

Kaplan, David
1974      The Anthropology of Authenticity: Everyman His Own Anthropologist.
          American Anthropologist 76:824–839.

Kaplan, Martha
1990      Meaning, Agency and Colonial History: Navosavakadua and the *Tuka*
          Movement in Fiji. American Ethnologist 17:3–22.

Kaplan, M. R.
1974      A Note on Nutini's "The Ideological Bases of Lévi-Strauss's Structuralism."
          American Anthropologist 76:62–65.

Kardiner, Abram
  1939    The Individual and His Society. New York: Columbia University Press.
  1945    Psychological Frontiers of Society. New York: Columbia University Press.

Karlan, Dean, and Jacob Appel
  2012    More Than Good Intentions: Improving the Ways the World's Poor Borrow, Save, Farm, Learn, and Stay Healthy. New York: Plume.

Karnow, Stanley
  1983    Vietnam: A History. New York: Penguin Press.

Karp, Ivan
  1974    Review: *Bangwa Kinship and Marriage* by R. Brain. American Anthropologist 76:137–138.

Katz, Stanley
  2002    The Path Breaking, Fractionalized Uncertain World of Knowledge. Chronicle of Higher Education, September 20, pp. B7–B9.

Keane, Webb
  1991    Delegated Voice: Ritual Speech, Risk, and the Making of Marriage Alliances in Anakalang. American Ethnologist 18(2):311–330.

Keen, David
  1999    The Uses of Famine (Review: *Famine Crimes* by A. de Waal). Times Literary Supplement, March 26, pp. 28–29.

Keesing, Felix
  1958    Cultural Anthropology: The Science of Custom. New York: Rinehart & Company.

Keesing, Roger
  1974    Theories of Culture. Annual Review of Anthropology 3:73–97.
  1981    Cultural Anthropology: A Contemporary Perspective, second edition. Fort Worth, TX: Holt, Rinehart and Winston.
  1985    Review: *Local Knowledge* by C. Geertz. American Ethnologist 12(3):554–555.
  1987    Anthropology as Interpretive Quest. Current Anthropology 28(2):161–176.
  1992    Review: *The Gender in the Gift*. Pacific Studies 15(1):129–137.

Keesing, Roger, and Felix Keesing
  1959    New Perspectives on Cultural Anthropology. New York: Holt, Rinehart and Winston.

Keller, George
  2001    Governance: The Remarkable Ambiguity. *In* In Defense of American Higher Education. P. G. Altbach, P. J. Gumport, and D. B. Johnstone, eds. Pp. 304–322. Baltimore, MD: Johns Hopkins University Press.

Keller, Ward
    1983    Shame and Stage Fright in Java. Ethos 11(3)152–165.

Kelly, John
    1990    History, Structure, and Ritual. Annual Review of Anthropology 19:119–150.
    1992    Fiji Indians and "Commoditization of Labor." American Ethnologist 19:97–120.

Kemper, Robert, and John Phinney
    1977    The History of Anthropology: A Research Bibliography. New York: Garland.

Kemper, Theodore
    2000    Toward Sociology as a Science, Maybe. Chronicle of Higher Education, August 11, p. B7–B8.

Kennedy, Gerard
    1978    Still More on Symbolic Interpretation. Current Anthropology 19(1):187–188.

Kerns, Virginia
    2003    Scenes from the High Desert: Julian Steward's Life and Theory. Urbana: University of Illinois Press.

Kerr, Clark
    1994a    Higher Education Cannot Escape History. Albany: State University of New York Press.
    1994b    Troubled Times for American Higher Education: The 1990s and Beyond. Albany: State University of New York Press.
    2001    The Uses of the University, fifth edition. Cambridge, MA: Harvard University Press.

Kidder, Tracy
    2004    Mountains Beyond Mountains: The Quest of Dr. Paul Farmer, A Man Who Would Cure the World. New York: Random House.

Kiefer, Christie
    1977    Psychological Anthropology. Annual Review of Anthropology 6:103–119.

Kiernan, Vincent
    2004    Company to Track Citations of Online Scholarship. Chronicle of Higher Education, March 19, p. A31.

Kim, Seung-Og
    1994    Burials, Pigs, and Political Prestige in Neolithic China. Current Anthropology 35(2):119–141.

King, Barbara
    2013    Why Does Jared Diamond Make Anthropologists So Mad? NPR, Cosmos and Culture. January 13. http://www.npr.org/sections/13.7/2013/01/14/

169374400/why-does-jared-diamond-make-anthropologists-so-mad (accessed October 5, 2017).

King, Irving
    1917    Review: *Democracy and Education* by J. Dewey. American Journal of Sociology 22(5):674–676.

King's College and Digital Science
    2015    The Nature, Scale and Beneficiaries of Research Impact. King's College London and Digital Science. https://www.kcl.ac.uk/sspp/policy-institute/publications/Analysis-of-REF-impact.pdf (accessed August 6, 2018).

Kingston, Sean
    2003    Form, Attention and a Southern New Ireland Life Cycle. Journal of the Royal Anthropological Institute 9:681–708.

Kipnis, Andrew
    2003    The Anthropology of Power and Maoism. American Anthropologist 105(2):278–288.

Kipp, Rita Smith
    1995    Conversion by Affiliation: The History of the Karo Batak Protestant Church. American Ethnologist 22(4):868–882.

Kirch, Patrick V., and Roger C. Green
    1987    History, Phylogeny, and Evolution in Polynesia. Current Anthropology 28(4):431–456.

Kirn, Walter
    2001    Remember When Books Mattered. New York Times Book Review, February 4, pp. 8–9.

Kiste, Robert C., and Mac Marshall
    1999    American Anthropology in Micronesia: An Assessment. Honolulu: University of Hawaii Press.

Klein, Joe
    2007    Nam and Pop (Review: *The Father of All Things* by T. Bissell). New York Times Book Review, March 4, p. 11.

Kloppenberg, James T.
    1992    Review: *John Dewey and American Democracy* by R. Westbrook. American Historical Review 97(3):919–920.

Knapp, A. Bernard
    1988    Ideology, Archaeology and Polity. Man 23:133–163.

Knauft, Bruce
    1979    On Percussion and Metaphor. Current Anthropology 20(1):189–191.
    1987    Reconsidering Violence in Simple Human Societies: Homicide among the Gebusi of New Guinea. Current Anthropology 28(4):457–500.

1996 Genealogies for the Present in Cultural Anthropology. New York: Routledge.

Kockelman, Paul
2003 The Meanings of Interjections in Q'eqchi' Maya. Current Anthropology 44(4):467–490.

Kolenda, Pauline
1984 Woman as Tribute, Woman as Flower: Images of "Woman" in Weddings in North and South India. American Ethnologist 11(1):98–117.

Kolowich, Steve
2016 The Water Next Time: Professor Who Helped Expose Crisis in Flint Says Public Science Is Broken. Chronicle of Higher Education, October.

Konrad, Monica
1998 Ova Donations and Symbols of Substance: Some Variations on the Theme of Sex, Gender and the Partible Body. Journal of the Royal Anthropological Institute 4(4):643–667.

Kotkin, Stephen
2007 In Africa, One Step Forward and Two Back. New York Times, July 8. https://www.nytimes.com/2007/07/08/business/yourmoney/08offtheshelf.html (accessed August 6, 2018).

Kottak, Conrad Phillip
1997 Anthropology: The Exploration of Human Diversity, seventh edition. New York: McGraw-Hill.
1999 The New Ecological Anthropology. American Anthropologist 101(1):23–35.
2005 Mirror for Humanity, fourth edition. New York: McGraw-Hill.

Krause, Elliott A.
1997 Death of the Guilds: Professions, States, and the Advance of Capitalism, 1930 to the Present. New Haven, CT: Yale University Press.

Krech, Shepard
1991 The State of Ethnohistory. Annual Review of Anthropology 20:345–375.

Kristof, Nicholas
2006 Aid: Can It Work (Review: *The White Man's Burden* by W. Easterly). New York Review of Books, October 5, pp. 41–44.
2007a Africa's World War. New York Times, June 14. https://www.nytimes.com/2007/06/14/opinion/14kristof.html (accessed August 6, 2018).
2007b Bono, Foreign Aid and Skeptics. New York Times, August 9. https://www.nytimes.com/2007/08/09/opinion/09kristof.html (accessed August 6, 2018).

Kroeber, Alfred

1935    History and Science in Anthropology. American Anthropologist 37(4):539–569.

1939    Cultural and Natural Areas of Native North America. University of California Publications in American Archaeology and Ethnology 38. Berkeley: University of California Press.

1943    Franz Boas: The Man. American Anthropologist 45(3, part 2):5–26.

1948    Anthropology. New York: Harcourt, Brace & World.

1944    Configurations of Cultural Growth. Berkeley: University of California
[1969]  Press.

Kroeber, Alfred, and Harold Driver

1932    Quantitative Expression of Cultural Relationships. University of California Publications in American Archaeology and Ethnology 29. Berkeley: University of California Press.

Kubota, Gary

2018    Ben Finney, a founder of the Polynesian Voyaging Society, dies at 83. Star Advertiser, December 31. https://www.staradvertiser.com/2017/05/24/breaking-news/ben-finney-a-founder-of-the-polynesian-voyaging-society-dies-at-83/ (accessed December 31, 2018).

Kuhn, Thomas S.

1970    The Structure of Scientific Revolutions, second edition. Chicago: University of Chicago Press.

Kuklick, Henrika

1976    Review: The Organization of Social Science in the United States. American Quarterly 28(1):124–141.

Kulick, Don

1993    Speaking as a Woman: Structure and Gender in Domestic Arguments in a New Guinea Village. Cultural Anthropology 8(4):510–541.

Kuper, Adam

1986    An Interview with Edmund Leach. Current Anthropology 27(4):375–382.

1994    Anthropological Futures. In Assessing Cultural Anthropology. R. Borofsky, ed. Pp. 113–118. New York: McGraw-Hill.

2007    Anthropology. Times Literary Supplement, March 30, p. 23.

2009    Great Grants. Times Literary Supplement, September 18. https://www.the-tls.co.uk/articles/private/great-grants/ (accessed August 6, 2018).

Kuper, Adam, and Jessica Kuper, eds.

1985    The Social Science Encyclopedia. Boston: Routlege and Kegan Paul.

Kurtz, Donald

1987    The Economics of Urbanization and State Formation at Teotihuacán. Current Anthropology 28(3):329–353.

Kurtz, Donald, and Mary Christopher Nunley
1993    Ideology and Work at Teotihuacan: A Hermeneutic Interpretation. Man 28:761–778.

Laboratory of Comparative Human Cognition
1978    Cognition as a Residual Category in Anthropology. Annual Review of Anthropology (7):51–69.
1979    What's Cultural About Cross-Cultural Cognitive Psychology. Annual Review of Psychology (30):145–172.

Lall, Rashmee Roshan
2013    Haiti to Plant Millions of Trees to Boost Forests and Help Tackle Poverty: Government-Backed Campaign Aims to Double Caribbean Country's Forest Cover by 2016. Guardian, March 28. https://www.theguardian.com/world/2013/mar/28/haiti-plant-millions-trees-deforestation (accessed October 5, 2017).

Lambek, Michael
1988    Spirit Possession/Spirit Succession. American Ethnologist 15(4):710–731.

Lamont, Michèle
2009    How Professors Think: Inside the Curious World of Academic Judgment. Cambridge, MA: Harvard University Press.

Lamphere, Louise, Helena Rogone, and Patricia Zavella
1997    Situated Lives. New York: Routledge.

Lampland, Martha
1991    Pigs, Party Secretaries, and Private Lives in Hungary. American Ethnologist 18(2):459–479.

Lancaster, C. S.
1976    Women, Horticulture, and Society in Sub-Saharan Africa. American Anthropologist 78(3):539–564.

Lane, Robert B.
1964    Review: *Primitive Social Organization*. American Anthropologist 66:151–153.

Lange, Charles
1965    Cultural Change. *In* Biennial Review of Anthropology. B. Siegal, ed. Pp. 262–297. Stanford, CA: Stanford University Press.

Langness, L. L.
1987    The Study of Culture, revised edition. Novato, CA: Chandler & Sharp.

Lapsley, Hilary
1999    Margaret Mead and Ruth Benedict. Amherst: University of Massachusetts Press.

Lariviere, Vincent, and Yves Gingras

2009     The Impact Factor's Matthew Effect: A Natural Experiment in Bibliomet-rics. Journal of the American Society for Information Science and Tech-nology. https://arxiv.org/abs/0908.3177 (accessed August 6, 2018).

Larson, Margali

1977     The Rise of Professionalism: A Sociological Analysis. Berkeley: University of California Press.

Lassiter, Luke Eric

2002     An Invitation to Anthropology. Walnut Creek, CA: AltaMira Press.

Lasswell, Harold

1940     Review: *Knowledge for What?* by R. Lynd. Public Opinion Quarterly 4(4):725–726.

Laughlin, Bridget

1975     Marxist Approaches in Anthropology. Annual Review of Anthropology (4):341–370.

Lawless, Andrew

n.d.     Dispelling the Myth: The Realities of Organ Trafficking. Professor Nancy Scheper-Hughes in interview. Three Monkeys Online. https://www.three monkeysonline.com/dispelling-the-myth-the-realities-of-organ-trafficking -professor-nancy-scheper-hughes-in-interview/ (accessed August 6, 2018).

Layton, Robert

1997     An Introduction to Theory in Anthropology. Cambridge, UK: Cambridge University Press.

Leach, Edmund

1965     Review: Le Cru et le Cuit. American Anthropologist 67:776–780.
1970     Claude Lévi-Strauss. New York: Viking.
1989     Review: *Works and Lives* by C. Geertz. American Ethnologist 16(1):137–141.

Leach, Helen

1999     Intensification in the Pacific. Current Anthropology 40(3):311–339.

Leaf, Murray

1979     Mind, Man, and Science: A History of Anthropology. New York: Columbia University Press.

Leavitt, John

1996     Meaning and Feeling in the Anthropology of Emotions. American Ethnol-ogist 23(3):514–539.

Lebra, Takie Sugiyama

1978     Japanese Women and Marital Strain. Ethos 6(1):22–41.

Lederman, Doug

2006     Will "Voluntary" Accountability Work? Inside Higher Ed, April 10. https://

www.goacta.org/news/will_voluntary_accountability_work (accessed August 6, 2018).

Lee, Richard
    1992    Art, Science, or Politics? The Crisis in Hunter-Gatherer Studies. American Anthropologist 94(1):31–54.

Lee, Stephanie
    2018    Sliced and Diced: The Inside Story of How an Ivy League Food Scientist Turned Shoddy Data into Viral Studies. BuzzFeed News, February 25. https://www.buzzfeed.com/stephaniemlee/brian-wansink-cornell-p-hacking?utm_term=.aoJ5ZpLLa#.wblAkrXX8 (accessed August 6, 2018).

Leerssen, Joep
    2007    National Thought in Europe. Amsterdam: Amsterdam University Press.

Lemann, Nicholas
    1997    The Bell Curve Flattened: Subsequent Research Has Seriously Undercut the Claims of the Controversial Best Seller. http://www.slate.com/articles/briefing/articles/1997/01/the_bell_curve_flattened.html (accessed October 5, 2017).

Le Vine, Robert
    1963    Culture and Personality. In Biennial Review of Anthropology. B. Siegal, ed. Pp. 107–145. Stanford, CA: Stanford University Press.
    1997    Culture and Personality. In The Dictionary of Anthropology. T. Barfield, ed. Pp. 102–103. Malden, MA: Blackwell.

Lévi-Strauss, Claude
    1963    Structural Anthropology. New York: Basic Books.
    1966    The Savage Mind. Chicago: University of Chicago Press.
    1967    The Story of Asdiwal. In The Structural Study of Myth and Totemism. E. Leach, ed. London: Tavistock.
    1969    The Raw and the Cooked. New York: Harper and Row.
    1981    The Naked Man. London: Jonathan Cape.
    1991    Conversations with Claude Lévi-Strauss. Chicago: University of Chicago Press.
    1994    Anthropology, Race, and Politics: A Conversation with Didier Eribon. In Assessing Cultural Anthropology. R. Borofsky, ed. Pp. 420–429. New York: McGraw-Hill.

Levy, Robert
    1992    Review: *The Apotheosis of Captain Cook* by G. Obeyesekere. New York Times, September 20. https://www.nytimes.com/1992/09/20/books/university-presses-did-captain-cook-have-it-coming.html (accessed August 6, 2018).

Lewenstein, B. V., and W. Baur

1991      A Cold Fusion Chronology. Journal of Radioanalytical and Nuclear Chemistry 152(1):273–297.

Lewis, Herbert

1998      The Misrepresentation of Anthropology and Its Consequences. American Anthropologist 100:716–731.

2001a     Boas, Darwin, Science, and Anthropology. Current Anthropology 42(3):381–406.

2001b     The Passion of Franz Boas. American Anthropologist 103(2):447–467.

Lewis, Oscar

1951      Life in a Mexican Village: Tepoztlán Restudied. Urbana: University of Illinois Press.

1956      Comparisons in Cultural Anthropology. *In* Current Anthropology: A Supplement to Anthropology Today. William Thomas, ed. Pp. 259–292. Chicago: University of Chicago Press.

1960      Tepoztlán: Village in Mexico. Fort Worth, TX: Harcourt Brace Jovanovich College Publisher.

Lewis-Kraus, Gideon

2016      The Trials of Alice Goffman. New York Times Magazine, January 17. https://www.nytimes.com/2016/01/17/magazine/the-trials-of-alice-goffman .html (accessed August 6, 2018).

Leyner, Mark

1997      Geraldo, Eat Your Avant-Pop Heart Out. New York Times, December 21. http://www.driftline.org/cgi-bin/archive/archive_msg.cgi?file=spoon -archives/baudrillard.archive/baudrillard_1998/baudrillard.9801&msgnum =9&start=454&end=724 (accessed August 6, 2018).

Li, Tania Murray

1998      Working Separately but Eating Together: Personhood, Property, and Power in Conjugal Relations. American Ethnologist 25(4):675–694.

Lightfoot, Kent G., and Gary M. Feinman

1982      Social Differentiation and Leadership Development in Early Pit House Villages in the Mogollon Region of the American Southwest. American Antiquity 47(1):64–86.

Lindesmith, Alfred, and Anselm Strauss

1950      A Critique of Culture-Personality Writings. American Sociological Review 15:587–600.

Lindholm, Charles

1997      Geertz, Clifford. *In* The Dictionary of Anthropology. T. Barfield, ed. Pp. 214–216. Malden, MA: Blackwell.

Lindsey, Lawrence
    2008    What the Iraq War Will Cost the US. CNN Money.com, January 11. https://money.cnn.com/2008/01/10/news/economy/costofwar.fortune/?postversion=2008011103 (accessed August 6, 2018).

Lingua Franca
    1995    Inside Publishing: The God That Sailed. Lingua Franca (March–April):15–16.

Linnekin, Jocelyn
    1991    Cultural Invention and the Dilemma of Authenticity. American Anthropologist 93(2):446–449.

Linton, Ralph
    1940    Acculturation in Seven American Indian Tribes. New York: Appleton.
    1945    The Scope and Aims of Anthropology. *In* The Science of Man in the World Crisis. R. Linton, ed. Pp. 3–18. New York: Columbia University Press.

Lippmann, Walter
    1922    Public Opinion. New York: Free Press Paperbacks.

LiPuma, Edward
    1983    On the Preference of Marriage Rules: A Melanesian Example. Man 18(4):766–785.

Lizot, Jacques
    1985    Tales of the Yanomami: Daily Life in the Venezuelan Forest. New York: Cambridge University Press.

Lock, Margaret
    2001    Twice Dead: Organ Transplants and the Reinvention of Death. Berkeley: University of California Press, 2001.

Lomnitz, Claudio
    1996    Review: Articulating Hidden Histories. American Ethnologist 23(1):147–148.

Lomnitz-Adler, Claudio
    1991    Concepts for the Study of Regional Culture. American Ethnologist 18(2):195–214.

Lord, Alfred
    1960    The Singer of Tales. Cambridge, MA: Harvard University Press.

Low, Setha
    1988    The Medicalization of Healing Cults in Latin America. American Ethnologist 15(1):136–154.

Lowie, Robert
    1937    The History of Ethnological Theory. New York: Holt, Rinehart and Winston.

1944      Franz Boas. Journal of American Folklore 57(223):59–64.

1947      Biographical Memoir of Franz Boas, 1958–1942. Vol. 24, Ninth Memoir. Washington, DC: National Academy of Sciences.

Lozazda, Carlos

2016      A Berkeley Sociologist Made Some Tea Party Friends—And Wrote a Condescending Book About Them. Washington Post, September 1. https://www.washingtonpost.com/news/book-party/wp/2016/09/01/a-berkeley-sociologist-made-some-tea-party-friends-and-wrote-a-condescending-book-about-them/?utm_term=.c2b2a39e201a (accessed October 5, 2017).

Lucas, Colin

1975      Power and the Panopticon (Review: *Discipline and Punish*). Times Literary Supplement, September 26, p. 1090.

Luhrman, T. M.

1984      Popul Vuh and Lacan. Ethos 12(4):335–362.

Lundberg, George

1939      Review: *Knowledge for What* by R. Lynd. American Journal of Sociology 45(2):270–274.

Lutzker, Adam, and Judy Rosenthal

2001      The Unheimlich Man-Oeuvre. American Ethnologist 28(4):909–923.

Lynch, Barbara

1982      The Vicos Experiment: A.I.D. Evaluation Special Study No. 7. Bureau for Latin America and the Caribbean US Agency for International Development, especially pp. ii–iv, 86ff.

Lynd, Robert

1939      Knowledge for What? The Place of Social Science in American Culture. Princeton, NJ: Princeton University Press.

Lyons, Thomas

2001      Ambiguous Narratives. Cultural Anthropology 16(2):183–201.

MacClancy, Jeremy

1990      Review: *The Gender in the Gift*. Man 25(3):559–560.

Mackey, Rob

2007      Wikipedia to Check I.D.'s (The Lede). New York Times, March 9. https://thelede.blogs.nytimes.com/2007/03/09/wikipedia-to-check-ids/ (accessed August 6, 2018).

Macleod, Malcolm R., et al.

2014      Biomedical Research: Increasing Value, Reducing Waste. Lancet 383(9912):101–104.

Maddox, Richard

1995    Revolutionary Anticlericalism and Hegemonic Processes in an Andalusian Town, August 1936. American Ethnologist 22(1):125–143.

Madrick, Jeff

2014    Seven Bad Ideas: How Mainstream Economists Have Damaged America and the World. New York: Knopf.

Mageo, Jeannette Marie

1996    Spirit Girls and Marines: Possession and Ethnopsychiatry as Historical Discourse in Samoa. American Ethnologist 23(1):61–82.

Magner, Denise

2000    Seeking a Radical Change in the Role of Publishing. Chronicle of Higher Education, June 16:A16–A17.

Malarney, Shaun Kingsley

1996    The Limits of "State Functionalism" and the Reconstruction of Funerary Ritual in Contemporary Northern Vietnam. American Ethnologist 23(3):540–560.

Malinowski, Bronislaw

1929    The Sexual Life of Savages in North-Western Melanesia: An Ethnographic Account of Courtship, Marriage, and Family Life Among the Natives of the Trobriand Islands, British New Guinea. New York: Halcyon House.

1935    Coral Gardens and Their Magic: A Study of the Methods of Tilling the Soil and of Agricultural Rites in the Trobriand Islands. New York: American Book Company.

1922    Argonauts of the Western Pacific. New York: Dutton & Company.
[1961]

Mangan, Katherine

2007    Business-School Accreditor Proposes Requiring Evidence of Influence of Faculty Research. Chronicle of Higher Education, August 6. https://www.chronicle.com/article/Business-School-Accreditor/122870 (accessed August 6, 2018).

2009    Law Schools Disdain Rankings but Dare Not Ignore Them, Authors Say. Chronicle of Higher Education, February 3. https://www.chronicle.com/article/Law-Schools-Disdain-Rankings/117331?cid=rclink (accessed August 6, 2018).

Mann, Michael

1993    Review: Unthinking Social Science by I. Wallerstein. British Journal of Sociology 44(2):362–363.

Maranda, Pierre

1979    Lévi-Strauss, Claude. In The International Encyclopedia of the Social Sciences, vol. 18. D. Sills, ed. Pp. 442–446. New York: Macmillan.

Marcus, George

1978    Status Rivalry in a Polynesian Steady-State Society. Ethos 6(4):242–269.

1982    Review: *Historical Metaphors and Mythical Realities* by M. Sahlins. Journal of the Polynesian Society 91(4):596–605.

1994    After the Critique of Ethnography: Faith, Hope, and Charity, but the Greatest of These Is Charity. *In* Assessing Cultural Anthropology. R. Borofsky, ed. Pp. 40–54. New York: McGraw-Hill.

1995    Review: *How "Natives" Think* by G. Marcus. Unpublished Ms.

1998    Ethnography Through Thick and Thin. Princeton, NJ: Princeton University Press.

Marcus, George, and Dick Cushman

1982    Ethnographies as Texts. Annual Review of Anthropology (11):25–69.

Marcus, George, and Michael M. J. Fischer

1986    Anthropology as Cultural Critique: An Experimental Moment in the Human Sciences. Chicago: University of Chicago Press.

Maren, Michael

1997    The Road to Hell: The Ravaging Effects of Foreign Aid International Charity. New York: Free Press.

Mark Ware Consulting

2008    Peer Review in Scholarly Journals: Perspective of the Scholarly Community—An International Study. Bristol, UK: Mark Ware Consulting.

Marr, David

1994    Review: *Understanding Vietnam* by N. Jamieson. Journal of Asian Studies 53(3):1005–1007.

Marrus, Michael

1998    The Enigma of the Century. New York Times Book Review, July 19, p. 8.

Marshall, Mac

1989    Rashomon in Reverse: Ethnographic Agreement in Truk. American Anthropologist 25:95–106.

Marshall, Wolfang

1999    Obituary: Eric R. Wolf. Anthropos 94:539–541.

Martin, Kay M.

1969    South American Foragers: A Case Study in Cultural Devolution. American Anthropologist 71:243–260.

Maschio, Thomas

1998    The Narrative and Counter-Narrative of the Gift: Emotional Dimensions of Ceremonial Exchange in Southwestern New Britain. Journal of the Royal Anthropological Institute 4(1):83–100.

Masco, Joseph
1995    "It Is a Strict Law That Bids Us Dance." Comparative Studies in Society and History 37(1):41–75.

Mason, Leonard
1959    Suprafamilial Authority and Economic Process in Micronesian Atolls. Humanites de l'Institut de Science Economique Appliquee 5(1):87–118.

Mass, Peter
2004    Professor Nagl's War. New York Times, January 11. https://www.nytimes.com/2004/01/11/magazine/professor-nagl-s-war.html (accessed August 6, 2018).

Massing, Michael
2007    Iraq: The Hidden Human Costs. New York Review of Books, December 20, pp. 82–86.

Massy, William, and Robert Zemsky
1994    Faculty Discretionary Time: Departments and the "Academic Ratchet." Journal of Higher Education 65(1):1–22.

Maurer, Bill
2003    Comment: Got Language? Law, Property, and the Anthropological Imagination. American Anthropologist 105(4):775–781.

Mauss, Marcel
1954    The Gift: Forms and Functions of Exchange in Archaic Societies London: Cohen and West (Essai sur le don. *In* Sociologie et anthropologie). Paris: PUF, 1925.

McCook, Alison
2018a   Duke's Mishandling of Misconduct Prompts New US Government Grant Oversight. Science, March 23. http://www.sciencemag.org/news/2018/03/duke-s-mishandling-misconduct-prompts-new-us-government-grant-oversight (accessed August 6, 2018).
2018b   Why the Ohio State University Decided to Go Public About Misconduct. Science, April 5. http://www.sciencemag.org/news/2018/04/why-ohio-state-university-decided-go-public-about-misconduct (accessed August 6, 2018).

McFeely, Eliza
2001    Zuni and the American Experience. New York: Hill and Wang.

McGee, R. Jon, and Richard L. Warms
2000    Anthropological Theory: An Introductory History. Mountain View, CA: Mayfield.

McHenry, Robert

2002    All Hail Oprah's Book Club. Chronicle of Higher Education, May 10, p. B17.

McIlwraith, Thomas

2017    Arthus Nole (1940–2015): Tahltan Elder, Raconteur, and Friends. *In* Historicizing Theories, Identities, and Nations. R. Darnell and F. Gleach, eds. Pp. 267–281. Lincoln: University of Nebraska Press.

2018    How "Public" Is Public Anthropology? Public Anthropologist, March 14. http://publicanthropologist.cmi.no/2018/03/14/how-public-is-public -anthropology/ (accessed August 6, 2018).

McLeod, Mark

1994    Review: *Understanding Vietnam* by N. Jamieson. American Historical Review 99(4):1382.

Mcmillen, Liz

1997    Judith Butler Revels in the Role of Troublemaker. Chronicle of Higher Education, May 23, pp. A14–A15.

McMurtrie, Beth

2008    US Could Look to Europe for Accountability Ideas. Chronicle of Higher Education, May 30. https://www.chronicle.com/article/US-Could-Look -to-Europe-for/17503 (accessed August 6, 2018).

McMurty, Larry

2001    Zuni Tunes. New York Review of Books, August 9, pp. 56–58.

McNutt, Marcia

2015    Data, Eternal. Science 347(6217):7.

Mead, Margaret

1928    Coming of Age in Samoa. New York: William Morrow.

1935    Sex and Temperament in Three Primitive Societies. New York: New
[1950]   American Library (Mentor).

1972    Blackberry Winter: My Earlier Years. New York: Morrow.

1973    Changing Styles of Anthropological Work. *In* Annual Review of Anthropology, vol. 2. B. J. Siegel, A. R. Beals, and S. A. Tyler, eds. Palo Alto, CA: Annual Reviews, Inc.

n.d.    S.v. Margaret Mead. http://www.abolitionistapproach.com/media/links/ p144/margaret-mead.pdf (accessed August 6, 2018).

Mead, Margaret, and Ruth L. Bunzel, eds.

1960    The Golden Age of American Anthropology. New York: George Braziller.

Medick, Hans

1987    "Missionaries in the Row Boat"? Ethnological Ways of Knowing as a Challenge to Social History. Comparative Studies in Society and History 29:76–98.

Mendelsohn, Daniel
    1999    After Waterloo. New York Times Book Review, August 29, pp. 15–17.

Merry, Sally Engle
    2011    Human Rights and Global Governance. Current Anthropology 52 (S3:S83–S95).
    2016    The Seductions of Quantification: Measuring Human Rights, Gender Violence, and Sex Trafficking. Chicago: University of Chicago Press.

Mervis, Jeffrey
    2018    Reporter's Notebook: House Budget Hearing Shows Science Chairman's Impact on NSF Peer Review. Science, March 16. http://www.sciencemag.org/news/2018/03/reporter-s-notebook-house-budget-hearing-shows-science-chairman-s-impact-nsf-peer (accessed August 6, 2018).

Messick, Brinkley
    1987    Subordinate Discourse: Women, Weaving, and Gender Relations in North Africa. American Ethnologist 14(2):210–225.

Miklikowska, Marta, and Douglas Fry
    2012    Natural Born Nonkillers: A Critique of the Killers-Have-More-Kids Idea. *In* Nonkilling Psychology. Daniel Christie and Joan Evan Pim, eds. Honolulu, HI: Center for Global Nonkilling.

Miller, Barbara D.
    2005    Cultural Anthropology, third edition. Boston: Pearson / Allyn and Bacon.

Miller, Daniel
    1991    Absolute Freedom in Trinidad. Man 26(2):323–341.

Miller, D. W.
    2001    Storming the Palace in Political Science. Chronicle of Higher Education, September 21, pp. A16–A17.

Miller, Laura
    2004    The Last Word: How Many Books Are Too Many? New York Times, July 18. http://www.nytimes.com/2004/07/18/books/the-last-word-how-many-books-are-too-many.html (accessed October 5, 2017).

Mills, David
    2008    Difficult Folk? A Political History of Social Anthropology. New York: Berghahn Books.

Mills, Donald
    1978    Review: *The Rise of Professionalism* by M. Sarfati. Contemporary Sociology 7(5):654–655.

Mills, Kathryn, ed.
    2000    Letters and Autobiographical Writings by C. Wright Mills. Berkeley: University of California Press.

Minds, Savage

n.d.    Posts from the "Public Anthropology" Category. Savage Minds (Notes and Queries in Anthropology—A Group Blog). https://savageminds.org/tag/ public-anthropology/ (accessed August 6, 2018).

Minturn, Leigh, and William W. Lambert

1964    Mothers of Six Cultures: Antecedents to Child Rearing. New York: John Wiley & Sons.

Mirsky, Jonathan

1998    The Mark of Cain. New York Review of Books, February 5, pp. 31–33.

Mitchell, Timothy

1989    The World as Exhibition. Comparative Studies in Society and History 31(2):217–236.

Mitchell, William

1988    The Defeat of Hierarchy: Gambling as Exchange in a Sepik Society. American Ethnologist 15(4):638–657.

Mitgang, Herbert

1991    Books of the Times: 2 Versions of the Long View of the Vietnam War. New York Times, January 26. https://www.nytimes.com/1991/01/26/books/ books-of-the-times-2-versions-of-the-long-view-of-the-vietnam-war.html (accessed August 6, 2018).

1993    Books of the Times: Echoes of the Vietnam War Are Still Resounding. New York Times, June 4. https://www.nytimes.com/1993/06/04/books/ books-of-the-times-echoes-of-the-vietnam-war-are-still-resounding.html (accessed August 6, 2018).

Monaghan, Peter

2009    What If You Pull a Literary Hoax and Nobody Notices? Chronicle of Higher Education, August 3. https://www.chronicle.com/article/What-if -You-Pull-a-Literary/47501 (accessed August 6, 2018).

Monastersky, Richard

2002    The Emperor's New Science. Chronicle of Higher Education, November 15, pp. A16–A18.

2005    The Number That's Devouring Science: The Impact Factor. Chronicle of Higher Education, October 14, pp. A12–A17.

Mooney, James

1896    The Ghost-Dance Religion and the Sioux Outbreak of 1890. Chicago:
[1965]    University of Chicago Press. [Originally published in 1896 as Part 2 of the Fourteenth Annual Report of the Bureau of Ethnology to the Secretary of the Smithsonian Institution, 1892–93.] Washington, DC: Government Printing Office.

Moore, Addison
    1916    Review: *Democracy and Education* by J. Dewey. International Journal of Ethics 26(4):547–550.

Moore, Ernest
    1917    Review: *Democracy and Education* by J. Dewey. Journal of Philosophy, Psychology, and Scientific Methods 14(14):384–389.

Moore, Jerry D.
    2004    Visions of Culture: An Introduction to Anthropological Theories and Theorists. Lanham, MD: AltaMira Press.

Morgan, Henry Lewis
    1962    League of the Iroquois. New York: Corinth Books.

Morris, Brian
    1987    Anthropological Studies of Religion: An Introductory Text. New York: Cambridge University Press.

Mosko, Mark S.
    1987    The Symbols of "Forest": A Structural Analysis of Mbuti Culture and Social Organization. American Anthropologist 89:896–913.
    1991    The Canonic Formula of Myth and Nonmyth. American Ethnologist 18(1):126–151.
    1995    Rethinking Trobriand Chieftainship. Journal of the Royal Anthropological Institute 1(4):763–785.
    1998    On Virgin Birth: Comparability and Anthropological Method. Current Anthropology 39(5):685–687.

Mowry, George
    1939    Review: *Knowledge for What* by R. Lynd. Mississippi Valley Historical Review 26(2):290–291.

Moyar, Mark
    2006    Triumph Forsaken: The Vietnam War, 1954–1965. New York: Cambridge University Press.

Mukhopadhyay, Carol, and Patricia Higgins
    1988    Anthropological Studies of Women's Status Revisited. Annual Review of Anthropology 17:461–495.

Mundkur, Balaji
    1978    The Alleged Diffusion of Hindu Divine Symbols in Pre-Columbian Mesoamerica: A Critique. Current Anthropology 19(3):541–581.

Munk, Nina
    2013    The Idealist: Jeffrey Sachs and the Quest to End Poverty. New York: Anchor.

Munn, Nancy
    1990    Constructing Regional Worlds in Experience: Kula Exchange, Witchcraft and Gawan Local Events. Man 25:1–17.
    1994    Review: Partial Connections. American Ethnologist 21(4):1012–1013.

Murphy, Robert
    1967    Cultural Change. *In* Biennial Review of Anthropology. B. Siegal, ed. Pp. 1–45. Stanford, CA: Stanford University Press.
    1979    Steward, Julian H. *In* International Encyclopedia of the Social Sciences: Biographical Supplement, vol. 18. D. Sills, ed. Pp. 744–746. New York: Macmillan.

Murray, Gerald
    2012    Competition Winner, California Series in Public Anthropology: A Haitian Tree Battle: Anthropology and the Devastated Forest. http://www.public anthropology.org/books-book-series/california-book-series/international -competition/a-haitian-tree-battle-anthropology-and-the-devastated-for est-by-gerald-f-murray/ (accessed October 5, 2017).

Murray, G.F., and M. E. Bannister
    2004    Peasants, Agroforesters, and Anthropologists: A 20-Year Venture in Income-Generating Trees and Hedgerows in Haiti. Agroforestry Systems 61:383-397.

Murray, Stephan
    1991    On Boasians and Margaret Mead: Reply to Freeman. Current Anthropology 32(4):448–452.
    1994    A Thirteenth Century Imperial Ethnography. Anthropology Today 10(5):15–18.

Myers, D. S., and John Myers
    2001    Walter Lippmann and John Dewey Debate the Role of Citizens in Democracy (Selected Moments of the 20th Century: History of Education). *In* A Work in Progress. D. Schugurensky, ed. Toronto: Ontario Institute for Studies of Education of the University of Toronto.

Myers, Fred
    1988    Locating Ethnographic Practice: Romance, Reality, and Politics in the Outback. American Ethnologist 15(4):609–624.

Nadel, S. F.
    1952    Witchcraft in Four African Societies. American Anthropologist 54:18–29.

Nader, Laura
    1994    Comparative Consciousness. *In* Assessing Cultural Anthropology. R. Borofsky, ed. Pp. 84–96. New York: McGraw-Hill.
    1997    Controlling Processes. Current Anthropology 38(5):711–737.

Nagl, John
  2002    Learning to Eat Soup with a Knife: Counterinsurgency Lessons from Ma-
          laya and Vietnam. Chicago: University of Chicago Press.
  2008    A Battalion's Worth of Good Ideas. New York Times, April 2. https://www
          .nytimes.com/2008/04/02/opinion/02nagl.html (accessed August 6, 2018).

Nanda, Serena, and Richard Warms
  2004    Cultural Anthropology, eighth edition. Belmont, CA: Wordsworth/
          Thomson Learning.

Naroll, Raoul
  1961    Review: *Evolution and Culture*. American Anthropologist 63:389–392.

Nash, Dennison, and Ronald Wintrob
  1972    The Emergence of Self-Consciousness in Ethnography. Current Anthro-
          pology 13(5):527–542.

Nash, June
  1981    Ethnographic Aspects of the World Capitalist System. Annual Review of
          Anthropology 10:393–423.
  1997    When Isms Become Wasms. Critique of Anthropology 17:11–32.

National Association for the Practice of Anthropology
  n.d.    The Practice of Anthropology. http://practicinganthropology.org/practic
          ing-anthro/ (accessed October 5, 2017).

Navasky, Victor
  1972    How We Got Into the Messiest War in Our History (Review: *The Best and
          the Brightest* by D. Halberstam). New York Times, November 12. https://
          archive.nytimes.com/www.nytimes.com/books/98/03/15/home/halberstam
          -best.html?mcubz=0 (accessed August 6, 2018).

Nelson, Robin, Julienne Rutherford, Katie Hinde, Kathryn Clancy
  2017    Signaling Safety: Characterizing Fieldwork Experiences and Their Im-
          plications for Career Trajectories. American Anthropologist. October 11.
          https://doi.org/10.1111/aman.12929 (accessed August 6, 2018).

Nettle, Daniel
  1997    On the Status of Methodological Individualism. Current Anthropology
          38(2):283–286.

Newbury, Colin
  1982    Review: *Historical Metaphors and Mythical Realities* by M. Sahlins. Journal
          of the Polynesian Society 91(4):606–609.

New Zealand Herald
  2005    Tiny Islands Find Cyclone Percy Packs a Punch. New Zealand Herald,
          March 2. http://www.nzherald.co.nz/nz/news/article.cfm?c_id=1&objectid
          =10113247 (accessed August 6, 2018).

Nicholson, Peter

    2007      The Intellectual in the Infosphere. Chronicle of Higher Education, March 9, pp. B6–B7.

NIH (National Institutes of Health)

    2017      NIH Mission and Goals, October 5. https://www.nih.gov/about-nih/what -we-do/mission-goals (accessed August 6, 2018).

Noble, David Watson

    1978      Review: *The Emergence of Professional Social Science* by T. Haskell. Journal of Southern History 44(2):318–319.

Nordstrom, Carolyn

    2004      Shadows of War: Violence, Power, and International Profiteering in the Twenty-First Century. Berkeley: University of California Press.

    2007      Global Outlaws: Crime, Money and Power in the Contemporary World. Berkeley: University of California Press.

NSF (National Science Foundation)

    2004      NSF 04-23 September 2004, Chapter III—NSF Proposal Processing and Review, A. Review Criteria. http://www.nsf.gov/pubs/gpg/nsf04_23/3.jsp (accessed August 6, 2018).

    2013      NSF 13-1 January 2013, Chapter III—NSF Proposal Processing and Review. http://www.nsf.gov/pubs/policydocs/pappguide/nsf13001/gpg_3.jsp#IIIA2 (accessed August 6, 2018).

    2015      NSF Higher Education Research and Development Survey Fiscal Year 2015, Table 16. Higher education R&D expenditures. https://ncsesdata.nsf .gov/herd/2015/html/HERD2015_DST_16.html (accessed August 6, 2018).

Nugent, Stephen

    1988      The "Peripheral Situation." Annual Review of Anthropology 17:79–89.

    1996      Postmodernism. *In* Encyclopedia of Social and Cultural Anthropology. A. Barnard and J. Spencer, eds. Pp. 442–445. New York: Routlege.

Oakes, Guy, and Arthur Vidich

    1999      Collaboration, Reputation, and Ethics in American Academic Life. Urbana: University of Illinois Press.

Obeyesekere, Gananath

    1992      The Apotheosis of Captain Cook: European Mythmaking in the Pacific. Princeton, NJ: Princeton University Press.

O'Brien, Michael J.

    1987      Sedentism, Population Growth, and Resource Selection in the Woodland Midwest: A Review of Coevolutionary Developments. Current Anthropology 28(2):177–197.

Ogle, Richard

    2007      Smart World. Cambridge, MA: Harvard Business School Press.

O'Hanlon, Michael
    1992    Unstable Images and Second Skins: Artifacts, Exegesis and Assessments in the New Guinea Highlands. Man 27:587–608.

O'Hara, Carolyn
    2014    How to Tell a Great Story. Harvard Business Review, July 30. https://hbr .org/2014/07/how-to-tell-a-great-story (accessed August 6, 2018).

Ohnuki-Tierney, Emiko
    1995    Structure, Event and Historical Metaphor: Rice and Identities in Japanese History. Journal of the Royal Anthropological Institute 1(2):227–253.

Okely, Judith
    1991    Defiant Moments: Gender, Resistance and Individuals. Man 26(1):3–22.

Oleson, Alexandra, and John Voss, eds.
    1979    The Organization of Knowledge in America, 1860–1920. Baltimore, MD: Johns Hopkins University Press.

Oliver, Douglas
    1959    Review: *Anthropologie Structurale*. American Anthropologist 61:506–512.

Omohundro, John T.
    2008    Thinking Like an Anthropologist: A Practical Introduction to Anthropology. New York: McGraw-Hill.

Open Science Collaboration
    2015    Estimating the Reproducibility of Psychological Science. Science 349(6251):943–951.

Opthof, Tobias, Ruben Coronel, and Michiel J. Janse
    2002    The Significance of the Peer Review Process Against the Background of Bias. Cardiovascular Research 56:339–346.

Orlove, Benjamin
    1980    Ecological Anthropology. Annual Review of Anthropology (9):235–273.
    1986    Barter and Cash Sale on Lake Titicaca: A Test of Competing Approaches. Current Anthropology 27(2):85–106.

Ortner, Sherry
    1984    Theory in Anthropology Since the Sixties. Comparative Studies in Society and History 26:126–166.
    1985    Acting Out Culture (Review: *Islands of History* by M. Sahlins). New York Times, June 9. https://www.nytimes.com/1985/06/09/books/acting-out -culture.html (accessed August 6, 2018).
    1995    Resistance and the Problem of Ethnographic Refusal. Comparative Studies in Society and History 37(1):173-193.

————, ed.

1999    The Fate of "Culture": Geertz and Beyond. Berkeley: University of Califor-
        nia Press.

2016    Dark Anthropology and Its Others: Theory Since the Eighties. Journal of
        Ethnographic Theory 6(1):47–73.

Osella, Caroline, and Filippo Osella

1998    Friendship and Flirting: Micro-Politics in Kerala, South India. Journal of
        the Royal Anthropological Institute 4(2):189–206.

Otto, M. C.

1920    Review: *Democracy and Education* by J. Dewey. Mississippi Valley Histori-
        cal Review 7(1):64–65.

Ouroussoff, Alexandra

1993    Illusions of Rationality: False Premises of the Liberal Tradition. Man
        28(2):281–298.

Outhwaite, William

1994    Habermas: A Critical Introduction. Stanford, CA: Stanford University
        Press.

Packer, George

2007    David Halberstam (Postscript). The New Yorker, May 7. https://www.new
        yorker.com/magazine/2007/05/07/david-halberstam (accessed August 6,
        2018).

Palmer, Gary, and William Jankowiak

1996    Performance and Imagination: Toward an Anthropology of the Spectacu-
        lar and the Mundane. Cultural Anthropology 11(2):225–258.

Panter-Brick, Catherine, et al.

2017    Resilience in Context: A Brief and Culturally Grounded Measure for Syr-
        ian Refugee and Jordanian Host-Community Adolescents. Child Develop-
        ment, June 15. https://publicanthropology.altmetric.com/details/21088723/
        news (accessed August 6, 2018).

Paredes, Anthony

2006    On Boas as Hamatsa. Anthropology News, March, p. 3.

Parini, Jay

1998    Delving into the World of Dreams by Blending Fact and Fiction. Chronicle
        of Higher Education, February 27, pp. B4–B5.

Parker, Christine

1995    Review: *Professionalism Reborn* by Eliot Freidson. Contemporary Sociol-
        ogy 24(4):387–388.

Parker, Seymour
    1988    Rituals of Gender: A Study of Etiquette, Public Symbols, and Cognition.
            American Anthropologist 90:372–384.

Parkin, David
    1993    Nemi in the Modern World: Return of the Exotic? Man 28(1):79–99.

Patai, Daphne
    1994    Sick and Tired of Scholars' Nouveau Solipsism. Chronicle of Higher Edu-
            cation, February 23, p. A52.

Patternson, Thomas C.
    2001    A Social History of Anthropology in the United States. New York: Berg.

Pauketat, Timothy, and Thomas Emerson
    1991    The Ideology of Authority and the Power of the Pot. American Anthropol-
            ogist 93(4):919–941.

Paul, Robert
    1989    Psychoanalytic Anthropology. Annual Review of Anthropology (18):177–
            202.

Peacock, James
    1968    Review: The Forest of Symbols by V. Turner. American Anthropologist
            70:984–985.
    1984    Symbolic and Psychological Anthropology: The Case of Pentecostal Faith
            Healing. Ethos 12:137-153.
    1997    The Future of Anthropology. American Anthropologist 99(1):9–17.

Peebles, Christopher S., and Susan M. Kus
    1977    Some Archaeological Correlates of Ranked Societies. American Antiquity
            42:421–448.

Pelto, Pertti
    1967    Psychological Anthropology. In Biennial Review of Anthropology. B. Sie-
            gal, ed. Pp. 140–208. Stanford, CA: Stanford University Press.

Peoples, James, and Garrick Bailey
    2009    Humanity: An Introduction to Cultural Anthropology. Belmont, CA:
            Wadsworth.

Pepper, Stephen
    1928    Review: The Public and Its Problems by J. Dewey. International Journal of
            Ethics 38(4):478–480.

Perry, Richard
    1992    Why Do Multiculturalists Ignore Anthropologists. Chronicle of Higher
            Education 4 (March):A52.

Peteet, Julie

1994 Male Gender and Ritual of Resistance in the Palestinian *intifada*: A Cultural Politics of Violence. American Ethnologist 21(1):31–49.

Petersen, Glenn

1995 Review: *How "Natives" Think* by M. Sahlins. Library Journal, April 15, p. 85.

Petrie, Matt

2007 NIH Awards Grants to 9 Consortia, Marking Shift Toward Interdisciplinary Research. Chronicle of Higher Education, September 7. https://www .chronicle.com/article/NIH-Awards-Grants-to-9/122017 (accessed August 6, 2018).

Piccini, Angela

1996 Filming Through the Mists of Time. Current Anthropology 37(1):S87–S111.

Pieters, Rik, and Hans Baumgartner

2002 Who Talks to Whom? Intra- and Interdisciplinary Communication of Economics Journals. Journal of Economic Literature 40:483–509.

Pike, Douglas

1983 The Vietnam War Recounted and Relived. New York Times, October 16. https://www.nytimes.com/1983/10/16/books/the-vietnam-war-recounted -and-relived.html (accessed August 6, 2018).

Pina-Cabral, Joao de

1993 Tamed Violence: Genital Symbolism in Portuguese Popular Culture. Man 28(1):101–120.

Piot, Charles

1995 Symbolic Dualism and Historical Process Among the Kabre of Togo. Journal of the Royal Anthropological Institute 1(3):611–624.

Podolefsky, Aaron, Peter Brown, and Scott Lacy

2011 Applying Anthropology: An Introductory Reader. New York: McGraw-Hill.

Poewe, Karla

2001 Politically Compromised Scholars, or What German Scholars Working under Missions, National Socialism, and the Marxist-Leninist German Republic Can Teach Us. American Anthropologist 103(3):834–837.

Poirier, Richard

1978 Of Inhuman Bondage (Review: *Discipline and Punish* by M. Foucault). Washington Post, January 29, pp. 1–4.

Polier, Nicole, and William Roseberry

1989 Tristes Tropes: Post-modern Anthropologists Encounter the Other and Discover Themselves. Economy and Society 18(2):245–264.

Pool, Robert
   1991     Postmodern Ethnography? Critique of Anthropology 11(4):309–331.

Postrel, Virginia
   2006     The Poverty Puzzle (Review: *The White Man's Burden* by W. Easterly). New York Times, March 19, p. 12.

Potter, Sulamith Heins
   1988     The Cultural Construction of Emotion in Rural Chinese Social Life. Ethos 16(2):181–208.

Pouillon, Jean
   1996     Lévi-Strauss, Claude. *In* The Social Science Encyclopedia. A. Kuper and J. Kuper, eds. Pp. 465–468. New York: Routledge.

Powdermaker, Hortense
   1945     Review: *The People of Alor* by C. DuBois. American Anthropologist 47:155–161.

Powell, J. W.
   1888     From Barbarism to Civilization. American Anthropologist 1(2):97–123.

Powers, Katherine
   1995     Review: *How "Natives" Think* by M. Sahlins. Boston Globe, June 11, p. 73.

Powers, Thomas
   1999     Oh, What an Ugly War. New York Times, January 10. https://archive.ny times.com/www.nytimes.com/books/99/01/10/reviews/990110.10powerst .html (accessed August 6, 2018).

Price, Barbara J.
   1977     Shifts in Production and Organization: A Cluster-Interaction Model. Current Anthropology 18(2):209–233.
   1982     Cultural Materialism: A Theoretical Review. American Antiquity 47(4):709–741.

Price, Michael
   2018     Some Scientists Publish More Than 70 Papers a Year. Here's How—and Why—They Do It. Science, September 12. https://www.sciencemag.org/ news/2018/09/some-scientists-publish-more-70-papers-year-here-s-how -and-why-they-do-it (accessed December 31, 2018).

Priest, Dana, and William M. Arkin
   2010     Monitoring America: Top Secret in America. Washington Post. http://proj ects.washingtonpost.com/top-secret-america/articles/monitoring-america (accessed October 5, 2017).

Prospect
   1998     What Is Academia For? Prospect (August–September). https://www

.prospectmagazine.co.uk/magazine/whatisacademiafor (accessed August 6, 2018).

Public Law

2007    110-69-August 9, America Competes Act, 121 STAT. 572-718. https://www
        .congress.gov/110/plaws/publ69/PLAW-110publ69.pdf (accessed August 6,
        2018).

Quiggin, John

2015    Rank Delusions. Chronicle of Higher Education, February 16. https://
        www.chronicle.com/article/Rank-Delusions/189919 (accessed August 6,
        2018).

Rabesandratana, Tania

2018    Universities are Worse than Drug Companies at Reporting Clinical Trials.
        Science, September 12. https://www.sciencemag.org/news/2018/09/univer
        sities-are-worse-drug-companies-reporting-clinical-trial-results (accessed
        Dec. 31, 2018).

Rappaport, Roy A.

1968    Pigs for the Ancestors: Ritual in the Ecology of a New Guinea People. New
[1984]  Haven, CT: Yale University Press.

1994    Humanity's Evolution and Anthropology's Future. In Assessing Cultural
        Anthropology. R. Borofsky, ed. Pp. 153–166. New York: McGraw-Hill.

1999    Ritual and Religion in the Making of Humanity. New York: Cambridge
        University Press.

Read, Brock

2006    Can Wikipedia Ever Make the Grade? Chronicle of Higher Education, Oc-
        tober 27, pp. A31–A36.

2007a   How Do You Cite Wikipedia on a History Paper? At Middlebury College,
        You Don't. A Professor Explains Why. Chronicle of Higher Education,
        February 1. https://www.chronicle.com/article/How-Do-You-Cite-Wiki
        pedia-on-a/122530 (accessed August 6, 2018).

2007b   Middlebury College History Department Limits Students Use of Wikipe-
        dia. Chronicle of Higher Education, February 16, p. A39.

Read, Dwight W., and Steven A. LeBlanc

1978    Descriptive Statements, Covering Laws, and Theories of Archaeology. Cur-
        rent Anthropology 19(2):307–335.

Rebel, Hermann

1989    Cultural Hegemony and Class Experience: A Critical Reading of Recent
        Ethnological-Historical Approaches. American Ethnologist 16(1–2):117–
        136, 350–365.

Redfield, Robert

1930    Tepoztlán, a Mexican Village: A Study in Folk Life. Chicago: University of Chicago Press.

1956    The Little Community and Peasant Society and Culture. Chicago: University of Chicago Press.

1957    The Primitive World and Its Transformation. Ithaca, NY: Cornell University Press.

Redman, Charles

1991    In Defense of the Seventies—The Adolescence of New Archeology. American Anthropologist 93(2):295–307.

Reeson, Nathan

2008    The Function of Dysfunction. Chronicle of Higher Education, June 30. https://www.chronicle.com/article/The-Function-of-Dysfunction/45866 (accessed August 7, 2018).

REF 2021

2017    What Is the REF? https://www.ref.ac.uk/about/whatref/ (accessed August 6, 2018).

Reff, Daniel

1991    Anthropological Analysis of Exploration Texts. American Anthropologist 93(3):636–655.

Regush, Nicholas

2000    Who Should Investigate: Looking at Conflict of Interest in Biomedicine, Part 2. ABC News Online, October 5. http://members.aol.com/nym1111111/darkness_in_el_dorado/documents/0070.htm (accessed June 2004).

Rensburger, Boyce

1996    As Others See Us. Anthropology News, October 12.

Research Excellence Framework

2015    Research Excellence Framework 2014: Overview Report by Main Panel C and Sub-panels 16-26. UOA 24. https://www.ref.ac.uk/2014/media/ref/content/expanel/member/Main%20Panel%20C%20overview%20report.pdf (accessed August 6, 2018).

Rhode, Deborah L.

2006    In Pursuit of Knowledge: Scholars, Status, and Academic Culture. Stanford, CA: Stanford University Press.

Rice, David

2000    Anthropologists as Spies. Nation, November 2. https://www.thenation.com/article/anthropologists-spies/ (accessed August 6, 2018).

Rice, Prudence M.

1981   Evolution of Specialized Pottery Production: A Trial Model. Current Anthropology 22(3):219–240.

1983   Serpent and Styles in Peten Postclassic Pottery. American Anthropologist 85(4):866–880.

Rich, Nathaniel

2016   Inside the Sacrifice Zone. New York Review of Books, November 10. http://www.nybooks.com/articles/2016/11/10/american-right-inside-the-sacrifice-zone/ (accessed October 5, 2017).

Richardson, J., and Alfred Kroeber

1940   Three Centuries of Women's Dress Fashions: A Quantitative Analysis. Berkeley: University of California Press.

Ricks, Thomas

2006   Fiasco: The American Military Adventure in Iraq. New York: Penguin Press.

Riddell, Roger

2007   Does Foreign Aid Really Work. New York: Oxford University Press.

Ridington, Robin

1988   Knowledge, Power, and the Individual in Subarctic Hunting Societies. American Anthropologist 90:98–110.

Rieff, David

1997   Charity on the Rampage: The Business of Foreign Aid. NomadNet (Foreign Affairs), January–February.

2002   A Bed for the Night: Humanitarianism in Crisis. New York: Simon & Schuster.

Riesman, David

1980   On Higher Education: The Academic Enterprise in an Era of Rising Student Consumerism. San Francisco, CA: Jossey-Bass.

Robben, Antonious

1989   Habits of the Home: Spatial Hegemony and the Structuration of House and Society in Brazil. American Anthropologist 91:570–588.

Robbins, Joel

1995   The Raw and the Cook. In These Times, June 26, pp. 32–34.

Robbins, Richard H.

2001   Cultural Anthropology: A Problem-Based Approach, third edition. Itasca, IL: F. E. Peacock Publishers.

2009   Cultural Anthropology: A Problem-Based Approach, fifth edition. Belmont, CA: Wadsworth.

Roberts, Michael
   1985       Ethnicity in Riposte at a Cricket Match: The Past for the Present. Compar-
                ative Studies in Society and History 27(3):401–429.

Robinson, Paul
   1983       From Suttee to Baseball to Cockfighting (Review: *Local Knowledge* by
                C. Geertz). New York Times, September 25. https://www.nytimes.com/
                1983/09/25/books/from-suttee-to-baseball-to-cockfighting.html (accessed
                August 6, 2018).

Rodin, Miriam, Karen Michaelson, and Gerald M. Britan
   1978       Systems Theory in Anthropology. Current Anthropology 19(4):747–762.

Rodman, Margaret
   1987       Constraining Capitalism? Contradictions of Self-Reliance in Vanuatu Fish-
                eries Development. American Ethnologist 14:712–726.

Rogge, A. E.
   1976       A Look at Academic Anthropology: Through a Graph Darkly. American
                Anthropologist 78:829–843.

Romer, Paul
   2016       The Trouble with Macroeconomics: Commons Memorial Lecture of the
                Omicron Delta Epsilon Society. The American Economist. https://paul
                romer.net/wp-content/uploads/2016/09/WP-Trouble.pdf (accessed August
                6, 2018).

Rosaldo, Michelle
   1983       The Shame of Headhunters and the Autonomy of Self. Ethos 11(3):135–151.

Rosaldo, Renato
   1989       Culture and Truth: The Remaking of Social Analysis. Boston: Beacon
                Press.

Roseberry, William
   1988       Political Economy. Annual Review of Anthropology 17:161–185.

Roseman, Sharon
   1996       "How We Built the Road": The Politics of Memory in Rural Galicia. Amer-
                ican Ethnologist 23(4):836–860.

Rosman, Abraham, and Paula Rubel
   1998       The Tapestry of Culture: An Introduction to Cultural Anthropology, sixth
                edition. New York: McGraw-Hill.

Ross, Andrew
   1995       The Raw and the Cook. Times Literary Supplement (May):11–13.

Ross, Dorothy
   1976       Review: *Advocacy and Objectivity: A Crisis in the Professionalization of*

*American Social Science, 1865–1905* by Mary O. Furner. Journal of Economic History 36 (June 2):468–470.

1978    Review: *The Emergence of Professional Social Science*. Journal of Economic History 38(2):494–499.

1991    The Origins of American Social Science. New York: Cambridge University Press.

Rossi, Ino

1976a    Cultural Ecology. *In* Encyclopedia of Anthropology. D. Hunter and N. Whitten, eds. Pp. 98–99. New York: Harper and Row.

1976b    Culture and Personality. *In* Encyclopedia of Anthropology. D. Hunter and P. Whitten, eds. Pp. 103–104. New York: Harper and Row.

Roston, Michael

2015    Retracted Scientific Studies: A Growing List. New York Times, May 28. https://www.nytimes.com/interactive/2015/05/28/science/retractions-sci entific-studies.html (accessed October 5, 2017).

Rothman, David J.

1978    Society and Its Prisons (Review: *Discipline and Punish*). New York Times Book Review, February 19, pp. 1, 26.

Ruby, Jay

2005    Anthropology as a Subversive Art: A Review of *Through These Eyes*. American Anthropologist 107(4):684–687.

Rueschemeyer, Dietrich

1995    Review: *In an Age of Experts* by S. Brint. Contemporary Sociology 24(4):388–390.

Rule, James

1997    Theory and Progress in Social Science. New York: Cambridge University Press.

Rumsey, Alan

2000    Agency, Personhood and the "I" of Discourse in the Pacific and Beyond. Journal of the Royal Anthropological Institute 6(1):101–115.

Rushforth, Scott

1994    Political Resistance in a Contemporary Hunter-Gatherer Society. American Ethnologist 21(2):335–352.

Russell, George

1978    Crime and Punishment (Review: *Discipline and Punish* by M. Foucault). Time Magazine, February 6.

Rutz, Henry

1987    Capitalizing on Culture: Moral ironies in Urban Fiji. Comparative Studies in Society and History 29:533–557.

Ruyle, Eugene E.

1973   Slavery, Surplus, and Stratification on the Northwest Coast: The Ethno-energetics of an Incipient Stratification System. Current Anthropology 14(5):603–631.

Rylko-Bauer, Barbara, Merrill Singer, and John van Willigen

2006   Reclaiming Applied Anthropology: Its Past, Present, and Future. American Anthropologist 108:178–190.

Sachs, Jeffrey

2005   The End of Poverty: Economic Possibilities for Our Time. New York: Penguin Books.

Sahlins, Marshall

1958   Social Stratification in Polynesia. Seattle: University of Washington Press.

1964   Culture and Environment: The Study of Cultural Ecology. In Horizons of Anthropology. S. Tax, ed. Pp. 132–147. Chicago: Aldine.

1981   Historical Metaphors and Mythical Realities: Structure in the Early History of the Sandwich Island Kingdom. In ASAO Special Publications, No. 1. Ann Arbor: University of Michigan Press.

1985   Islands of History. Chicago: University of Chicago Press.

1988   Deserted Islands of History. Critique of Anthropology 8(3):41–51.

1989   Captain Cook at Hawaii. Journal of the Polynesian Society 98(4):371–423.

1993   Waiting for Foucault. Cambridge, UK: Prickly Pear Press.

1995   How "Natives" Think: About Captain Cook, for Example. Chicago: University of Chicago Press.

2005   Culture in Practice: Selected Essays. Zone Books: New York.

Sahlins, Marshall, and Elman Service, eds.

1960   Evolution and Culture. Ann Arbor: University of Michigan Press.

Said, Edward

1988   Michel Foucault, 1926–1984. In After Foucault. J. Arac, ed. Pp. 1–11. New Brunswick, NJ: Rutgers University Press.

Salmond, Ann

1993   Whose God, or Not? Social Analysis 34(December):50–55.

Salome, Frank

1976   Adaptation, Cultural. In Encyclopedia of Anthropology. D. Hunter and N. Whitten, eds. Pp. 4–5. New York: Harper and Row.

Salzman, Philip Carl

1994   The Lone Stranger in the Heart of Darkness. In Assessing Cultural Anthropology. R. Borofsky, ed. Pp. 29–39. New York: McGraw-Hill.

Samuels, David

1996   "These Are the Stories That the Dogs Tell." Cultural Anthropology 11(1):88–118.

Sanderson, Stephen

1977     Evolution, Evolutionism, Social (and Cultural). *In* The Dictionary of Anthropology. T. Barfield, ed. Pp. 172–177. Malden, MA: Blackwell.

1997     Cultural Materialism. *In* The Dictionary of Anthropology. T. Barfield, ed. Pp. 96–98. Malden, MA: Blackwell.

Sangren, P. Steven

1988     Rhetoric and the Authority of Ethnography; "Postomodernsm" and the Social Reproduction of Texts. Current Anthropology 29(1):405–435.

2007     Anthropology of Anthropology? Further Reflections on Reflexivity. Anthropology Today 23(4):13–16.

Sanjek, Roger

1991     The Ethnographic Present. Man 26(4):609–628.

Saris, A. Jamie

1996     Mad Kings, Proper Houses, and an Asylum in Rural Ireland. American Anthropologist 98(3):539–554.

Saunders, George

1995     The Crisis of Presence in Italian Pentecostal Conversion. American Ethnologist 22(2):324–340.

Savage, Charlie

2017     Post-Snowden Efforts to Secure NSA Data Fell Short, Report Says. New York Times, June 16. https://www.nytimes.com/2017/06/16/us/politics/nsa -data-edward-snowden.html (accessed October 5, 2017).

Scheper-Hughes, Nancy

1987     The Best of Two Worlds, the Worst of Two Worlds: Reflections on Culture and Field Work among the Rural Irish and Pueblo Indians. Comparative Studies in Society and History 29(1):56–75.

1993     Death Without Weeping. Berkeley: University of California Press.

1995     The End of Anthropology (Review: *After the Fact* by C. Geertz). New York Times, May 6. https://www.nytimes.com/1995/05/07/books/the-end-of -anthropology.html (accessed August 6, 2018).

2000     The Global Traffic in Human Organs. Current Anthropology 41(2):191–224.

2003     Commodity Fetishism in Organs Trafficking. *In* Commodifying Bodies. Nancy Scheper-Hughes and Loïc Wacquant, eds. Pp. 31–62. Thousand Oaks, CA: Sage.

2011     The Rosenbaum Kidney Trafficking Gang. Counterpunch, November 30. http://www.counterpunch.org/2011/11/30/the-rosenbaum-kidney-trafficking-gang (accessed August 6, 2018).

Schieffelin, Edward

1976     The Sorrow of the Lonely and the Burning of the Dancers. New York: St. Martin's Press.

1983     Anger and Shame in the Tropic Forest. Ethos 11(3):181–191.

Schmidt, Peter

2008a    Most Colleges Chase Prestige on a Treadmill, Researchers Find. Chronicle of Higher Education, November 21, p. A14.

2008b    Studies Link Use of Part-Time Instructors to Lower Student Success. Chronicle of Higher Education, November 21. https://www.chronicle.com/ article/Use-of-Part-Time-Instructors/35149 (accessed August 6, 2018).

2009a    Researchers Say Lack of Wage Data Clouds Debate of Part-Time Faculty Members. Chronicle of Higher Education, May 19.  https://www.chronicle .com/article/Researchers-Say-Lack-of-Wage/47607 (accessed August 6, 2018).

2009b    US Faculty Members Feel a Lack of Clout, International Survey Finds. Chronicle of Higher Education, June 12. https://www.chronicle.com/ article/US-Faculty-Members-Feel-a/47318 (accessed August 6, 2018).

Schneider, David

n.d.     Blurb for *Race, Language, and Culture* by F. Boas in a University of Chicago Press advertisement. American Anthropologist.

Schneider, Jane

1999     Obituary: Eric Robert Wolf. American Anthropologist 101(2):395–399.

Schneider, Jane, and Rayna Rapp

1995     Articulating Hidden Histories: Exploring the Influence of Eric R. Wolf. Berkeley: University of California Press.

Schultz, Emily A., and Robert H. Lavenda

2001     Cultural Anthropology: A Perspective on the Human Condition, fifth edition. Mountain View, CA: Mayfield.

Schwartz, Theodore

1972     Review: *The Ritual Process* by V. Turner. American Anthropologist 74:904–908.

Schwartzman, John

1977     Art, Science, and Change in Western Society. Ethos 5:239–262.

Schwenkel, Christina

2009     The American War in Contemporary Vietnam. Bloomington: Indiana University Press.

Scott, David

1992     Conversion and Demonism: Colonial Christian Discourse and Religion in Sri Lanka. Comparative Studies in Society and History 34(2):331–365.

Scott, Wilbur

　　1994    Review: *Understanding Vietnam* by N. Jamieson. Contemporary Sociology 23(2):246–247.

Scull, Andrew

　　1990    Review: *The System of Professions* by A. Abbott. Isis 81(1):148–149.

　　2007    Scholarship of Fools. Times Literary Supplement, March 23, p. 3.

Scupin, Raymond

　　2008    Cultural Anthropology: A Global Perspective. Upper Saddle River, NJ: Pearson / Prentice Hall.

Secor, Laura

　　2002    We're Here to Help You (Review: *A Bed for the Night* by D. Rieff). New York Times Book Review, November 3, p. 20.

Sen, Amartya

　　2006    The Man Without a Plan (Review: *The White Man's Burden* by W. Easterly). Foreign Affairs, March–April. https://www.foreignaffairs.com/reviews/review-essay/2006-03-01/man-without-plan (accessed August 6, 2018).

Senior, Jennifer

　　2016    Review: In *Hillbilly Elegy*, a Tough Love Analysis of the Poor Who Back Trump. New York Times, August 11. https://www.nytimes.com/2016/08/11/books/review-in-hillbilly-elegy-a-compassionate-analysis-of-the-poor-who-love-trump.html (accessed October 5, 2017).

Seron, Carroll

　　2002    Review: *Professionalism* by E. Freidson. Contemporary Sociology 31(5):551–552.

Service, Elman

　　1955    Indian-European Relations in Latin America. American Anthropologist 25:411–423.

　　1958    A Profile of Primitive Culture. New York: Harper.

　　1962    Primitive Social Organization: An Evolutionary Perspective. New York: Random House.

　　1968    Cultural Evolution. *In* International Encyclopedia of the Social Sciences, vol. 5. D. Sills, ed. Pp. 221–228. New York: Macmillan.

Shane, Scott, Nicole Perltoth, and David E. Sanger

　　2017    Security Breach and Spilled Secrets Have Shaken the NSA to Its Core. New York Times, November 12. https://www.nytimes.com/2017/11/12/us/nsa-shadow-brokers.html?_r=0 (accessed August 6, 2018).

Shankman, Paul

　　1984    The Thick and the Thin: On the Interpretive Theoretical Program of Clifford Geertz. Current Anthropology 5(3):261–279.

1986    Review: *Islands of History* by M. Sahlins. American Anthropologist 88:767–768.

Sheehan, Paul
1988    A Bright Shining Lie: John Paul Vann and America in Vietnam. New York: Vantage.

Shelley, Louise I.
1979    Review: *Discipline and Punish* by M. Foucault. American Journal of Sociology 84(6):1508–1510.

Shore, Bradd
1983    Paradox Regained: Freeman's Margaret Mead and Samoa. American Anthropologist 85(4):935–944.
1991    Twice-Born, Once Conceived: Meaning Construction and Cultural Cognition. American Anthropologist 93(1):9–27.

Shore, Cris
1996    Anthropology's Identity Crisis. Anthropology Today 12(2):2–5.

Shore, Cris, and Susan Wright
2000    Coercive Accountability. *In* Audit Cultures. Marilyn Strathern, ed. Pp. 57–89. London: Routledge.
2015    Audit Culture Revisited: Rankings, Ratings, and the Reassembling of Society. Current Anthropology 56(3):421–444.

Shostak, Marjorie
1983    Nisa: The Life and Words of a !Kung Woman. New York: Vintage Books.

Shott, Michael
1992    On Recent Trends in the Anthropology of Foragers: Kalahari Revisionism and Its Archaeological Implications. Man 27(4):843–871.

Shweder, Richard
1985    A Slash-and-Burn Intellect (Review: *The View from Afar* by C. Lévi-Strauss). New York Times, April 14. https://www.nytimes.com/1985/04/14/books/a-slash-and-burn-intellect.html (accessed August 6, 2018).
1988    The How of the Word (Review: *Works and Lives* by C. Geertz). New York Times, February 28. https://www.nytimes.com/1988/02/28/books/the-how-of-the-word.html (accessed August 6, 2018).

Sica, Alan
2001    Review: *Chaos of Disciplines* by A. Abbott. Theory and Society 30(6):829–836.

Sidrys, Raymond V.
1976    Classic Maya Obsidian Trade. American Antiquity 41(4):449–464.

Silva, Edward, and Sheila Slaughter
   1984      Serving Power: The Making of the Academic Social Science Expert. West-
             port, CT: Greenwood Press.

Silver, Harold
   1979      Review: In Search of Social Science. History of Education Quarterly
             19(2):277–281.

Simpson, Christopher, ed.
   1999      Universities and Empire: Money and Politics in the Social Sciences during
             the Cold War. New York: New Press.

Singer, Merrill
   2000      Why I Am Not a Public Anthropologist. Anthropology News 41(6):6–7.

Singer, Milton
   1961      A Survey of Culture and Personality Theory and Research. *In* Studying
             Personality Cross-Culturally. Bert Kaplan, ed. Pp. 9–90. New York: Harper
             and Row.
   1977      On the Symbolic and Historic Structure of American Identity. Ethos 5:431–
             454.

Sivaramakrishnan, K.
   1995      Colonialism and Forestry in India: Imagining the Past in Present Politics.
             Comparative Studies in Society and History 37(1):3–40.

Sixty Minutes
   2008      Dr. Farmer's Remedy for World Health. CBS News, May 4. http://www
             .cbsnews.com/stories/2008/05/01/60minutes/main4063191.shtml (accessed
             August 6, 2018).

Smart, Barry
   1985      Michel Foucault. New York: Routledge.

Smelser, Neil, ed.
   1973      Karl Marx on Society and Social Change. *In* The Eighteenth Brumaire of
             Louis Bonaparte 1852. Chicago: University of Chicago Press.

Smith, Adam
   2008      No End of It. Times Literary Supplement, May 23, p. 8.

Smith, Carol
   1997      Reconceptualizing "Wolfian" Anthropology and the Peasantry. American
             Anthropologist 99(2):381–383.

Smith, David
   1993      Review: *Unthinking Social Science* by I. Wallerstein. Contemporary Sociol-
             ogy 22(5):759–760.

Smith, Geri
   2000      Atrocities in the Amazon? BusinessWeek, December 18, pp. 21–24.

Smith, Mark
    1994     Social Science in the Crucible: The American Debate over Objectivity and Purpose, 1918–1941. Durham, NC: Duke University Press.

Smith, Philip
    1987     Transhumant Europeans Overseas: The Newfoundland Case. Current Anthropology 28(2):241–250.

Smith, T. V.
    1929     Review: *The Public and Its Problems* by J. Dewey. Philosophical Review 38(2):177–180.

Smolin, Lee
    2007     The Trouble with Physics: The Rise of String Theory, the Fall of a Science, and What Comes Next. New York: First Mariner Books.

Snow, Dean R.
    1969     Ceramic Sequence and Settlement Location in Pre-Hispanic Tlaxcala. American Antiquity 14(2):131–145.

Social Science Research Council
    2017     Fellowships and Grants > Dissertation Proposal Development Fellowship (DPDF) Program—DPDF Selection Criteria for Students. http://www.ssrc.org/fellowships/dpdf-fellowship/ (accessed August 6, 2018).

Social Sciences and Humanities Research Council of Canada
    2009     Apply for Funding / Standard Research Grants—Evaluation. http://www.sshrc-crsh.gc.ca/funding-financement/programs-programmes/standard_grants_subventions_ordinaires-eng.aspx (accessed August 6, 2018).

Sorenson, Richard E.
    1972     Socio-Ecological Change among the Fore of New Guinea. Current Anthropology 13(3–4):349–383.

Spencer, Jonathan
    1989     Anthropology as a Kind of Writing. Man 24:145–164.
    1996     Symbolic Anthropology. *In* Encyclopedia of Social and Cultural Anthropology. A. Barnard and J. Spencer, eds. Pp. 535–539. New York: Routledge.

Spindler, George
    1955a    Review: The Modal Personality Structure of the Tuscarora Indians As Revealed by the Rorschach Test. American Anthropologist 57:171–173.
    1955b    Sociocultural and Psychological Processes in Menomini Acculturation. Berkeley: University of California Press.
    1962     Review: *Culture and Personality* by A. Wallace. American Anthropologist 64:1320–1322.

————, ed.

1978      The Making of Psychological Anthropology. Berkeley: University of California Press.

Spindler, George, and Louise Spindler

1959      Culture Change. *In* Biennial Review of Anthropology. B. Siegal, ed. Pp. 37–66. Stanford, CA: Stanford University Press.

Spiro, Melford E.

1968      Culture and Personality. *In* International Encyclopedia of the Social Sciences. D. Sills, ed. Pp. 558–563. New York: Macmillan.

1979      Whatever Happened to the Id? American Anthropologist 81(1):5–13.

Sponsel, Leslie

1977      Ecological Anthropology. *In* The Dictionary of Anthropology. T. Barfield, ed. Pp. 137–139. Malden, MA: Blackwell.

Spradely, James P., and David W. McCurdy

1975      Anthropology: The Cultural Perspective. New York: John Wiley & Sons.

Stahl, Ann Brower

1993      Concepts of Time and Approaches to Analogical Reasoning in Historical Perspective. American Antiquity 58(2):235–260.

Stapel, Diederik

2014      Faking Science: A True Story of Academic Fraud. https://errorstatistics .files.wordpress.com/2014/12/fakingscience-20141214.pdf (accessed August 6, 2018).

Staples, James

2003      Disguise, Revelation and Copyright: Disassembling the South Indian Leper. Journal of the Royal Anthropological Institute 9:295–315.

Stark, Andrew

2006      Spot the Manager. Times Literary Supplement, August 11, p. 28.

Starobin, Paul

2013      Does It Take a Village? Jeffrey Sachs Dazzled the Development World with His Plan to End Poverty. But Now Critics Say There's No Way to Prove Whether It Works. Foreign Policy, June 24. http://foreignpolicy.com/2013/ 06/24/does-it-take-a-village/ (accessed August 6, 2018).

Stasch, Rupert

2003      Separateness as a Relation. Journal of the Royal Anthropological Institute 9:317–337.

Steadman, Lyle B., and Charles F. Merbs

1982      Kuru and Cannibalism? American Anthropologist 84:611–627.

Steel, Ronald

1988      The Man Who Was the War (Review: *A Bright Shining Lie* by N. Sheehan).

New York Times, September 25. https://www.nytimes.com/1988/09/25/books/the-man-who-was-the-war.html (accessed August 6, 2018).

Stein, Felix
  2017    Anthropology's "Impact": A Comment on Audit and the Unmeasurable Nature of Critique. Journal of the Royal Anthropological Institute 24:10–29.

Steiner, David
  1992    Review: *John Dewey and American Democracy* by R. Westbrook. Political Theory 20(3):515–518.

Steiner, George
  1999    Work in Progress (Review of *The Arcades Project* by Walter Benjamin). Times Literary Supplement, December 3, pp. 3–4.

Steponaitis, Vincas P.
  1981    Settlement Hierarchies and Political Complexity in Nonmarket Societies: The Formative Period of the Valley of Mexico. American Anthropologist 83(2):320–363.

Steward, Julian
  1955    Theory of Cultural Change: The Methodology of Multilinear Evolution. Urbana: University of Illinois Press.
  1968    Cultural Ecology. *In* International Encyclopedia of the Social Sciences, vol. 3. D. Sills, ed. Pp. 337–344. New York: Macmillan.

Stewart, Pamela, and Andrew Strathern
  2016    Breaking the Frames. New York: Springer International.

Stichcombe, Arthur
  1990    Review: *The System of Professions* by A. Abbott. Contemporary Sociology 19(1):48–50.

Stirrat, R. L.
  1984    Sacred Models. Man 19:199–215.

Stocking, George
  1976    Ideas and Institutions in American Anthropology: Thoughts Toward a History of the Interwar Years. *In* Selected Papers from the American Anthropologist, 1921–1945. G. Stocking, ed. Pp. 1–50. Washington, DC: American Anthropological Association.

Strathern, Andrew
  1985    Review: *Pigs for the Ancestors*. American Ethnologist 12:374–375.

Strathern, Marilyn
  1988    The Gender of the Gift: Problems with Women and Problems with Society in Melanesia. Berkeley: University of California Press.
  1992    Response. Pacific Studies 15(1):149–159.

————, ed.

   2000    Audit Cultures: Anthropological Studies in Accountability, Ethics and the Academy. Oxford, UK: Routledge.

Surowiecki, James

   2007    The Piracy Paradox. The New Yorker, September 24, p. 90.

Sutton, Douglas

   1990    Organization and Ontology: The Origins of the Northern Maori Chiefdom, New Zealand. Man 25(4):667–692.

Swidler, Nina

   1992    Kalat: The Political Economy of a Tribal Chiefdom. American Ethnologist 19(3):553–570.

Tarter, Andrew

   2016    Haiti Is Covered with Trees. EnviroSociety, May 19. http://www.envirosociety.org/2016/05/haiti-is-covered-with-trees/ (accessed August 6, 2018).

Taussig, Michael

   1980    The Devil and Commodity Fetishism in South America. Chapel Hill: University of North Carolina Press.

Taylor, Peter

   1993    Review: Unthinking Social Science by I. Wallerstein. Annals of the Association of American Geographers 83(3):551–553.

Templer, Robert

   1999    Shadows and Wind: A View of Modern Vietnam. New York: Penguin.

Tennekoon, N. Serena

   1988    Rituals of Development: The Accelerated Mahavali Development Program in Sri Lanka. American Ethnologist 15(2):294–310.

Tenner, Edward

   2018    The Efficiency Paradox: What Big Data Can't Do. New York: Knopf.

Thayer, James Steel

   1983    Nature, Culture, and the Supernatural among the Susu. American Ethnologist 10(1):116-132.

Thomas, Julian

   1987    Relations of Production and Social Change in the Neolithic of North-West Europe. Man 22:405–430.

Thomas, Landon

   2006    Confessing to the Converted. New York Times, February 19. https://www.nytimes.com/2006/02/19/business/yourmoney/confessing-to-the-converted.html (accessed August 6, 2018).

Thomas, Nicholas
  1996      Cold Fusion. American Anthropologist 98(1):9–16.

Thomas, William, ed.
  1956      Current Anthropology: A Supplement to Anthropology Today. Chicago:
           University of Chicago Press.

Thornton, Robert
  1983      Narrative Ethnography in Africa, 1850–1920: The Creation and Capture of
           an Appropriate Domain for Anthropology. Man 18(3):502–520.

Throsby, David
  2007      Dismal Still. Times Literary Supplement, September 7, p. 25.

Thurnwald, Richard
  1936      Review: *Sex and Temperament in Three Primitive Societies* by M. Mead.
           American Anthropologist 38:663–667.

Ticker, The
  2009      National Science Foundation Announces Pentagon-Financed Research
           Awards. Chronicle of Higher Education, October 2. https://www.chronicle
           .com/blogs/ticker/national-science-foundation-announces-pentagon
           -financed-research-awards/8317 (accessed August 6, 2018).

Tierney, Patrick
  2000      Darkness in El Dorado: How Scientists and Journalists Devastated the
           Amazon. New York: Norton.

Time
  2005      18 Heroes. Time Magazine, November 7, pp. 79–81.

Tocqueville, Alexis de
  1840      Democracy in America, vols. 1 and 2. New York: Random House.
  [1945]

Toren, Christina
  1988      Review: *Islands of History*. Critique of Anthropology 8(1):113–118.

Townsend, Robert
  2005      New Study Highlights Prominence of Elite PhD Programs in History. Per-
           spectives  (October):15–17.

Trask, Haunani-Kay
  1985      Review: *Islands of History* by M. Sahlins. American Ethnologist 12:784–785.

Trautmann, Thomas
  1992      The Revolution in Ethnological Time. Man 27(2):379–397.

Triandis, Harry, Roy Malpass, and Andrew Davidson
  1972      Cross-Cultural Psychology. *In* Biennial Review of Anthropology. B. Siegal,
           ed. Pp. 1–84. Stanford, CA: Stanford University Press.

Trigger, Bruce
  1991      Constraint and Freedom—A New Synthesis for Archeological Explana-
            tion. American Anthropologist 93(3):551–569.

Trotter, Robert, Jean Schensul, and Kristin Kostick
  2015      Theories and Methods in Applied Anthropology. *In* Handbook of Methods
            in Cultural Anthropology, H. Russell Bernard, and Clarence Gravlee, eds.
            New York: Rowman & Littlefield.

Trow, Martin
  2001      From Mass Higher Education to Universal Access: The American Ad-
            vantage. *In* In Defense of American Higher Education. P. G. Altbach, P. J.
            Gumport, and D. B. Johnstone, eds. Pp. 110–143. Baltimore, MD: Johns
            Hopkins University Press.

Turnbull, Colin
  1987      The Mountain People. New York: Simon and Schuster.

Turner, Victor
  1967      The Forest of Symbols: Aspects of Ndembu Ritual. Ithaca, NY: Cornell
            University Press.
  1968      Myth and Symbol. *In* International Encyclopedia of the Social Sciences,
            vol. 10. D. Sills, ed. New York: Macmillan.
  1969      The Ritual Process: Structure and Anti-Structure. Chicago: Aldine.
  1974      Dramas, Fields, and Metaphors: Symbolic Action in Human Society.
            Ithaca, NY: Cornell University Press.
  1975      Symbolic Studies. *In* Annual Review of Anthropology, vol. 4. B. Siegal, ed.
            Pp. 145-161. Palo Alto, CA: Annual Reviews.

United Kingdom's Research Councils
  n.d.      Embedding Public Engagement in Research. https://www.ukri.org/public
            -engagement/research-council-partners-and-public-engagement-with
            -research/embedding-public-engagement/ (accessed August 6, 2017).

University of North Carolina
  1997      Toward a Public Anthropology: Strategies and Prospects. University Ga-
            zette, March 26. http://gazette.unc.edu/archives/97mar26/file.54.html (no
            longer available).

UpFront
  2007      Profiles in Sycophancy. BusinessWeek, August 13, p. 12.

Utley, Francis Lee
  1974      The Migration of Folktales: Four Channels to the Americas. Current An-
            thropology 15(1):5–27.

Van Der Werf, Martin
  2009      Clemson Assails Allegations That It Manipulates "US News" Rankings.

Chronicle of Higher Education, June 4. https://www.chronicle.com/article/
Clemson-Assails-Allegations/47295 (accessed August 6, 2018).

Vance, J. D.
2016    Hillbilly Elegy: A Memoir of a Family and Culture in Crisis. New York:
        Harper.

Vansina, Jan
1961    Oral Tradition. Chicago: Aldine.
1966    Kingdoms of the Savanna. Madison: University of Wisconsin Press.
1968    L'evolution du Royaume Rwanda des Origines a 1900. Bruxelles (New
        York): Johnson Reprint.

Vaux, Tony
2001    The Selfish Altruist: Relief Work in Famine and War. Sterling, VA: Earth-
        scan.

Veblen, Thorstein
1918    The Higher Learning in America. New York: Huebsch.

Vedantam, Shankar
2006    Ants Are First Non-Humans To Teach, Study Says. Washington Post, Jan-
        uary 16. https://www.washingtonpost.com/archive/politics/2006/01/16/
        ants-are-first-non-humans-to-teach-study-says/229cec1b-6291-4667-b624
        -993cb4dc14c8/?utm_term=.ba434bb80d07 (accessed August 6, 2018).

Verdery, Katherine
1998    Transnationalism, Nationalism, Citizenship, and Property: Eastern Europe
        Since 1989. American Ethnologist 25(2):291–306.

Vergano, Dan
2000    *Darkness* Shadows Pursuit of Anthropology. USA Today, October 2. http://
        members.aol.com/nym1111111/darkness_in_el_dorado/documents/0203
        .htm (accessed June 2004).

Veysey, Laurence
1975    Who's a Professional? Who Cares? (Review: *Advocacy Objectivity* by
        M. Furner). American History 3(4):419–423.

Vicos
n.d.    Vicos: A Virtual Tour. http://courses.cit.cornell.edu/vicosperu/vicos-site/
        cornellperu_page_3.htm (accessed October 5, 2017).

Vidal, John
2005    Feed the World (Review: *The End of Poverty* by J. Sachs). Guardian, April
        22. https://www.theguardian.com/books/2005/apr/23/highereducation
        .news2 (accessed August 6, 2018).

Viegas, Susana de Matos
2003    Eating with Your Favourite Mother: Time and Sociality in a Brazilian

Amerindian Community. Journal of the Royal Anthropological Institute 9:21–37.

Vincent, Joan

1986     System and Process, 1974–1985. Annual Review of Anthropology (15):99–119.

Vogel, Gretchen, and Kai Kupferschmidt

2017     A Bold Open-Access Push in Germany Could Change the Future of Academic Publishing. Science, August 23. http://www.sciencemag.org/news/2017/08/bold-open-access-push-germany-could-change-future-academic-publishing?utm_campaign=news_weekly_2017-08-25&et_rid=79380147&et_cid=1511582 (accessed October 5, 2017).

Voget, Fred

1963     Cultural Change. In Biennial Review of Anthropology. B. Siegal, ed. Pp. 228–275. Stanford, CA: Stanford University Press.

1973     The History of Cultural Anthropology. In Handbook of Social and Cultural Anthropology. J. Honigmann, ed. Pp. 1–88. Chicago: Rand McNally.

1975     A History of Ethnology. New York: Holt, Rinehart and Winston.

Voosen, Paul

2015     Amid a Sea of False Findings, the NIH Tries Reform. Chronicle of Higher Education, March 16, p. A12. https://www.chronicle.com/article/Amid-a-Sea-of-False-Findings/228479 (accessed August 6, 2018).

Walker, Rob

2003     The Media Thing. New York Times Book Review, November 2, p. 34.

Wallace, Anthony F. C.

1952     The Modal Personality Structure of the Tuscarora Indians as Revealed by the Rorschach Test. Washington, DC: US Government Printing Office.

1961     Culture and Personality. New York: Random House.

1966     Review: The Revolution in Anthropology by I. C. Jarvie. American Anthropologist 68:1254–1255.

Wallace, Anthony F. C., and Raymond Fogelson

1962     Culture and Personality. In Biennial Review of Anthropology. B. Siegal, ed. Pp. 42–78. Stanford, CA: Stanford University Press.

Wallerstein, Immanuel

1974     The Modern World System, vol. 1. New York: Academic Books.

1980     The Modern World System, vol. 2. New York: Academic Press.

1989     The Modern World System, vol. 3. New York: Academic Press.

2001     Unthinking Social Science: The Limits of Nineteenth-Century Paradigms. Philadelphia: Temple University Press.

Ward, F. Champion
    1969    Review: *The Academic Revolution* by C. Jencks and D. Riesman. Ethics 80(1):74–75.

Warren, Kay B.
    2006    Perils and Promises of Engaged Anthropology: Historical Transitions and Ethnographic Dilemmas. *In* Engaged Observer: Anthropology, Advocacy, and Activism. Victoria Sanford and Asale Angel-Agani, eds. Pp. 213–227. New Brunswick, NJ: Rutgers University Press.

Wasley, Paula
    2007    Faculty-Productivity Index Offers Surprises. Chronicle of Higher Education, November 16, pp. A10–A12.
    2008    Tests Aren't Best Way to Evaluate Graduates' Skills, Business Leaders Say in Survey. Chronicle of Higher Education, January 23. https://www.chronicle.com/article/Tests-Arent-Best-Way-to/114460 (accessed August 6, 2018).

Wasserstrom, Jeffrey
    1998    Are You Now or Have You Ever Been . . . Postmodern? Chronicle of Higher Education, September 11, pp. B4–B5.

Watanabe, John M., and Barbara B. Smuts
    1999    Explaining Religion Without Explaining It Away: Trust, Truth, and the Evolution of Cooperation in Roy A. Rappaport's "The Obvious Aspects of Ritual." American Anthropologist 101(1):98–112.

Waters, Lindsay
    2001    Rescue Tenure from the Tyranny of the Monograph. Chronicle of Higher Education, April 20, pp. B7–B10.

Watkins, Bari
    1976    Review: *Advocacy and Objectivity. A Crisis in the Professionalization of American Social Science, 1865-1905* by Mary O. Furner. History and Theory 15(1):57–66.

Watson, James B.
    1969    Review: *Pigs for the Ancestors.* American Anthropologist 71:527–529.

Weber, Max
    1958    The Protestant Ethic and the Spirit of Capitalism. New York: Charles Scribner's Sons.

Weiner, Annette
    1976    Women of Value, Men of Renown: New Perspectives on Trobriand Exchange. Austin: University of Texas Press.
    1988    The Trobrianders of Papua New Guinea. New York: Holt, Rinehart, and Winston.

Weintraub, Ariene

    2008    Teaching Doctors—Or Selling to Them? BusinessWeek, August 11, pp. 26–28.

Weintraub, Philipp

    1941    Review: *Knowledge for What* by R. Lynd. Philosophical Review 50(3):323–325.

Wellmon, Chad, and Andrew Piper

    2017    Publication, Power, and Patronage: On Inequality and Academic Publishing. Critical Inquiry, October 2. http://criticalinquiry.uchicago.edu/publi cation_power_and_patronage_on_inequality_and_academic_publishing/ (accessed October 5, 2017).

Wengle, John

    1984    Anthropological Training and the Quest for Immortality. Ethos 12(3):223–244.

Wenner-Gren Foundation

    n.d.    Programs. Post-Ph.D. Research Grants. Application Procedures. Project Description Questions. http://www.wennergren.org/programs/post-phd -research-grants/application-procedures/project-description-questions (accessed October 5, 2017).

Werbner, Pnina

    2001    The Limits of Cultural Hybridity: On Ritual Monsters, Poetic License and Contested Postcolonial Purifications. Journal of the Royal Anthropological Institute 7(1):133–152.

Westbrook, Robert

    1991    John Dewey and American Democracy. Ithaca, NY: Cornell University Press.

    1992    Review: *The Origins of American Social Science* by D. Ross. Journal of American History 79(2):613–615.

    1994    Review: *Intellect and Public Life* by T. Bender. Journal of American History 80(4):1497–1498.

Westen, Drew

    1984    Cultural Materialism: Food for Thought or Bum Steer? Current Anthropology 25(5):639–653.

Westhoff, Laura

    1995    The Popularization of Knowledge: John Dewey on Experts and American Democracy. History of Education Quarterly 35(1):27–47.

Whalen, Michael E.

    1981    Cultural-Ecological Aspects of the Pithouse-to-Pueblo Transition in a Portion of the Southwest. American Antiquity 46(1):75–92.

Whipple, Mark
    2005    The Dewey-Lippmann Debate Today: Communication Distortions, Reflective Agency, and Participatory Democracy. Sociological Theory 23(2):156–178.

White, Leslie
    1959    The Evolution of Culture. New York: McGraw-Hill.
    1968    Culturology. *In* International Encyclopedia of the Social Sciences, vol. 3. D. Sills, ed. Pp. 547–551. New York: Macmillan.

White, Richard
    1992    Assessing the Consequences. American Ethnologist 19(1):155–159.

Whitehead, Neil
    1995    The Historical Anthropology of Text: The Interpretation of Raleigh's *Discoverie of Guiana*. Current Anthropology 36(1):53–74.

Whiteley, Peter
    1987    The Interpretation of Politics: A Hopi Conundrum. Man 22:696–714.

Whiting, Beatrice Blyth, ed.
    1963    Six Cultures: Studies in Child Rearing. New York: John Wiley & Sons.

Whiting, Beatrice Blyth, and John W. M. Whiting with Richard Longabaugh
    1975    Children of Six Cultures: A Psycho-Cultural Analysis. Cambridge: Harvard University Press.

Whiting, J. W. M., et al.
    1966    Field Guide for a Study of Socialization. Six Cultures Series, vol. 1. New York: John Wiley & Sons.

Whitman, Alden
    1978    Carter Mourns Anthropologist: Margaret Mead Is Dead of Cancer at 76. New York Times, November 16, p. A1.

Whitten, Norman
    1988    Toward a Critical Anthropology. American Ethnologist 15(4):732–742.

WIC, Margaret Mead
    n.d.    S.v. "Margaret Mead. Tribute to Greatness." http://www.wic.org/bio/mmead.htm (accessed August 6, 2018).

Wiebe, Robert
    1967    The Search for Order, 1877–1920. New York: Hill and Wang.

Wierzbicka, Anna
    1984    Apples Are Not a "Kind of Fruit": The Semantics of Human Categorization. American Ethnologist 11(2):313–328.
    1988    Emotions Across Culture: Similarities and Differences. American Anthropologist 90(4):982–983.

Wikipedia (various entries accessed October 5, 2017)
  Anthropology
  Boat People
  Carlos Castaneda
  Cold Fusion
  Confessions of an Economic Hit Man
  Edward Snowden
  The End of Poverty
  Franz Boas
  The Golden Bough
  Hillbilly Elegy
  John Ioannidis
  Noam Chomsky
  Operation Bid Rig
  Primum non nocere
  Project Camelot
  Pukapuka
  The Structure of Scientific Revolutions
  Thomas Samuel Kuhn
  Vietnam War
  Vietnam War Casualties
  William Easterly

Wilk, Richard
  2013     Anthropology Until Only Yesterday. American Anthropologist, August
           20. http://onlinelibrary.wiley.com/doi/10.1111/aman.12038_1/full/ (accessed
           October 5, 2017).

Williams, Vernon
  1991     Review: *Franz Boas—Social Activist* by M. Hyatt. Transforming Anthro-
           pology 2(2):18.

Williams, Wendy, and Stephen Ceci
  2007     Does Tenure Really Work? Chronicle of Higher Education, March 9,
           p. B16.

Willis, Paul
  1981     Learning to Labor. New York: Columbia University Press.

Wilsdon, James, et al.
  2015     The Metric Tide: Report of the Independent Review of the Role of Metrics
           in Research Assessment and Management. HEFCE. http://www.hefce.ac
           .uk/pubs/rereports/year/2015/metrictide/ (accessed August 6, 2018).

Wilson, Godfrey, and Monica Wilson
  1945     The Analysis of Social Change, Based on Observations in Central Africa.
           Cambridge, UK: Cambridge University Press.

Wilson, Robin

1998    Harvard Professors Are Cited Most by Major Academic Journals, Study
Finds. Chronicle of Higher Education, October 28. https://www.chronicle
.com/article/Harvard-Professors-Are-Cited/104518 (accessed August 6,
2018).

2009    Downturn Threatens the Faculty's Role in Running Colleges (Attack
on Faculty Governance: Professors Decry Lost Influence). Chronicle of
Higher Education, February 6, p. 1.

Wissler, Clark

1914    The Influence of the Horse in the Development of Plains Culture. American Anthropologist 16:1–25.

1917    The American Indian: An Introduction to the Anthropology of the New
World. New York: McMurtrie.

Wobst, H. Martin

1978    The Archaeo-Ethnology of Hunter-Gatherers or the Tyranny of the Ethnographic Record in Archaeology. American Antiquity 43(2):303–309.

Wolcott, Harry

2007    The Middleman of MACOS. Anthropology and Education Quarterly
(38):195–206.

Wolf, Eric

1957    Closed Corporate Peasant Communities in Mesoamerica and Central Java.
Southwestern Journal of Anthropology 13:1–18.

1969    American Anthropologists and American Society. *In* Concepts and
Assumptions in Contemporary Anthropology. S. A. Tyler, ed. Pp. 3–11.
Athens: University of Georgia Press.

1974    Anthropology. New York: Norton.

1980    They Divide and Subdivide and Call It Anthropology. New York Times,
December 14, p. 20.

1982    Europe and the People Without History. Berkeley: University of California
Press.

1990    Facing Power—Old Insights, New Questions. American Anthropologist
92:586–596.

1999    Cognizing "Cognized Models." American Anthropologist 101(1):19–22.

Wolf, Eric, and Joseph Jorgensen

1970    Anthropology on the Warpath in Thailand. New York Review of Books,
November 19, pp. 26–35.

Wolf, Martin

2007    How the Bottom Billion Are Trapped (Review: *The Bottom Billion* by
P. Collier). Financial Times, May 13. https://www.ft.com/content/4858ed7e
-0178-11dc-8b8c-000b5df10621 (accessed August 6, 2018).

Worsley, Peter
    1984    A Landmark in Anthropology (Review: *Europe and the People Without History*). American Ethnologist 11(1):170–175.

Worster, Donald
    2001    A River Running West: The Life of John Wesley Powell. New York: Oxford University Press.

Wright, Austin
    2009    U. of Alaska Journalism Students to Embed with Combat Team in Iraq. Chronicle of Higher Education, July 27. https://www.chronicle.com/article/U-of-Alaska-Journalism/47476 (accessed August 6, 2018).

Wyndham, Susan
    1995a    Making a Meal of Cook. Star-Times, July 30, p. C8.
    1995b    Scholars at Sea on Cook's Endeavors. Australian, July 20, p. 1.

Yagoda, Ben
    1998    Using an Electronic Data Base to Detect Current Clichés. Chronicle of Higher Education, July 10, p. B6.

Yalman, Nur
    1964    Review: *La Pensee Sauvage* by C. Lévi-Strauss. American Anthropologist 66:1179–1182.

Yang, Mayfair Mei-Hui
    1989    The Gift Economy and State Power in China. Comparative Studies in Society and History 31(1):25–54.

Yetish, Gandhi, et al.
    2015    Natural Sleep and Its Seasonal Variations in Three Pre-Industrial Societies. Current Biology 25(21:2862–2868). http://www.cell.com/current-biology/fulltext/S0960-9822(15)01157-4 (accessed October 5, 2017).

Yunus, Muhammad
    2007    Creating a World Without Poverty: Social Business and the Future of Capitalism. New York: Public Affairs.

Zaid, Gabriel
    2003    So Many Books. Philadelphia: Paul Dry Books.

Zubrow, Ezra
    1972    Environment, Subsistence, and Society: The Changing Archaeological Perspective. Annual Review of Anthropology 1:179–206.

Abbott, Andrew, 16, 49, 110, 115, 128, 206
Abdul Latif Jameel Poverty Action Lab
    (J-PAL), 154, 155, 178–80, 226
Abui. *See* Atimelang
academic accountability. *See* accountabil-
    ity; faculty accountability
academic advancement, 119
    advancing knowledge and, 29, 107–9,
        150
    "benefitting others" and, 146
    "bump and go" citation pattern and, 113,
        130 (*see also* citation patterns)
    "do no harm" paradigm and, 41 (*see also*
        *under* "do no harm" paradigm)
    mentors and, 116
    public appearance and the politics of,
        108–10
    public engagement and, 146, 211
    publications and, 19, 26–27, 107, 134–35
    *See also* accountability standards; faculty
        accountability; status advancement
Academic Analytics, 197–99
academic careerism. *See* accountability
    standards; publications: quantity (vs.
    quality) of
academic standards of accountability. *See*
    accountability standards
accountability, 32, 33, 121, 197, 203
    definition and scope of the term, 33, 34
    "do no harm" paradigm and, 34, 121,
        202, 204
    pressure on universities for greater,
        200–203, 222–23
    public engagement and, 132
    *See also* faculty accountability
accountability standards, 107–9, 116,

120–21, 133, 145, 146, 202, 203, 213,
    220–22
administrators, anthropologists, and,
    107, 145–46, 202–3, 207, 212, 213,
    215, 222, 228
administrators, government officials,
    and, 222
changing control over, 202–4
faculty wishing to change, 204
framed in terms of publications, 25,
    29–30, 36, 43, 197 (*see also* publica-
    tions: quantity [vs. quality] of)
hegemonic-like structures and, 145, 202,
    213, 215
metric assessment standards, 202–5,
    210–13, 222, 228–30
transparency and, 35, 36, 156, 158, 188
universities and, 27–29, 34, 202–3
using flexibility in accountability
    standards to facilitate change,
    215–16
*See also* faculty accountability; intellec-
    tual advances: in cultural anthro-
    pology; publications: quantity (vs.
    quality) of
activism, 131, 176–77, 180
    objectivity and, 11, 12, 121 (*see also under*
        objectivity)
    scholar-activists, 14, 214 (*see also* Boas,
        Franz; Farmer, Paul; Mead,
        Margaret)
    universities seeking to limit faculty's,
        11
    *See also* advocacy
administrators and anthropologists, 25,
    141, 215–17, 222

administrators and anthropologists
(*continued*)
accountability standards, metrics, and,
107, 145–46, 202–3, 207, 212, 213,
215, 222, 228
animosity between, 143, 217
collaboration and, 163
disconnect between, 143
advocacy, 11–14. *See also* activism
*Advocacy and Objectivity: A Crisis in the
Professionalization of American Social
Science, 1865–1905* (Furner), 11–13
African societies, witchcraft among, 6–7
Agroforestry Outreach Project, 150–52
Albert, Bruce, 170–71
Alor Island, 68. *See also* Du Bois, Cora
America COMPETES Act (ACA) of
2007, 32, 186
American Anthropological Association
(AAA), 158, 209, 212
Boasians and, 20–21
codes of ethics, 27, 138, 141
El Dorado Task Force, 139, 209
journals, 42, 114, 206
membership, 127, 206
Napoleon Chagnon and, 139–40
Principles of Professional
Responsibility, 159
Yanomami and, 139–40, 209
*See also American Anthropologist*
*American Anthropologist*, 124–25
book reviews, 42, 73–74
books not reviewed in, 42, 83, 90–91
comparison articles (controlled) in, 223
Geertz's writings and, 42, 83, 85, 91
lack of subfield integration in articles
published in, 22–23
"Public Anthropologies" section, 124
special issue honoring Roy Rappaport, 79
Americentrism. *See* Vietnam War:
American ethnocentrism in
analytics in higher education. *See*
Academic Analytics
Angell, Marcia, 13
anthropological messages, structures that
enhance, 178–80
anthropological publications, xi, 214, 228
and the advancement of knowledge,
xi–xii, 215, 216, 218, 229–30
in *American Anthropologist*, 22–23

diversity of topics, 228
public audiences and, 217, 219, 225, 228
"purity," "pollution," and the "turned
inward" quality of many, 115, 128,
207–8 (*see also* cultural anthropologists: "turned inward" quality)
standards in assessing, 215, 216, 229–30
(*see also* accountability standards;
publishing standards)
winners and losers in the push to
publish uncertain, ambiguous
knowledge, 119–21
*See also* anthropology departments:
faculty publications; publications;
publishing
anthropological subfields, 21–23. *See also*
cultural anthropology: specialized
studies and specializations within
anthropologists, 16, 18
engagement with other professionals,
72, 77, 79, 85, 87, 92–93, 95, 104, 106,
113 (*see also* citations)
establishing a distinct intellectual
identity, 116
finances, 121, 134–35
historical changes in the number of, 127,
206–7
reproducing themselves, 16, 17, 19, 133
who have spoken out about social and
political issues, 9 (*see also* activism;
advocacy)
why they don't follow in the footsteps of
Boas, Mead, and Farmer, 11–15
*See also* cultural anthropologists; *specific
topics*
anthropology, xi–xii, 9, 15
definition and scope of, 15, 17–18
Eric Wolf's characterization of,
226n71 (*see also* Wolf, Eric: on
anthropology)
reproducing itself, 16, 17, 19, 133
traditions in, 49–50
uncertain public status, 205–6
universities and, 19 (*see also* anthropology departments)
*See also* cultural anthropology; *specific
topics*
*Anthropology as Cultural Critique* (Marcus
and Fischer), 96, 97nn143–45, 99, 100,
101n156, 103, 104

anthropology courses, 17, 18, 37
  on public anthropology, 125
  *See also* Man: A Course of Study
anthropology degrees completed,
      diminishing number of, 206–7
anthropology departments, 15–18, 21, 128,
      215–16
  administrators and, 25 (*see also* adminis-
      trators and anthropologists)
  applied anthropology and, 133
  competition with other departments,
      22, 120
  disciplinary integration vs. intellectual
      fragmentation within, 23
  faculty assessments and, 212 (*see also*
      faculty accountability)
  faculty publications, 120, 206, 208 (*see
      also* anthropological publications)
  finances, 120
  how departmental structure shapes the
      discipline's self-image, 19–23
  status, 117–18, 120
  *See also specific topics*
anthropology faculty, 28. *See also under*
      anthropology departments
anthropology journals, 42, 85, 114, 206.
      *See also American Anthropologist*;
      peer-review process
"anthropology of anthropology," xii, 24
anthropology professors. *See* faculty
anti-structural rituals, 80
anti-structure, 82, 131, 132
Antrosio, Jason, 208
Appel, Jacob, 155
Appiah, K. Anthony, 137
applied anthropologists, 17, 133
applied anthropology, 21, 150–51
  differentiating between public anthro-
      pology and, 128–30
  mainstream academic anthropology
      and, 133
  nature of, 130, 133
  roots/origins, 129
  straddling of the academic/nonaca-
      demic divide, 17
  uses and connotations of the term, 130
*Applied Anthropology* (journal), 17, 129
Arab countries, women and gender roles
      in, 8
Arab Spring, 225

Arkin, William, 183–84
Asad, Talal, 90n128, 98n149
assessment standards. *See* accountability
      standards
Atimelang (Alor Island, East Nusa
      Tenggara, Indonesia), 68–70
attrition warfare in Vietnam War, 190,
      192–93

bands (stage of cultural evolution), 73
Banerjee, Abhijit, 154–56, 178, 179
Bangladesh, 180
Bannister, M. E., 151–53, 155
Barrett, Stanley, 46
Barth, Fredrik, 174
Basken, Paul, 38–39
Beaglehole, Earnest, 61–62
Beaglehole, Pam, 61–62
Beals, Ralph, 136, 158
*Bell Curve, The* (Herrnstein and Murray),
      161
Beltrán, Pedro, 144
Benedict, Ruth, 126–27
beneficence, 134. *See also* "benefitting
      others"
"benefitting others" (paradigm), 124, 131,
      133–46, 208, 217–21
  advancing knowledge and, 218
  complications in, 145
  vs. "do no harm," 31, 32, 123, 124, 139,
      216
  nature of, 145
  *See also* collaboration; public
      anthropology
Berdahl, Robert, 202
Bloland, Sue Erikson, 229
Boas, Franz, 9
  activism, 9, 131, 132, 158
  Alfred Kroeber and, 51, 52, 116
  characterizations of, 19, 20
  contextual analysis and, 6n6
  evolution, evolutionists, and, 20, 51
  in historical context, 19, 20
  public engagement, 126, 127
  racist theories, race and culture, and,
      9, 131
  readership, 126, 127
  skepticism regarding historical
      speculation used in wide-ranging
      comparisons, 51

Boas, Franz (continued)
    students of (and Boasians), 20–21, 51–52,
        116
    writings, 9, 51
        letter to The Nation, 158
        The Mind of Primitive Man, 9
Borofsky, Amelia, 160
Bourdieu, Pierre, 214
Bourgois, Philippe, 142, 174–75, 214
BRAC (organization), 180
Brandeis, Louis, 158
Brazil, 139, 170–72. See also Yanomami
breast implants, 13–14
"broader impacts," 32–33, 35, 187
    defined, 32–33
Burke, Peter, 43–44
Burton, Sandra, 58–59
Butterfield, Fox, 191, 193

California Series in Public Anthropology,
    37, 125
capitalism, 90n130, 91, 93
capitalist mode of production, 90n130
career advancement. See academic
    advancement
careerism. See accountability standards;
    publications: quantity (vs. quality) of
Carey, Benedict, 53–54, 56
Castaneda, Carlos, 58–59
Center for a Public Anthropology, 170,
    171, 187–88, 192
    Community Action Project, 170, 171
Chagnon, Napoleon, 139–41, 160–61
chiefdoms (stage of cultural evolution), 73
Chomsky, Noam, 14–15
citation patterns, "bump and go," 79, 87,
    106, 113, 130
citation system, 120, 221
citations, 197, 216
    citation counts and quantity of, 65, 78,
        79, 85–87, 94–95, 104–5, 197, 198,
        204, 216
    and faculty accountability and credibil-
        ity, 30, 114, 115, 118, 120, 197
    and quality of writings, 34–35, 113
    reasons for, 45, 65, 77–78, 85
    significance and implications of, 113
citizenship, global, 18
Clark, William, 109, 197
Clayton, Victoria, 38, 221

Clifford, James, 101n156, 118
    citations to, 104–5
    on colonial domination, 135
    on ethnography and ethnographers,
        98, 135
    postmodernism and, 97n142, 117–18 (see
        also Writing Culture)
    See also Writing Culture
closed corporate communities, 7
collaboration, 26, 31–32, 161–64, 169
    across subfields, 23
    for bringing ideas to life beyond the
        academy, 31, 225–27
    challenges and complications involved
        in, 162–64
    examples of (see also Yanomami blood
        samples)
        Man: A Course of Study, 164–67,
            169
        Partners in Health (PIH), 10, 162,
            167–69, 179, 226
    as a strategy for change, 162
    See also cultural anthropology: building
        a broader constituency of support
        for; cultural anthropology: exog-
        amy problem of; interdisciplinary
        studies
collaborative articles across subfields,
    number of, 23
Colley, Linda, 21–22
Collins, Francis, 34, 203
colonialism, 7, 135
    anthropology and, 129, 133–35, 141
Colson, Elizabeth, 45
Coming of Age in Samoa (Mead), 10,
    100n153, 177
commodity-oriented economies, 102
"common good," advancing the. See
    "benefitting others"
common ground, 174
communities, 82
Community Action Project (Center for a
    Public Anthropology), 170, 171
comparative analysis, 3. See also compari-
    sons: controlled
comparative fallacy, 59, 65, 71, 161, 224
comparisons
    controlled, 6–8 (see also comparative
        analysis)
    used to ask big questions, 223–25

confirmation (of research findings), 48, 54, 56, 112, 156
  objectivity and, 11, 13, 35
  transparency and, 34–36, 56, 158, 160
  *See also* replicability of studies; reproducibility
controlled comparisons. *See* comparisons: controlled
Cook, James, 92n135
  apotheosis (as *Lono*), 63–65, 95
  background, 66
  death, 87, 91–92
  Makahiki and, 64, 91–92
  Marshall Sahlins and, 62–63, 87, 91, 93, 95 (*see also* Sahlins–Obeyesekere controversy)
  voyages of, 126
  third voyage, 62–63, 65, 91, 126
Cook Islands. *See* Pukapukans
Coordinated Investigation of Micronesian Anthropology (CIMA), 142–45, 217, 218
*Cows, Pigs, Wars, and Witches: The Riddles of Culture* (Harris), 75–77. *See also* Harris, Marvin
crisis in cultural anthropology, 196–204
  hegemonic-like structures and, 207
  and paradigm shift, 24–25, 195–97, 204
  *See also Advocacy and Objectivity*
"crisis of representation," 97, 99
Crossen, William, 191–92
cultural anthropologists
  problems facing, 204–5, 210–13 (*see also* crisis in cultural anthropology)
  cultural anthropology's diminished role, 205–7
  hesitancy to challenge the status quo, 207–10
  role of, 163
  "turned inward" quality, 115, 204, 225, 227, 228 (*see also under* anthropological publications; cultural anthropology: exogamy problem of)
  who have made contributions to broader society, 8–11 (*see also specific topics*)
  why they fail to change public policy, 173–77
  *See also* anthropologists; *specific topics*
cultural anthropology, xi–xii, 1
  building a broader constituency

of support for, 216–27 (*see also* collaboration)
  choice facing the field of, 228
  controversies in, 59–66
  current status of, 205–6
  diminished role of, 205–7
  dominating trends in, 66–67
    assessing cultural ecology, 72–80
    assessing culture and personality, 67–72
    assessing interpretations of myths, symbolism, and ritual, 80–87
    assessing postmodernism, 96–106
    assessing the (Re)Turn to History, 87–95
  ethnographic tools of, 3–8
  exogamy problem of, xi, 218, 225, 228 (*see also* collaboration; cultural anthropologists: "turned inward" quality)
  how departmental structure shapes the discipline's self-image, 19–23
  potential, 1
  "pure," 208
  scope of, 18
  specialized studies and specializations within, 18–19, 117 (*see also* anthropological subfields)
    problems with specialization, 119
  ways academic contexts shape the practice of, 15–19
  *See also* anthropology; crisis in cultural anthropology; *specific topics*
cultural context, understanding, 3–6
cultural critique, 100, 101, 205
  defined, 205
  *See also Anthropology as Cultural Critique*
cultural distinctions and cultural boundaries, 174
cultural domination, law of, 73
cultural ecology, assessing, 72–80
cultural evolution, 72–73
  stages of, 73
  theory of, 72–73 (*see also Evolution and Culture*)
  *See also* cultural materialism
cultural materialism, 72, 75, 76. *See also* cultural evolution
cultural reproduction, 63, 91, 92n135

culture and personality
  assessing, 67–72
  models for conceptualizing the relation
    between, 69–70
Curriculum Development Associates
  (CDA), 166–67
Cushing, Frank Hamilton, 129

Dahl, Ophelia, 179
Darwin, Charles, 196
Davis, John, 46
Davis, Wade, 208
Daws, Gavan, 93
Deaton, Angus, 121
deforestation problem in Haiti, 152–53
Dewey, John, 162–63
Diamond, Jared, 208–9, 223
disciplinary integration, 23. *See also*
  collaboration; interdisciplinary
  studies
diversity, organization of. *See* organization
  of diversity
"do no harm" paradigm, 27–28, 32, 34, 41,
  204
  AAA's codes of ethics and, 27, 138, 141
  AAA's Principles of Professional
    Responsibility and, 138
  accountability and, 34, 121, 202, 204
  and advancing knowledge, 41, 121
  vs. "benefitting others," 31, 32, 123, 124,
    139, 216
  faculty interests and, 40, 41, 121, 145,
    210
  Hippocratic Oath and, 136 (*see also*
    "first, do no harm")
  moving beyond "do no harm" to helping
    improve people's lives, 217–21
  overview and nature of, 27–28
  principles on which it centers, 28
  problems with, 121, 136–37, 141, 210, 217
  vs. public anthropology paradigm, 27,
    40, 123, 133, 139, 145, 196, 211
  specialization and, 119
  universities and, 27, 32, 34, 121, 202
  Vietnam War and, 181
Don Juan, 58–59
Dorsey, George A., 129
Doughty, Paul, 144
Douglas, Mary, 115, 128, 207–8
Dow, Peter, 164–67

Du Bois, Cora
  Atimelang and, 68–70
  on child-rearing practices, 67, 68, 70
  on culture and personality, 67–71
  honors and positions held by, 131
  research methodology and, 68, 69, 71
Dubois, Laurent, 152–53
Duflo, Esther, 154–56, 178, 179

East Sepik (province in Papua New
  Guinea), 67–68
ecology
  "new," 76
  *See also* cultural ecology
Edgewater (district of San Francisco),
  174–75
education. *See* anthropology courses;
  anthropology degrees completed;
  teaching anthropology
Educational Development Center (EDC),
  165–67
educational reform movement, 164
Educational Services Incorporated (ESI),
  164–65
Edwards, Marc, 198
Eggan, Fred, 223–24
elementary school programs, 164. *See also*
  Man: A Course of Study
Ely, Richard T., 12–13
Ember, Carol, 21
Ember, Melvin, 21
Erikson, Erik H., 229
Errington, Frederick, 71n76
ethical issues
  AAA's codes of ethics, 27, 138, 141
  *See also* "do no harm" paradigm
ethnic conflict, reduction of, 174
ethnic groups and the organization of
  ethnicity, 174. *See also specific topics*
ethnocentrism, 101. *See also under* Vietnam
  War
ethnographers, 142. *See also specific topics*
ethnographies, 219–20
  standards for assessing, 100
  *See also specific topics*
Eubanks, Virginia, 222
European Union (EU) and National
  Security Administration (NSA), 182,
  184
Evans-Pritchard, E. E., 129

*Evolution and Culture* (Sahlins and
Service), 72–73, 74n85, 77
evolutionary potential, law of, 73
explanation, interpretive. *See*
interpretivism

fabricating data, 35, 48, 57n46
faculty, 203. *See also* academic advance-
ment; status; status advancement
faculty accountability, 197
fostering alternative forms of, 43,
145–46, 204, 213
Abhijit Banerjee, Esther Duflo, and
Dean Karlan, 154–56
in anthropology, 158–61
Gerald F. Murray, 150–54
Jeffrey Sachs, 147–50
transparency and, 156–58
public anthropology and, 40
*See also* accountability standards
Falgout, Suzanne, 143
Fanelli, Daniele, 54
Farmer, Paul, 8, 10–11, 179–80, 214
Fassin, Didier, 176–77
Federal Bureau of Investigation (FBI) and
Nancy Scheper-Hughes, 185–86
female subordination, 8. *See also* gender
roles
Fenton, William, 20
fiction, anthropological works of, 58–59
Filiu, Jean-Pierre, 225
Finney, Ben, 130
"first, do no harm," 27, 136, 217. *See also* "do
no harm" paradigm
Firth, Raymond, 127–28
Fischer, Michael M. J., 96, 97n143, 101,
103–5, 118
*Anthropology as Cultural Critique*, 96,
97nn143–45, 99, 100, 104
citations to, 104–5
on crisis of representation, 99
on ethnography, 96, 99n151, 100, 101n156
postmodernism and, 117–18
Flynn, Michael, 182
Foucault, Michel, 87–89, 89n127
citations to, 93, 94
*Discipline and Punish: The Birth of the
Prison*, 89
Eric Wolf and, 91–94
Marshall Sahlins and, 92–94

(Re)Turn to History trend and, 87, 88
Frank, Barney, 178n14
fraud, 47–48, 53, 55, 58, 59, 61. *See also*
retractions in academic publishing
Frazer, James, 116, 126–27
Freidson, Eliot, 163n106
French police and prisons, 176
Frost, Robert, 227–29
funding. *See* research funding
Fung, Archon, 181
Furner, Mary, 11–13, 25, 27

Geertz, Clifford, 5, 15–16
and analysis of symbols, myths, and
rituals, 80–81, 83–84
citations to, 85–86, 115
on culture, 83
*The Interpretation of Cultures*, 42, 83–84,
91
on interpretive explanation, 50
Lévi-Strauss and, 84–86
on Obeyesekere, 64
on science and anthropology, 50
on thick description, 83
Victor Turner and, 84–86
*Gender of the Gift, The* (Strathern), 96,
101–4
gender roles, 7–8, 102
Margaret Mead and, 67–68, 70, 101,
106
Giáp, Võ Nguyên, 190
gift-oriented economies, 102
Givens, David, 209
Glasziou, Paul, 35–36, 157
global citizenship, 18
Goldacre, Ben, 157–58
Goldschmidt, Walter, 101n156
Golub, Rex, 208
good
definitions, 123–24
doing, 123 (*see also* "benefitting others")
Goodenough, Ward, 217
Graeber, David, 27, 199–200, 209–10
Graham, Mary, 181
Gramsci, Antonio
hegemonic-like structures and, 211, 212
on hegemony, 24–27, 207
grant proposals/grant applications, 33, 44,
108, 109, 200, 216. *See also* National
Science Foundation

grants, 34, 108, 202, 203
  NIH and, 33, 34
  *See also* National Science Foundation
guest authorship, 26
Gwari, witchcraft among, 6–7

Haiti, 179
  deforestation problem, 152–53
  Partners in Health (PIH) and, 168–69,
    179
  reforesting, 150–55, 218
Halberstam, David, 189, 191–92
Haro, Lia, 149–50
Harris, Marvin, 46, 76, 101n156
  activism, 131
  citations to, 77, 78
  cultural ecology and, 72
  on ecological/evolutionary theory/
    cultural materialism, 75
  on evolution, 77
  positivism of, 50
  Roy Rappaport and, 76–77
  writings, 75–77
Hawaii, 93
  Sahlins and, 62–65, 87–88, 91, 92n135,
    95, 106
  third voyage of James Cook, 62–63, 91
Hawaii Pacific University, 18
Hawaiian Cultural Renaissance, 130
Hawaiian rituals, 64, 91–92, 92n135
health care. *See* medical research; Partners
  in Health
hegemon/hegemony
  elements of, 25
  Gramsci's concept of, 24–26, 207
hegemonic-like structures (of the
  academy), 24, 43, 44, 162, 163, 202,
    207, 213, 226, 227, 229
  academic publishing and, 25–26, 36–39,
    207, 213, 215, 230
  accountability standards and, 145, 202,
    213, 215
  challenging, 109–10, 210
  funding agencies and, 32–34
  Gramsci and, 207, 211, 212
  historical perspective on, 215
  limitations, 212
  overview and nature of, 25, 31–32
  public anthropology paradigm and,
    131–33, 211

that shape cultural anthropology,
    understanding the, 213–15
  universities and, 34–36
hegemonic-like system, embracing the,
    230
Hereniko, Vilsoni, 135
heroin addicts, 174–75
Herrnstein, Richard, 161
hierarchies, social, 82, 132. *See also* status
  hierarchy
High Plains, Indians of the, 224
Higher Education Act of 1965 (HEA),
    201
historical anthropology, 63, 91
history. *See* (Re)Turn to History trend
Hochschild, Arlie, 219–21
Holmberg, Alan, 143–44, 218
Holy, Ladislav, 223
homeless, 175
Horton, Richard, 55
Hughes, David, 198
human interrelatedness, models of, 82

Ik people in Uganda, 136, 137
informants, 99, 101, 136, 138n51, 141, 222
Innovations for Poverty Action (IPA), 154,
    155, 178
intellectual advances
  anthropologists and, 107
  anthropology departments and, 19, 215,
    216
  and benefitting others, 29, 121, 218
  career advancement and, 29, 107–9, 150
    (*see also* academic advancement)
  in cultural anthropology, standards to
    measure, 49–53 (*see also* account-
    ability standards)
  assessing whether researchers are
    living up to, 53–66
  defining, 203
  exogamy problem and, 225
  funding and, 29, 44, 108, 121 (*see
    also under* National Science
    Foundation)
  generated by publications, questioning
    the, 43–47
  broadening the critique, 47–49
  taking note of positive, 106–7
  traditions in anthropology and, 49–50
  universities and, 29, 107–8

validity of studies and, 53
*See also* cultural anthropology:
    dominating trends in; intellectual
    progress
intellectual competence, assessment of,
    25–26, 29–31, 37, 40, 204. *See also*
    accountability standards
intellectual progress, 49, 80, 84, 87, 96, 109
    accountability and, 107
    anthropology's commitment to, 21
    culture and personality studies and,
        70, 71
    historical perspective on, 43–44
    publications and, 35–36, 51, 52, 79–80,
        107–8, 114, 118, 210, 215, 216
    (Re)turn to History studies and, 92
    *See also* intellectual advances
interdisciplinary studies, 15, 16, 18. *See*
    *also* collaboration; disciplinary
    integration
*Interpretation of Cultures, The* (Geertz), 42,
    83–84, 91
Interpreting Myths, Symbols, and Rituals
    trend, 66, 110
    assessing interpretations of myths,
        symbolism, and ritual, 80–87
interpretive theory and interpretive
    analysis, 83, 84
interpretivism, 50, 51
Ioannidis, John, 47, 54
Islamic states, 7–8, 225

Jamieson, Neil, 189
Jarvie, J. C., 101
Jones, Robert J., 146, 211
Jorgensen, Joseph, 158–59
journals. *See* anthropology journals
J-PAL (Abdul Latif Jameel Poverty
    Action Lab), 154, 155, 178–80, 226
Jump, Paul, 199, 200–201

Kardiner, Abram, 68–69
Karlan, Dean, 154–56
Karnow, Stanley, 190
Kennedy, Edward M., 144
Kerns, Virginia, 116
Kidder, Tracy, 179–80
Kim, Jim Yong, 179
King, Barbara, 208, 223
Kiste, Robert C., 143

Kluckhohn, Clyde, 15
knowledge. *See* intellectual advances;
    intellectual progress
Kroeber, Alfred, 21, 51–52, 116
Kuhn, Thomas S., 32n69
    on paradigm shifts, 24–25, 195–97, 229
    on paradigms, 24–26, 195
    on rejection of ideas that challenge the
        consensus, 109
Kuper, Adam, 50, 108

LaCour, Michael, 56
Lambert, William W., 71n78
Lamont, Michèle, 109
Lee, Stephanie, 56–57
Lemann, Nicholas, 161
Lévi-Strauss, Claude
    anthropologists and, 106
    on anthropology, 81, 135, 226n71
    citations to, 85–86
    Clifford Geertz and, 80–81, 84–86
    on colonialism, 135
    criticism of, 81, 84
    on myths, 80, 81
    overview, 81
    Victor Turner and, 83–85
Lewis, Oscar, 14, 60–61
lineage unity, principle of, 224
Linton, Ralph, 21
Lippmann, Walter, 162–63
Lowie, Robert, 101n156, 116
Lynch, Barbara, 144–45

MacLeod, Malcolm, 157
Makahiki, 64, 91–92
Malinowski, Bronislaw, 3–4, 52
Man: A Course of Study (MACOS),
    164–67, 169
Marcus, George E., 101n156, 118, 205
    *Anthropology as Cultural Critique*, 96,
        97nn143–45, 99, 100, 104
    citations to, 104–5
    on crisis of representation, 99
    on ethnography and ethnographers, 98,
        99nn151–52, 100, 101n156
    postmodernism and, 96, 99, 100, 117–18
    (*see also Writing Culture*)
Marshall, Mac, 142–43
Marx, Karl, 213
Mason, Leonard, 53

matrilocality, 62
McCormack, Todd, 179
McNutt, Marcia, 123, 146
Mead, Margaret, 8–11, 71, 126–28, 131
　activism, 10
　Chambri/Tchambuli and, 71n76
　cultural, personality, and, 68, 70
　as cultural icon, 9–10
　gender and, 67–68, 70, 101, 106
　overview and characterizations of, 9–10,
　　67
　writings, 67
　　*Coming of Age in Samoa*, 10, 100n153,
　　　177
measles vaccination, 55–56, 140
medical publications, 26, 35–36, 47
　retracted, 53–56
medical research
　controversies in, 13–14
　fraud in, 47–48, 54, 157–58
　methodological problems in, 35–36, 47,
　　54, 156–57
　transparency in, 55–56, 157–58
　*See also* National Institutes of Health
Melanesians, 101, 102
mentors, 116
Merry, Sally Engle, 200, 222
metric assessment standards. *See under*
　accountability standards
Micronesians, 142–45, 217, 218
Millennium Villages Project, 147–50, 154
minimum publishable units, 26–27
Minturn, Leigh, 71n78
modernism, 97
Mooney, James, 20, 129, 131
Morduch, Jonathan, 147
Morgan, Lewis Henry, 20
Mullainathan, Sendhil, 178
Munk, Nina, 147–50, 154
Murray, Charles, 161
Murray, Gerald F., 150–54
　reforestation in Haiti, 150–55, 218
Muslim women, 7–8
myths, 63–66, 91
　self-affirming, 19–24
　*See also* Interpreting Myths, Symbols,
　　and Rituals trend

Nadel, S. F., 6–7, 119, 224
Nader, Laura, 7–8, 119, 223–24

narcissism of small differences (Freud),
　130
National Cancer Institute (NCI), 170–71
National Institutes of Health (NIH),
　33–34, 134, 203
National Science Foundation (NSF),
　32–33, 134, 186–88, 201
　Center for a Public Anthropology and,
　　187–88
　Congress and, 187–88, 192, 203
　Educational Development Center
　　(EDC) and, 165, 166
　funding/grants, 32–34, 164–67, 186–88,
　　201, 204, 205
　　for anthropology, 187, 205–6
　　values and criteria for, 32–33, 44, 108,
　　　134, 203
　MACOS and, 164–67
　Project Outcome Reports and, 33,
　　186–88
　"Proposal and Award Policies and
　　Procedures Guide," 187
National Security Administration (NSA),
　Edward Snowden and, 182–85, 192
Native Americans, 224
Nazism, 9
Neel, James, 139–41, 170
neo-evolution. *See* cultural evolution;
　cultural materialism
New Guinea. *See* Trobriand Islanders;
　Tsembaga Maring tribe
Ninov, Victor, 54
nongovernmental organizations (NGOs),
　121, 153, 180
Nosek, Brian, 57
Nupe, witchcraft among, 6–7

Oberholzer, Emil, 68–69
Obeyesekere, Gananath, 63–66
　on Sahlins, 92, 95
　*See also* Sahlins–Obeyesekere
　　controversy
objectivity
　advocacy, activism, and, 11–14, 121
　*Advocacy and Objectivity* (Furner), 11–13
　anthropology and, 50
　connotations of the term, 13
　definitions of the term, 11, 121
　ethnographies and, 98–99
　nature of, 11, 13, 14

postmodernism and, 97–99
publication and, 28–29
research transparency and, 29, 35
universities and, 28–29, 121
O'Hara, Carolyn, 222
Oliver, Douglas, 164
opiate addiction, 174–75
Oransky, Brian, 30
organ trafficking, 185–86
organization of diversity (model of culture
and personality), 69–70
originality of research, 107, 109–10
Ortner, Sherry, 205

Pacific Islanders, 64, 135. *See also specific
cultures*
Palmer, Bruce, 190–91
Papua New Guinea, 52, 103. *See also* East
Sepik; Trobriand Islanders
paradigm shift(s)
crisis in cultural anthropology and,
24–25, 195–97, 204
and the recycling of paradigms, 45
Thomas Kuhn on, 24–25, 195–97, 229
paradigms, 24
status of, 24
testing, 24–25
Thomas Kuhn on, 24–26, 195
*See also specific paradigms*
participant-observation, 3, 4
Partners in Health (PIH), 10, 162, 167–69,
179, 226
patrilinearity, 61–62
Pauling, Linus, 14
peer-review process, 38–39, 116
Peregrine, Peter, 21
personality. *See* culture and personality
Peru, 143–44
pharmaceutical industry, 157–58, 181
*Pigs for the Ancestors* (Rappaport), 74–75,
79. *See also* Rappaport, Roy A.
Piper, Andrew, 28–30
Plains Indians, 224
police, French, 176
Polier, Nicole, 101n156
political engagement, 11. *See also* public
engagement
Polynesia, 52, 61, 65, 127, 130
Polynesian atolls, 5, 52–53, 61–62, 159–60
Polynesian Voyaging Society, 130

Pool, Robert, 99n150, 101n156
*Poor Economics: A Radical Rethinking of the
Way to Fight Global Poverty* (Banerjee
and Duflo), 154–55, 178, 179
positivism, 49–51
postmarital residence, 61–62
postmodernism, 63, 66, 110, 117–18, 214–15
assessing, 96–106
James Clifford, George Marcus, and,
96, 97n142, 99, 100, 117–18 (*see also
Writing Culture*)
objectivity and, 97–99
poverty, extreme, 147
poverty reduction, 121, 147–49, 152–55, 178.
*See also* Millennium Villages Project;
*Poor Economics*
Powell, John Wesley, 20, 131
power and resistance, 89
power structures and power relations, 142
prestige. *See* status (and prestige)
Priest, Dana, 183–85
*Primitive Social Organization: An
Evolutionary Perspective* (Service),
73–74, 76
*Prison Worlds: An Ethnography of the
Carceral Condition* (Fassin), 176
prisons, French, 176–77
production, modes of, 90n130
professional advancement. *See* academic
advancement
professors. *See* faculty
"progress." *See* intellectual progress
Project Camelot, 159
Project Outcome Reports, 33, 186–88,
187n38
public advocacy. *See* advocacy
public anthropology, 133
coining of the term, 125, 129, 130
courses on, 125
definitions, meanings, and uses of the
term, 125
differentiating between applied
anthropology and, 128–30
education in, 124, 125
nature of, 125, 126, 129
origins, 129, 130
and related terms, 125
and university prestige, 216
writings on, 124–25
*See also* "benefitting others"

public anthropology paradigm, 133, 145–46
  alternative names for, 123–24
  vs. "do no harm" paradigm, 27, 40, 123,
    133, 139, 145, 196, 211
  focus on outcomes, 216
  and the future, 212, 218, 230
  hegemonic-like structures and, 131–33,
    211
  implications of, 213, 218
  nature of, 27, 126
  placing it in historical contexts, 126–28
  ramifications of, 213, 230
public engagement, 9, 33n73, 125–28, 146,
  221
  and change, 214
  hegemonic-like structures limiting, 133
  and "pure" vs. "impure" work, 208
  why a more socially engaged public
    anthropology has not taken root,
    131–33
  See also public anthropology
Public Issue Anthropology program at
  University of Guelph, 125
publication bias, 158. See also publications;
  publishing standards
publications, 28–29
  accountability standards framed in
    terms of, 25, 29–30, 36, 43, 197
  coauthoring and number of authors of,
    26
  creative, 35
  intellectual progress and, 35–36, 51, 52,
    79–80, 107–8, 114, 118, 210, 215, 216
  as measure of intellectual competence,
    25–26
  peer-review process, 38–39, 116
  quantity (vs. quality) of, xi–xii,
    25–31, 34, 112, 117, 204, 215, 218, 225,
    229–30
  retractions, 35, 53–57
  standards for assessing, 30–31, 107, 113,
    114 (see also publishing standards)
  and status, 28–30, 34–35, 48, 128
  and status advancement, 28–29, 37,
    114–18, 120, 228
  and tenure, 25, 30, 36–38, 113–14, 120,
    210
  transparency and, 29, 31, 35, 36, 38, 156,
    159 (see also transparency)

universities and, 25, 28–30, 228
  See also anthropological publications;
    publishing
"publish or perish," 207. See also publications: quantity (vs. quality) of
publishing, academic
  hegemonic-like structures (of the
    academy) and, 25–26, 36–39, 207,
    213, 215, 230
  how focus on publishing fits into
    pursuit of status, 114–18
  problematic nature of specialization
    under these conditions, 119
  See also anthropological publications;
    publications
publishing standards, 34, 38, 107, 109. See
  also anthropological publications:
    standards in assessing; peer-review
    process; publications: standards for
    assessing
Pukapukans, 3, 5–6, 61, 62, 159–60
Pwojè Pyebwa (Tree Project). See
  Agroforestry Outreach Project

Quechua highlanders, 143–44

racial differences in intelligence, 161
Rappaport, Roy A.
  citations to, 77–79
  criticisms of, 75, 75n89
  cultural adaptation and, 74
  cultural ecology and, 72, 74–77
  Harris, Sahlins, Service, and, 76, 77
  Julian Steward and, 76
  on traditions in anthropology, 49–50
  on Tsembaga, 74, 76, 80
  writings honoring, 79, 80, 106
Redfield, Robert, 14, 60–61
Redfield-Lewis controversy, 14, 60
reforesting Haiti, 150–55, 218
religion, 114
Rensberger, Boyce, 46–47, 60
replicability of studies, 14, 33–34,
  47–49, 53. See also confirmation;
    reproducibility
replication of uniformity (model of culture
  and personality), 69–70
reproducibility, 34, 35, 47–49, 55, 203. See also
  confirmation; replicability of studies

Research Excellence Framework (REF),
197, 199, 200, 212
research funding
funding agencies and hegemonic-like
structures, 32–34
and intellectual advances, 29, 44, 108,
121
*See also* grants; National Science
Foundation: funding/grants
research transparency. *See* transparency
resistance
anthropology of, 205
Foucault on, 89
power and, 89
retractions in academic publishing, 35,
53–57
Rhode, Deborah, 29, 31, 108, 113, 115, 117
Rich, Nathaniel, 220
rites of passage, stages in, 82
ritual and environment, 75
*Ritual Process: Structure and Anti-Structure,*
*The* (Turner), 82
rituals, 75, 80. *See also* Interpreting Myths,
Symbols, and Rituals trend
"Road Not Taken, The" (Frost), 227–29
Romer, Paul, 36
Rosaldo, Michelle, 98n149, 104n164
Roseberry, William, 101n156
Rosenbaum, Levy Izhak, 185–86
Rule, James, 44–45, 110, 205

Sachs, Jeffrey, 147–50, 152, 154, 155
Sahlins, Marshall
cultural ecology and, 72
Elman Service and, 73, 76, 77, 106
Foucault and, 92–94
Hawaii and, 62–65, 87–88, 91, 92n135,
95, 106
*Historical Metaphors and Mythical*
*Realities*, 63, 91, 92n135
*Islands of History*, 91, 92n135, 93
James Cook and, 62–63, 87, 91, 93, 95
(Re)Turn to History trend and, 87, 88
*See also Evolution and Culture*
Sahlins–Obeyesekere controversy, 63–66,
88, 92, 95, 106
comparative fallacy and, 65
intellectual progress resulting from,
95

and the minimal differences between
Sahlins and Obeyesekere, 64
overview, 62–63
resolution of, 111, 113
Salzman, Philip Carl, 45–46, 59
Samoa. *See Coming of Age in Samoa*
Scheper-Hughes, Nancy, 142, 185–86, 192,
214
Schonberg, Jeff, 174–75
*Schoolhouse Politics: Lessons from the Sputnik*
*Era* (Dow), 165
science and intellectual progress, 49–50
scientific communities, Kuhn on, 32n69
Scientific Investigation of Micronesia
(SIM), 142–45
scientific research, aim of, 50
Seaborg, Glenn T., 55
Senior, Jennifer, 219
Service, Elman
citations to, 77, 78
cultural ecology and, 72–74, 76
*Evolution and Culture*, 72–73, 74n85, 77
Julian Steward and, 76, 106
levels of integration concept, 76
Marvin Harris and, 76, 77
Roy Rappaport and, 76, 77
Sahlins and, 73, 76, 77, 106
on stages of cultural evolution, 73, 76
sexuality and sexual practices, 8, 177
Sharp, Andrew, 130
Shore, Cris, 199, 204
Six Cultures Project, 71–72
Smolin, Lee, 36, 48
Snowden, Edward, 182–85, 192
social advocacy. *See* advocacy
social engagement of anthropologists, 133.
*See also* public engagement
social integration, 73
levels of, 73, 74, 76, 106
social solidarity, tribal, 73
social stratification. *See* hierarchies; status
socialization, models of, 69–70
Society for Applied Anthropology, 129, 133
Solow, Robert, 154–55
Spicer, Edward H., 58
Sputnik era, 164, 201. *See also Schoolhouse*
*Politics: Lessons from the Sputnik Era*
stabilization, principle of, 73
Starr, Paul, 209–10

status (and prestige)
of anthropologists, 108, 114–16 (*see also* status advancement)
"do no harm" paradigm and, 121
of faculty, 11, 13, 116, 128 (*see also* status advancement)
publications and, 28–30, 34–35, 48, 128
relative status and zero-sum pursuit of status, 115
of universities, 28, 117, 121, 200, 216
status advancement, 11, 108, 118
chase/drive for, 114–15, 118, 120, 229, 230
problems in the, 116–17
publications and, 28–29, 37, 114–18, 120, 228
of universities, 30, 36, 120, 227, 228
*See also* academic advancement
status competitions between departments or between universities, 120
status hierarchy, 82, 116, 126, 132
status rivalry, 5, 159–60
status seeking. *See* status advancement: chase/drive for
Stevenson, Matilda C., 129
Steward, Julian H., 51–52, 72, 73, 106, 116
Stocking, George, 22, 127
storytelling, power of, 221–23
Strathern, Marilyn, 200
citations to, 104–6
*The Gender of the Gift*, 96, 101–4
subfield integration, lack of, 23
Sydenham, Thomas, 136
symbols. *See* Interpreting Myths, Symbols, and Rituals trend

targeted transparency as means for enhancing public attention, 180–82, 192–93
Edward Snowden and the NSA, 182–85, 192
Nancy Scheper-Hughes and the FBI, 185–86
National Science Foundation (NSF), 186–88
Vietnam War, 189–92
Tarter, Andrew, 152–53
teaching anthropology, 120, 128. *See also* Man: A Course of Study

*Teachings of Don Juan, The* (Castaneda), 58–59
Tenner, Edward, 211–12
tenure, 38, 114, 210
administrators' coercive power and, 25
denial of, 209
publications and, 25, 30, 36–38, 113–14, 120, 210
Tepoztlán, 14, 60–61
Thompson, Nainoa, 130
Tikopia, 127
transparency, 156–58
accountability standards and, 35, 36, 156, 158, 188
anthropology and the lack of, 120
and confirmation of research findings, 34–36, 56, 158, 160
"do no harm" paradigm and, 31, 34
emphasis on, 29, 35, 36
ethnographies and, 129, 159
importance, 34–36, 156, 158, 181
limited, 35, 38
nature of, 31, 159
publications and, 29, 31, 35, 36, 38, 156, 159
roles in anthropology, 158–59
*See also* targeted transparency as means for enhancing public attention
tree-planting project. *See* Agroforestry Outreach Project
tribes (stage of cultural evolution), 73
tributary mode of production, 90n130
Trobriand Islanders, 4, 52
Tsembaga Maring tribe, 74, 76, 77n93, 80
(Re)Turn to History trend, 87, 88, 92, 95, 110
assessing the, 87–95
Turnbull, Colin M., 137
Turner, Victor, 80–86, 131
Tyler, S. A., 101n156

unilineal descent organization, 224
universities
and accountability standards, 27–29, 34, 202–3
"do no harm" paradigm and, 27, 32, 34, 121, 202
finances, 29, 30
hegemonic-like structures and, 34–36

intellectual advances and, 29, 107–8
objectivity and, 28–29, 121
pressure for greater accountability,
    200–203, 222–23
publications and, 25, 28–30, 228
status advancement, 30, 36, 120, 227, 228
status and prestige, 28, 117, 121, 200, 216
University of Global Health Equity
    (UGHE), 169

van Gennep, Arnold, 82
Vance, J. D., 219, 221
Vicos, 143–45
Vicos Project, 142–44, 218
Vicosinos, 144, 145, 218
Viet Cong
    resilience, 191
    search-and-destroy missions against, 191
Vietnam Veterans Memorial, 189
Vietnam War, 189–92
    academic neglect of Vietnam during,
        191, 193
    American ethnocentrism in, 190
    anthropologists and, 193
    "do no harm" paradigm and, 181
    U.S. strategy of attrition in, 190–93
visiting anthropologists, 134–36

Wakefield, Andrew, 55–56
Wallace, Anthony, 67, 69–72, 110
Wansink, Brian, 56–57
Weber, Max, 114–15
Weil, David, 181
Weiner, Annette, 52
Wellmon, Chad, 28–30
Westinghouse Learning, 166
Westmoreland, William, 190–92
White, Leslie, 72–73, 76
White, Tom, 179
Whiting, Beatrice, 71–72
Whiting, John, 71–72
Wilsdon, James, 199
witchcraft, 6–7
witchcraft accusations, 7
Wolf, Eric, 93
    on anthropologists, 158–59
    on anthropology, 16n38, 45, 93, 226n71

capitalism and, 90n130, 91, 93
citations to, 93, 94
on closed corporate communities, 7
on forms and modes of production,
    90n130
Foucault and, 87, 91–94
Julian Steward and, 52, 116
myth of disciplinary integration and, 22
on responses to colonization in
    Mesoamerica and Central Java, 7
Sahlins and, 87, 92, 93
on trade, 90
(Re)Turn to History trend and, 87, 88
writings, 158–59
    *Europe and the People Without History*,
        42, 52, 88–90, 90n128, 116, 208, 223
women
    Muslim, 7–8
    sexuality and, 8
    *See also* gender roles
Wright, Susan, 199, 204
*Writing Culture* (Clifford and Marcus), 96,
    97n142, 98–100, 99n150, 103–4

Yanomami, 139
    American Anthropological Association
        and, 139–40, 209
    "benefitting others" and, 140, 170
    Brazilian politicians and, 139
    collaboration and, 162
    controversies regarding, 111, 139–41,
        160–61, 170–72
    James Neel and, 140, 141, 170
    Napoleon Chagnon and, 139–41, 160–61,
        209
    violence, 139, 160
    writings on, 111n175
*Yanomami: The Fierce Controversy
    and What We Can Learn From It*
    (Borofsky), 170
Yanomami blood samples, 140
    campaign to return, 170–72, 192–93
Yunus, Muhammad, 153

Zacharias, Jerrold, 164–65
Zaid, Gabriel, 41–42
Zanmi Lasante. *See* Partners in Health

# ABOUT THE AUTHOR

**DR. BOROFSKY** is the Director of the Center for a Public Anthropology and a Professor of Anthropology at Hawaii Pacific University. Including this book, he is the author or editor of eight books dealing with constructions of knowledge in the Pacific islands—such as *Making History* (1987) and *Remembrance of Pacific Pasts* (2000)—and the current state of cultural anthropology, including *Assessing Cultural Anthropology* (1994) and *Yanomami* (2005). As this book explains, his present work focuses on drawing anthropology—with its powerful tools and insights—into addressing key problems faced by societies around the world.

CPSIA information can be obtained
at www.ICGtesting.com
Printed in the USA
LVHW081944110721
692416LV00012B/1318